The Great Self-Improvement Sourcebook

The Great

SELF-IMPROVEMENT

Sourcebook

Hundreds of Ways to Improve Yourself
Physically, Mentally, Financially and Socially
From Absolutely Free to Fabulously Expensive

RUTH WINTER

E. P. DUTTON • NEW YORK

The names and services in *The Great Self-Improvement Sourcebook* were considered by the author for inclusion based on reputation, but satisfaction is exclusive to the individual and therefore cannot be guaranteed. Prices and services naturally are both subject to change.

For information contact: E.P. Dutton, 2 Park Avenue, New York, N.Y. 10016

Library of Congress Cataloging in Publication Data
Winter, Ruth
  The great self-improvement sourcebook.
  1. Health. 1. Success. 3. Finance, Personal. 4. Health—Information services—United States—Directories. 5. Success—Information services—United States—Directories. I. Title.
RA776.5.W53   640   79-16490

ISBN: 0-525-93075-2 (cloth)
ISBN: 0-525-93083-3 (paper)
Published simultaneously in Canada by Clarke, Irwin & Company Limited. Toronto and Vancouver

10 9 8 7 6 5 4 3 2 1

First Edition

Contents

Foreword

We live in a competitive world. We are constantly being evaluated and reviewed. But more than that we live in a world where knowledge and ability are highly valued. You want to be your best—and it's just good sense to do everything you can to live up to your potential.

If you want to feel your best, look your best, and receive the latest information and the best services (many completely free) directly delivered to your mailbox, this is the book for you. This compendium of kits, programs, courses, books, films, activities, and advice is yours, and the expertise of thousands of professionals is at your fingertips.

This book has been several years in the making. Ruth Winter, who has written more than a dozen books, wanted to keep all the facts as close to reliable as possible. We cannot guarantee any of the services or other mail-away equipment; but we can guarantee that we've tried our best to get you the most direct, clear, and reliable information that was available to us on each subject.

You'll find a myriad of tips and techniques in this super-compilation. We all hope that it brings you whatever you want.

Connie Schrader

Preface

Why try to improve yourself?

Because the quest is the best!

By taking even the first steps toward making yourself more educated, more attractive, financially better off, physically stronger, increasingly capable, you begin to leave behind tension, depression, and even aging.

Tension is born of frustration and lethargy. Depression is a helpless inability to act, as well as a feeling of worthlessness. And people are old only when they are no longer interested in learning new things and receiving stimulation from the world around them.

The quest for self-improvement is a natural, even biological, need. Notice how carefully children and animals explore new surroundings— out of a need to master their environment. This sense of mastery, or "competence," according to psychoanalysts, grows with each successful dealing with the external world.

Competence—knowledge of the ability to master a variety of situations—leads to self-esteem. In order to enjoy yourself and get the most out of living, you have to like yourself. If you are truly to seek self-improvement, you have to be self-centered.

Behavioral psychologists today emphasize that self-centeredness is the key to achieving happiness and satisfaction in life. Being self-centered does not imply that you are selfish. It means that you view yourself as the center of your own, personal world. You do what *you* want to do; what's good for *you*.

Therefore, set your goals for yourself alone. Of course, they have to be realistic. If you sing in a monotone, for instance, you can't learn to be an opera star, but you can increase your appreciation of music. You may not have the strength and coordination to become an Olympic champion, but you can pursue a sport which you enjoy and which improves your physical fitness.

Decide for yourself what your motivations are for a particular self-improvement pursuit. Are your goals real or only for show? What is truly important to you about them? Satisfaction will ultimately come from self-improvement activities based upon a realistic evaluation of what you *can* and what you *want* to do.

But whatever your goals and pursuits, you are lucky to be alive today. The sources of self-improvement—all kinds of improvement—are almost infinite. In this volume, only a small percentage of facilities could be described. Some are unique, many are national, and most are available in some form no matter where you live. If you cannot find a particular course or facility you would like to try, adult schools, Y's, and commercial establishments are constantly seeking to meet demands. There are educational and vocational brokers and government agencies which will refer you to the closest source or actually help set up a local facility for you.

In all categories, the names and addresses of national resources have been provided. If there are no facilities listed in your phone book, check the central organization or contact a similar facility in another area for referral. All sources in this book are willing to provide information.

Read on. Take the first step in the wonderful quest to improve yourself and your life. Some of the pursuits are easy. Some are extremely difficult. Some are fabulously expensive and many are absolutely free.

ACKNOWLEDGMENTS

The author wishes to thank for their invaluable assistance: Jory Graham, Illinois correspondent; Glena Pfennig, Texas correspondent; Helen Smith, Georgia correspondent; Dolly Wageman, California correspondent; Robin Winter, Florida correspondent; and Jeanne Weisman of Short Hills, New Jersey, and Dorothy Cohen of West Orange, New Jersey, and all the many people working in the self-improvement field who gave generously of their time and knowledge.

I dedicate this book to my family, who were patient while I pursued self-improvement.

PART I

Build a Better Body

What Is Physical Fitness?
How Fit Are You?

How physically fit are you right now?

Before you answer that question, there is an important fact that you must recognize: There is a lot more to fitness than playing tennis or bowling or even jogging. You can be a weight lifter and press 350 pounds of steel, but if you cannot run 100 yards without getting out of breath, you are not physically fit. You can be a marathon runner and finish first, but if you cannot lift sufficient weight for your size, you are not physically fit.

Physical fitness consists of three basic components:

1. *Strength:* This is what most people consider fitness. But what is strength for one person may be weakness for another. Developing and maintaining the strength of your muscles is, of course, very important.

2. *Endurance:* You can be strong but have no endurance. You have to be able to maintain physical activity for a reasonable period of time to be fit.

3. *Flexibility:* This becomes more and more important as you get older. The stiffness of old age can be prevented or minimized if you keep your body flexible. In fact, more than half the lower backaches people suffer from are due to poor tone and lack of litheness in the back and abdominal muscles.

Here are some ways to test your physical fitness and to find out where you should start on your self-improvement shape-up program. If you have any physical condition that could be adversely affected by even the simple movements described in the following section, do not do the tests without checking with your physician.

TEST YOUR PHYSICAL FITNESS

The Stork Test

This test determines minimal physical fitness.

Stand on one foot, like a stork. Close your eyes, and with your hands on your hips, try to hold this position while you count to 15. If you can complete the count without falling over, you are in at least fair physical condition.

The Arc

The arc tests endurance, particularly in your back and abdominal muscles.

Lie on your stomach with your arms stretched out in front of you; be sure to keep your head down. Raise your right arm and left leg, then your left arm and right leg. Do not let your arms and legs touch the floor. Hold each position for at least 1 minute. If you can do this without strain, your endurance is pretty good.

The Elasticity Estimator

This exercise tests the flexibility of your muscles. Sit on the floor with your legs extended in front of you. Stretch your arms out in front of you, reach slowly toward your toes, and hold the most extended position that you can reach for 4 seconds. Do not push or jerk forward; your reach should be slow and easy.

Distance Reached	Your Flexibility Fitness
7 inches beyond toes	Excellent
3 inches beyond toes	Good
To toes	Average
3 inches from toes	Needs improvement
7 inches from toes	Are you stiff and out of shape!

The Best Test for Cardiovascular Fitness

Your heartbeat is a live giveaway when it comes to your physical condition. The fewer number of beats per minute—providing, of course, that you do not have a condition that affects the electrical system of your heart—the better shape you are in. The less your heart beats per minute, the less work it has to do to meet normal body needs.

CHECK YOUR RESTING HEARTBEAT

After you have awakened in the morning but while you are still in bed, take your pulse. The lower your pulse rate is, the higher your fitness level. Count the pulse beats in your wrist or in your neck for 30 seconds, and multiply by 2. If your *resting* heartbeat is:

Beats Per Minute	Your Fitness Level
51–61	Excellent
62–69	Good
70–76	Average
77–84	Needs improvement
85 or over	You are certainly out of shape.

CHECK YOUR ACTIVE HEART RATE

Step up and down a stair or a platform 13 to 20 inches high, 30 times a minute, for 4 minutes. Then take your pulse rate for 30 seconds 1 minute, 2 minutes, and 4 minutes after you stop. Add the three 30-second pulse rates together.

Total Beats	Your Fitness Level
199 or more	Poor
150 to 170	Good
133 to 149	Very good
132 or less	You are in great condition.

What should the maximum level of your heartbeat during exercise be? Here is how you can find out:

Take the number 220

Subtract your age

Subtract the number 40

The answer is the maximum heartbeat for which you should aim. A forty-year-old man, for example, should aim for 140 beats per minute.

A Test of Strength

Your grip is an indication of your total body strength. Grab a new tennis ball or a hard rubber ball in your dominant hand, and dent it with your fingertips. If you cannot hold the grip for 30 seconds, your total body strength is probably below par.

The Pinch-of-Fat Test

Too much fat is an indication of lack of physical fitness. So take a ruler, and measure. Pinch your "spare tire," the skin just above your hipbone. How thick is it?

Amount of Fat	**Your Fitness Level**
½ inch or less	Excellent
¾ inch	Good
1 inch	Average
More than 1 inch	You are too fat and out of shape.

CLINICS FOR TESTING STRESS

There are medically supervised exercise programs that involve cardiovascular stress testing. If you want to know the condition of your heart and arteries without undergoing complicated X rays or even surgery, stress testing (the monitoring of your heart and blood pressure as you exercise) is your best choice. It is hoped that in the not too distant future, stress testing will be part of every regular physical examination. Such testing is especially important because a resting electrocardiogram may seem perfectly normal, but an exercise electrocardiogram may show a gross abnormality in the same person.

More than 200 clinics, hospitals, and university medical centers now provide this service. Many centers require a physician's referral. Therefore, the expense of stress testing is often reimbursable under private health insurance or hospital service plans, particularly if you have had a heart problem in the past.

If you are over forty, have not exercised in a number of years, or have suffered a heart attack in the past, it would be wise for you to shape up in a medically supervised facility. New programs are being opened all the time. Here is just a sampling of well-established facilities.

The Aerobics Center, 12100 Preston Road, Dallas, Texas 75230, (214)239-7223. Dr. Kenneth H. Cooper, the man who made aerobics famous, is founder and director of the Aerobics Center. The center is comprised of three divisions: the Cooper Clinic, the Aerobics Activity Center, and the Institute for Aerobics Research.

The Cooper Clinic is a professional organization that specializes in medical examinations, including stress testing, and dietary and exercise recommendations. The Institute for Aerobics Research studies exercise and its relation to the prevention and rehabilitation of disease, and the Aerobics Activity Center is a facility where medically prescribed and supervised aerobic programs are performed.

The Aerobics Center is situated on eighteen acres in northern Dallas. Visitors are welcome to view the facility and, for a $5 guest fee, to use the outdoor jogging tracks (one-half mile and one-quarter mile), indoor jogging track, swimming pool, handball-racquetball courts, tennis courts, basketball arena, exercise equipment (Cybex, Universal, Nautilus), sauna, steam, and whirlpool. Computer terminals on which Activity Center members can record their workouts are located at the center's locker counter. At the end of each month, a computerized printout is sent to each member, giving recorded workouts and number of aerobic points earned. All recorded information is also used by the Institute for Aerobics Research in their longitudinal study to determine the role exercise plays in the prevention of coronary heart disease.

The Aerobics Center offers a parent-child program. From Monday to Friday, no one under the age of eighteen is allowed in the facility. But in an effort to encourage family participation in an aerobics program, the center invites parents who are members to bring their children on Saturdays from 9:00 A.M. to 2:00 P.M. and from 6:00 to 9:30 P.M. There is also a medically supervised exercise class designed especially for individuals with diagnosed coronary disease and other conditions requiring medical supervision. All exercises are prescribed and supervised by the professional staff of the Aerobics Activity Center and the Cooper Clinic. This class meets Monday to Friday, 7:00 to 8:00 A.M.

Membership in the center for one year is $500 for men and $300 for women.

Cardio-Metrics Institute, 295 Madison Avenue, New York, New York 10017, (212) 889-6123. This facility opened six years ago as a diagnostic center for the detection of coronary heart disease and to aid the medical community in developing exercise programs for their patients. Although the institute has many corporate clients, the majority of its patients are physician referrals and people who have read about the institute and wish to come in for testing and to have an exercise program developed for them.

The first step at Cardio-Metrics is an examination by a cardiologist. The doctor listens to your heart and takes your blood pressure, interprets your resting electrocardiogram, and takes your family and personal medical history. A nurse then straps numerous wires to your body and hooks up a pressure cuff to your arm, and you walk a treadmill that can be adjusted to simulate steeper and steeper hills.

Midway through the test, your nostrils are clamped shut, forcing you to breathe through your mouth into a respirometer just long enough to measure your body's oxygen-handling ability. The more fit you are, the longer the test runs, and the steeper the treadmill is. A cardiologist monitors your active electrocardiogram until your heartbeat gradually reaches 85 percent of capacity (a number figured on the basis of your age). By observing your heartbeat, blood pressure, oxygen consumption, and electrocardiogram, the staff at Cardio-Metrics can determine the overall condition of your cardiovascular system, but its primary function is to determine whether you have any serious blockage of one or more of the blood vessels of the heart that supply the heart with oxygen. Blockage of this nature can cause a heart attack.

A large percentage of the institute's clients are postcoronary patients referred by their physicians for stress testing and the appropriate exercise prescription. Exercise programs are designed specifically for each individual according to his or her capacity and need. For instance, one woman, a fifty-two-year-old company president, had suffered a severe heart attack before coming to Cardio-Metrics. An exercise program designed for her increased her cardiac capacity 10 percent within three months. She is no longer so fatigued at the end of the day, and the goal set for her is an increase of 25 percent.

In addition to stress testing, exercise, and its in-house exercise training center, Cardio-Metrics also performs the following diagnostic procedures:

ECHOCARDIOGRAPHY/PHONOCARDIOGRAPHY

This procedure is used primarily to detect the function of the valves of the heart. A technician places a transducer on the patient's chest; this device sends harmless sound waves through the heart. A tracing is produced on recording paper indicating the heart-valve motion, which is interpreted by a cardiologist.

PULMONARY FUNCTION STUDIES

This procedure is used to determine if there is any abnormality in the amount of air your lungs can hold (restrictive lung disease) or if there is a limitation of airflow in and out of the lungs (obstructive lung disease). After a maximum inhalation the patient exhales into a mouthpiece as rapidly as possible.

TWENTY-FOUR-HOUR HOLTER MONITORING

This procedure is helpful in determining hidden abnormalities in the rhythm of the heart. During a twenty-four-hour Holter Monitoring Study, the patient carries a small tape recorder that records his or her electrocardiogram throughout the entire period.

At Cardio-Metrics, you pay $190 for testing if you are a cardiac patient. Cardiac patients who wish exercise programs and five sessions of supervised exercise pay $265. If you are not a heart patient, you pay $215 for testing and exercise programs.

Fitness Systems, Inc., Atlantic Richfield Plaza, P.O. Box 71606, Los Angeles, California 90071, (213)488-9949. Fitness Systems, Inc., is a leader in providing a variety of highly professional physical fitness services to business and industry. FSI has assisted major companies across the nation in evaluating fitness program alternatives, developing facility layouts and equipment requirements, recommending implementation and operating procedures, and managing in-house exercise facilities and programs. In addition to these services, FSI maintains a fully equipped exercise facility, Fitness Center of America, in Atlantic Richfield Plaza.

The center offers physiological testing equipment, cardiovascular and skeletomuscular exercise equipment, an indoor jogging track, lockers and changing facilities, a pool, and a sauna. The center is open Monday to Friday from 7:00 A.M. to 7:00 P.M., with alternate hours for men and women. (Women's hours are limited.) There is a $100 initiation fee and monthly dues of $36 for men and $20 for women.

FSI's conditioning program is designed to enhance total fitness, with an emphasis on cardiovascular conditioning through exercise. Program participants are given personally tailored fitness programs designed by FSI exercise physiologists. These exercise prescriptions are based on the individual's health and exercise history, fitness objectives, and physiological tests (percentage of body fat, muscular strength and flexibility, and respiratory capacity and heart rate at rest and in response to moderate activity). Participants are retested periodically to assess their progress and upgrade their programs.

Although FSI's principles of exercise physiology remain the same, their application is tailored to the specific needs of the company or the individual. Whether at the Atlantic Richfield Plaza center, at a company's in-house facility, or in a private home, participants in FSI programs have evidenced significant physiological benefits. After four months on the program, those carrying out their thirty- to forty-minute programs two to three times a week experience, on the average, a 30 percent improvement in cardiovascular condition, a 10 percent reduction in body fat, and substantial increases in overall strength and flexibility.

WHY PURSUE PHYSICAL FITNESS?

So you have tested your physical fitness and found that there is certainly room for improvement. Why bother? You have heard the one about the wag who said the only exercise he gets is carrying the coffins of his friends who exercise. And you have probably heard the other one about the person who said that when he feels like exercising, he just lies quietly until the feeling goes away.

The truth of the matter is that exercise is one of the best and quickest ways to improve your health and your looks. It also improves your mood.

People who exercise have half the heart disease rate that people who do not exercise have. And if a physically fit person suffers a heart attack, he or she is more likely to survive it. Sedentary people have a greater incidence of diabetes, ulcers, and other internal ailments. Furthermore, an estimated 80 percent of the cases of low back pain can be traced to lack of physical activities. Repeated experiments have shown that exercise improves the action of your heart, blood circulation, and breath. It improves muscle tone and certainly helps you control your weight. If you are physically active, you will adapt better to stress, show less muscle tension, and experience less fatigue. You will tend to age more slowly, have lower blood pressure and greater breathing capacity, and remain more flexible both mentally and physically.

Some people need more exercise than others. The mesomorphs (those with large muscle mass and large bones) need more physical activity to keep in shape and maintain normal weight. The ectomorphs (those with slender skeletons and long, narrow hands and feet) can sit down at a desk all day and not get fat. Their appetite is lower, and as they become less mobile, it continues to drop. However, modern society makes it difficult for mesomorphs, ectomorphs, or anyone else to get sufficient exercise. For example, using an electric typewriter instead of a manual one can mean two to three pounds of added fat per year for the typist.

The fact that more and more younger women are falling prey to heart attacks is believed to be due not only to stress but also to the fact that housework has become too easy. With machines to do the physical labor, today's women are not getting the exercise that their mothers and grandmothers did.

In order to achieve and maintain physical fitness, you have to engage in some activity that raises your pulse rate to 70 to 80 percent of its capacity. (The satisfactory capacity rate for the average adult is probably 140 to 160 beats per minute.)

How much exercise do you need? The optimum frequency is one hour every day. But because you may not be able to exercise daily, you should try to have a minimum of one hour, divided into at least three segments, per week. Because a burst of activity can put undue strain on your heart if you are not in shape, you should not start an exercise program unless you are going to keep it up regularly.

Age is no barrier to exercise; there is a conditioning program for everyone. But physical problems can begin at an early age. Hardening of the arteries may be evident even in youth. Therefore, before you embark on any strenuous physical fitness program, check with your physician. There are specific programs, as you will see, for postcoronary patients and for others with physical limitations.

How can you tell whether your exercise program is too strenuous? If breathlessness and pounding of your heart do not subside within ten minutes after exercise, if marked weakness or fatigue persists two hours later, or if you are still fatigued the next day, you have overdone it. You should get medical advice before proceeding farther.

Motivation

All right, you know exercise is good for you, and you have tried to exercise before, but—you got bored and soon dropped out. How can you motivate yourself?

Keep a journal: The prime tool of the behavioral psychologists is the written record. Make a chart for yourself with short-term goals every few days or weeks. Mark a place for measurements such as girth and poundage. Set specific rewards, something you would really like to do or to buy, for reaching each goal.

Work out with a friend, relative, or lover: Companionship in working out can be both pleasant and motivating, especially if there is some competition involved.

Do not strain yourself. Your enthusiasm will last longer if you do not feel uncomfortable because you are in pain.

Change exercise locations regularly: The idea is to keep moving and avoid boredom. You can even change rooms at home occasionally.

Change the order of your exercises: This also helps to avoid boredom. But *always* do your warm-up exercises (see pages 11-12) first.

Start at the same time each day: This will not eliminate boredom, but it will help you find the time to fit exercise into your daily routine.

Finish with cool-down exercises: These exercises, which are the same as the warm-up exercises, prevent lightheadedness and chills.

Choose something you really like: If you pursue a sport or exercise program that you really enjoy, chances are you will stick with it longer.

EXERCISES

Recommended Warm-up Exercises

Warm-up exercises should be done before embarking on *any* sort of exercise program. They are designed to promote better breathing and to limber up major muscle groups. And although they are aimed at getting you ready for more strenuous things, they are themselves beneficial.

DEEP BREATHING

This routine will warm up your respiratory system.
Starting Position: Stand at attention, with your arms at your sides.
Count 1: Rise on your toes. As you do, make small inward circles with your arms as you slowly raise them, and inhale deeply. At the end of movement, your arms should be extended overhead.
Count 2: Reverse your circles with your arms. Move them downward while lowering your heels and exhaling.
This exercise should be done slowly and rhythmically.

BACK STRETCHER

This exercise will condition lower back and thighs as well as warm you up.
Starting Position: Stand with your feet apart and your arms extended overhead.

Count 1: Bend forward from the hips, knees bent, and swing your arms downward between your legs.

Count 2: Return to starting position.

Do the Back Stretcher 5 times.

THE BICYCLE

This is a general warm-up for the heart and lungs. It is also strengthens legs and hip muscles.

Starting Position: Lie on your back, raise your hips and legs, supporting your hips with your hands, to bicycle-pumping position.

Count 1: Pump your legs slowly, as if peddling a bicycle, for 30 seconds, breathing deeply.

Count 2: Increase speed of peddling action, and continue to pump your legs at this increased speed for another 30 seconds.

Basic Exercise Program

If performed every day for 15 minutes, these basic exercises will put you in good physical shape and keep you there. They are physiologically designed to strengthen your muscles, keep them flexible, and increase your endurance. Because each exercise is meant for a specific group of muscles and joints, do not do any one that might involve an area of your body with which you have some trouble, such as a knee or your neck, without checking with your physician first.

EXERCISES FOR GENERAL FLEXIBILITY AND A TRIMMER WAIST

THE STRETCHER

Starting position: Stand erect with your feet spread apart.

Count 2: Reach high with your hands as you rise on your toes.

Count 2: Return to starting position.

Do this a minimum of 4 and a maximum of 10 times.

THE TWISTER

Starting position: Sit on the floor with your legs apart, hands out wide.

Count 1: Touch your right hand to your left toe, keeping your left arm back and horizontal. Return to starting position.

Count 2: Then touch your left hand to your right toe, and return to starting position.

Do this exercise a minimum of 6 times and a maximum of 15 times.

THE SIDE BENDER

Starting position: Stand erect, with your feet spread shoulder width apart, your left hand on your left hip, and your right arm extended at shoulder height.

Count 1: Bend your trunk to the left, reaching over and beyond your head with your right arm. Return to starting position.
Count 2: Repeat to the opposite side.
Do the Side Bender 10 times.

EXERCISES TO TONE THE CHEST AND ARMS

These exercises strengthen and tone up the arms and chest muscles.

KNEE PUSH-UP
Starting position: Lie prone, with your hands outside your shoulders, fingers pointing forward.
Count 1: Straighten your arms, keeping your back straight as you push yourself up.
Count 2: Return to starting position.
Do a minimum of 5 and a maximum of 15 push-ups.

CHEST PRESS
Starting position: Sit or stand erect. Clasp your hands, with palms together, close to your chest.
Count 1: Press your hands together as hard as you can, maintaining pressure.
Count 2: Move your locked hands up and down your chest.
Do this exercise a minimum of 5 and a maximum of 10 times.

EXERCISES TO TRIM THE THIGHS

To slim and trim your thighs and strengthen them, do these three exercises.

QUARTER KNEE BENDS
Starting position: Stand erect, with your hands on your hips and your feet comfortably apart.
Count 1: Bend your knees to 45-degree angle, keeping your heels on the floor.
Count 2: Return to starting position.
Do a minimum of 4 and a maximum of 20 Quarter Knee Bends.

SITTING LEG RAISE
Starting position: Sit erect on a chair, with your hands on the sides of the chair seat and your legs extended slightly forward on the floor.
Count 1: Raise your left leg waist-high, and hold it there for a count of 5. Lower your left leg to the floor.
Count 2: Raise your right leg, hold it there for a count of 5, and lower it to the floor.
Do this exercise a minimum of 5 and a maximum of 15 times.

SIDE-LYING LEG LIFT

Starting position: Lie on your right side, with your legs extended and your arms above your head on the floor.

Count 1: Raise your left leg as high as possible. Lower your leg to starting position.

Count 2: Turn over onto your left side. Raise your right leg as high as possible. Lower your leg to starting position.

Do a minimum of 4 and a maximum of 15 Leg Lifts.

THE SIT-UP

This exercise eliminates that bulge, flattens the tummy, and strengthens the abdominal muscles.

Starting position: Lie on your back, with your arms crossed on chest and your hands grasping opposite shoulders.

Count 1: Curl up to a sitting position.

Count 2: Curl down to a starting position.

Do a minimum of 4 and a maximum of 15 Sit-ups.

BACK LEG SWING

This exercise will tighten the derriere.

Starting position: Stand erect behind a chair, with your feet together and your hands on the chair for support.

Count 1: Lift your left leg back as far as possible. Return to starting position.

Count 2: Repeat with your right leg.

Do this exercise a minimum of 6 and a maximum of 20 times.

THE PUSH-UP

This exercise strengthens the arms, shoulders, and chest muscles.

Women should do the Push-up as follows:

Starting position: Kneel, with your arms out in front of you and your hands on the floor.

Count 1: Lower your trunk to the floor.

Count 2: Push up to starting position.

Men should do the Push-up as follows:

Starting position: Lie face down, with your hands flat on the floor and the soles of your feet upward, toes down.

Count 1: With body straight raise your trunk from the floor, keeping your body straight and your elbows straight.

Count 2: Lower yourself to the floor.

THE HIGH-STEPPER

This exercise benefits your entire body and raises your pulse rate.

Starting position: Stand erect, with your elbows bent, your fists clenched.
Count: Run in place, pumping your knees and arms vigorously.
  Do this exercise 15 to 20 times.

Sources

Stretching. Bob Anderson, P.O. Box 767, Palmer Lake, Colorado 80133.
Anderson, a physical education graduate of California State University at
Long Beach, has developed stretching into an art. He maintains that it
increases a person's overall level of performance, whether for fitness or
competition, and that it is related to a general feeling of well-being. He
teaches not only the physical aspect of regular stretching and exercise but
also the mental aspect of these activities. He provides stretching charts
for twenty-three sports, including golf, tennis, wrestling, and walking, at
$2 each or $25 for all twenty-three charts. He also has a book, *Stretching,*
for $8.50 postpaid.

Feet First. Millions of Americans today are playing, instead of watching,
popular games such as tennis, racquet ball, golf, basketball, skiing,
hockey, and many others. Yet, according to Maurita Robarge, professor
of kinesiology at the University of Wisconsin at LaCrosse and physical
fitness expert, most of the bodies that are generating this activity have
been conditioned for nothing more strenuous than sitting in the grand-
stands or in front of the television set. A starting point for the superac-
tive life, Robarge says, is at the bottom: the feet and legs.

PUBLICATION

Foot Kinetics, Maurita Robarge. Scholl, Inc., 150 East Huron, Eighth
Floor, Chicago, Illinois 60610. Robarge has developed a fitness exercise
program that she calls *foot kinetics* for Scholl, the international foot-care
specialists. For tips on making the right moves for toe-to-total fitness,
send $.35 to cover the cost of postage and handling.

Isometric Exercises

Isometric exercises involve muscle contractions without movement. They
can be done anywhere and at anytime and are very good when you are
confined to one position for a long time, as you are, for example, in an
airplain, in a car, or behind a desk. They can help you maintain muscle
strength and increase circulation, but by themselves they cannot keep
you physically fit. Isometric exercises should not be done by persons
suffering from high blood pressure or other ailments that may be aggra-
vated by sudden exertion. Hold each contraction for the count of five and
repeat two or three times.

The Organ-grinder. Push one hand against the other hand; then clasp hands and pull one hand against the other.

The Thinker. Push your forehead against your palms; then push the back of your head against your palms.

The Bird. Push the back of your hands against a doorjamb; then push your palms in the same manner.

The Sampson. Stand in a doorway with your arms at your sides, fully extended. Push your palms against the doorjamb and try to straighten arms. Push your palms overhead against the top of the door and try to straighten arms.

The Siesta. Sit with your back against one doorjamb, and push your right foot against the other doorjamb; then push your left foot in the same manner.

On Your Knees. Sit on a chair, and place your hands on your knees. Use your hands to resist spreading your knees apart, thereby exercising the shoulder, hip, and forearm muscles.

Double Cross. Sit on a chair. Cross your right foot over the left. Press with your right heel against the resistance of your left instep. Reverse your feet and repeat. This exercises your leg muscles.

PUBLICATIONS

The following publications can be obtained from the President's Council on Physical Fitness, Superintendent of Documents, Washington, D.C. 20402:

Introduction to Physical Fitness (No. 017-000-00122-1). Self-testing activities, graded exercises, and jogging guidelines; information on exercise and weight control for adults. 28 pages. The price is $.60.

Adult Physical Fitness (No. 040-000-00026-7). Explains health and other benefits of regular vigorous exercise; progressive, five-level programs for men and women; sections on weight lifting exercises, water activities, and daily fitness opportunities. 64 pages. The price is $1.50.

The Fitness Challenge in the Later Years (No. 017-062-00009-3). For older men and women, exercises and activities carefully selected to combat problems of aging and to promote flexibility, balance, and cardiovascular fitness; includes self-scoring system. 28 pages. The price is $.75.

The following publication can be obtained from American Medical Association Publications, P. O. Box 821, Monroe, Wisconsin 53566.

The ABC's of Perfect Posture (OP 320). The price is $.65.

Basic Bodyworks for Fitness and Health (OP 428). The price is $.75.

EXERCISE CLASSES

Commercial establishments and community groups all over the United States are now offering exercise classes. There is enough variety so that you can choose one that best fits your needs and interests. There are even mail-order exercise classes available on tapes and in books. Here is a sample of the classes available:

Body Works, 65 West 54th Street, New York, New York 10019, (212) 757-6224. This exercise program based on Larry Ross's unique isolation method is for spot conditioning, firming and toning common trouble spots such as buttocks, thighs, and lower abdomen. The program is designed for men and women and young adults "who wish to beautify, firm and strengthen the body (in addition to relieving tension)." The Body Works program does not involve calisthenics; it is not machine-oriented. You will be taught how your muscles function correctly and independently while enjoying the benefits of isolations. In effect, it is training the body, as opposed to just working out. Personal attention is the keynote. The staff of instructors conducts classes limited to twelve students and sees to it that each individual receives all the attention he or she needs. Many successful and famous people take part in the classes, which are graded beginners, intermediates, and advanced. Advanced classes require strength, stamina, and concentration. There are also special classes for pregnant women. Most clients subscribe at the special rate of twelve classes per month for $60, which is what they recommend for superior body maintenance. There are also other rates, ranging from twelve classes for three months at $96 to forty classes over four months for $200 and unlimited classes for $75 a month and $600 a year. Also available are sauna and steam facilities as well as masseurs and masseuses who give Swedish body massage (no intermingling of the sexes).

TAPE

Body Works Exercise Class on Tape, Body Works Maternity Exercise Class on Tape. Send $9.95 plus $1.25 postage and handling.

Kounovsky Physical Fitness Center, 25 West 56th Street or 24 West 57th Street, New York, New York 10019, (212)246-6415. Classes for women, men, and children. Nicholas Kounovsky, a Russian-born physical fitness expert, will not reveal who his clients are. "My studios," he says, "are the only private studios that are *really* private. Only those students who themselves wish to announce that they attend do so." Jackie Kennedy Onassis has told people she attended, as did her sister and many other celebrities. Kounovsky is one of the pioneers in physical fitness exercise techniques, and he has created a program entitled *Sixometry*, based on anatomy, physiology, and mechanics. First, the beginner takes Sixometric tests to measure his or her degree of fitness in six important categories: endurance, suppleness, balance, strength, speed, and coordination. Then, a program of exercises may be chosen, suited to the individual's needs and goals.

"Becoming fit doesn't mean you have to strain muscles," Kounovsky insists. He believes exercise should be fun as well as relaxing. Classes are held in several large, airy, mirrored rooms equipped with mats, trapezes, dumbbells, and an NAK gym. The NAK gym is Kounovsky's development. It is triangular-shaped, with an overhead crossbar that enables you to perform many of the exercises done on the trapeze but much lower to the floor and therefore safe to use alone at home.

The center offers a test lesson for $10 that includes measuring your physical fitness to determine the exercise program you need. The center is open Monday to Friday, 8:00 A.M. to 8:00 P.M., and Saturday and Sunday, 9:00 A.M. to 2:00 P.M. The monthly fees are $30 for one weekly class, $58 for two weekly classes, and $84 for three weekly classes. Ten lessons cost $75 (you set the time period); 20 lessons, $140; ten half-hour private lessons, $140.

PUBLICATION

Joy of Feeling Fit, Nicholas Kounovsky. New York: Avon Books, 1971. Gives more than 300 of Kounovsky's exercises, along with innumerable exercise charts, diagrams, and health tips. The price is $3.95.

Lilian Rowen Exercise Studio, 225 East 79th Street, New York, New York 10021, (212)YU 8-5561. A no-nonsense, no-frills course of exercise to improve your body. Courses are held daily from 9:00 A.M., run fifty minutes each and cost $10 per class. There are also afternoon and evening classes. Cheaper by the semester. Three months at $8 a lesson with a maximum of six in a class. There is also a six-week course, the Y's Way to a Healthy Back, which is given at the studio. It is designed to prevent muscular tension in neck and back areas through a program of gentle muscle toning, stretching, and relaxing. 12 lessons, $100.

PUBLICATION

The Working Woman's Body Book, Lilian Rowen. New York: Rawson Associates, 1978. Rowen shows the busy working woman how to recognize her problem areas and how to help yourself. The price of this paperback is $4.95.

RECORDING

Shape up with Lilian Rowen. This record-slide presentation permits an individual or group to follow Rowen's regimen. The program can be used by community groups who want to shape up together. The price of the color slides and record, $19.95; black-and-white illustrated brochure and record, $6.95.

Manya Kahn Salon, 12 East 68th Street, New York, New York 10021, (212)288-1300. If you were casting the part of a strict, Russian ballet director, you would choose Manya Kahn immediately. She is a no-nonsense person who has taught many of the beautiful people to shape up. Born in Russia, she came to the United States at the age of sixteen; she performed and later taught classical ballet. Gradually, she developed a new system of exercise based on a slow stretch–breathe–relax technique that she calls *body rhythms*. This natural system strengthens, reshapes, and revitalizes the muscle structure of the entire body. Many of her clients have been referred to her by physicians. Her body rhythms can help eliminate back pains caused by poor posture and are also good for prenatal, postnatal, and postoperative care. In 1963, Kahn was appointed to the New York State Legislative Committee on Sports and Physical Fitness as a member of the Citizen's Advisory Committee.

Her salon is an elegant town house. She personally weighs and measures every client and charts a program to meet their individual needs. In addition to body rhythms, clients can undergo a relaxing heat therapy treatment, a scientific facial, a body massage, and a foot massage. They are also taught relaxation techniques. A woman can visit New York, stay at a hotel, and take advantage of Ms. Kahn's 10-day Wonder Course, which consists of 10 two-hour sessions for $350. Women who want to sample the program can take an introductory two-hour session for $30. Rates vary all the way up to 100 two-hour sessions for $2,500.

PUBLICATION

Body Rhythms: A New Approach to Exercise, Manya Kahn. New York: E. P. Dutton, 1977. Those who cannot come to New York or who cannot afford the full services of the salon in person will welcome this book. It re-creates the complete Manya Kahn Health and Beauty Program that has reshaped and rejuvenated many of the country's most prominent, fashionable, and beautiful women. Many photographs illustrate the body rhythms in detail. The price is $14.95.

RECORDING

Manya Kahn has also created a two-record album that follows the entire program in the book page by page. The oral direction and musical background make it easy to follow and add enjoyment to the entire program. The price is $14.95.

Manya Kahn Body Rhythms, a New Approach to Exercise Through Sight and Sound. If you buy both the record and book, the price is $25.

Nickolaus Exercise Centers, 509 Fifth Avenue, New York, New York 10017, (212)986-9100. There are Nickolaus Centers in Philadelphia, Long Island, and Connecticut, as well as the six in Manhattan. The Nickolaus Centers, called the "first universities of the body," provide a system of supervision essential to a systematic program of exercise that you can continue throughout your life with enjoyment and with steady improvement. Students receive constant encouragement, based on their specific physical needs, problems, and goals. The carefully structured movements of the Nickolaus Technique are a series of thirty head-to-toe exercises performed in a set sequence under close supervision. Each exercise has its own breathing pattern, and each is designed to exercise a specific part of the body naturally, without machines or apparatus. These thirty movements were devised by Richard Nickolaus during a research grant at Duke University. They represent, in a highly concentrated form, years of experience with the human body and of scientific research into the body's nature and functions.

Each movement in the technique contributes to the total effect of toning and refining every muscle individually and all muscles together. When performed properly, in correct sequence, the exercises can help bring a sense of balance to your life as well as to your body. Nickolaus believes that the connection between body and mind is one of the factors frequently overlooked in exercise programs. Stimulating the body will also stimulate the brain, release tension in the muscles, activate the glands, and coordinate the nervous system. The most common feeling reported by students at the end of a session is exhilaration.

With a set discipline of only two hours a week, the Nickolaus Technique can prepare you for any task—skiing, tennis, dancing, even childbirth—while adding a new dimension to your life as you become more in touch with your body, mind, interests, and emotions.

The program costs $165 for three months, $440 per year; a special half-hour lesson is offered at noontime, 5:15 P.M. and 5:45 P.M. for $90 for three months. There is no contract. Classes are coeducational.

PUBLICATION

What It Takes to Feel Good: The Nickolaus Technique. New York: Viking, 1978. $12.95 in bookstores. $13.95 direct from Nickolaus. The book contains the 30 step program of exercise for men and women of any age that can put you in shape for only two hours per week, without gadgets, pills or any other devices.

RECORDINGS

Exercise Bag, $8.00 direct from Nickolaus. Two 15 minute cassettes with illustrated pamphlet packaged in an exercise bag. Warm Up I and Warm Up II.

Warm Up/Cool Down for Runners, $9.50 direct from Nickolaus. A 15 minute cassette for runners.

Exercise Club, $29.50 plus $1.00 handling charge direct from Nickolaus. Complete 6 month home exercise program on three cassettes with a spiral-bound book. It's like having a Nickolaus instructor right in your own home to give you lessons at your convenience.

Ron Fletcher Studio for Body Contrology, 9549½ Wilshire Boulevard, Beverly Hills, California 90212, (213)278-4777. The studio offers a therapeutic exercise system that works on the theory that the slow and careful alignment of the body from the feet up and the correction of muscular imbalances bring about a better shape, better health, improved posture, a heightened sense of physicality, and an appreciation of what studio director Ron Fletcher refers to as the "Divine Gift of the Body." Deep breathing is stressed to increase circulation and stimulate the flow of oxygen to the muscles and vital organs of the body, bringing about more total elimination of body wastes, including fat. There is a first-rate nutritionist on the staff, Hermien Lee, who offers a program called "Weigh of Life," which analyzes your eating patterns and teaches you about yourself and how to eat. Eight private sessions with Lee are $250.

Ron Fletcher was a dancer and choreographer, with training in body mechanics and kinesiology. Some of his students are Candice Bergen, Susan Blakely, Dyan Cannon, Cher, Sandy Duncan, Goldie Hawn, Ali MacGraw, Doris Duke, Shirley Jones, Donna McKechnie, Valerie Perrine, Katherine Ross, Barbra Streisand, and Raquel Welch, but Ron points out that not all his students are *names*, "not by any measure." The studio is open to both men and women.

Sessions are by appointment only, and minimum attendance is twice weekly. Although there are other students in the studio at any session, each person receives individual attention. There is always a waiting list, but new students are worked in as quickly as possible. The studio is now under the management of Diana Severino, a Juilliard graduate with an advanced degree in dance. There is a staff of five. The fees are $140 for the first ten sessions and $110 for every ten after that. A single private session with Ron costs $75.

PUBLICATION

Every Body Is Beautiful, Ron Fletcher. Philadelphia: J. B. Lippincott Company, 1978, $14.95. The book gives easy to follow exercises that have kept the "stars" slim and shining. Ron is now in the process of developing cassette tapes.

DANCE CLASSES

Dancing is not only good exercise but also social and fun. Here is a sampling of some of the courses available.

Aerobic Dancing Inc., Corporate Headquarters, 18907 Nordhoff Street, Northridge, California 91324, (213)885-0032. Dance centers: New Jersey, (201)386-9180; New York, (212)752-0040; Baltimore, (301)523-4400; San Diego, (714)299-5062; North Hollywood, California, (213)982-4111. Classes are held at the centers and at Ys and churches in thirty-four states. You can telephone corporate headquarters or a center near you to obtain the schedule of classes in your area. Aerobic Dancing is simple, vigorous dancing for nondancers that takes the place of jogging. It firms the figure and the muscles and is fun.

The program started in South Orange, New Jersey, by Jacki Sorensen when she taught a group of six women in the basement of a church under the auspices of the YMCA. There are now more than 300 Aerobic Dancing courses. Jacki is president of the corporation and conducts and coordinates nationwide clinics in public schools and colleges, as well as research projects in Aerobic Dancing. *Aerobic* means "with oxygen." Any activity that causes your body to demand and use oxygen is aerobic, and Jacki calls her program *Aerobic Dancing* because it makes your body demand and use oxygen. She choreographs a new sequence of dances for each twelve-week Aerobic Dancing course. This allows new students to enter this lifetime fitness program and also provides the regular students with changes that make Aerobic Dancing challenging and exhilarating. In each course, she incorporates movements for toning muscles in all areas of the body and at the same time strengthening the heart and lungs.

Any man or woman can participate in Aerobic Dancing because it is choreographed for nondancers at three levels. Most new students are not physically fit, so they begin dancing their way to fitness at the "walking" level. In time, they are able to "jog" and then to "run" the dances. Every person succeeds at his or her own level. Skill and technique are not important; having fun is. A forty-five- to sixty-minute class begins with a choreographed warm-up to get the body systems ready for dancing. Six to ten Aerobic Dances follow, to such songs as "In the Mood" and "Rock Around the Clock." The class ends with a choreographed gradual cool-down. The cost is $2 to $5 per class, depending on the locale.

Albert Butler Dance Studios, 24 West 57th Street, New York, New York 10019, (212)757-6660. Called the "Cartier of dancing schools," the Albert Butler Dance Studios has a fifty-year history of excellent teaching. Classes consist of about thirty students who share an airy, beautiful studio ballroom. Social dancing—American, Latin, and international—is taught. Among the dances taught are the lindy, the Peabody, and the advanced hustle. Pupils are about evenly divided between the sexes. Classes take one hour. Eight group lessons cost $45, ten hours of private instruction are $300. There are no contracts.

Boston Dance Academy, 138 Newbury Street, Boston, Massachusetts 02116, (617)247-8009. In this unique approach to dance education, highly qualified instructors employ teaching methods that allow them to focus on each student's individual needs. Classes are offered in all levels, from fundamental to advanced, in modern, ballet, pointe, jazz, jazz-ballet, and creative movement. The Boston Dance Company, the academy's resident company under the artistic direction of Diane I. Crawford, offers the advanced student performing experience. The fee for ten weeks of 1½-hour classes is $35.

Jon Devlin's Dancercise Club, 1845 Broadway (between 60th and 61st Streets), New York, New York 10023, (212)245-5200; 157 East 86th Street (between Lexington and Third Avenues), New York, New York 10028, (212)831-2713; 2005 Hoyt Street, Fort Lee, New Jersey 07024, (201)944-5527. Jon Devlin's Dancercise Club is designed to promote good breathing and posture; tone muscles; release tension; develop coordination, grace, and poise; and increase endurance and circulation. It is stretch without strain, an exhilarating rather than exhausting activity. Devlin has combined the best features of calisthenics, dance, yoga, isometrics, and Tai Chi Chuan for his program. The instructors are professional dancers, who have been further trained in Devlin's method. Rates are ten classes for $55, twenty classes for $65, 50 classes for $200 and one hundred classes for $375. Private lessons $30 an hour or $15 a half hour.

Esther Nelson Workshops for Teachers in Movement, Dance and Music, P.O. Box 403, Kingsbridge Station, Bronx, New York 10463, (212) 548-6112. Workshop director Esther Nelson offers a unique method of reaching your children and developing their creative potential through the magic of movement, dance, and music. Nelson works directly with young children as the teachers watch. She shares with the teachers techniques for developing body awareness; working out a well-balanced program; adapting to different size, age, and ability groups; working with handicapped children; and creating your own material.

Those who teach teachers, those who work directly with the very young, and most importantly, the very young themselves, benefit from these dancing games. For information and availability, contact the workshop.

Joy of Movement Center, 536 Massachusetts Avenue, Cambridge, Massachusetts 02139, (617)492-4680. The philosophy behind the Joy of Movement Center is that dance is for everyone: for the young and the old, for those who dance for fun, for exercise, and for recreation, as well as for the professional dancer. Part of what makes the center unique is that it values all forms of dance and movement and is prepared to offer them with professional-quality instruction to those seeking either professional or recreational education. The Joy of Movement Center teaches classes in over fifty forms of dance and movement, including ballet, modern dance, jazz, disco, swing, tap, ballroom, exercise, yoga, Tai Chi Chuan, various forms of ethnic dance, creative movement, and movement for pregnant and postpartum women. Among the more unusual courses they offer are the Joy of Movement, which is an improvisational dance and movement exploration of joyous energy as it relates to the music of humankind throughout the ages; Movement for Nondancers, which concentrates on body work using plastiques, natural movement, and improvisational techniques to improve body strength, flexibility, and coordination; Group Improvisation, which explores the potential of the group as a highly creative, organic structure; and Feeding Ourselves: Confronting Weight Problems, which uses creative movement, improves body image, and raises energy levels to help change the ways people eat.

Courses cost $50 for a ten-week semester, plus a $5 registration fee. However, for Feeding Ourselves, the fee is $175 for a three-hour weekly session for 10 weeks. Discounts are available for those taking more than one course.

Ibrahim Farrah School of Near East Dance, LeRoy Rehearsal Studios, 743 Eighth Avenue, New York, New York (212)595-1677. Ibrahim Farrah is a director and choreographer who began his Middle Eastern dance career in the 1960s; he has performed all over the United States, Europe, and the Middle East. In 1971, he was awarded a grant for field research to study cultural dance traditions in the Middle East. He and his staff promote Near Eastern dance as an art form. The classes are of an "educational and noncommercial nature" and are geared not only to persons who are professional dancers but also to enthusiasts of dance who are studying for the sake of knowledge alone.

There is a $5 registration fee. Individual classes are $4 for professionals and $5 for nonprofessionals. A class card for ten lessons over a three-week period costs $30 for professionals and $35 for nonprofessionals.

Morocco Mideastern Dance Studio, 150 West 75 Street, New York, New York 10023, (212)799-1272 or 580-2731. Morocco, a teacher, author, and lecturer on Middle Eastern dance, believes that Middle Eastern dance promotes body control, natural tightening and toning of muscles, weight loss, grace, coordination, and heightened self-confidence. She teaches a variety of dances while authentic, recorded music plays. She concentrates on oriental dance (what the public erroneously refers to as *belly dance*). Classes last a little over an hour. A single lesson costs $6.

Serena Studios, 138 West 53d Street, New York, New York 10019, (212)245-9603 or 247-1051. One of the best-known belly dancers in the eastern United States, Serena is an entertainer, poet, and teacher. She evolved her technique from the natural movements of Middle Eastern dances. There are infinite steps and combinations in her dance, each an elaboration of, or derived from, a purely natural body movement. She believes that her dance is the essence of feminine creativity in a framework of genuine oriental music. You not only develop grace from belly dancing; you exercise every muscle. The fundamental class covers body positions, stretches, and simple dances. The beginners class is a program of body movements, accents, and footwork to the five fundamental rhythms. Finger cymbals are not required, and no previous training is necessary. The intermediate class provides an introduction to complex step and arm movements with cymbal coordination; shimmy and vibrations are taught. The advanced class covers development of a dance sequence with integration of steps. Serena also offers an advanced professional course, workshops with videotape, and live music and costume making. If you are interested, you can come and observe for fifteen minutes free of charge. Classes are $5 per hour; ten lessons cost $45. Private lessons are available for $20 per hour, $10 for half an hour.

If you would like to try it at home, Serena has worked out the exercises on pages 25-28 for you. These exercises will introduce you to some of the basic movements of this ancient art. With practice, you should be able to combine them into dances of your own. Slow music—oriental or Middle Eastern—is a must.

BODY MOVEMENTS

Basic Posture: This is referred to throughout the exercises. It requires (1) a high, expanded rib cage, (2) shoulders held down, (3) a slightly arched back, (4) abdomen held in, and (5) spine elongated.

Deep Knee Bend: This exercise firms and strengthens thighs and calves. (1) Start with the Basic Posture. (2) Slide one leg straight out in back of you, and slowly descend until your back knee touches the floor. Your front leg should be slightly turned out so that you do not lose your balance; your foot should be flat on the floor. (3) Now slowly rise, maintaining an erect posture.

Arch and Contraction: (1) Start with (a) legs straight, (b) one heel off the floor so that your weight is on the other foot, (c) shoulders pushed way back so that you can feel yourself stretching, (d) head erect, chin level, (e) rib cage high, (f) arms down at sides. Your entire body should form a C. (2) Bend your knees, push your pelvis and shoulders forward and contract the midsection (abdomen and rib cage) of your body. You should look as if you are recoiling gracefully from a poke in the stomach. If you have done this correctly, there will be a crease all the way around the front of your

Fundamental Body
Positions of the SERENA
TECHNIQUE

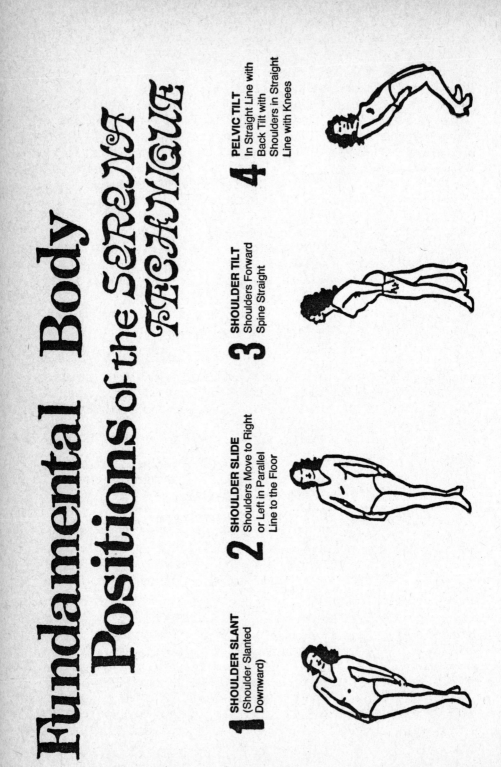

1 SHOULDER SLANT
(Shoulder Slanted
Downward)

2 SHOULDER SLIDE
Shoulders Move to Right
or Left in Parallel
Line to the Floor

3 SHOULDER TILT
Shoulders Forward
Spine Straight

4 PELVIC TILT
In Straight Line with
Back Tilt with
Shoulders in Straight
Line with Knees

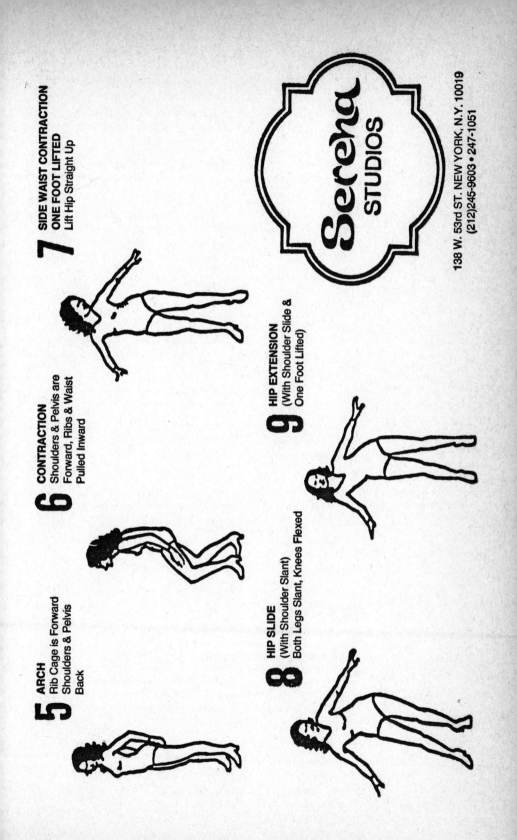

7 SIDE WAIST CONTRACTION
ONE FOOT LIFTED
Lift Hip Straight Up

6 CONTRACTION
Shoulders & Pelvis are
Forward, Ribs & Waist
Pulled Inward

5 ARCH
Rib Cage is Forward
Shoulders & Pelvis
Back

9 HIP EXTENSION
(With Shoulder Slide &
One Foot Lifted)

8 HIP SLIDE
(With Shoulder Slant)
Both Legs Slant, Knees Flexed

Serena
STUDIOS

138 W. 53rd ST. NEW YORK, N.Y. 10019
(212)245-9603 • 247-1051

waistline. (3) While maintaining the contraction, push back with your knees until your legs are straight. Then, leading with your rib cage, move out of the contraction back into your original posture. Each step of this exercise should be done very slowly, and needless to say, it is wonderful for the stomach muscles.

Hip Extension: (1) Start with the Basic Posture. Throughout this exercise, one foot should be firm on the floor, and knees should be slightly flexed. (2) Very slowly lift up your left hip and left heel, transfer your weight to your right foot, and at the same time, move your shoulders to the right, keeping them level. You should feel your waist muscles stretch. (3) Return to the Basic Posture. Repeat the Hip Extension in the opposite direction.

ARM MOVEMENTS

Rounded Arm Movement: (1) Assume a relaxed posture. (2) Start out with your arms at your sides, but slightly rounded at elbows; your hands and fingers should be loose. (3) Make a full circle, leading with your elbows. Keeping your shoulders down, lift your arms out to the sides and gradually up until they are directly over your head. They should remain slightly curved; the hands should point toward each other. (4) Now cross your wrists so that your palms face toward you and slowly bring your arms down in front of you to your sides. As you lower your arms at approximately face-level, the wrists become uncrossed. This is a slow, smooth movement that should look relaxed and soft.

Figure Eight Arm Movement: (1) Start with a relaxed posture, your arms at your sides. Throughout this exercise, your arms should remain long and loose, not bent at the elbow. (2) Keeping your arms down, bend your wrists, and bring the backs of your wrists toward each other so that your palms are turned out, away from you. (3) As your wrists are about to meet, turn your hands over so that the palms are up, as if you were offering a gift. Now, slowly move your arms behind your hips. (4) Turn your hands over, and bring your arms foward, leading with your wrists.

RECORDINGS

Dance Class with Serena. Two records and an instruction booklet make this set a must for the student who is unable to attend classes at Serena's studio in New York. Serena's instructions are given in a "voice over" with the music to which the dance is taught. This is followed by music alone, so that the student can practice with the music after she has learned the steps. The instruction booklet is fully illustrated, and the text is geared to accompany the recordings. The price is $10 postpaid.

Dancer pendant, designed for the oriental dancer, reflects the grace and beauty of the dance. Gold or silver color, $5, direct from Serena.

T'ai Ch'i: How to Do Less and Accomplish More, YES Educational Society, 1035 31st Street, N.W., Washington, D.C. 20007, (202) 338-7676. The ancient Chinese discipline of relaxed movement is taught in this workshop. Once the body is given a chance to relax *within* action, there is a natural tendency to reevaluate the assumptions about work and effort that you have carried with you since childhood. Through the workshop, you learn to rediscover and appreciate the effects of gravity on your movements, to apply the basic techniques for centering and freeing the body in a balanced way, and to integrate the sense of effortlessness into all your activities. Essentially, the result will be to reduce stress and increase awareness and efficiency. Taoism, the profound philosophy behind Tai Chi Chuan is discussed in relation to health, diet, sleep, self-defense, professional technique, and personal psychology. For both beginning and advanced students. The fee is $45.

2 Sporting Self-Improvement

Exercise, movement, and dance classes can, of course, be appreciated for their own worth. But they also provide excellent preparation for a sports activity. Once your body is in shape, you can pursue any number of activities with maximum enjoyment. However, it is the height of folly to be only a weekend athlete. You must keep at it.

If you are not in top condition, the mere fact that your muscles get tired while you play does not mean that you are having a healthy workout. And remember that sudden vigorous exercise without proper conditioning and warm-up exercises (see pages 11-12) can be suicidal. Your heart must warm up sufficiently to benefit from the exercise. Your best yardstick is the pulse test (see page 5). And before you pursue any vigorous sport, you should of course have a thorough medical checkup, including a cardiac stress test (see page 6).

All right, so you are fit enough to pursue a sport. Which sport should you choose? Here are some factors you should consider:

1. You have to choose a sport that you like and will continue to like without becoming bored.

2. You have to have the physical capacity to participate in the sport you choose. If you have bad knees, you probably will not be able to ski. If your elbow hurts, tennis is not for you. If your arm or shoulder gives you trouble, even golf may be too hard on you. If you have a weak cardiovascular system, squash would certainly not do anything for you except perhaps send you to that big squash court in the sky.

3. You have to be able to afford the sport. Some activities, such as skiing or horseback riding, can be very expensive; others, such as jogging or weight lifting, can be inexpensive or even free.

4. You have to pick an activity that is convenient. Will it require other people who may be hard to find when you want to play? Are the facilities too far from your home of office? Does the sport require too much time? Is it too seasonal?

5. If you want to select a sport for fitness, choose one for just that, *not* to become a champion. Such an activity has to challenge your body, not your timing, swing, or agility. Practicing a sport to improve your ability to compete requires specific training and is what competitive atheletes do. There is nothing wrong with wanting to improve your game. That is part of the fun of pursuing fitness through sports. But your main goal should be more realistic and ultimately more beneficial: conditioning.

SELECTING A SPORT

Bicycling

An excellent fitness-building activity, especially as far as the heart is concerned, bicycling develops the leg and back muscles and builds endurance. At an average speed and on good road conditions, you will burn about 400 calories per hour. Pedaling over hilly terrain will, of course, increase both the expenditure of calories and energy and muscular strength.

You should plan a regular bicycling route. A good way to increase endurance is to travel over flat land for five to ten minutes while you warm up and then up and down hills for twenty minutes. If you plan a bicycle trip of several miles, be sure to eat at least two hours before starting out to avoid stomach cramps. Carry some energy snacks with you such as fruit or candy bars to supply you with energy if you should need it.

There are several inexpensive gadgets that can make your bike stationary for use inside your home during inclement weather. This is a good investment if you are serious about using your bike as a means of achieving and maintaining physical fitness.

See also Part V, Chapter 9 (Hosteling page 336).

Fencing

Swordsmanship, whether for sport or for deadly combat, has been practiced for centuries. With the decline of dueling, fencing became popular as a vigorous sport for both men and women. It provides poise and self-assurance; develops coordination, speed, and agility; and generally contributes to physical fitness.

Amateur Fencing League of America, 601 Curtis Street, Albany, California 94706. The league is the official governing body for amateur fencing in America; it is a nonprofit, tax-exempt corporation staffed by volunteers devoted to the development of the sport. It organizes and conducts fencing events at the local, sectional, and national levels; establishes the rules, and sets up international competitions, including the Olympics and the Pan American Games; and generally encourages fencing and disseminates knowledge about it.

The AFLA publishes *American Fencing* six times a year. It is distributed to all league members and to subscribers throughout the fencing world.

You can receive a single copy of *How to Understand and Enjoy the Sport of Fencing and Questions & Answers about Amateur Fencing League of America* free of charge by writing to the league.

National Fencing Coaches Association of America, Hatfield Road, R.D. 1, Mahopac, New York, (914) 628-7263. The association is a professional society of fencing teachers, coaches, and others with a vocational interest in the sport. Its aim is to promote fencing and conduct clubs. You can write to NFCAA for the name of a fencing facility near you. The organization publishes a journal, *Swordmaster.*

Gymnastics

The sport has grown in popularity since recent Olympics made stars of the gymnasts, when the grace and beauty of their movements were seen by millions of people on their home television screens. This is basically an activity for the young, although some variations are suitable for adults under careful supervision. On the whole, gymnasts are an extremely fit group of athletes; they do not overdevelop any one part of the body. In tests to detect flexibility performed at the Institute of Sports Medicine at Lenox Hill Hospital in New York, gymnasts came in first, with a score of 93 percent. (Football players came in second, at 57 percent.)

If you undertake gymnastics, make sure that your teacher is qualified and that the equipment is kept in good order. Gymnastics classes are available at Ys, and commercial programs are springing up.

Gymatlanta, Arden Zinn Studio, 2192 Blakely Drive, Atlanta, Georgia 30324, (404) 875-9088. This is one of the largest and best-known programs in the South. Adult or children's gymnastics costs $30 a month for unlimited classes employing Ardenics, developed by Arden Zinn, a system that includes total body exercises to shape and tighten hips, thighs, and abdomen as well as generally put you into good shape.

National Association of College Gymnastic Coaches (Men), c/o Dr. Robert D. Peavy, president, Washington State University, Pullman, Washington 99164. This group of gymnastics coaches at colleges and universities aims to improve gymnastics participation at all levels. The association sponsors research, national and regional Coach of the Year awards, All American certification of collegiate gymnasts, Honor Coach awards, Citizens Hall of Fame awards, and other programs to honor gymnasts.

Handball

Handball is a vigorous game that provides a maximum of exercise in a minimum of time. It promotes agility and endurance and burns a spectacular 600 calories per hour. A warm-up prior to play is essential. And please note that the demands that handball makes on ligaments and joints may cause arm, shoulder and leg problems for people in their middle or later years.

U.S. Handball Association, 4101 Dempster Street, Skokie, Illinois 60076, (312) 673-4000. Several million handball players belong to this organization, which establishes rules and sponsors tournaments. *Handball*, a bimonthly publication is included in the membership which is $10 annually, $25 for 3 years, or $150 for lifetime. Membership also includes eligibility to play in the USHA tournaments.

Ice Skating and Roller Skating

These excellent sports are usually learned in childhood, but they can be enjoyably mastered at any time. Skating is good for the pelvis and legs, is excellent for fitness and endurance when done on a regular basis, and burns about 640 calories an hour. It is also an inexpensive social activity. If skating is to be your major method of fitness training, you should supplement it with exercises for the upper body.

Jogging

An estimated 7 million Americans have taken up this efficient and inexpensive way to gain physical fitness. Regular jogging conditions the heart to do more work with less effort. It also increases the efficiency of the respiratory system by strengthening the muscles that aid breathing. It uses up about 720 calories per hour. Before you begin a jogging program, it is definitely advisable to have a cardiac stress test (see page 6).

Jogging clothes should be loose and comfortable. You should not wear restricting, rubberized, or plastic garments. Such garments cause increased sweating, which will not produce real weight loss and which can be dangerous. Wear shoes that fit properly and have firm soles, good arch support, and pliable tops. (Do not wear sneakers.) Wear two pairs of socks: a smooth nylon or rayon pair against the skin and a heavy cotton or wool pair over these.

HOW TO JOG

Run in an upright position with your back straight and your head up. Avoid looking at your feet. Your arms should be held slightly away from your body; your elbows should be bent; and your forearms should be parallel to the ground. To reduce the tightness that sometimes occurs while jogging, occasionally shake and relax your shoulders. Try to land on the heel of the foot and rock forward so that your weight comes off the ball of your foot for your next step. Keep your steps short, and breathe deeply with your mouth open. Do not hold your breath. If you become overly tired or uncomfortable, slow down, walk, or stop completely.

WHEN AND WHERE TO JOG

Most people who jog in the early morning stick to it. Those who jog in the evening are less likely to keep to a schedule. In any event, avoid jogging during the first hour after eating or during extremely cold and hot weather. Running tracks and grassy fields are the best places to do your jogging; they are safest and easiest on the feet. Try to avoid hard running surfaces at least for the first few weeks. Varying your jogging route and location can add interest to your program.

A BASIC JOGGING PLAN

First week: Jog 40 seconds (100 yards); walk 1 minute (100 yards). Repeat 9 times.

Second week: Jog 1 minute (150 yards); walk 1 minute (100 yards). Repeat 8 times.

Third week: Jog 2 minutes (300 yards); walk 1 minute (100 yards). Repeat 6 times.

Fourth week: Jog 4 minutes (600 yards); walk 1 minute (100 yards). Repeat 4 times.

Fifth week: Jog 6 minutes (900 yards); walk 1 minute (100 yards). Repeat 3 times.

Sixth week: Jog 8 minutes (1,200 yards); walk 2 minutes (200 yards). Repeat 2 times.

Seventh week: Jog 10 minutes (1,500 yards); walk 2 minutes (200 yards). Repeat 2 times.

Eighth week: Jog 12 minutes (1,700 yards); walk 2 minutes (200 yards). Repeat 2 times.

By the eighth week, you would be in top physical condition and can set your own jogging pace.

Warning: If you experience any of the following symptoms, stop jogging immediately, and do not jog again until you have consulted your physician.

Pain or exertion under the breastbone, which feels as if someone is pressing against your rib cage. The pain may move or radiate to other areas of the upper body, such as the neck, cheek, shoulders, arms, or back.

A choking sensation during exertion.

Severe pain in the front portion of your shins or ankles when walking or jogging.

JOGGING YOUR FEET

Millions are running for fun and fitness. In jogging, the foot makes heel-to-toe contact with the ground as body weight is transferred from the heel, over the arch, and then pushed off the toes. In running, only the ball of the foot makes contact with the ground, and speed is of concern. For both running and jogging, there is a very short time when neither foot is on the ground. This suspension phase is what burns calories, requiring as much as three times more energy than walking.

PUBLICATION

Where the Action Is: A Run-Down on Running Tips. Scholl, Inc., 150 East Huron, Eighth Floor, Chicago, Illinois 60611. Send $.35 to cover postage and handling.

Road Runners Club of America, 6913 Westlawn Drive, Falls Church, Virginia 22042. What has 30,000 legs and runs 400,000 miles a week? It's the Road Runners Club of America (RRCA). Founded in 1958, the organization has eighty-eight chapters, with new ones being added monthly. Located in thirty-five states from coast to coast, the local clubs promote long-distance running both for persons seeking camaraderie through a regular physical fitness program and for highly trained competitive runners. The clubs sponsor weekly or twice-a-month programs that include races, fun runs, and/or Run for Your Life fitness events.

RCA has been the force behind the Run for Your Life Program, which centers on noncompetitive jogging events aimed at people of all ages and both sexes who simply like to run for fun and health. The club has its own Personal Fitness Program, which is open to members and nonmembers; publishes a quarterly national newsletter, *Footnotes;* schedules lectures, seminars, clinics, and an annual convention; and actively promotes the sport of long-distance running. Members range in ability from Olympians to two- to three-mile-a-day joggers just trying to keep fit. All walks of life are represented, and participation can take many forms. You can join one of the local chapters. If there is no chapter in your area, you can become a member-at-large. Or you may want to start a Road Runners Club in your own community. (Of course, already existing clubs that promote and sponsor running events on a regular basis are also welcome to join this national organization.)

You don't have to be a member to participate in the Personal Fitness Program. Just register before the end of the third month of any of the six-month periods, and estimate your mileage goal. Your award depends only on the total mileage you attain, regardless of your initial estimate. Keep a record of your mileage throughout the six months. Miles run prior to registration but during the six-month period can be included. Report your final mileage to the RRCA Personal Fitness Program coordinator on a form that will be furnished, and you will receive your award. There is a registration fee of $3 for RRCA members and $4 for nonmembers.

Martial Arts

The martial arts have a double advantage: They are good exercise, and they teach you how to defend yourself. Interest in these activities reached its peak in the early 1970s, but there are still thousands of devoted practitioners of all ages, stages, and incomes. The modern martial arts had their beginnings in India, where Buddhist monks used certain body motions both as mental and physical exercises, and as an effective method of defending their beliefs. The founder of the Zen sect, Bodhidharma, is reputed to have brought the Indian technique to China. The Chinese had their own form of unarmed combat, Kempo, which dated back to 3000 B.C. The Chinese and Indian techniques were merged, and further refinements from Mongolia, Korea, and Vietnam were added.

Meanwhile, the Japanese had developed their own hand-and-foot combat, tekot, which developed into the sumo style of wrestling. But by the thirteenth century, Japanese warriors charged with keeping peace in the country found sumo too slow. They added Kempo's faster, more aggressive movements and called it *jujitsu*. Later, Okinawan tricks of self-defense were added to jujitsu, making it a highly skilled art.

By the latter part of the nineteenth century, modern weapons put a crimp in the ancient art of jujitsu. A young Japanese, Jigoro Kano, then took the physical exercise and rough and tumble of jujitsu and added the concepts of gentleness and self-defense. He called his new sport *judo*. He opened a school to teach it in 1882. One of Kano's disciples brought judo to the United States in 1902. A few West Coast colleges showed some interest, but the sport did not really develop in this country until after World War II, when American soldiers brought back tales of great feats performed by practitioners of the martial arts. By 1953, judo had gained acceptance by the American Athletic Union and had become a competitive sport on a national scale.

What is judo's great appeal today? One of Kano's original objectives in developing judo was that anyone—male or female, young or old—could do it. And, indeed, with proper instruction, anyone can. Don Pohl, secretary of the U.S. Judo Federation, reports that approximately 250,000 individuals participate in judo. Half or more are introduced to it through the local Y or neighborhood judo club. There are about 100,000 registered rank holders, half of them under the age of seventeen. Women now constitute about 10 percent of the active judo participants.

What about karate? There are four kinds: Japanese, Korean, Okinawan, and Burmese. It is a far more aggressive sport than judo. The word *karate* means "empty hand," and those who become proficient in it are quite capable of swiftly killing someone with their bare hands. Its basic techniques include punches, kicks, strikes, and steps, all delivered with maximum speed, strength, accuracy, and coordination.

If you stick with karate and become proficient, it usually takes from two to three years to become a first-degree black belt. You start with a white belt; then proceed to yellow, green, purple, brown, and finally, black. To achieve the ranks, you must take a test before the headmaster. There are seven degrees of black belt and it ususally takes twenty-five years to become a seventh dan. In fact, out of the 10,000 enrollees at the Karate Institute in New York, only 50 adults have achieved black belt status.

The martial arts can be excellent for fitness, particularly for flexibility and muscular strength. However, if they are not done properly, they can easily result in serious injury. You must make sure that your instructor is properly trained.

Here is a list of the basic martial arts discipline.

Aikido: Similar to judo except that the wrists of the opponent (rather than the clothing) are grabbed. The movements are smooth, and the throwing technique takes advantage of the natural motion of the body. No choking or bone-breaking holds are allowed.

Judo: Invented in 1882 (the same time as American volleyball). It is based on jujitsu. A competitive sport of grappling, wrestling, and body throws.

Jujitsu: An ancient Japanese technique of bare-handed fighting. It was used by Japanese warriors to kill or maim the enemy.

Karate: Used to transform the whole body into a fighting weapon. It is more aggressive than judo.

Kung Fu (Gung Fu): Chinese karate. It uses more clawing and stabbing hand blows. Soft-style kung fu emphasizes speed; hard-style kung fu emphasizes power and the opponent's vulnerability.

Tai Chi Chuan: Chinese dancelike exercises aimed at promoting health. All the movements (unlike those of yoga) are natural to the body and can be done without strain.

The following associations can provide referrals to martial arts teachers:

Society of Black Belts International, Inc., P.O. Box 580, Summit, New Jersey 07901, (201)273-1337. The society has a registry of more than 1,000 authentic black belts in various systems and styles of all martial arts (judo, jujitsu, aikido, karate, kung fu, and so on) from around the world. Even if a prospective instructor's name is not registered, the society can assist you in contacting other organizations that can verify the person's credentials.

U.S. Judo Federation, R.R. 21, Box 519, Terre Haute, Indiana 47802, (812)299-9264. This organization, which was founded in 1952, has a membership of more than 25,000. It supervises the technical aspects of the sport, such as refereeing, judging, testing of ranks, and conducting tournaments. Through the federation's Teachers' Institute and Teachers' Placement Service, you can check credentials or find a certified teacher near you.

Skiing

Skiing has grown in popularity in recent years. More than 6 million Americans now ski, and surprisingly, skiing has a relatively low injury rate. For every 1,000 people who don their skis on a given day, fewer than 4 will have accidents requiring medical treatment. Skiers can do a lot to avoid injury on the slopes by keeping fit through exercise, even in the off-season.

Downhill skiing promotes leg and back development as well as agility. Nordic, or cross-country, skiing which is growing in popularity, builds endurance. Skiing can be fun, healthy, and of course, expensive.

GETTING IN SHAPE

Skiing is more difficult than it seems at first glance; it demands strenuous use of the abdominal muscles, front thigh muscles, rear thigh muscles, and calf muscles—muscles that seldom get a workout from normal daily activities. If more skiers started to get in shape at least six weeks before their first outing, many injuries could be averted. Pre-ski body-conditioning classes are offered at numerous gyms, Ys, schools, and ski shops.

If no such facilities are available near you, practice the following exercises: Raise your right leg in front of you approximately 12 inches from the floor. Keeping the leg extended, slowly lower yourself to a full squat without letting your foot hit the ground. Return to a standing position. Now do the same with your left leg. Repeat the whole procedure 5 times, gradually increasing to 10 times with each leg.

Of course, year-round conditioning is one of your best defenses against injury. Daily stretching exercises such as side leg lifts, half squats, and bent-knee sit-ups or jogging or bicycling three or four times a week are excellent conditioners (see pages 11-14). You should also do on-the-spot muscle warm-ups before starting down the trail.

INJURIES

In skiing, the principal injuries are to the heel area, but there are also chronic knee injuries and, of course, broken legs.

If you wear down the outside edges of the heels of your shoes walking, if you have to hop to initiate a turn on skis, if you depend too much on your outside ski, or if you turn better in one direction than in another, visit a foot specialist. He or she can prescribe placement of devices between the boot and the ski to facilitate even distribution of your weight. In skiing, as in other sports, correction of foot problems will make you a better athlete.

Ill-fitting or inadequate equipment is a prime cause of skiing accidents. If you are a beginner, don't buy; instead, rent the best gear possible until you get some idea of whether you will keep up with the sport and what you will need.

EQUIPMENT SKIS

Unless you intend to be a downhill racer, don't take extra long skis. At the very most, your skis should be about as long as you are tall or shorter. Lengthy skis are hard to manipulate, and if you fall forward, you are more likely to get hurt. Also look for skis with an antifriction device, a small disk on the underside of the ski that allows it to rotate and pop off automatically if you should fall.

BINDINGS

When purchasing bindings, look for those designed to release your skis quickly in case you fall. Have them fitted by an expert. Have the ski pro examine your bindings before you start out. It costs very little and can save you a lot of pain and medical bills. The National Ski Patrol frequently offers a free binding check at ski areas.

BOOTS

Shop for boots from a reputable dealer; don't look for bargains. Higher boots are now in vogue because it is claimed that they protect the ankle from injury. However, if you fall sharply forward, high boots can cause a fracture, not prevent it.

CLOTHING

Blue jeans, heavy sweaters, and woolen mittens are not recommended. After a spill or two, they can become wet and may even freeze. Look for nonskid gear. Avoid slippery, shiny garments; they are so dangerous in an unexpected slide down a slope that some resorts will not allow anyone wearing them on ski lifts. Dress in layers; you'll be warmer. Don't forget thermal underwear and socks and waterproof mittens or gloves. Wear protective goggles to cut down the glare from the sun and snow, and apply antichap lip balm and suntan lotion.

SOME TIPS

For the first skiing during the season, try to ski before one o'clock. By one, the slopes really get crowded, and people are tired from the morning's efforts, increasing the likelihood of accidents.

Always try to ski with a buddy. If one of you gets hurt, the other can seek help. If you are alone, stick to main trails and well-traveled slopes so that if you do get hurt, you can get help fast. If you fall, relax as you hit the surface. It may save you a broken bone.

U.S. Ski Association, Eastern Division, 22 High Street, Brattleboro, Vermont 05301, (802)257-7113. More than 30,000 members belong to this organization, which promotes the development of skiing skills, ski competition, and formation of ski clubs. It examines and certifies qualified amateur instructors. It also lobbies on behalf of skiers at state and federal levels and offers a comprehensive package of cash benefits such as discount tickets. The association also maintains an information office; publishes two tabloid newspapers, *Skier* and *Ski Competition East;* and offers travel packages, recreational ski series, and insurance plans.

American Ski Teachers Association of Nature Teknik, Camelback Ski Area, Tannersville, Pennsylvania 18372, (717)629-1661. Founded in 1960, this organization certifies ski instructors. It sets standards, improves teaching techniques, and maintains a library. It also has a placement service, cosponsors competitions, and publishes the annual *Directory of Certified Ski Instructors*, a booklet called *Skiing for Beginners*, and a teacher's manual. Check with this association to find a good skiing instructor.

Swimming

Swimming is an excellent sport for all-around body development and endurance training. It is also good for people recovering from hip, ankle, and knee problems because it is a non-weight-bearing sport. (On the other hand, because it is non-weight-bearing, it is not as effective for the muscles involved in maintaining posture.) At average speed and stroke, swimming uses about 500 calories per hour.

Aqua Dynamics. Physical Conditioning Through Water Exercises. Superintendent of Documents, U.S. Government Printing Office, Washington, D.C. 20402, No. 040-000-00360-6. Swimming is one of the best physical activities for people of all ages and for many persons who are handicapped. Vigorous water activities can make a major contribution to flexibility, strength, circulatory endurance. With the body submerged in water, blood circulation automatically increases to some extent; the pressure of water on the body also helps promote deeper ventilation of the lungs. With well-planned activity, both circulation and ventilation increase still more. Increased flexibility work is performed more easily in water because of the lessening of gravitation pull. A person immersed to the neck in water experiences a loss of 90 percent of weight. This means the feet and legs of a 130-pound individual immersed in water support only 13 pounds. Thus, individuals and especially older people with painful joints or weak leg muscles will usually find it possible and comfortable to move in the water. It is much easier to do leg straddle or stride stretches in water than on the floor. Many individuals can do leg bobbing or jogging in the water that they could never do on land. The exercises in this thirty-two-page booklet are fun. The price is $.75.

Tennis

A spectacularly popular sport in the 1960s and 1970s, tennis can be a fine way to keep fit if it is played vigorously. It stimulates endurance, flexibility, and balance and burns about 500 calories an hour. It should, of course, be played for fun, as well as for fitness.

United States Tennis Association, 51 East 42nd Street, New York, New York 10017, (212)949-9112. The motto of this group is "Tennis: The Sport for a Lifetime." A lifetime membership is $200. An annual membership for an adult is $13 per year. A Junior Membership for those twenty-one years and under is $6 and a Family Membership is $25. For membership, you will receive: twelve issues of *World Tennis Magazine*, the association's official publication, plus twenty-four issues of *Tennis USA*, a newsletter. You will also receive information and discounts on many USTA teacher training workshops and other events and a 2 percent discount on USTA publications. You will be eligible to play in any USTA sanctioned tournament and you will have your tournament record considered for ranking. You will help promote tennis development in your area. One third of your fee is returned to your sectional association.

U.S. Tennis Association Education and Research Center, 729 Alexander Rd., Princeton, New Jersey 08540, (609)452-2580. USTA maintains an annotated list of publications. The materials are classified for easy reference. If you have any questions about topics not covered in the publication list, you can contact the association; it is a clearinghouse for educational information on all aspects of tennis.

PUBLICATIONS

Here are some of the publications offered (at a 10 percent discount for USTA members):

Conditioning Exercises, Margaret Court. 1974. Exercises for stretching, speed, footwork, strength, and stamina. Three pages, $.25.

Stan Smith's Guide to Better Tennis, Stan Smith. Stan Smith analyzes and corrects the mistakes most commonly made by weekend players. Instruction covers all the strokes and is accompanied by action photos and artwork. Forty-eight pages, $2.95.

The Complete Pocket Tennis Strategist, Donald Sonneman. 1974. You can keep this small handbook in the pocket of your tennis shorts to guide you as you play. It provides the overall game plan for singles and doubles, and details the tactics used to implement the appropriate strategy. Fifty-six pages, illustrated, $1.50.

The Inner Game of Tennis, W. Timothy Gallway. New York: Random House, 1974. This best seller is about the game that takes place in your mind when you play tennis. It is aimed at overcoming all mental habits that inhibit excellence in performance. Gallway's thesis is that changing the feelings you have about play and competition is the key to improving your game. One hundred forty-two pages, $7.95.

Advanced Tennis, Chet Murphy. 1970. In addition to a review of the basic strokes, this booklet covers supplementary shots for the more advanced player and includes chapters on play situations and doubles strategy. Seventy-one pages; illustrated; $2.50.

TENNIS WORKSHOPS

John Gardiner's Tennis Ranch on Camelback, 5700 East McDonald Drive, Scottsdale, Arizona 85253, (602)948-2100. This is the in tennis place of the beautiful people. It has twenty-four championship tennis courts under the supervision of an internationally recognized staff. The teaching court, reportedly the most complete in the world, is equipped with a closed-circuit television system, a motion picture screening room, and many unique training aids. Special tennis clinics for groups are held throughout the year. Six casas, some with their own tennis court and pool, provide deluxe accommodations for four couples with complete hotel service. There are forty-one two-bedroom condominium cottages with fireplaces and complete kitchens. The eight-day, seven-night tennis clinic is $850 per person, double occupancy in casita guest bedroom. This fee includes all meals, saunas, two massages, Jacuzzi service charges, taxes, and twenty-two hours of tennis instruction. Air fares are extra, of course. Contact your travel agent or the tennis ranch for reservations.

World of Tennis Resort, World of Tennis Square, Austin, Texas 78734, (512)261-6300 or (800)531-5001. Set in the beautiful hill country of Texas, World of Tennis is a year-round resort and conference center with superior tennis instruction and full-service resort facilities. The complex consists of a trilevel clubhouse that provides lodge rooms, indoor tennis courts, pro shop, saunas, steam rooms, whirlpools, and a 125-person dining room serving gourmet meals and health-oriented lunches. The clubhouse features a racquet-shaped swimming pool, 1,500-seat stadium court, and sixteen lighted courts. Completely furnished town houses are available in two-, three-, and four-bedroom units. Special features include fireplaces, wet bars, outdoor grills, washers and dryers, double ovens and dishwashers, and of course, tennis courts right outside. Cliff Drysdale is the resident touring professional, and Billy Freer is director of tennis. Miniclinics are held every weekend, and six-day, five-night clinics for adults are scheduled regularly. Billy and his staff of pros also conduct youth clinics in the summer. There is a complete conference package, including a steward to serve you throughout each meeting day, secretarial assistance, a party each evening, and unlimited use of the tennis and spa facilities. Championship golf (twenty-seven holes), water-skiing, sailing and fishing on Lake Travis, horseback riding, and hiking in the hill country are also available. Rates for lodge rooms in the clubhouse range from $45 to $50; furnished town houses cost $60 per bedroom. Weekend miniclinics are $99 per person, double occupancy; the six-day, five-night clinics are $350 per person, double occupancy. The conference package costs $69 per person, double occupancy.

Rod Laver Tennis-Letset Resorts, Inc., 5310 Indigo, Houston, Texas 77096, (713)661-7298. A variety of tennis vacation packages are available at Rod Laver resort facilities at April Sound, Texas, (713)588-1101, and Palmetto Dunes on Hilton Head Island, South Carolina. For Villa rooms, call toll free outside South Carolina (800) 845-6130). For Hyatt Hotel, call toll free (800) 228-9000. All facilities offer luxurious accommodations. You decide on the amount of tennis instruction per day, what additional tennis activities you would like to participate in, and whether you want two, three, or five days of tennis. Instructors are trained in the Laver method of instruction. There is Supervised Tennis Play, a unique concept in tennis vacations offering activities such as round robin tournaments for men, women, and mixed doubles; Beat the Pros matches for advanced players; Australian-style play; action drills; and other tennis activities, all under the watchful eyes of the Laver teaching professionals. There is videotape with instant replay, automatic ball machines, and the *Courtside Companion*, an instructional diary.

The resorts offer swimming, boating, golf, horseback riding, and other recreational activities. The Court 'n Clinic Tennis Holiday includes five nights' deluxe accommodations, ten hours of on-court tennis instruction and drills, eight to ten hours of Supervised Tennis Play, welcome cocktails, the *Courtside Companion*, additional court play (subject to availability), and full resort guest privileges for $315 to $470 single occupancy, $225 to $320 double occupancy, depending on resort. The Weekender Clinic includes two nights' deluxe accommodations, seven hours of on-court instruction, welcome cocktails, the *Courtside Companion*, additional court play (subject to availability), and full resort guest privileges for $170 to $175 single occupancy, $145 to $150 double occupancy.

Ramey Tennis Schools, Route 6, Owensboro, Kentucky 42301, (502)771-4723. Mrs. William Ramey, the director, is a certified professional U.S.P.T.A. affiliated with the U.S. Tennis Association. She offers tennis camps for adults in Indiana, Illinois, Minnesota, Ohio, and Kentucky. All are on college campuses and are staffed by qualified professionals who teach the Ramey method of tennis instruction. There are also special weekends and a "Ladies Only" week at the camp's indoor tennis club headquarters in Kentucky.

The Adult Weekends, Adult Week Camps, and Holiday Camps have as their object the teaching of tennis, the sport for a lifetime, in a manner that will improve the student's performance and self-confidence. Each session offers instruction for beginners as well as advanced players, and there are opportunities for competitive play and unlimited court time. Special help is given to coaches and teachers who attend and wish to learn advanced drills, corrective techniques, and training methods, as well as to improve their own games. There is limited enrollment in each session, with one instructor to each four persons. An organized schedule is followed, and each participant receives a complete stroke analysis with recommendations for correcting form. Those with such ailments as tennis elbow are shown which stroke is causing the difficulty and how to correct the problem. Videotape instant replay is used in each program, and ball machines are available for drills and practice. Lectures and movies supplement on-court sessions. With hard work, a participant often makes a whole summer's advancement in one session. Better footwork, smoother strokes, and greater confidence are the easily recognized results of time spent in the program. Costs average $295 per week and $175 for weekends for a single or double room, meals, and instructions. Write to headquarters for schedules and costs in your area.

Platform Tennis

Platform tennis is growing in popularity because it has many advantages over regular court tennis. Its playing area is smaller than the regular court but bigger than a Ping-Pong table. It was invented by two weather-frustrated tennis players on a dreary fall afternoon in 1928. Today more than half a million play platform tennis. There are more than 7,000 courts, and more are popping up everywhere as individuals and recreation departments become aware of the popularity of the sport. It is competitive, social, mentally challenging, and excellent exercise, and you can learn to play it well in a month. And more important, you can play it all year round, outside and at night.

The court looks like a traditional tennis court, but it is one-fourth the size, and it is a platform made of wooden slats. Many courts are heated underneath so that you can play in cold, snowy weather. All you need is a seventeen-inch perforated paddle made out of metal, wood, or plastic and costing $10 to $35; a hard sponge-rubber ball; a good pair of sneakers. One manufacturer has already designed a special platform tennis shoe for $25. There are no uniform dress requirements.

American Platform Tennis Association, 52 Upper Montclair Plaza, Upper Montclair, New Jersey 07043, (201)783-5325. The association promotes and regulates the game of platform tennis and publishes an official rules guide. Write for more information.

Walking

Walking is an excellent, practical exercise. You don't need to train for it, you can do it alone at any time and practically anywhere. To promote fitness, you should keep up a brisk, steady pace (about 4 miles per hour, or 1 mile every fifteen minutes). You can use up about 250 calories per hour.

You can also be more relaxed. A study by researchers at the University of Southern California compared the effects of a fifteen-minute walk at a moderate pace and a single dose of a mild tranquilizer. The measurements were made with an electromyograph, a machine that measures muscle tension. They found that the walk at a rate sufficient to raise the heart rate to 100 beats per minute was more relaxing than the tranquilizer and that the effect persisted for at least one hour.

A BASIC WALKING PLAN

First week: Walk at a brisk pace for 10 minutes (or for a shorter time if you become uncomfortably tired), walk slowly or rest for 3 minutes. Again walk briskly for 10 minutes, or until you become uncomfortably tired.

Second week: Walk at a brisk pace for 15 minutes (or for a shorter time if you become uncomfortably tired). Walk slowly for 3 minutes.

Third week: Jog 20 seconds (50 yards), or walk as fast as you can for 1 minute (100 yards). Then walk at a slow pace for 1 minute (100 yards). Repeat 12 times.

Fourth week: Jog 20 seconds (100 yards), or walk as fast as you can for 2 minutes (200 yards). Then walk at a slow pace 1 minute (100 yards). Repeat 12 times.

By the end of the fourth week, you should be ready to take up a jogging program, or you can continue your walking regimen.

Weight Lifting

This sport has undergone a renaissance for men and has been taken up by women. Twenty-five Ys in the Los Angeles area alone have weight lifting programs for women, and many other Ys and health clubs are setting up programs.

Female and male weight lifters have different goals. Men generally want to lift heavier and heavier weights as an exercise in strength; whereas women use weights to condition the body. Most women start with eight-pound weights and work up to twenty-five-pound ones. They work out at least three times a week. The immediate effect is a better-contoured body, but the long-range effects are psychological as well as physical. Women report that they feel better and have the satisfaction of knowing that they are physically strong.

PRESIDENTIAL SPORTS AWARD

Because goals are important in any self-improvement pursuit, the President's Council on Physical Fitness has set requirements for a council award:

ARCHERY

1. Shoot a minimum of 3,000 arrows.
2. No more than 60 arrows in any one day may be credited to the total.
3. Minimum target distance is 15 yards. In field or roving archery, there should be 14 different targets, each at 15 or more yards.

BACKPACKING

1. Backpack for a minimum of 50 hours.
2. No more than 3 hours in any one day may be credited to the total.
3. Weight of pack must be at least 10 percent of body weight.

BADMINTON

1. Play badminton for a minimum of 50 hours.
2. No more than 1½ hours in any one day may be credited to the total.
3. Play must include at least 25 matches (best 2 of 3 games) of singles and/or doubles.

BASKETBALL

1. Play basketball and/or practice basketball skills for a minimum of 50 hours.
2. At least 15 of the 50 hours must be in organized league or tournament games.
3. No more than 1 hour in any one day may be credited to the total.

BICYCLING

1. Bicycle for a minimum of 600 miles (more than five gears), or bicycle for a minimum of 400 miles (five gears or less).
2. No more than 12 miles in any one day may be credited to the total (more than five gears); no more than 8 miles in any one day may be credited to the total (five or fewer gears).

BOWLING

1. Bowl a minimum of 150 games.
2. No more than 5 games in any one day may be credited to the total.
3. The total of 150 games must be bowled on not less than 34 different days.

CANOE OR KAYAK

1. Paddle for a minimum of 200 miles.
2. No more than 7 miles in any one day may be credited to the total.

CLIMBING

1. Climb under Alpine-type conditions for a minimum of 50 hours.
2. No more than 3 hours in any one day may be credited to the total.

EQUITATION
1. Ride on horseback a minimum of 50 hours.
2. No more than 1 hour in any one day may be credited to the total.

FENCING
1. Practice fencing skills for a minimum of 50 hours.
2. No more than 1 hour in any one day may be credited to the total.
3. At least 30 of the 50 hours must be under the supervision of an instructor.

FIGURE SKATING
1. Skate for a minimum of 50 hours.
2. No more than 1½ hours in any one day may be credited to the total.
3. Skating should include figure-eight work (patch), free skating, ice dancing.

FITNESS WALKING
1. Walk for a minimum of 125 miles.
2. Each walk must be continuous, without pauses for rest, and the pace must be at least 4 miles per hour (15 minutes per mile).
3. No more than 2½ miles in any one day may be credited to the total.

GOLF
1. Play a minimum of 30 rounds of golf (18 holes).
2. No more than one 18-hole round a day may be credited to the total.
3. No motorized carts can be used.

GYMNASTICS
1. Practice gymnastic skills and/or compete in gymnastics for a minimum of 50 hours.
2. No more than 2 hours in any one day may be credited to the total.
3. Practice must include work in at least one-half of the recognized events (2 of 4 for women and girls, 3 of 6 for men and boys).
4. Particiate in at least 4 organized competitions.

HANDBALL
1. Play a minimum of 150 games.
2. No more than 4 games in any one day may be credited to the total.

ICE SKATING
1. Skate for a minimum of 200 miles.
2. No more than 6 miles in any one day may be credited to the total.

JOGGING

1. Jog for a minimum of 125 miles.
2. No more than 2½ miles in any one day may be credited to the total.

JUDO

1. Practice judo skills for a minimum of 50 hours.
2. At least 30 of the 50 hours must be under the supervision of a qualified teacher.
3. No more than 1 hour in any one day may be credited to the total.

KARATE

1. Practice karate skills for a minimum of 50 hours.
2. At least 30 of the 50 hours must be under the supervision of a qualified instructor.
3. No more than 1 hour in any one day may be credited to the total.

RACQUET BALL

1. Play a minimum of 150 games.
2. No more than 4 games in any one day may be credited to the total.

ROLLER SKATING

1. Skate for a minimum of 50 hours.
2. No more than 1½ hours in any one day may be credited to the total.

ROWING

1. Row a rowboat for a minimum of 50 miles, or row a wherry for a minimum of 100 miles, or row a shell for a minimum of 120 miles.
2. No more than 1½ miles in any one day may be credited to the total (rowboat); no more than 3 miles in any one day may be credited to the total (wherry); no more than 3½ miles in any one day may be credited to the total (shell).

RUNNING

1. Run for a minimum of 200 miles.
2. Run continuously for at least 3 miles during each outing. No more than 5 miles in any one day may be credited to the total. Longer runs are not discouraged, but miles counted toward the 200-mile total must be spread over at least 40 outings.
3. Average time must be 9 minutes or less per mile (27 minutes for 3 miles, 45 minutes for 5 miles, and so on).

SAILING

1. Sail for a minimum of 50 hours (practice and/or competition).
2. No more than 2½ hours in any one day may be credited to the total.

SCUBA DIVING OR SKIN DIVING
1. Scuba or skin dive or train for diving for a minimum of 50 hours.
2. No more than 1 hour in any one day may be credited to the total.
3. Total time must include at least 15 logged dives on 15 separate days under the Safe Diving Standards of one of these groups: National Association of Skin Diving Schools, National Association of Underwater Instructors, Professional Association of Diving Instructors, the National YMCA, or the Underwater Society of America.

SKIING (ALPINE)
1. Ski for a minimum of 50 hours.
2. No more than 3 hours in any one day may be credited to the total.

SKIING (NORDIC)
1. Ski for a minimum of 150 miles.
2. No more than 10 miles in any one day may be credited to the total.

SOCCER
1. Play soccer or practice soccer skills for a minimum of 50 hours.
2. At least 30 of the 50 hours must be under the supervision of a coach or official.
3. No more than 1 hour in any one day may be credited to the total.

SOFTBALL
1. Play softball or practice softball skills for a minimum of 50 hours.
2. At least 20 of the 50 hours must be in organized league or tournament games.
3. No more than 1 hour in any one day may be credited to the total.

SQUASH
1. Play squash for a minimum of 50 hours.
2. No more than 1½ hours in any one day may be credited to the total.
3. Total must include at least 25 matches (3 of 5 games) of singles and/or doubles.

SWIMMING
1. Swim for a minimum of 25 miles (44,000 yards).
2. No more than ¾ mile (1,320 yards) in any one day may be credited to the total.

TABLE TENNIS
1. Play table tennis for a minimum of 50 hours.

2. At least 20 of the 50 hours must be in organized league or tournament play.

3. No more than 1 hour in any one day may be credited to the total.

TEAM HANDBALL

1. Play team handball or practice team handball skills for a minimum of 50 hours.

2. At least 20 of the 50 hours must be in organized league or tournament games.

3. No more than 1 hour in any one day may be credited to the total.

TENNIS

1. Play tennis for a minimum of 50 hours.

2. No more than 1½ hours in any one day may be credited to the total.

3. Total must include at least 25 sets of singles and/or doubles (tie-break rules may apply).

VOLLEYBALL

1. Play volleyball or practice volleyball skills for a minimum of 50 hours.

2. At least 10 of the 50 hours must be in organized league or tournament games.

3. No more than 1 hour in any one day may be credited to the total.

WATER SKIING

1. Water ski for a minimum of 50 hours.

2. No more than 2 hours in any one day may be credited to the total.

WEIGHT TRAINING

1. Train with weights for a minimum of 50 hours.

2. No more than 1 hour in any one day may be credited to the total.

3. A workout must include at least 8 weight exercises, each performed a minimum of 10 times.

Qualifying Standards for Presidential Sports Award

The President's Council on Physical Fitness will award you a Presidential Sports Award Certificate, emblem, and pin if you complete the qualifications for any one of the sports listed in this section. Qualification is based on fifty hours of participation spread over at least fifty activity sessions within a period of four months. Concessions are made only in sports for which seasons may be short or for which access to facilities may be limited. In such cases, the fifty-hour activity requirement may be reduced. This is a very effective way to encourage yourself to stick to a fitness program. For a free logbook in which to keep your official record, write to:

Presidential Sports Award
President's Council on Physical Fitness and Sports
Room 3030
Donohoe Building
400 Sixth Street, S.W.
Washington, D.C. 20201

When you have completed your program, send $4 to the same address to receive your awards.

IMPROVING PERFORMANCE

How can you improve your athletic ability in any sport?

Dr. Robert Nideffer, former associate professor of psychology at the University of Rochester and now director of Enhanced Performance Associates (see page 52), offers this sound and basic advice: Relax, rehearse, and pay attention. When you learn to relax and to keep your attention on your objective, your performance will improve tremendously.

First, he says, you have to sit down and take a good look at yourself and your ability to play at that sport. You have to analyze your strengths and weaknesses. Everyone has different points of stress. Where do *your* problems occur when you are playing? What are *your* stresses? Then you have to learn one of the relaxation techniques, whether it's TM or biofeedback or progressive relaxation (see Part III, Chapter 8). When you feel under stress or know you are about to tighten, you must practice your relaxation technique.

Nideffer says that every sport offers the opportunity to relax. You can do it during a football huddle, between points in tennis, while a foul shot is being taken in basketball. The more skilled you become at the relaxation technique, the more quickly you can relax. He explained that relaxation is so important because the more tense and anxious you become during performance, the more likely you are to lose your ability to control your attention. And that is when you are going to make mistakes and not perform up to your best ability. Attention, like relaxation, is helped by rehearsal. The more you rehearse, the easier it is for you to concentrate and the less likely you are to be distracted by interference. Some games require you to pay attention to a lot of different things at once. If you are a quarterback in football or a member of a volleyball team, for example, you have to keep an eye on your teammates as well as on your own duties. If you play golf, the focus of your attention is much narrower. That's why analyzing your strengths and weaknesses is important. You have to figure out whether the interference ("psychological noise") comes from outside or from inside your head.

Enhanced Performance Associates, 12468 Bodega Way, San Diego, California 92128, (714)487-3750, Robert M. Nideffer, Ph.D., president. This organization is hired by police departments, athletic teams, businesses, and individuals to help them assess and manage stress and to improve performance. Programs include workshops, training of in-house personnel, and individual treatment. Workshop costs vary according to length and content, with a minimum of $500 per day plus expenses. Individual treatment typically involves four 45-minute sessions at $50 per session.

PUBLICATIONS

The Inner Athlete: Mind Plus Muscle for Winning, Robert M. Nideffer. New York: Thomas Y. Crowell Company, Publishers, 1976. Price: $8.95.

A.C.T.: Attention Control Training, Robert M. Nideffer and Roger Sharpe. New York: Wyden Books, 1978. Price: $8.95.

How to Put Anxiety Behind You, Robert M. Nideffer and Roger Sharpe. Briarcliff Manor, N.Y.: Stein & Day Publishers, 1978. Price: $8.95.

Predicting Human Behavior: A Theory and Test of Attentional and Interpersonal Style, Robert M. Nideffer. San Diego, Calif.: Enhanced Performance Associates, 1979. Price: $19.95.

3 Improving Your Health

It's very difficult to improve any aspect of your life if you are not feeling well. The zest for the quest for self-improvement is best fueled by energy produced by a healthy body. If a hidden physical or emotional ailment is diagnosed and successfully treated, your whole outlook on life improves, and all things look brighter. You'll even look better. Most of us don't hesitate to visit a beauty parlor or barbershop and spend money on toiletries and clothes to keep ourselves looking good. But how many of us realize that one of the best cosmetics is good health? If you don't believe that, just remember what you looked like the last time you were sick or had a hangover.

We also don't think twice about taking our cars for a periodic tune-up and laying out several thousand dollars for a new machine we consider a necessity, not a luxury. Yet, when it comes to keeping ourselves in good health—doing those things that will maintain our bodies and prevent things from going wrong and improving those things that do go wrong—most of us are reluctant. We don't want to spend the time or money for medical care, and we secretly believe that if we don't let a doctor look for a problem, there won't be any problem.

Would you hook up your seat belt if the law didn't require you to do so? When was your last physical checkup? Why are we so reluctant to practice prevention?

All of us have heard tales of someone who passed a health examination with flying colors, only to drop dead on the way out of the doctor's office. And periodically, some professor of medicine will announce that health checkups are useless or too expensive and that diseases cannot be prevented by early detection. Nevertheless, the question remains: Can checkups really prevent illness and improve health?

The answer is *yes!* Screening programs have shown that surprising numbers of us are walking around unaware that we have a problem that could benefit from medical attention. For example, statistics evolved from health examinations at Kaiser Permanente Multiphasic Testing Center in California, show that 1 out of every 3 individuals has a condition warranting a doctor's care, 1 out of every 50 has undetected high blood pressure, 1 out of every 100 has hidden diabetes, and 1 out of every 500 has undetected heart disease.

The Preventive Medicine Institute–Strang Clinic in New York, a pioneer in the field, examined 150,000 adults between 1963 and 1972. More than 900 malignancies and 7,500 premalignant conditions were uncovered; that is, the clinic found previously unsuspected conditions in about 50 out of every 1,000 patients. In another 30,000 patients, or about 200 out of 1,000, other abnormalities ranging from anemia and hypercholesterolemia (high blood fats) to high blood pressure and abnormal electrocardiograms were found and called to the attention of the patients with advice for corrective action. Appropriate medical attention for these previously undiagnosed conditions can be conservatively estimated to have saved 1,000 lives and prevented disease in another 10,000 individuals.

Whether or not we practice prevention, it is true that the statistics show we are living longer. At the turn of the century, most Americans died by their forties. Today, life-spans for women are approaching an average of eighty years and seventy-five years for men. What accounts for this? In the past, infectious diseases killed us quickly; today, chronic diseases kill us slowly. Consequently, today, we have time for therapy.

Chronic illnesses can be treated and either cured or controlled so that we can enjoy our longer lives to the fullest.

Of course, you don't want to find out that you have even a minor health problem, let alone a serious one. But if you do have such a condition and it can be cured or controlled so that you can continue to feel well and vigorous or better than you do now, then the payoff from prompt medical detection is worth the cost and the trouble.

What constitutes a good health examination? Here are the basic elements:

History: This should include any symptoms you may have, any illnesses or operations you have had in the past, a record of your parents' and grandparents' and other close relatives' major ailments, your immunizations, drugs or medicines you take, whether you have any allergies, what kind of diet you follow, and the kind of life you lead.

Physical examination: This will begin with a check of your blood pressure, pulse, temperature, and general appearance. The doctor will check your body for swellings, lumps, or tender areas and look into your mouth, eyes, ears, throat, and other body openings. To be truly thorough, an examination should include manual and sigmoidoscopic examinations of the rectum and lower colon, particularly if you are over forty years old.

Laboratory tests: These should include blood and urine tests, as well as a Pap test for women. Chest X rays and electrocardiograms should also be performed periodically.

Computerized health screenings have grown in popularity in the past decade. Technology has made it easy to do many tests at once and at lower cost. Health screening examinations have also become a fringe benefit for many corporations and union members. Companies know that whatever they pay for screening they receive back tenfold by preventing the loss of valuable personnel through sickness. However, it is important to understand that health screenings are *not* a substitute for personal medical care. They do not treat; they only diagnose. And the information detected at a screening is of little value unless followed up with therapy under medical supervision.

This chapter describes some of the top screening programs in the nation, as well as organizations seeking to help people improve their health by correcting bad habits. This section of Chapter 3 deals directly with medical facilities and health-oriented organizations but other portions of this book discuss other topics—diet, dentistry, mental health, and exercise—that are central to the vital issue of health. And no aspect of self-improvement is more important than improving and maintaining your health.

HEALTH PROFILES

Medical Datamation, Southwest and Harrison, Bellevue, Ohio 44811, (419)483-6060. Medical Datamation provides a computerized system for assessment of health status. It allows you to obtain a variety of health information. All assessments are processed from information obtained through a series of questionnaires.

A questionnaire (see pages 56-59) determines your Health Risk Index. If you fill it in and send it to Medical Datamation, you will receive an evaluation of your life-style, hereditary patterns, and current medical problems. The information you provide will be used to project major health problems that you will most likely encounter in the coming years and to suggest "action items" to help avoid serious illness. In addition, the report that you receive will provide a comparative assessment of your "health age" and your chronological age. You may, for example, find that you have the health status of someone who is thirty-eight, even though you are only thirty. The cost is $8.

A four-page questionnaire provides a Complete Medical History Profile, as well as the Health Risk Index. The medical history summarizes past and current problems and projects potential problems based on reported symptoms. This profile is valuable for beginning or updating a home health file. The cost is $10.

An eight-page questionnaire provides a Life Quality Report, in addition to the Complete Medical History Profile and your Health Risk Index. The Life Quality Report assesses your emotional health and your satisfaction with your current life-style and environment. The cost is $12.

Medical Datamation also provides sixteen information booklets on such subjects as sexual problems, diet, and health hazards. These booklets were developed by the company and are only available through its office. They are free to those who have filled in the questionnaire.

Lifestyle Assessment Questionnaire, University of Wisconsin— Stevens Point Foundations, Inc., Stevens Point, Wisconsin 54481. The $5 fee for this questionnaire includes the computer analysis and return mailing. This questionnaire is similar to the one on pages 56-59 and was developed by a group of researchers working to understand how life-style and environment affect health.

GETTING A THOROUGH CHECKUP AT ONE OF THE CLINICS

If you wish to have a thorough medical checkup with all the latest equipment, you would be wise to go to one of the nation's leading clinics.

Boston, Massachusetts

Lahey Clinic, 605 Commonwealth Avenue, Boston, Massachusetts 02215, (617)262-4900. Patients are referred to this clinic by their physi-

Your Health Risk Index Questionnaire

A questionnaire designed to provide an analysis of your medical history, current habits, and other factors that influence your life expectancy.

Questionnaire: Unit Number:

NOTE: *Read instructions provided and follow directions carefully. If you consider a question too personal, you may skip it. Medical Datamation warrants that it will provide medical reports resulting from this questionnaire to you and/or your designated medical facility, if applicable, and it will not otherwise release your reports without your written consent.*

1-203

IDENTIFICATION

10 Name
   Last Name, First Name, Middle Name

11 Today's Date   Mo. — Da. — Yr.

12 Date of Birth   Mo. — Da. — Yr.

15 __ Female   16 __ Male

17 Height __ ft. __ in.   18 Weight ____ lbs.

PERMANENT HOME ADDRESS

19 Street

20 City

21 State or Province

22 Zip

23 Country

1-603

DEMOGRAPHIC Background

Race

10 __ American Indian

11 __ Black

12 __ Caucasian

15 __ Other

Family income level

16 __ Low

17 __ Middle

18 __ High

Religious Preference

65 __ Catholic

66 __ Jewish

67 __ Protestant

69 __ Other

2-104

ILLNESSES and MEDICAL PROBLEMS

2-105

10 — Alcoholism
11 — Anemia-sickle cell
12 — Bleeding trait
13 — Bronchitis, chronic

Cancer
14 — Breast
15 — Cervix
16 — Colon
17 — Lung
18 — Uterus
19 — Other cancer
20 — Cirrhosis - liver
21 — Colitis - ulcerative
22 — Depression
23 — Diabetes
24 — Diabetes, uncontrolled
25 — Emphysema
26 — Fibrocystic breasts

Heart problem
27 — Heart attack
28 — Coronary disease
29 — Rheumatic heart
30 — Heart valve prob.
31 — Heart murmur
32 — Enlarged heart
33 — Heart rhythm prob.
34 — Other heart prob.

High blood fats, specify.
50 — Cholesterol
51 — Triglycerides
52 — High blood pressure
53 — High blood pressure, uncontrolled
54 — Obesity - more than 20 lbs overweight
55 — Pneumonia
56 — Polyps in colon
57 — Rheumatic fever
58 — Rheumatic fever, with resultant heart murmur
59 — Stroke
60 — Suicide attempt
61 — Tuberculosis

No   Yes   In the past year, have you had -
62 — Chest pain on exertion, relieved by rest?
63 — Shortness of breath lying down, relieved by sitting up?
64 — Unexplained weight loss, more than 10 lbs?
65 — Unexplained rectal bleeding?
66 — Unexplained vaginal bleeding?

listed by placing a checkmark in the appropriate column.

M-Most of time   S-Some of time   R-Rarely or none

	M	S	R	
10				Feel sad, depressed?
11				Wish to end it all?
12				Feel tense and anxious?
13				Worry about things generally?
14				More aggressive, hard-driving than friends?
15				Have an intense desire to achieve?
16				Feel optimistic about the future?

FAMILY MEDICAL HISTORY (Blood Relatives)

Check items that apply for your blood relatives. Your blood relatives include your children, brothers, sisters, parents, and grandparents.

30 — Do not know my family medical history.
(Go to question 50)

Yes	No	Illness	Yes	No	Illness
31		Anemia-sickle cell	36		High blood press.
32		Bleeding trait	37		Mental illness
33		Cancer	38		Stroke
34		Diabetes (sugar)	39		Suicide
35		Heart disease	40		Tuberculosis

Yes   No   Check the items that apply.

Yes
50 — Father died of a heart attack before age 60?
51 — Mother died of a heart attack before age 60?
52 — Mother or sister had cancer of the breast?
53 — Did your mother take DES (diethylstilbestrol) when she was pregnant with you?

HABITS and RISK FACTORS

Your habits influence your ability to achieve and maintain good health and long life. The questions on this page concern factors that are known to influence your health.

4-201

EXERCISE

Specify the amount of exercise you get each day.

Yes No

10 ___ None or very little

The equivalent of-

11 ___ 10 flights of stairs, or 1 mile walking

12 ___ 20 flights of stairs, or 2 miles walking

13 ___ Over 20 flights of stairs, or over 2 miles walking

SMOKING

Yes No Do you-

14 ___ Smoke a pipe and inhale 5 or more times/day?

15 ___ Smoke cigars and inhale 5 or more times/day?

16 ___ Currently smoke cigarettes?

17 ___ Have a history of cigarette smoking, but stopped?

If no longer smoking, specify number of years since you stopped.

18 ___ 1 yr.   21 ___ 4 yrs.   24 ___ 7 yrs.

19 ___ 2 yrs.   22 ___ 5 yrs.   25 ___ 8 yrs.

20 ___ 3 yrs.   23 ___ 6 yrs.   26 ___ 9 yrs.

If you have ever smoked cigarettes, specify amount and duration.

Daily amount   Number of years

27 ___ 1/2 pack/day or less   31 ___ Less than 1 year

28 ___ 1/2 to 1 pack/day   32 ___ 1 to 5 years

29 ___ 1 to 2 packs/day   33 ___ 5 to 10 years

SELF-CARE

The early evaluation of symptoms, self-exams, and various professional health exams are important in detecting diseases. Regular medical follow-up is important in keeping problems under control and avoiding complications.

Yes No Have you-

10 ___ Ever had a chest x-ray?

11 ___ Had an abnormal chest x-ray?

12 ___ Ever had an EKG (Electrocardiogram)?

13 ___ Had an abnormal EKG?

14 ___ Had a TB skin test?

15 ___ Had a positive TB skin test?

16 ___ Had eyes checked in past two years?

17 ___ Had hearing tested (audiometry) in past 2 years?

18 ___ Had dental exam in the past year?

Do you-

19 ___ Regularly follow your physician's advice?

20 ___ Plan annual medical symptom review with your physician or health service?

21 ___ Plan annual rectal exam after age 30?

WOMEN (Men go to "Tests")

Yes No Do you or have you-

30 ___ Had a PAP test within past year?

31 ___ Had at least three PAP tests in past 5 years?

32 ___ Had an abnormal PAP test in past?

33 ___ Plan annual PAP tests in the future?

34 ___ Check your breasts once a month for lumps?

35 ___ Have a breast exam by a doctor once yearly?

results. If measured more than once, use most recent value.

Blood Pressure | Cholesterol

Systolic	Diastolic	Cholesterol
40 ___ 120 or less	45 ___ 82 or less	50 ___ 180 or less
41 ___ 140	46 ___ 88	51 ___ 210
42 ___ 160	47 ___ 94	52 ___ 240
43 ___ 180	48 ___ 100	53 ___ 270
44 ___ 200 or more	49 ___ 106 or more	54 ___ 300 or more

INFORMATION

Check items for which you would like educational information.

60 ___ Alcohol	68 ___ Legal problems
61 ___ Birth Control	69 ___ Loneliness
62 ___ Diet	70 ___ Marital problems
63 ___ Drug abuse	71 ___ Medical emergencies
64 ___ Emotional problems	72 ___ Self-breast exam
65 ___ Exercise	73 ___ Sexual problems
66 ___ Financial problems	74 ___ Smoking
67 ___ Health hazards	75 ___ Venereal disease

CONCLUSION

Yes   No

80 ___   ___   Do you have any other problem not covered
by this questionnaire?

Please give us your opinion of this system.

81 ___ Great   83 ___ Generally good, criticism minor

82 ___ Good   84 ___ Don't like it

Thanks for completing this questionnaire. Please review for
accuracy. then mail.   © Medical Datamation 1977

ALCOHOL

Yes   No

35 ___   ___   Do you currently drink alcohol?

36 ___   ___   Did you formerly drink alcohol but stopped?

If you have ever drunk alcohol. specify details.

Amount per week	Number of years
37 ___ Less than 2 drinks/wk.	42 ___ Less than one year
38 ___ 2 to 10 drinks/wk.	43 ___ 1 to 5 years
39 ___ 10 to 25 drinks/wk.	44 ___ 5 to 10 years
40 ___ 25 to 40 drinks/wk.	45 ___ 10 to 20 years
41 ___ Over 40 drinks/wk.	46 ___ Over 20 years

TRAUMA, ACCIDENTS and OTHER HAZARDS

Yes   No   Do you-

47 ___   ___   Often carry a weapon at work or otherwise?

48 ___   ___   Have an arrest record for a violent crime?

49 ___   ___   Drive after drinking or taking drugs?

How many miles do you travel in a car or other motor vehicle each year
(average is 12,000 miles)?

50 ___ Up to 10,000	52 ___ 15,000 to 20,000
51 ___ 10,000 to 15,000	53 ___ Over 20,000

What percent of the time do you wear a seat belt?

54 ___ 0 to 25%	56 ___ 50% to 75%
55 ___ 25% to 50%	57 ___ 75% to 100%

What percent of the time do you wear a shoulder strap?

58 ___ 0 to 25%	60 ___ 50% to 75%
59 ___ 25% to 50%	61 ___ 75% to 100%

cians or they can come on their own. The Periodic Examination Program at Lahey is designed for corporations that send executives or employees to it for annual examinations (for which the corporations pay). Or you can arrange to undergo these periodic examinations as an individual patient.

If you participate in this program, you receive a medical questionnaire to complete and return to Lahey prior to your arrival. At the clinic, a staff physician conducts a comprehensive history and physical examination. Based on this examination, laboratory tests, X rays, and consultations are ordered to detect diseases for which there are no current symptoms and to evaluate disabilities as a result of known illnesses. Typical tests ordered include laboratory blood and urine analyses, electrocardiogram with exercise tolerance, chest X rays, eye pressure, proctoscopy, timed vital capacity (for respiratory evaluation), Pap smear (for women), and blood fat levels. The results of the examination will be discussed with you by your physician. Recommendations are made for treatment of any abnormalities detected, as well as for prevention of those conditions for which the patient is considered to be at risk. Should an abnormality be detected, you have the option of having additional studies and treatment at the clinic or having the results forwarded to your physician for follow-up care.

The initial examination generally requires two days. Subsequent visits are usually completed in one or two days. Interim appointments for monitoring significant abnormalities are available if desired. Hospitalization is permitted only for treatment of those abnormalties that cannot be treated in the ambulatory facilities. Initial examinations average $300 to $350 (based on the clinic's current fees), but the cost can vary, depending on specific tests ordered by the examining physician. Subsequent annual visits average less but also vary according to the number of tests ordered. General fee adjustments are, of course, made from time to time. The waiting time for appointments is six to eight weeks.

California

Palo Alto Medical Clinic, 300 Homer Avenue, Palo Alto, California 94301 (415)321-4121 (Central Appointment Desk: Extension 542), John R. Johnson, executive administrator. Two to four weeks' advance notice is recommended for the clinic's full examination, which takes one day unless further tests are indicated. You do not need a physician's referral and can contact the clinic directly. The average cost is $250.

Chicago, Illinois

George and Anna Portes Cancer Prevention Center of Chicago, 33 West Huron Street, Chicago, Illinois 60610, (312)440-7100. The motto of this center, founded in 1943 and the first of its kind in the Midwest, is "An ounce of detection is worth a pound of cure." Its focus is on early detection among the apparently well. The center's current volume of 125 examinees per day is one of the largest handled by an overall health examination center anywhere in the world. The automated multiphasic screening system aids the center's physicians by performing certain tests, recording and evaluating results, keeping detailed records, and delivering reports. The system uses a computer, which is located on the premises. This makes it possible for a comprehensive examination to be completed in approximately three hours.

You are eligible for admission to the center, by appointment, if you consider yourself in good heath. If you are currently being treated by a physician, a note of referral is required because the center does not want to interfere with any medical treatment you may be getting.

If the health screening indicates a medical problem in need of immediate attention, a note to the private doctor is given to the examinee at the time of the examination, and the examinee is instructed to contact his or her physician immediately. The physician is sent a report about any less urgent conditions as expeditiously as possible once all data are recorded.

Each examinee is encouraged to return to the center about two weeks after the initial screening for a consultation with one of the center's doctors. This review of medical findings is included in the basic fee. If you choose not to make a consultation appointment, a brief summary of the medical findings of your examination, in layman's terms, will be sent to you through the mail. In either case, the complete medical report is sent, with your approval, to your family physician or whatever physician you may indicate. The full procedure costs $85. It covers the following physician examinations: physical, gynecological, proctoscopic, SMAC 21, serology, Pap smear for all women, two X rays, twelve-lead EKG, complete blood count, and eleven other procedures, including stool and urine analyses, thermography for all women, and sickle-cell screening where indicated, as well as the consultation. There is an additional fee for breast X rays (mammogram) and sputum cytology (for smokers or those in high-risk occupations). At present, there is a three- to four-week wait for appointments.

Cleveland, Ohio

Cleveland Clinic Foundation, 9500 Euclid Avenue, Cleveland, Ohio 44106, (216)444-2200. This nonprofit organization, founded in 1921, has four divisions in its sixteen-building complex: a 1,008-bed hospital, outpatient facilities, research, and education. The professional staff numbers more than 330 full-time, salaried physicians and scientists practicing forty medical and surgical subspecialties; they are assisted by approximately 400 physicians in specialty training programs. The staff also includes a nutritionist who will help you to change your eating habits gradually if the doctors recommend a new diet for you. About 3,000 patients are treated in the clinic each working day.

The clinic is well known for heart diagnosis and therapy. It also offers an Executive Health Program. The basic examination usually includes the following: history and physical examination, screening survey (urinalysis and blood tests), chest X ray, resting electrocardiogram, special fat studies, lung function test, Pap test and pelvic examination for women, eye pressure test (for people over forty), and sigmoidoscopy (for people over forty). The examination takes about two days, and reservations should be made six to eight weeks in advance. Meals and lodging are available at the Park Plaza Hotel, in the Cleveland Clinic Complex, 96th and Carnegie Avenues. Free shuttle buses provide continuous scheduled transportation between the clinic and the hotel. A descriptive leaflet, *Cleveland Clinic Executive Health Program,* is free on request.

The results of X rays and laboratory studies, as well as a detailed report, are sent at a later date to you or, if you wish, to your personal physician. Confidentiality is strictly maintained. This helps calm anxieties over health problems feared to be detrimental to career opportunities and encourages full investigation of symptoms and complaints. A report will be sent to a designated officer of your company, if you wish, if you sign a written release.

The total cost for the basic examination is approximately $299. If other tests are deemed necessary, additional fees will be charged.

Dallas, Texas

Cooper Clinic, 12100 Preston Road, Dallas, Texas 75230, (214)239-7223. The clinic's basic aims are evaluation, education, and motivation of patients toward a reorientation of their living patterns in ways that will counter coronary risk factors. Physical examinations are performed, with special attention focused on the performance and efficiency of the heart and lungs. These are followed by recommendations for enhancement of general health and improvement in cardiovascular and pulmonary fitness. The physical performance test and diagnostic evaluation are designed to measure fitness, and you must have had a complete history, a physical examination, and a resting electrocardiogram within three months before being tested.

A maximum-performance stress test is conducted, with frequent blood pressure determinations both during exercise and after several minutes of recovery. You must fast for a minimum of two hours before the test. Following your examination, you will receive specific recommendations for your physical conditioning and your dietary program. The examination takes one to one and a half hours, including resting. The charge is $82. EKG $97.

Minnesota

Mayo Clinic, Rochester, Minnesota 55901, (507)284-2511, Earl T. Carter, M.D., Ph.D., chairman, preventive and internal medicine. This famous clinic, which is synonymous with a thorough checkup and which often solves diagnostic problems that others could not, has several programs within the Division of Preventive Medicine. One full day is required for the ordinary health checkup, but frequently during that first day the need for further studies is detected, so that a longer stay is required. The clinic offers all the conventional diagnostic services, including pulmonary function studies and stress EKG studies. Special attention is given to those who have recently returned from overseas, to detect "imported" problems.

Many companies have contracts with the division's Executive Health Program. Individuals being evaluated under this program must be employed by a firm that has made an agreement for evaluation of its employees. However, individuals can arrange for health examinations at the Mayo Clinic without a physician's referral or company arrangement; the usual waiting time is ten to twelve months. However, it should be emphasized that patients with significant medical problems need not wait for prompt care. Prices range from $200 to $400, depending on the tests that are required.

New York City

Eastern Women's Center, 14 East 60th Street, New York, New York 10022, (212)832-0033. This licensed clinic for gynecological health and abortion was founded in 1971 to provide patient-oriented medical services within a supportive and friendly environment. Counseling supplements medical care and provides women with information needed to make informed decisions regarding their health care. The center is under the direction of a gynecologist. The available services include abortion (to the twelfth week); pregnancy testing (Monday to Saturday); gynecological examinations, birth control information, and contraceptive care (Tuesday, Wednesday, and Friday); venereal disease diagnosis and treatment; and free Pap testing (Monday evenings and Wednesday mornings). Medical backup is provided by New York Hospital. The center also holds frequent workshops and programs. Charges are: abortion, $150 with local anesthesia, $185 with general anesthesia (New York Medicaid accepted); pelvic and breast examination and blood pressure, $20; Pap smear, $7; gonorrhea culture, $4; IUD insertion, $50; diaphragm fitting, $15. There is no charge for pregnancy testing or for birth control pills.

Executive Health Examiners, 777 Third Avenue, New York, New York 10017, (212)486-8900. Also has offices in Morristown, NJ (201)540-0177, and Stamford, CT, (203)348-7500. One of the most complete examination services, EHE (which was founded in 1959) provides complete physical and psychological evaluations, including pulmonary analysis, cardiac stress testing, and emotional stress testing. Individuals may contact them directly or ask a physician for a referral. A special Ladies' Day is held each Thursday afternoon. Only women are examined, and they have access to a female gynecologist. Tests require three hours and average $150. The waiting time for appointments is one to two weeks.

Preventive Medicine Institute–Strang Clinic, 55 East 34th Street, New York, New York 10016, (212)683-1000. A pioneer in early cancer detection, the Strang Clinic at Memorial Hospital for Cancer and Allied Diseases was founded in 1940 by Dr. Elise Strang L'Esperance.

The Strang Clinic currently serves about 20,000 patients a year. The comprehensive examination for men and women thirty-five and over takes about 2½ hours, and there is a health review examination for those under thirty-five. Additional services include the Digestive Disease Center, gynecological examinations, exercise tolerance test (stress test), and counseling services for overweight persons and smokers. You do not need a doctor's referral. The comprehensive examination costs $150; the health review costs $110. A 20 percent fee reduction for men and women over sixty-five is available upon request. There is also a limited patient fund available for those who cannot afford the fees. A free brochure describing the clinic's services and prices is available.

Since its inception, the Strang Clinic has never had a woman patient die of cancer of the cervix. Its survival statistics for other detected cancers are much better than national averages.

In 1963, the clinic became an independent, nonprofit center in its own building at its present location. In the years that followed, the clinic, which until then had been devoted largely to cancer detection, broadened its work to cover diagnosis, research, and detection of all the major chronic and controllable diseases. In 1966, it became the clinical division of the Preventive Medicine Institute. Strang believes very strongly in educating the layperson. It was at the Strang Clinic that Dr. George Papanicolaou amassed clinical evidence to support his Pap test for uterine cancer.

Vincent Astor Diagnostic Service, New York Hospital, 525 East 68th Street, New York, New York 10021, (212)472-5753 or 472-5754. The service was established by members of the professional staff of New York Hospital to provide complete diagnostic facilities for ambulatory patients. Professional services are provided entirely by members of the attending staff of the Cornell Medical Center, and specialists in all branches of medicine and surgery are available for consultation. A comprehensive examination includes chest X ray, electrocardiogram, eye examination, hearing test, pulmonary function test, nineteen laboratory procedures, proctosigmoidoscopy, and Pap smear (for women). Should the examining physician decide that additional laboratory studies, X rays, or consultations are needed, appointments will be arranged at your convenience, and charges will be made at the prevailing New York Hospital rates. The full examination requires about 3½ hours and costs $250.

BREAK BAD HABITS: SAVE MONEY AND LIVE LONGER AND BETTER

Many of our problems are the result of our life-styles. We eat too much, drink too much, smoke too much. We don't get enough rest, exercise, or emotional outlets. Furthermore, we are not just a migraine headache or a bladder problem, we are whole human beings. There are many facilities around the nation that are concerned with the entire person. Most of them believe we each have a responsibility for our own health, and some of them contend that there are numerous minor health problems that we can diagnose and treat ourselves. The centers described in this section offer information and therapy for those who wish to improve the way they live so that they can have longer, healthier lives.

Your Life-Style Profile, printed on the following page, allows you to evaluate your own pluses and minuses when it comes to your habits and environment. Once you add up your score, you can begin your efforts to improve your health. There are many sources in the chapter that will help you.

California

Anaheim Memorial Hospital, 111 West La Palma, Anaheim, California 92803, (714)774-1450, Andrea Manes, director. This hospital sponsors a community-service program of health education classes in preventive medicine. Among the courses offered are: how to deal with stress, how to stop smoking, cancer support classes, diabetes information, weight reduction, cardiopulmonary resuscitation, and health lectures. Some courses are free; for others, a moderate fee is charged.

Center for Health Enhancement Education and Research (CHEER), Department of Medicine, University of California, Los Angeles, School of Medicine, Los Angeles, California 90024, (213)226-2622. Charles Kleeman, professor of medicine, director. This is one of the first major centers established to study the role of health habits and life-style changes in the prevention of disease and the promotion of health. A primary aim of the center is to carry out metabolic, cardiovascular, epidemiologic, and psychosocial research in relation to health enhancement generally and in relation to the role of life-style change in the prevention and control of hardening of the arteries in particular.

One of CHEER's focal points is the residential program, established in 1979, in which participants and their spouses undergo an intensive

Your Lifestyle Profile

Indicate by circling or checking only the signs that apply to you.

The plus (+) and minus (−) signs next to some numbers indicate more than (+) and less than (−).

Exercise

Amount of physical effort expended during the workday: mostly

Heavy physical, walking, housework ●   Desk work ▶

Participation in physical activities — (skiing, golf, swimming, etc.) (lawn mowing, gardening, etc.)?

Daily ●   Weekly ▶   Seldom ■

Participation in a vigorous exercise program?

3 times Weekly ●   Weekly ▶   Seldom ■

Average miles walked or jogged per day?

1+ ●   −1 ▶   None ■

Flights of stairs climbed per day?

10+ ●   −10 ▶   None ■

Nutrition

Are you overweight?

No ●   5 to 19 lbs. ▶   20 + lbs. ■

Do you eat a wide variety of foods — something from each of the following five food groups:

(1) meat, fish, poultry, dried legumes, eggs or

Drugs

Do you take drugs illegally?

No ●   Yes ■

Do you consume alcoholic beverages together with certain drugs (tranquilizers, barbiturates, antihistamines or illegal drugs)?

No ●   Yes ■

Do you use pain-killers improperly or excessively?

No ●   Yes ■

Tobacco

Cigarettes smoked per day?

None ●   −10 ▶   10+ ■

Cigars smoked per day?

None ●   −5 ▶   5+ ■

Pipe tobacco pouches per week?

None ●   −2 ▶   2+ ■

Personal Health

Do you experience periods of depression?

Seldom   Occasionally   Frequently

Road and Water Safety

Mileage per year as driver or passenger?

−10,000 ●   10,000+ ▶

Do you often exceed the speed limit?

No ●   by 10 mph+ ▶   by 20 mph+ ■

Do you wear a seatbelt?

Always ●   Occasionally ▶   Never ■

Do you drive a motorcycle, moped or snowmobile?

No ●   Yes ▶

If yes to the above, do you always wear a regulation safety helmet?

Yes ●   No ■

Do you ever drive under the influence of alcohol?

Never ●   Occasionally ■

Do you drive when your ability may be affected by drugs?

Never ●   Occasionally

Are you aware of water safety rules?

Yes ●   No ▶

cereals; (4) fruits; (5) vegetables?

Each day ● | 3 times Weekly ▶

Alcohol

Average no. of bottles (12 oz.) of beer per week?
0 to 7 ● | 8 to 15 ▶ | 16+ ■

Average no. hard liquor (1½ oz.) drinks per week?
0 to 7 ● | 8 to 15 ▶ | 16+ ■

Average no. of glasses (5 oz.) of wine or cider per week?
0 to 7 ● | 8 to 15 ▶ | 16+ ■

Total no. of drinks per week, including beer, liquor, and wine?
0 to 7 ● | 8 to 15 ▶ | 16+ ■

Sub totals

No | Occasionally ▶ | Frequently ■

Do you get enough satisfying sleep?
Yes ● | No ▶

Are you aware of the causes and dangers of VD?
Yes ● | No ▶

Breast self-examination? (If not applicable, do not score.)
Monthly ● | Occasionally ▶

Sub totals

General

Average time watching TV per day (in hours)?
0 to 1 ● | 1 to 4 ▶ | 4+ ■

Are you familiar with first-aid procedures?
Yes ● | No ▶

Do you ever smoke in bed?
No ● | Occasionally ▶ | Yes ■

Do you always make use of clothing and equipment provided for your safety at work? (If not applicable, do not score.)
Yes ● | Occasionally ▶ | No ■

Sub totals

Scoring Section

Count total number of ● ▶ ■   1 point for each ●▶■   3 points for each ●   5 points for each ▶   Your total score _____

Your Lifestyle Profile will indicate where lifestyle changes should be made; but only if you answer the questions as objectively as possible.

Excellent: 34-45: You have a commendable lifestyle based on sensible health habits and lively awareness of personal health.

Good: 46-55: You have a sound grasp of basic health principles. With a minimum of change you can develop an excellent lifestyle pattern.

Risky: 56-65: You are taking unnecessary risks with your health. Several of your lifestyle habits are based on unwise personal choices which should be changed if potential health problems are to be avoided.

Hazardous: 66 and over: Either you have little personal awareness of good health habits or you are choosing to ignore them. This is a danger zone — but with a conscientious effort to improve basic living patterns even hazardous lifestyles can be modified and potential health problems overcome.

REPRINTED WITH THE PERMISSION of Journal American Insurance/Winter 1977-78

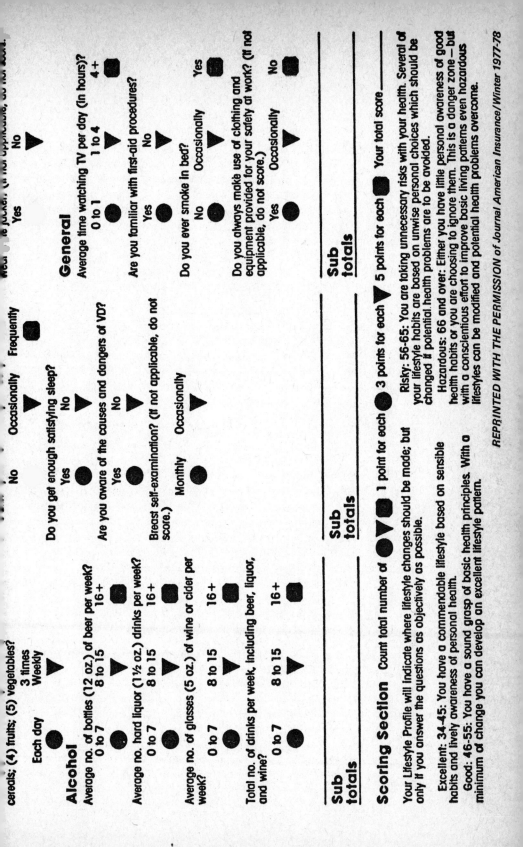

four-week, live-in experience in "wellness" education. The major goal of this program is the learning of responsibility for improving one's own health. Participants are encouraged to develop a new life-style that will favor optimum health. The program emphasizes reduction and prevention of high blood pressure, obesity, blood fats, smoking, and diabetes mellitus, all of which are known to contribute to heart disease, diseases of the blood vessels, and chronic lung, liver, eye, and kidney diseases. Participants live in hotel-like accommodations and take their meals together, choosing from a variety of appealing menus consisting of foods that are within prescribed dietary restrictions. Medical supervision by members of the UCLA faculty is provided, along with follow-up support for several years after the participants have completed the residential program.

Future plans call for the development of health enhancement programs that can be adapted by various groups in the community, especially for schoolchildren so that they can learn the principles of a health-enhancing life-style at an early age. A projected program will be for industrial workers whose companies wish to develop comprehensive, self-sustaining health programs. CHEER also plans to act as a consultant and participant in helping various small communities to develop their own health enhancement programs. Information about fees will be provided upon request.

Wellness Resource Center, 42 Miller Avenue, Mill Valley, California 94941. John Travis, M.D., M.P.H., founded the Wellness Resource Center in 1975 after his residency in preventive medicine at Johns Hopkins Medical School. He felt that medical, nursing, and other graduate schools taught mainly urgent but superficial issues concerned with getting people to function again and that once that is accomplished, little is done until the next symptom arises. He designed the *Wellness Workbook* for students, clients of health professionals, and ordinary people; it contains many of the tools that he found useful in his own growth and evolution, as well as a reading list and resource guide that allow the reader to continue on his/her own path. The *Wellness Workbook* is designed to introduce you to factors that affect your health in ways you may not have realized before, to allow you to become more aware of the role those factors are playing in your life, to show you ways you can take charge of many areas in your life that are presently not working well, and to encourage you to find your own unique path by using a wide variety of readily available resources. The book includes wellness evaluation tests, step-by-step instructions in different methods of meditation, recommendations for specific exercises, instructions on how to keep a psychological journal, a miniature biofeedback thermometer, and specific tools for making changes in your life. *Wellness Workbook for Health Professionals*, $60 including a $25 computer processing.

More Effective Living, Kaiser Permanente Medical Centers, Office of

Community Services, 5755 Cottle Road, San Jose, California 95123, (408)578-0300, Sarah J. Nasser, coordinator. A health education series is jointly sponsored by the Kaiser Permanente Medical Center at Santa Teresa and Santa Clara and two local community colleges. The adult education classes are open to health-plan members and community residents.

PUBLICATION

Medical Self-care Magazine, P.O. Box 717, Inverness, California 94937. Dr. Tom Ferguson, medical editor of *CoEvolution Quarterly* and a graduate of Yale Medical School, started *Medical Self-care* to give lay people access to existing medical tools and information. He and his co-workers believe that you *can* take more responsibility for your own good health. They believe you can learn to handle stethoscopes and blood pressure cuffs, administer breast self-examinations and Pap smears, and in some cases, carry out elementary surgery. "Self-care practitioners learn to heed the messages of their own bodies—and to appreciate the importance of exercise, proper nutrition, relaxation, and habit control in leading healthier lives." A descriptive brochure is free, a sample copy is $2.50, and a year's subscription is $10.00.

Among the courses offered are:

Introduction to Effective Communication Skills, Effective Marriage Communications, Learning to Relax/Body Balance, Self-discovery through the Arts, Assertion Training, Living with Children/Adolescents, Freedom as a Way of Life, How to Handle Stress, and Stretching Your Dollar. Because all classes are noncredit and nongraded, emphasis is placed on relaxed, meaningful experiences. Fees range from $3 to $15, and some courses are free.

Colorado

Aspen Health Center, Aspen Meadows, P.O. Box 1092, Aspen, Colorado 81611, (303)925-3586. This is part of the nonprofit Aspen Institute for Humanistic Studies. A forward-looking project, its programs have been designed primarily to prevent illness, rather than to treat the person who is already mentally or physically ill. The program seeks to tune up the physical body, refresh the spirit and mind, and demonstrate that good health and a sense of well-being can be attained by almost anyone. Because we live in a time of tension, insecurity, and dynamic change, we should try to prevent stress from becoming distress.

Although the center's primary function is to conduct a health program for the Aspen Executive Program and other conferences sponsored by the institute, it is open to the general public for single treatments and for planned programs for longer periods.

The entire program is directed by specialists in the fields of recreation and physical education and therapy.

The center offers a complete fitness program, including gymnasium, sauna, steambath, whirlpool, massage, and facials. A new program is the cardiopulmonary testing and conditioning lab. Facilities are open summer and winter. Rates are $4 for sauna, steam, cold plunge, and whirlpool; $10 for complete body massage; $10 for facial treatment; and $4 for exercise class.

Idaho

Healthwise, Inc., 111 South Sixth, Boise, Idaho 83702, (208)345-1161, Donald W. Kemper, director. This self-care education program motivates parents to handle routine family health problems. The program format allows any primary-care professional to present a practical and effective self-care course with a minimum of personal research and preparation.

Healthwise is designed to build on the common sense that most young parents possess. The result is better-informed, better-motivated people who will play a more active roll in their family's health. Common colds, flu, backaches, headaches, and childhood illnesses are part of every family's health problems. Healthwise provides the information, skills, and encouragement needed for young families to address such problems responsibly, without overreliance on health professionals.

The educational format utilizes a group learning approach. Carefully prepared handbooks, videotapes, and instructors' guides assure the basic continuity and quality of the program. Ten-color videotapes present facts on each session's key topics and demonstrate useful skills. The *Healthwise Handbook*, which is provided to each participant, is a comprehensive guide to most routine health concerns. The program is usually presented in ten weekly sessions lasting two hours each. Cost information will be sent upon request. The *Healthwise Handbook* is $22.

Kentucky

Holistic Health Center, 1412 North Broadway, Lexington, Kentucky 40505, (606)233-4273. Dr. Walter Stoll, the center's medical director, is a family practitioner who teaches his patients self-care on an individual basis. He believes patients should take a greater share of the responsibility for their health, and he emphasizes the role of mental and emotional factors. He also makes use of some nontraditional techniques, including biofeedback, transactional analysis, meditation, and aerobic exercises. He maintains that 75 percent of sickness is preventable and that we have come to depend too heavily on doctors. His message is that we all have a lot of capabilities that we haven't gotten in touch with and that we have a great deal to do with whether we are sick or well. He teaches many ways to doctor yourself, but he cautions that if you are ever in doubt, or if pain or sickness persists, you should call your doctor. He offers the following to the public by mail for $1.50 each: *Patient Brochure and Self-Help Manual.* 27 pp. (It tells you all about what you should expect from your doctor and vice versa and how to treat minor illnesses.)

The following are patient information protocols:

1. Nose Drops, How to Use
2. Angina Pectoris
3. Arthritis
4. Biofeedback
5. Bursitis
6. Colitis
7. Common Cold
8. Constipation
9. Costo-Chondritis
10. Diabetes Mellitus
11. Elimination of Refined Carbohydrates (Total)
12. Fever, What to Do
13. Headache
14. Humidification
15. Hypertension
16. Hyperventilation Syndrome
17. Low Back Syndrome
18. Otitis Medica
19. Pelvic Inflammatory Disease
20. Peptic Ulcer
21. Prostatitis
22. Sinusitis
23. Transient Ischemic Attacks
24. Vomiting and/or Diarrhea

Maine

Self-activation Program, Maine Medical Center, Portland, Maine 04102, (207)871-0111, Eleanore Irish, R.N., M.P.H., Department of Community Medicine, director. Courses are free and similar to the other self-help programs in other parts of the country. Check with the center for scheduling.

Minnesota

Duluth Community Health Center Free Clinic, 2 East 5th Street, Duluth, Minnesota 55805, (218)722-1497, Mary A. Massey, director. "Concerned, caring and confidential" describes this facility. It is private and nonprofit, and it is the only alternative health-care facility in the area. This is basically a neighborhood-type clinic that was started by a group of concerned residents to serve a population that, for one reason or another, cannot, or chooses not to, receive health care from the established health-care system. The clinic firmly believes that health care is a human right.

The staff includes a full-time nurse practitioner who cares for the entire person, a male VD technician who has experience and expertise in working with those problems, and a certified lab assistant who heads the laboratory. The director organizes and coordinates the clinic; a volunteer coordinator is the direct supervisor of the many community volunteers who donate their time to the clinic. The volunteer staff includes pregnancy counselors, physicians, nurses, medical technologists, pharmacists, certified lab assistants, and medical and nursing students. Many other concerned people handle the nonmedical jobs.

A health-care program is held at a different senior citizens eating facility each week to serve the community's elderly. General Medical Night, which is held on alternate Tuesdays, gives people who feel they have no access to the established medical profession a chance to see a physician. There is a sliding fee scale; that is, each person pays only what he or she can afford. For some, this means no charge; for others, a small fee. *No one* is ever refused care for financial reasons.

The Role of Wellness in the Work Place, Health Central Institute, 240 Brookdale Towers, 2810 57th Avenue N., Minneapolis, Minnesota 55430, (612)566-0180.

The increasing interest in healthy living today is awesome. Even more important is the potential practical benefits for corporations, their families, and the societies in which they function. Conferences are planned in the interest of employers and other policymakers. The objectives are to introduce the philosophy of health promotion and high level wellness. There are demonstrations and/or presentations of specific components of health promotion and wellness programs including personal responsibility, nutritional awareness, stress management, physical fitness, and environmental sensitivity. The process involves all participants in a critical assessment of health promotion and wellness in terms of its role in the work place. The assessment looks at myths and realities, practical applications, impact on costs/benefits, productivity, whether people feel better and other questions which will help employers make better decisions regarding their involvement.

The HCI presents frequent programs to promote health in the workplace at the request of industry.

New Jersey

Center for Self-regulation and Biofeedback, Carrier Foundation, Belle Mead, New Jersey 08502, (201)874-4000, E. S. Paul Weber, M.D., director. Biofeedback, the use of electronic monitoring equipment to show a person's state of relaxation, is used at this private clinic. Relaxation methods are used as part of behavior therapy to facilitate change. The state of deep relaxation facilitates the uncovering of thought and emotional patterns and increases the effectiveness of direct, active intervention through the use of imagery and verbal suggestions as therapy for emotional problems.

New York

Energetic Living, Capital Area Health Maintenance Organization Planning Council Inc., 1201 Troy-Schenectady Road, Latham, New York 12110, (518)783-3110, Gerry Matheson, Ed.D., director. This innovative program focuses on weight control, physical fitness, and stress reduction. Participants learn a variety of skills that they can apply in their daily living; these skills are designed to improve and maintain health. Participants learn how to use nutrition effectively and how to perform enjoyable physical activities that can be practiced in their homes. They are taught how to reduce tension and cope with stress through energetic living. Participants wear clothing appropriate for exercising. Classes are small. The fees are $30 for Capital Health Plan subscribers and $40 for non-subscribers.

North Carolina

Bad Habits Clinic, Duke University, Durham, North Carolina 27706, (919)684-2887, Dr. Patrick Boudewyns, director. Kicking the smoking habit is difficult but possible, according to Dr. Robert Shipley, director of the smoking control program. In the past, the most successful lasting treatment has been the use of rapid smoking, which requires the client to puff every six seconds until smoking becomes intolerable. Because a large majority of the people treated at the clinic are over forty; have symptoms of heart trouble, high blood pressure, or emphysema; and have smoked for many years, there is concern that the rapid-smoking treatment might cause heart attacks. A similar but safer method, regular-paced aversive smoking, is used instead, with a very good success record.

The therapy includes relaxation training through self-hypnosis and deep breathing exercises to help the individual in combating urges to smoke. It also includes "cognitive ecology," that is, getting rid of such rationalizations as "I'll gain too much weight," "I can't do it," and "I'm only smoking low-tar cigarettes anyway."

The Bad Habits Clinic (formerly known as the Behavior Change and Self-Control Program) also seeks to help essentially normal people overcome a variety of other ingrained behavior patterns, including insomnia, overeating, tension, and excessive fears (phobias). The smoking program is six sessions scheduled within eight days. Follow up by letter and phone call. Schedule information is sent free upon request.

PUBLICATION

Community Health Education: The Lay Advisor Approach, Connie Service and Eva J. Salber, editors, Health Care Systems, P.O. Box 2932, Durham, North Carolina 27705. There is much current interest in health promotion, preventive medicine, and the importance of individual responsibility in health care. This book describes in detail an approach that puts these concepts into practice. A model community health education program with broad applicability has been developed, utilizing the existing personal and group strengths of a community to promote health in its fullest sense. This program identifies those laypeople in every community to whom friends, relatives, and neighbors turn for help, advice, and support. It trains them in promotive health practices, prevention of disease, early recognition of illness, the use of community resources, and appropriate referral. Strengthened by the training, these lay advisors can continue to serve their communities by assisting troubled individuals and by disseminating health information through established community networks. Health Care Systems, the book's publisher, is a subsidiary of Duke University Medical Center. The book costs $6.50.

Oregon

Barefoot Mothers, Community Health and Education Center, 433 West 10th, Eugene, Oregon 97401, (503)485-5782. Two registered nurses, Dorothy Lematta and Karen Bain, have designed this unique program, which takes untrained, uncertain, and uninformed women and, through education and training, turns them into "barefoot mothers." (The name *barefoot* is derived from the paramedic program in China known as *barefoot doctors*.) The goal of the program is to produce mothers who are well educated, self-assured, and assertive. They are taught how to communicate specific data to health professionals and how to understand their answers. They know how to exercise discretion in utilizing a health-care provider. These women, in turn, become a resource to their friends. Included in the course are home nursing, home physical examinations, awareness of normal childhood development, practical herbal remedies, principles of nutrition, home safety, sexuality, emotional well-being, family dynamics, and proper care of the sick child. The system uses books, films, and spin-off teaching (in which each mother is responsible for teaching others some of what she has learned).

Barefoot Mothers is part of the Community Health and Education Center (CHECK), which provides a wide range of medical services. There is twenty-four-hour physician coverage, but the emphasis is on self-help. Fees are based on ability to pay.

Virginia

Health Activation Network, division of Interactive Services, Inc., P.O. Box 923, Vienna, Virginia 22180, (703)938-4447. Health activation is an approach to health care and health education that incorporates health rights, skills, and responsibilities, with emphasis on wellness. It focuses on what you can do for yourself. Through health activation, you can accept more responsibility for your own health care and that of your family; learn skills in observing, describing, and handling common illnesses, injuries, and emergencies; increase your awareness and knowledge about wellness and about common health problems; and learn how to use health-care resources such as services, facilities, personal insurance, and medications more effectively and economically.

Organized in 1976, the Health Activation Network has programs nationwide for users and providers of health care services. It is a nonprofit organization supported in part by grants from the Sandoz Foundation and serves to coordinate the national effort. It offers the Black Bag Learning Series. The training concentrates on the development of skills and knowledge of self in areas that relate to the contents of the black bag: stethoscope, sphygmomanometer, otoscope, oral and rectal thermometers, tongue depressor and dental reflector, and high-intensity light, along with self-care instructions and a family health history packet. Copies of the Guide cost $15.00, the Health Activation Diary costs $10.00, and the Family Black Bag costs $79.50. Health Activation Network also publishes a quarterly newsletter; a subscription is $25.00 per year. A two-year membership in a Health Activation Club is $10.00; a copy of the *Health Activation for Senior Citizens Course Guide* is $25.00.

West Virginia

Greenbrier Clinic, White Sulphur Springs, West Virginia 24986, (800)624-6070. If you want a complete physical checkup while you are having a wonderful time, the fully staffed Greenbrier Clinic is the place for you. You stay at the hotel. The clinic, which is attached to the hotel building, requires three mornings of tests. The general examination includes a health history, physical examination, sigmoidoscopy, chest X rays, EKGs at rest and after exercise, routine laboratory studies, blood chemistry and serology, urinalysis, eye pressure test, and visual and hearing tests. When indicated by a history or examination, a variety of other tests, such as X rays and cardiac stress testing (see page 6), and other studies are performed and charges are at the current rates in the area. This service is very popular with captains of industry and with celebrities, who fly in on their private planes and land at the hotel's own airport. The fee for the general examination is $275. Additional tests and studies are performed at current rates in the area.

(See Greenbrier health spa, page 134.)

MEDICAL INFORMATION

Center for Medical Consumers and Health Care Information, Inc., 237 Thompson Street, New York, New York 10012, (212)674-7105. The staff of the center comes from Judson Memorial Church and Consumer Action Now's Council. The church, located on Washington Square in Greenwich Village, has a history of providing health services to the community that dates back to the early 1900s; the council is a New York–based environmental and consumer organization founded in 1970. The two groups formed the center in May 1976 because they felt that changes in the quality of medical care will come from informed consumers.

The center runs a free telephone health library. More than 140 tapes are available; each is three to eight minutes in length. A variety of health topics are covered, from hypertension to how to choose a psychiatrist. You can call (212)674-7100 and ask to hear any one of the tapes listed in the library brochure. To receive a copy of the brochure, send a stamped, self-addressed, business-size envelope to the center.

The center's medical reference library for laypeople is open Monday to Friday from 9:00 A.M. to 5:00 P.M.; on Wednesdays, it remains open until 8:00 P.M. Most of the books at your disposal were written for laypeople, but some are the same texts or publications used by doctors and medical students. You can look up such information as the side effects of your prescription drugs, your doctor's credentials, or your own illness. You may also learn about alternatives to traditional medicine, such as yoga, folk medicine, acupuncture, and meditation.

Tel-Med, New Jersey, (609)452-2882; California, (202)453-2260. These are only two of Tel-Med's phone-in health information services. When you call, you can receive medically approved advice in answer to questions ranging from "When should I see a psychiatrist?" to "How can I decrease the risk of a heart attack?" All calls are answered by an operator who will play a specific tape that you request or who will assist you in finding the most suitable tapes on the subject you wish to know about. A Tel-Med exchange can handle up to ten calls simultaneously. The tapes are from three to five minutes in length and use easy-to-understand language. One of the goals of Tel-Med is to help you recognize early symptoms of health problems that require a physician's care. The information they provide can help you to understand and deal with your ailments, including ulcers, high blood pressure, diabetes, and arthritis. Tel-Med began under the auspices of University of California physicians at the Sacramento Medical Center. The service is now widely available throughout the country. If you cannot find a location near you, call your local medical society. You can also call either of the numbers listed here.

PUBLICATION

Health Facts is a consumer bulletin published by the center six times a year. Each issue explains a particular health- or medical-care question in laypeople's terms and presents the reader with the consensus of informed opinion on the subject. Where there is a difference of opinion, that too is presented. Preventive medicine and how to get good-quality medical care are stressed.

To get on the center's mailing list, send a donation of $6 (the center is an independent, nonprofit, tax-exempt organization); this will put you on the list for one year. In addition to the publications, you will receive notices of the center's activities.

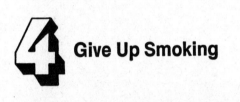

4 Give Up Smoking

If you smoke, one of the best ways that you can improve your health, your looks, your smell, and your budget is to give up the filthy habit. If you stop smoking right now, there will be a rapid decline of the carbon monoxide in your blood over the first twelve hours; over the next few weeks, coughing, sputum production, and shortness of breath will lessen. A woman who stops smoking by the fourth month of pregnancy no longer runs an increased risk of stillbirth or prenatal death related to smoking. Deterioration of lung function in the smoker who has quit is arrested. Death rates from heart disease, chronic bronchitis, and emphysema also drop. During the first few years after you stop, the risk of cancer of the lung, larynx, and oral cavity decline; and after ten to fifteen years, it approximates that of nonsmokers.

You have heard all the health risks. You know that cigarette smoking causes premature coronary heart disease and that the lung cancer risk factor is ten times more prevalent among smokers than among nonsmokers. Smokers also have more nonmalignant but often just as fatal respiratory diseases.

PUBLICATIONS

Clearing the Air: A Guide to Quitting Smoking, Department of Health, Education, and Welfare Publication No. (NIH) 78-1647, prepared by Office of Cancer Communications, National Cancer Institute, Bethesda, Maryland 20014. This booklet contains a variety of tips and helpful hints on how to stop smoking and how to make your own personal efforts a little easier. Many people have quit "cold turkey" without the aid of professional help or a special program, and many have given up cigarettes by replacing them with new habits or using a special gimmick. Successful methods are as different as the people who use them. Pick the ideas that make sense to you, and follow through; you will have a much better chance of success. The booklet also includes descriptions of formal programs using group therapy or individual counseling methods, and descriptions of other sources on quitting. The booklet is free.

Why Do You Smoke? Department of Health, Education, and Welfare, Publication No. (NIH) 78-1822, Superintendent of Documents, U.S. Government Printing Office, Washington, D.C. 20402. This booklet is designed to provide you with a score on each of six factors that describe many people's smoking behavior. Your smoking may be characterized by only one of these factors or by a combination of them. This test will help you identify what you use smoking for and what satisfaction you think you derive from it. Three questions represent positive feelings people get from it, the fourth asks for negative feelings such as anger and anxiety, the fifth concerns psychological addiction to smoking, and the sixth is about habit smoking, which is purely automatic. Learn what it is that you get out of smoking before you decide whether you can forego the satisfactions it gives you or can find other ways to achieve them. Send for the booklet; it can help you make up your mind. Free.

If You Want to Give up Cigarettes, American Cancer Society, 777 Third Avenue, New York, New York 10017 (212)371-2900. The society and its chapters have prepared this booklet, which contains case histories, a score card, and numerous behavioral techniques you can use to kick the habit. For a copy, call your local ACS chapter, or write to headquarters. The booklet is free.

Also free are the periodic Stop Smoking Clinics run by the society and its chapters. To find out when the next clinic will be held in your area, call your local chapter, or write to headquarters. The clinics are free.

Smokenders, Memorial Parkway at Prospect Street, Phillipsburg, New Jersey 08865, (201)454-HELP. Founded in 1969 by Dr. Jon Rogers and Jacquelyn Rogers of Easton, Pa., this is the oldest and largest smoking cessation organization of its kind. With the professional assistance of her husband, who is a dentist, and the support of their four children, Mrs. Rogers embarked on an intensive research project to acquire knowledge and expertise to create a cessation technique for herself that was both effective and "painless." It does not involve willpower, medicine, hypnosis, psychoanalysis, or group therapy. At no time is the member expected to "confess" or in anyway embarrass himself or herself. On the contrary, an integral part of the approach is the creation of a sense of self-worth and of a renewed belief in one's own capabilities. It is a pleasant, step-by-step course of instruction designed to disconnect the smoker from the smoking habit. The program is conducted nationwide, as well as in Canada and Norway. The first step is to introduce the prospective member of Smokenders at a free public meeting, at which the structure and the cost of the program are explained. The program itself consists of eight weekly meetings, approximately two hours per session, held at hospitals, schools, churches, lodges, hotels, community centers, and other such facilities. For the first five weeks, the members smoke as much as they wish while achieving the proper attitude, and disconnecting all the conditioned responses through a structured technology. When Cut-Off Day (the day after the fifth meeting) arrives, the person is physiologically and psychologically prepared to quit.

Frequent reunions are organized by members for added reinforcement. Smokenders maintains periodic contact with all graduates for one full year after completion of the program. Graduates can attend any one additional Smokender meeting, anywhere in the world, at no charge. Or if they wish to go through the entire program again, they will receive a 50 percent discount. Among the celebrities who have successfully completed the program are ex-Secretary of Health, Education, and Welfare Joseph Califano, actress Lauren Bacall, singer-composer Barry Manilow, and actress Rosemary Harris. Smokenders programs have been presented for employees of the Center for Disease Control in Atlanta; the Department of Health, Education, and Welfare in Washington; and in over a hundred of the nation's largest corporations, including AT&T, IBM, Xerox, and Exxon.

Brochures are available free. The fee (which includes all materials) is not uniform throughout the country, but averages $250 to $350.

Smoking Cessation Program, Center for Behavioral Medicine, Department of Psychiatry, Hospital of the University of Pennsylvania, 34th Street and Spruce Street, Philadelphia, Pennsylvania 19104, (215)662-3503. Ovide F. Pomerleau, Ph.D., director, Michael Pertschuk, M.D., associate director. The method for inducing smoking cessation developed at the Center for Behavioral Medicine illustrates a number of basic concepts in behavior modification. The procedure, using an integrated sequence of instructions, has three main phases: reduction of smoking, cessation of smoking, and the maintenance of nonsmoking.

The first problem, keeping the smoker in the program, is dealt with by requiring a prepaid fee that is not returned if the smoker drops out of treatment; however, part of the fee *is* refunded for following therapeutic instructions.

Treatment is carried out in a small group of approximately ten smokers, which makes possible social reinforcement for compliance while still focusing on the problems of the individual. Treatment consists of eight 1½-hour weekly sessions. Follow-up consists of five additional sessions, spread out at increasing intervals over the next ten months to sustain treatment gains by withdrawing support gradually.

In the first week, the participant is taught to keep a daily written record of his or her smoking, showing time, mood, and situation. Over the next three weeks, a reduction in smoking rate is accomplished through the use of various contingency management techniques, such as publicly stated quotas and designated nonsmoking situations. Another technique involves putting cigarettes, ashtrays, and matches in separate places. The participant purchases only enough cigarettes to meet daily quotas. All these tools help to establish a delay between the urge to smoke and the act of inhaling.

The group goal of abstinence is purposely delayed over the first three weeks until a reduction to a rate of five to ten cigarettes a day is achieved. This provides many smokers with their first successful experience in controlling some aspects of smoking.

During the abstinence period, several new techniques are introduced: the ultimate aversive consequences of smoking are now emphasized for the first time, and participants are taught to imagine their personal fears of the health effects of sustained smoking whenever they experience a craving for cigarettes. They are encouraged to make the transition from ex-smoker to nonsmoker by referring to themselves as nonsmokers, by learning to dislike the smell of cigarette smoke from others, and so on. Patterns that reinforce a sense of physical well-being, such as exercise and deep muscle relaxation are also encouraged.

In the follow-up phase, the group continues to meet occasionally, providing support and encouragement for nonsmoking, and the staff remains available to give assistance if problems arise. Throughout treatment, rewards for behavior that leads to nonsmoking is used, rather than punishment for smoking. Resumption of smoking is presented as a failure of technique, not of the individual, and the smoker is encouraged to try again.

Initial results of the program have been favorable. A summary of treatment outcome for the first forty-eight smokers seen in therapy indicates that 65 percent of the participants were abstinent at the end of the two-month treatment and 46 percent continued to be abstinent a median of 11.1 months after the end of treatment. The combined percentage of abstinent (46 percent) and improved (35 percent) suggests a high degree of effectiveness for the present approach.

The cost of the program is $50, plus a $50 commitment fee. The full commitment fee can be earned back. An initial evaluation fee of $15 is charged.

Ochsner Clinic, 1514 Jefferson Highway, Jefferson Parish, New Orleans, Louisiana 70113, (504)834-7070. This clinic is one of the pioneers in the campaign against smoking. In addition to regular checkup services, it offers special pulmonary tests for smokers. The Ochsner Foundation offers an antismoking program that includes five treatment days and eight weeks of follow-up. The smoker is given a guarantee that he or she will discontinue cigarettes. The cost of the program is $300. The tests that constitute the clinic's regular physical checkup take 1½ to 5 days to administer; costs range from $225 to $550 for the antismoking program. Reservations should be made four to six weeks in advance.

See Part 3, Chapter 7, "Hypnosis" (page 217).

5 Controlling Your Weight

QUIZ YOURSELF ON WEIGHT CONTROL

This miniquiz will help you to assess what you know about losing weight and keeping it off. In the case of weight control, what you don't know *can* harm you. So answer the questions, and see how your answers stack up with those of the experts. Respond on the basis of what you feel and believe, as opposed to what you know intellectually.

True or false:

1. Losing weight requires enormous willpower.
2. Some people have large appetites and just naturally overeat.
3. Food often seems to jump into my mouth!
4. Some people have absolutely no imagination.
5. My mind and body are really two separate parts of me.
6. My imagination isn't as real as my everyday actions.
7. The only really effective way to lose weight is to go on a strict diet.
8. Failing at weight control means something is wrong with me.
9. Trying to talk yourself out of overeating usually doesn't work.
10. The more often I gain weight back, the harder it is to keep the weight off.

The answer to *all* these questions is False.

1. False. Willpower is a negative concept. People think they either have it or lack it. Actually, it is possible to develop *self-control*, learned responses through which *you* decide on the outcome. Step-by-step self-control allows you to learn to eat some food and flush the rest down the toilet or to pour water over food—without an "iron will."

2. Not true. Overeating is learned and so is appetite to a large (no pun intended) degree. The heavier you are, the better you may have learned overeating skills. These can be unlearned and replaced with more normal eating patterns and appetite.

3. False. You have learned to put it there and thus can learn to keep food out. We are not just helpless victims of our binges.

4. Not true. The ability to imagine is something we are born with. Some people develop their capacity more than others. Do you worry? If you do, then you are using negative imagery. It is possible to use the same skills to learn positive imagery.

5. Not true. How you feel and what you say to yourself affect how you eat. Our minds often signal eating instructions that our bodies obey, even when we are not really hungry. Conversely, our bodies signal pain, fatigue, and the like and our minds misinterpret these signals, causing us to eat. It is important to change your *mind* to change your weight.

6. False. In some cases, the image is more real than the object. For example, people often get a mental picture of a food and tend to overeat it in real life—without actually tasting the food. Blindfold yourself next time, and eat. Roll the food around on your tongue. Does it taste as good as you imagined it would? Many people find that it does not, that they eat with their images rather than with their taste buds.

7. False. Restrictive dieting or following fad diets works for a short time only, if at all. Usually people cannot continue on restrictive diet; they go off them and gain the weight back. Or they go on a diet (often called the *wagon*) and conjure up images of all they will eat when they lose weight (and are off the wagon). They proceed to do just that and gain the weight back. It is much better not to have a wagon mentality. Instead, one should learn to eat all kinds of foods in varying quantities.

8. Not true. Overweight people are generally no different from people whose weights are normal. They are not saner or less sane. Usually diet or thinking patterns are the culprit. Change those, and you may become more successful.

9. False. Talking to yourself *does* work. For many, however, the talk has been negative, with negative outcomes. It is possible to give yourself positive instructions, to hear them, and to act accordingly. Listen to your head the next time you binge. Learn to give yourself positive instructions: "I can put this food away and do something more constructive. I just have to try and then do it." "I can handle feeling tense, bored, and so on. It's okay. Food won't take care of the feeling." "Get going! March! Get out of the kitchen, now!"

10. False. Weight gain may mean that you have tried the same approach repeatedly and that you are *expecting* to gain it back. Try a new approach, one that attacks the problem in a new way. Allow for the possibility of some day being more normal-weighted (not thin if that is unrealistic). Think in terms of setting yourself up for success.

Quiz by Frances Stern, Ph.D., director, Behavioral Awareness Institute (see page 94).

LOSE WEIGHT AND KEEP IT OFF!

You already know that losing weight is one of the most dramatic ways to improve your health and your appearance. You have probably tried every new "easy" diet that has come into vogue and found that losing weight may be easy but keeping it off is next to impossible.

Statistics show that less than 5 percent of dieters are able to maintain their weight reduction. Why? Why do we start out with the best of intentions, only to fail? Why do we go from diet to diet, always seeking the seemingly unattainable goal of lasting leanness?

Dr. Margaret Mackenzie, an anthropologist at the University of California at Berkeley, believes that obesity is an incurable disease, at least for those who do not recognize it as a cultural, rather than a medical, problem. Writing in *Bariatric Medicine* in 1977, she said: "The stereotype of the fat, happy person must be the strongest candidate for the most inaccurate myth in American culture," she explains. "The obese are in despair. They share the disapproval of themselves that others have of them. To it they add remorse, self-hatred, and hopelessness at their failure to stop eating when they know it would mean the loss of the weight they see as the source of their problems. Why can they not stop eating when there is nothing they feel they want to achieve more?"

According to Dr. Mackenzie, American culture defines an adult as "self-centered, competent, morally responsible, rational, productive, and independent. The obese contradict every one of these American values. If they were competent, responsible, and rational, they would simply stop eating—and without help from anyone else." Dr. Mackenzie notes that it is difficult to hide obesity. Nicotine in the lungs is invisible, alcoholism may be hidden, but the results of an addiction to food are irrevocably public. The obese are outcasts because "they show their failure to achieve the goals the culture sets for everyone."

Mackenzie believes that if weight loss is to be maintained, we must first understand the role of food as a culture symbol and its meaning to us. If we can comprehend that the refrigerator has replaced the hearth as the heart of the home in our society, we will be better able to change our eating habits and to stay thin and gain self-esteem by feeling competent and in control.

Dr. Theodore Rubin, author of *Forever Thin* and *The Thin Book by a Formerly Fat Psychiatrist*, maintains that overweight people have remarkably little tolerance of anxiety and frustration. They want quick results in weight loss. But if weight reduction is to be effective, loss of pounds must be second to emotional changes.

"Obese people have a preoccupation with food and weight that truly thin people, even those who happen to be heavy for a time, generally don't have," Dr. Rubin says. "It is a preoccupation far out of proportion to anything that can even indicate a hunger for food. They constantly think of food. They do not feel satisfied after eating because this is not what tempted them to eat in the first place. They eat out of a compulsive necessity, and they don't know why."

Dr. Harvey Einhorn, a New Jersey internist specializing in nutrition and metabolic diseases and a former officer of the American College of Nutrition, believes he knows why: "The tense, anxious individual who overeats is perfectly obvious. So is the person with financial, marital, or environmental problems. But the most common and least recognized reason for overeating is mild depression. Almost all fat people have latent insecurities. In fact," he continues, "you can tell a lot about people's emotional histories by the foods they choose to overeat. Security foods, for example, are milk, eggs, and butter. They are the foods of infants. They give a sense of the warmth of infancy. Reward foods include cake, cookies, ice cream, and chocolate. The obese person often says: 'I know I shouldn't have eaten it, but I ate it anyway.' That shows a subconscious desire to reward themselves following a difficulty or frustration. A man who feels the need to show the world that he is masculine seeks grown-up foods: beer, pretzels, steak, and potatoes. When he eats them, he tells the world that he is a 'man.' "

Aside from the emotional, cultural, and cosmetic reasons for losing weight and keeping it off, the best reason for reducing is your health. If you are more than 30 percent overweight, you may be seriously endangering your well-being. Medical authorities and insurance statisticians agree that the obese do not live as long as those of normal weight. Overweight puts an extra burden on your back and feet, for example, and you are more likely to develop problems with them, such as severe osteoarthritis (the wear-and-tear disease). If you are overweight and you need an operation, there is a greater risk from the anesthesia. It takes the surgeon more time to perform the operation, and not infrequently, the instruments are too small to cut through the fat. If you are overweight, you probably have more skin problems than you would otherwise have. You may also have elevated blood fats, and you may secrete more insulin. Your chances of developing hardening of the arteries and diabetes are greatly increased. In fact, many times the only treatment for adult diabetics is loss of weight. The same holds true for persons with high blood pressure; when they diet and lose pounds, their blood pressure may fall without medication.

Well, perhaps you know you should lose weight. Perhaps you want to lose weight and keep it off, but you have failed in all your previous attempts. What can you do? First of all, you can get rid of misconceptions. Dr. Michael J. Mahoney, associate professor of psychology at Pennsylvania State University, lists these common ones:

Exercise is not very useful in reducing and just makes you hungrier.

If you are not successful at reducing, you lack willpower.

Weigh yourself every day to aid reducing.

Eliminate all fats and carbohydrates if you want a quick method of losing weight.

Obesity is a symptom of deep personality problems that require prolonged psychotherapy.

Most weight problems are inherited.

Dr. Mahoney points out that most of the popular diets are so drastic that you cannot stay on them. The Stillman (water) and Atkins (carbohydrate) diets require dramatic changes, and because they are not nutritionally safe, you can stay on them for only a few weeks. Even if you stay on them for several months and lose twenty or thirty pounds, you will not develop an alternate way of eating or an alternate style of living. Consequently, when you stop the diet, you will return to the very patterns that got you into trouble in the first place. And a yo-yo pattern of dieting may damage your health.

A firm believer in behavior modification as a means of losing weight, Dr. Mahoney maintains that a combination of gradual weight loss and a change in eating behavior is the only permanent and safe way to reduce. He points out that 100 calories a day (a mere glass of beer or a handful of peanuts) make a difference of 10 pounds a year. And if you are willing to accept a gradual weight loss, you are going to be doing a lot more good for your heart and arteries. So far, the evidence suggests that the faster you lose weight, the greater the likelihood that you will put it on again.

There is a basic equation, Dr. Mahoney points out: Calories consumed in excess of calories spent equals overweight. Physical activities, therefore, are very important in weight loss. "It is a combination of diet restriction or dietary reappraisal and changes in physical activity pattern. Many people consume fewer calories than their normal weight peers but are so sedentary in their life-styles that they cannot even afford to consume 1,500 calories a day, yet cutting back on those 1,500 calories would be dangerous. You've got to have 1,000 to 1,200 calories a day in order to get minimal nutritional needs."

As for heredity, there is certainly strong evidence that obesity tends to run in families. But Dr. Mahoney says that evidence does not indicate that overweight is genetic. Rather the significant factor may be family eating patterns. There are rare instances of hereditary disease that is characterized by obesity. There is also an inherited body build that may make you less tolerant of higher calories than another person.

Dr. Mahoney believes there is some evidence to refute the widely held belief that 3,500 calories equal 1 pound. For some individuals, 3,200 calories equal 1 pound; for others, 3,800 calories equal 1 pound. Some people are "fast fat burners" who can eat more and not gain weight; they have a higher metabolic rate.

Another myth that Dr. Mahoney debunks is that you can cut out carbohydrates and fats and lose weight faster. "That is incorrect. You will lose weight more slowly, and you will destroy some lean body mass in the process. The diet must include fats, proteins, and carbohydrates." The doctor and his colleagues at Penn State firmly believe that "if you can't live with something, don't start it. If you are starting on a diet of cottage cheese and fish, you should ask yourself: 'Could I live with that the rest of my life?' If the answer is no, don't start it."

Dr. Mahoney explains that if you take smaller portions of whatever foods you enjoy, you can lose weight. If you remove one extension phone in your home, you will save about ten pounds a year because of the number of steps involved. If you take the farthest parking place rather than the closest one, or if you use a stairway rather than the elevator, you can have a dramatic effect on your weight. "Remember, it takes a reduction of only 100 calories a day to make a difference of 10 pounds a year."

The idea that it is natural to develop a middle-age spread is also a myth, the doctor maintains. "That is the result of a reduction in physical activity without corresponding reduction in caloric intake. It happens if you continue to eat the same quantities and type of food that were appropriate when you were an active, growing person, even though your food needs decline each year."

Like the other behavioral psychologists quoted in this section, Dr. Mahoney believes that you should not blame your failure to diet successfully on some mysterious inner force. "Recent evidence shows that self-control is not an inborn strength that some people possess and others lack. The successful reducer does not owe his or her success to an inherited personality trait. Self-control is a complex but learnable set of personal skills. The reason some people reduce so easily while others fail repeatedly is not one of willpower. Although age, activity, and metabolism do play an important part, the major difference lies in learnable skills."

Regardless of your age, past history of failures, or degree of obesity, you can learn to control your weight effectively and permanently. Many methods and diets are described in this section. The emphasis is on behavioral techniques because these seem the most successful with the largest number of people. But the best of all possible diets is, of course, the one that works for *you*.

CALORIE COUNT

Here is a list of some commonly consumed foods. Can you guess their calorie content? June Hemphill of the Diet Workshop prepared this quiz.

1. 3-ounce martini
2. ½-cup potato salad
3. 12-ounce can of beer
4. 1 sugared doughnut
5. 12-ounce can of cola
6. 12-ounce can of ginger ale
7. 1 ounce peanuts
8. 1 large chocolate shake
9. ¾-ounce peanut butter cup
10. 1 serving of apple pie a la mode
11. 1 peanut butter and jelly sandwich
12. 3 one-inch pieces of nut fudge
13. 1 ounce corn chips
14. 1 slice of chocolate cake with frosting

Answers

1. 168	**5.** 160	**9.** 130	**13.** 160
2. 164	**6.** 130	**10.** 534	**14.** 400
3. 155	**7.** 166	**11.** 438	
4. 233	**8.** 365	**12.** 576	

If you are dieting, you should avoid all the items on this list. For a more complete calorie counting list, send a large, self-addressed, stamped envelope to:

The Diet Workshop, Inc.
111 Washington Street, Suite 301
Brookline, Maryland 02146

BEHAVIOR MODIFICATION TECHNIQUES FOR WEIGHT LOSS

There is no one definition of behavior modification. Generally, it involves dealing with the feelings, thoughts, and behavior, in this case, concerning food, and using clever, easy techniques to counteract actions that lead to particular behavior patterns, in this case overeating. Behaviorists, for instance, accept the fact that it is more difficult to diet than it is to quit smoking. You can stop using cigarettes altogether and never smoke again, but you cannot eliminate eating. You have to face it constantly. You have maintained a series of eating patterns for many years. They are relatively resistant to change. Therefore, a gradual change makes more sense than a drastic one.

People who want to lose weight are always looking for a miracle cure, an easy, magic way to take off pounds and keep them off. Of course, there is no such method, although it is often promised. The closest thing to a permanent cure for overeating that you can live with can be achieved through behavior therapy. You gradually change your life-style until you can eat in such a way that you lose weight and maintain the weight loss. The techniques vary. Some programs assume that by now you know what to eat and what not to eat and so do not even give you a low-calorie diet. Most programs are not geared to rapid weight loss. They believe in a gradual change of behavior.

The Little Changes That Help a Lot

Here is a summary of the behavior modification techniques used in the programs described in this chapter.

Keep a written record of what you eat: This technique is common to all programs. You write down everything you put in your mouth from morning to night, seven days a week, until you can see a pattern emerging. In this way you will discover when your dangerous periods are and how much you actually eat.

Always eat in the same place: By eating in one place, you will begin to associate that place with food. You can be in control of what you eat and discourage yourself from eating when you would rather be in another place.

Do nothing else while eating: If you are watching television or reading a magazine or talking on the telephone, you may eat more and enjoy it less than you would if you concentrated on what you were doing.

Don't bring it home: If you don't have fattening snacks and rich foods in the house, you won't be tempted to eat them. What you receive when you eat out will be minimal compared with what you would eat if you had it in the house.

Do your food shopping after you have had a full meal: You are less likely to be tempted by fattening foods if you shop on a full stomach than you will be if you shop on an empty one.

Use smaller plates: Smaller plates and smaller portions can do a great deal to help you reduce your food intake.

Take smaller bites, and chew, chew, chew: Another well-established behavior modification technique is to take small bites, to savor your food, and to lay down your fork as you chew each mouthful at least ten times.

Always leave some food on your plate: This helps break the habit you developed in childhood, when you were encouraged to finish everything. Don't eat just because it's there.

Break the pattern: Change mealtimes to very irregular schedules before you try to reduce your intake. This helps both to break old habits and to make you more aware of what you are eating.

Eat half your food raw each day: Fresh food in its natural state can be more satisfying and more filling.

Pinpoint the dangerous times: Find out when you are likely to down those fattening snacks or to overeat, and arrange to reprogram your time. Make sure you are taking a walk or doing something else enjoyable at those times instead of eating.

Wear a surgeon's mask when preparing food: Many people sample food as they prepare it without even realizing that they are doing so. Wearing a surgeon's mask (usually available at a drugstore or surgical supply store) will easily prevent this unconscious habit.

Give up one treat per day: By eliminating one glass of beer or two slices of bread, you can do away with 100 calories a day. If you *have* to have pretzels or ice cream or some favorite treat, cut back somewhere else.

Take only half your portion: Keep the serving bowls in the kitchen. Take only half of what you normally eat. Perhaps you will not go back for the rest. Even if you do, you are likely to take less if the bowl is in another room, rather than conveniently in front of you.

Park far away: When you go somewhere by car, park in the farthest reasonable parking space or get off a distance from your regular stop when riding public transportation so that you have to walk. It can use up many calories.

Take the stairs instead of the elevator: You can get rid of more calories by climbing stairs than you can playing tennis or jogging. A 150-pound person burns up 14 calories climbing stairs. Multiply this by the number of times a day that you need to go from one floor to another, and you will see how beneficial using the stairs can be.

Enlist the help of your spouse and/or friends: If people help you in your efforts, rather than hinder you, you can do a lot better. Learn how to answer when someone says to you, "Oh, a little bit won't hurt."

Watch the liquor: Some drinks are more fattening than others. For example, gin and tonic has a lot more calories than white wine, and Scotch on the rocks is less fattening that rum or rye whiskey.

Holidays don't have to revolve around food: Plan other activities for the holidays. Many a lavish meal during a festivity has dashed the dieting aspirations of the well-intentioned. Prepare yourself mentally before going to a party, and rehearse your answers so that you can turn down high-calorie treats automatically.

Choose the smaller portions offered on the menu when eating out: You don't need the big portion. Take advantage of the increasing number of menus offering low-calorie dishes.

Give yourself nonfood rewards: This is a hard habit to break because food was used as a reward in childhood. By giving yourself something you like other than food when you have achieved a goal, you can overcome the "sweet for a treat" routine.

Level with yourself before you get out of bed in the morning: Tell yourself that there is no one or nothing to blame for your overweight except yourself and that throughout the day you are going to do your best to avoid the pitfalls presented by high-calorie, overly salted, and junk foods, all of which you dearly love to eat.

CLINICS FOR WEIGHT CONTROL: BEHAVIORAL MODIFICATION TECHNIQUES

Florida

Nutrition and Bariatrics Associates, Cedars of Lebanon Health Care Center, Suite A, 1295 Northwest 14th Street, South Building, P.O. Box 520793, Miami, Florida 33152, (305)545-7666. This is a privately staffed and licensed group of physicians specializing in the treatment of over-weight individuals as well as balancing body chemistry. The weight control program utilizes protein-sparing modified fast (PSMF) and be-havioral modification to assist the patient in making the necessary life-style changes. The protein fast is used to achieve rapid weight loss by completely restricting food intake. Compensation for the absence of food is managed by the use of protein supplements, minerals, and vitamins. This regimen ensures that most of the weight loss will be fat rather than lean muscle tissue and vital organs. Weekly weight loss varies from individual to individual; the average is approximately ⅓ to ½ pound per day.

Because patient needs are different, Nutrition and Bariatrics Asso-ciates offers both an Outpatient Program and a Hospital Program. Outpatient Program patients visit the clinic regularly for medical and behavior therapy. While the patient is on the PSMF diet, blood chemis-tries are taken every second week to assure that no problems exist.

The Hospital Program is for patients with complex medical problems or patients who experience difficulty establishing the fast. They are admit-ted to Cedars of Lebanon Health Care Center. The length of stay depends largely on the nature and extent of the patient's problem, but the usual hospitalization is five days, from Sunday afternoon to Friday morning. Data are continually collected to monitor the progress of the program and to ensure its effectiveness. Basic research is also ongoing, and results of the studies are reported to interested professionals in the health-care field.

Behavior modification is a required part of the program. Both group and individual sessions are available.

Balancing Body Chemistry (BBC) is a program in which the person's state of chemical balance is determined by the use of extensive blood tests, urine and fecal studies, EKG, a complete physical examination, and a hair analysis for trace mineral balances. The essence of this program is recognizing that the human body is a natural chemistry set. Theoretically, when that chemistry set is in a state of perfect balance, the body will then experience perfect health. Chemical balance is accomplished by an individualized and customized nutritional and supplementation program based on the results of the initial and continuing testing. The basic balancing program lasts for a period of approximately eight weeks, during which time the patient's progress is constantly monitored and recorded.

After the initial program, maintaining a balanced body chemistry becomes a situation in which the patients will require continued monitoring from time to time. This time is determined by the patients' individual state of balance and by his or her adherence to the specific program.

Balanced body chemistry is determined both by certain genetic factors and by environmental factors. Some of the environmental factors that disturb chemical balance are the air that we breathe, the toxins in the foods that we eat, the amount of stress we must deal with, and our attitude toward accepting total responsibility for our health.

The initial examination and evaluation for the Outpatient Program costs $200; this covers the first and second weeks' visits. Subsequent weekly visits cost $35 each, including medical follow-up and nutritional supplements. The average charge for the Hospital Program is $1,000, including doctors' fees and medical, psychological, and nutritional evaluations. Group behavior modification sessions are $20. Balancing Body Chemistry costs $500; there are additional charges for the prescribed supplements, which can be purchased at the dispensary in the program's offices.

Maryland

Behavioral Weight Control Program, Randolph Medical Center, 4701 Randolph Road, Rockville, Maryland 20852, (301)770-5664, Paul Levine, director. This program, which is based on the techniques developed at the University of Pennsylvania (see page 92) and elsewhere, employs behavioral modification techniques. The director, Paul Levine, was once grossly overweight himself, and after going through countless weight reduction regimens, he decided to design his own program. He found the behavioral technique to be the best and established this successful program. The program has been designed to promote gradual and continued weight loss. This is accomplished by teaching you how to modify your response, exposure and susceptibility to the factors responsible for your overweight.

The facility is nonmedical and is divided into three stages. The first is diagnostic and entails three sessions. This is followed by a ten-session self-management phase and finally by an extended follow-up phase.

The first appointment is private and involves a case history, the identification of important determinants of your food intake and energy expenditure, and diagnosis of how you could best be helped. The other sessions are with groups of twelve people; these meet once a week for 1½ hours. During this phase, attention is paid to such issues as habitual patterns of ingestion and energy expenditure, perceptions of hunger and satiety, life-styles, attitudes, and thoughts and feelings about weight and food. The follow-up phase is based on your needs. It may take the form of a simple periodic weight check, or it may involve continued active participation in the program.

The minimum enrollment is thirteen weeks, and the fee is $185.

Pennsylvania

Center for Behavioral Medicine, Department of Psychiatry, University of Pennsylvania Hospital, 1140 Gates Building, Philadelphia, Pennsylvania 19104, (215)662-2818. The yo-yo dieting that so many people resort to is not a good idea. The center's staff believes that cycles of gradual weight gain followed by sudden loss through crash diets can lead to a profound sense of failure and discouragement.

The center's program is designed to help you break up these self-defeating habits and develop a way of life conducive to comfortable weight control. The initial objective is an immediate, significant weight loss, demonstrating that controlled eating practices are both possible and desirable. The long-range goal is to establish dietary and activity patterns that can be sustained for a lifetime. The patient learns to maximize his or her chances of achieving a stable pattern of weight control by learning gradually, over the course of an entire year, to modify the habits that led to obesity.

Treatment takes place in small groups on an outpatient basis. The first eight weekly treatment sessions are devoted to behavioral management and dietary modification techniques. In the transition phase, four biweekly meetings provide the foundation for more independent functioning and help you develop a better grasp of "energy dynamics." In the follow-up phase, eight monthly meetings are devoted to solving individual problems.

The preliminary screening interview is $25. The fee for the treatment, transition, and follow-up phases is $25 per session.

Institute for Behavioral Education, Suite 105, 1000 Valley Forge Circle, King of Prussia, Pennsylvania 19406, (215) 783-0150, Henry A. Jordan, M.D., director. Formerly located in the Department of Psychiatry of the Hospital of the University of Pennsylvania, this program has moved to a new address, although its staff is still affiliated with the university. Dr. Jordan and Dr. Leonard Levitz pioneered the treatment of obesity through behavior therapy, and many behavioral weight loss programs are based on their research. The institute's Behavioral Weight Control Program is conducted in group sessions that meet once a week for one hour. Each treatment group is limited to eight patients and is conducted by a professional therapist.

The staff feels that it is apparent that obesity and eating disorders "are neither caused nor maintained by any single factor. Obesity can be the result of numerous biological (physical and metabolic), psychological, cultural, familial, and environmental determinants. Such influences, which vary greatly from one individual to another, lead to important differences in the behaviors involved in overeating and underactivity. Because a variety of factors can lead to the same result, excessive weight, it is essential that treatment be carefully individualized if long-term success is to be realized. The program promotes gradual and continued weight loss by teaching the patient how to modify his/her response, exposure, and susceptibility to the factors responsible for overweight. It is this strategy that provides the basis for self-control.

The program is divided into three phases: a three-session diagnostic phase, a fifteen-session treatment phase, and an extended follow-up or consolidation phase.

The self-modification treatment techniques that are used are based on psychological principles of learning, motivation, and behavior change. During treatment, attention is paid to such issues as the patient's habitual patterns of ingestion and energy expenditure, perceptions of hunger and satiety, family interactions and life-style, and attitudes, thoughts, and feelings toward weight and food.

The follow-up phase is based on the patient's needs and may take the form of periodic weight checks or continued group meetings. All patients are followed for at least one year; for some patients, longer follow-up periods are advisable.

Patients accepted for the program usually weigh at least 20 percent more than their desired body weight. However, there are two exceptions: a person who has been gaining consistently over an extended period of time (two to three pounds per year for last four years) and wants to prevent further weight gain; a person who has lost weight, is close to his/her ideal weight, and is now interested in learning how to maintain this weight loss.

Each applicant is required to attend a free one-hour introductory session. During this session, details of the program are explained, and individual questions are answered. Fees are $100 for the three-week diagnostic phase, $375 for the fifteen-week treatment program, $20 for each biweekly follow-up session; and $15 for each monthly follow-up session.

PUBLICATION

Eating Is Okay, Henry Jordan, M.D., Leonard Levitz, Ph.D., and Gordon Kimbsell, Ph.D. New York: Rawson Associates, 1977 (hardcover); New York: New American Library, 1978 (paperback). This book emphasizes behavioral techniques rather than calorie counting. The price of the hardcover edition is $7.95; the price of the paperback edition is $1.50.

New Jersey

Institute for Behavioral Awareness, 810 South Springfield Avenue, Springfield, New Jersey 07081, (201)376-8744. Frances Meritt Stern, Ph.D., director. The institute uses behavior modification along with other creative techniques, one of which is called *mind tripping*. Founded in 1973, this program emphasizes developing a healthy, positive self-image, rather than just losing weight. There is no badgering or punishment for cheating. There are no bad foods, only bad quantities. You are provided with clear, complete instructions on how to eat, not what to eat. You are taught how to monitor your thoughts and how to pattern your thinking in constructive ways that tend to produce successful weight loss. You also learn creative alternatives to overeating that can increase your ability to cope.

Mind trips are really positive daydreams, constructive fantasies that can help you deal with the temptation to overeat. The mind trips aid relaxation and introduce a picture you can call up when you need it to help you deal with your overeating problem. Dr. Stern, for example, dreams of a chocolate fudge sundae that she can imagine tasting and feeling. Every once in a while she eats one to refuel her imagination.

Here are a few mind trips she teaches:

Favorite place: You escape to a place where you feel safe, secure, and free. Nothing can harm you there. You feel good. Some people make up a variation on this trip, such as a magic carpet or the seaside. You can recall your favorite vacation spot. While on your escape trip you may find your desire to eat has vanished.

Up scene and testimonial dinner: These are designed to make you like yourself. You picture the tributes being given you by others and how you look before the crowd. This can keep you from feeling blue and then stuffing your mouth for comfort.

Doors: Dr. Stern makes a lot of use of imaginary doors. She finds that if you have a friend or relative or co-worker who is a thorn in your side and you imagine that person behind a door, you can slam it and say, "You're not going to get in my way anymore." She also recalls one very fat woman who imagined opening a closed door. Behind it she saw her husband with a box of chocolates. She had never consciously realized before, and neither had her husband, that he encouraged her to eat.

Aversion trip: This one is used in an emergency when you are tempted to eat a very fattening beloved food. You have to picture something awful in that food—worms, bugs, or other repulsive things—so that if you ate it, you would be sick. You can also picture yourself in a dire situation with the tempting food present. The idea is to associate the food with something unpleasant.

Dr. Stern, who was once very overweight, said that you can learn to enjoy food and yet maintain a normal weight without resorting to a restrictive diet. You can learn to listen to what you are saying to yourself about food and to utilize your intelligence to gain control of your eating. The learning program consists of weekly sessions of approximately one and a half hours. These sessions are conducted by a professional leader. You work with a small group of other people who share similar eating problems. Separate classes are held for men and women. There is also an adolescent program. The cost of a 15 week program is $225, paid in installments. Sessions are 1½ hours. Individual sessions cost $300 and are 35 minutes per week for 15 weeks. The Institute for Behavioral Awareness offers a mail-order package: *How to Use Your Head to Lose Weight and Keep It Off.* $30. It includes:

Specific, easy-to-do strategies to increase changes in thinking behavior and eating habits.

Specific information on how and why these strategies work, and how to keep them working.

A copy of the book, *Mind Trips to Help You Lose Weight,* co-authored by Dr. Stern. This book helps you step-by-step to use your imagination for weight control. It provides 50 easy-to-follow strategies, proven techniques for more permanent weight control.

A STEM Dot. A self-monitoring device that offers you feedback on the imagery techniques and tells you when you are calm, cool and relaxed.

The book alone, *Mind Trips to Help You Lose Weight,* can be found in bookstores or ordered directly from IBA for $9.95.

Washington, D.C.

Georgetown University's Diet Management Program, 2233 Wisconsin Avenue, N.W., Washington, D.C. 20007, Suite 324, Aaron M. Altschul, Ph.D., director, Division of Nutrition, (202)625-2018, Mary Ellen Fediuk, administrative director, (202)625-2064, William Ayers, M.D., medical director, (202)625-7685. The Georgetown program is a weight reduction clinic for the treatment of obesity and a research organization for the study of obesity and the weight loss process. The Diet Management Program approaches the problem of obesity in three ways: behaviorally, educationally, and nutritionally. One of the clinic's major concerns is with obesity as a medical risk factor associated with coronary heart disease, high blood pressure, and diabetes. Therefore, counseling is directed at modifying high-risk dietary life-styles as well as at weight reduction.

Private sessions on an individual basis cover a five-month period for $360. The first session is an hour and a half. The second session is an hour, and other sessions are each a half hour in length. For a free introductory session to decide whether a program is appropriate for you, call (202) 625-3674.

MEDICAL PROGRAMS FOR WEIGHT LOSS

Health and diet are intimately connected with each other. Of course, no one who has a serious medical problem should embark on a diet regimen without the supervision of a physician. And in cases where drugs are used, of course only a physician can legally prescribe them.

The programs described here are under the supervision of physicians.

American Society of Bariatric Physicians, Suite 300, 5200 South Quebec Street, Englewood, Colorado 80110, (303)779-4833, Wilmer L. Asher, M.D., director of professional affairs. This organization was formed more than twenty-five years ago to encourage excellence in the care of the overweight person. It has fostered research, postgraduate education, and the dedication of its members. The society is primarily the voice of physicians specializing in nutrition and weight control. It does not offer advice directly to the general public, but it will provide you with a list of members in your area.

"The bariatrician believes the overweight person is entitled to and deserves comprehensive health care," Dr. Asher says. "Obesity is often accompanied by other serious medical conditions such as diabetes, high blood pressure, elevated cholesterol levels, premature heart attacks, and numerous additional complications. The society believes that the overweight person should have a medical history taken and should have a complete physical examination before embarking on any kind of reducing program."

Modified Fasting Program, Metabolic and Nutrition Service, Newark Beth Israel Medical Center, 201 Lyons Avenue, Newark, New Jersey 07112, (201)926-7550, Dr. Marvin A. Kirschner, director. Aimed at patients who are a minimum of 50 pounds overweight, this program uses a carefully monitored diet limited to 325 calories a day. Dr. Kirschner emphasizes that the 325-calorie fasting technique should never be attempted without strict, coordinated medical control and monitoring. Patients with coexisting medical problems may require a brief period of hospitalization at the outset so that their medication and dietary regimens can be regulated. Patients are then seen each week on an outpatient basis throughout their weight loss period. Psychological and dietary counseling are part of the program. Some patients may experience menstrual irregularities; some, hair loss or a sensation of cold. The program usually succeeds in placing patients who have to lose 100 pounds or more at their desired weight within five to seven months without interrupting their normal work or life programs. The program's success rate is an estimated 80 percent; whereas fad diets average 10 to 15 percent success at the end of four years. Most patients are not hospitalized; instead, they attend a weekly clinic, where they are monitored, tested, and provided with the following week's supply of supplements. Dr. Kirschner says that in many cases patients are able to discontinue medications for high blood pressure or diabetes because the effects of the supplements and fasting eliminate the need. As patients approach their weight goal, they are reintroduced to food and transferred to a sensible maintenance program planned for them by a dietician. The program costs about $200 a month, or $10 per pound of desired weight loss.

Nutrition and Bariatrics Associates, Cedars of Lebanon Health Care Center, 1295 Northwest 14th Street, Suite A, South Building, P.O. Box 520793, Miami, Florida 33152, (305)545-7666, Leonard Haimes, M.D., director. This group of licensed physicians specializes in the treatment of overweight individuals. Using a system of complete medical and behavioral therapy, the program utilizes the protein-sparing modified fast (PSMF) to encourage a weight loss that the patient can maintain. It also stresses a change of life-style, which the patient learns through the use of behavior therapy. PSMF is used to achieve rapid weight loss by completely restricting food intake. To compensate for the absence of food, the patient is given medically prescribed amounts of protein supplements, minerals, and vitamins. This regimen ensures that most of the weight lost during the fast will be fat, rather than lean muscle tissue. The amount of weight actually lost each week varies from individual to individual, but most people will lose from ⅓ to ½ pound of true fat per day.

Approximately one day after the PSMF program is begun, Dr. Haimes says, a condition called *ketosis* occurs; this acts as a natural hunger reduction mechanism. Although most people do not actually feel hungry on this diet, psychological factors tend to influence how they feel physically. This is modified through group and individual behavior therapy and lectures. Because needs differ from individual to individual, two types of programs are offered for patients: the Outpatient Program and the Hospital Program. These services are going to be supplemented with a residential program, which is now being developed. Outpatient Program patients visit the clinic regularly for medical and behavior therapy. While the patient is on the PSMF diet, blood chemistries are taken every second week to make sure that no problems exist. The Hospital Program is for patients who have complex medical problems or who experience difficulty with the fast. They are admitted to Cedars of Lebanon Health Care Center. The length of stay depends on the nature and extent of the patient's problem, but the usual hospitalization is five days, from Sunday afternoon to Friday morning. Data are continually collected to monitor the progress of the program and to ensure its effectiveness. Basic research also continues, and results of the studies are reported to interested health-care professionals.

Behavior therapy is a required part of the program. You can choose your format. A half-hour individual session costs $50; a two-hour group session costs $20; the lecture series costs $100 for eighteen sessions (one hour each) but is included without additional charge to those participating in other aspects of the program. The waiting period to enter the program is about three weeks. The fee for the Outpatient Program is $200 for the initial examination and evaluation and includes the first and second weeks' visits. After that, each weekly visit costs $35, including medical follow-up and nutritional supplements.

Rice Diet Program, Duke University Medical Center, Durham, North Carolina 27710, (919)684-3418. This diet was originated by Dr. Walter Kempner in the early 1940s. He became interested in obesity because he considered it a "derangement in cellular metabolism" and a major cause of vascular complications, particularly high blood pressure. He began treating edema (the accumulation of salt-containing fluid in the bodies of patients with blood vessel, heart, and kidney disease) with a strict or modified rice diet. Rice, he reasoned, was a low-calorie, relatively high-carbohydrate, low-protein, low-fat, cholesterol-free, salt-free food. In one of his first cases, Dr. Kempner reported that a patient on the rice diet lost 63 pounds in a little more than two weeks without the aid of any medication (drugs had been tried before). The rice diet is now famous internationally, and patients come from all over the United States and other countries to stay in Durham and to eat at the Rice House.

When you first arrive at Duke, you undergo a complete diagnostic survey before decisions regarding treatment are made. The examination, X rays, and special studies included in this survey require three to five days for completion. Treatment, which begins immediately following the examination, might last for only a few weeks; but more often, it continues for several months and sometimes as long as a year. Much depends on your condition and your cooperation. Dr. Kempner and his associates make the rounds at the Rice House each day, seven days a week, to monitor and direct the activities of the patients.

Throughout your time in Durham, you stay, not in the hospital, but in a private home or at a motel or hotel nearby. The Rice House is owned privately, rather than by the hospital or the physicians, and it is operated exclusively for the program's patients. Its primary function is to prepare and serve the special diets prescribed. There are a few rooms in the Rice House, but they are usually reserved for younger patients who are not accompanied by their parents and for patients who cannot walk.

This is not an easy diet to follow, and it takes a relatively long time. However, it can have spectacular results for the grossly overweight and for those suffering from high blood pressure, arteriosclerosis, heart and kidney disease, and diabetes mellitus.

The cost of the diagnostic survey varies according to the tests needed, but on an outpatient basis, it generally runs between $700 and $900, which is payable in full upon completion of the examination. If hospitalization is found necessary, additional charges will depend on the type of accommodations and the length of the stay. Accommodations for Rice House diet patients start at $80 per week for a semiprivate room, special diet, and limited personal attention. The charge for the special diet only is approximately $45 per week. The present standard fee (unchanged for twenty years) for the total services of Dr. Kempner and his colleagues is $150 per week, including certain special studies. This fee is based on uninterrupted treatment. There is no adjustment in fees for any absence prior to completion of the program. An occasional additional test, X ray, or consultation with another specialist may be necessary but will probably not amount to much additional money. Weekly fees can be paid in advance if you wish, but they *must* be paid at the end of each month. Checkout studies, done during the last few days of a patient's stay, usually cost between $125 and $175. Most patients are advised to return from time to time for complete reevaluation and sometimes for further treatment. The costs for this range from $550 to $650. Insurance may pay for much of the cost, but the patient is responsible for seeing that all fees are paid.

Doctors

Robert Atkins, 400 East 56th Street, New York, New York 10022, (212)PL8-2110. Author of *Dr. Atkins' Diet Revolution* (New York: David McKay Co., 1972) and *Dr. Atkins' Superenergy Diet* (New York: Crown Publishers, 1976). Dr. Atkins is famous for his low-carbohydrate diet. He is a graduate of Cornell University Medical College and medical director of Diet Revolution Centers, Inc.

Hilda Bruch, 1600 Holcombe Boulevard, Houston, Texas 77030, (713)790-1872. Dr. Bruch is a psychiatrist and author of *The Golden Cage: The Enigma of Anorexia Nervosa* (New York: Basic Books, 1978). She specializes in the treatment of eating disorders.

George Christakis, chief, Nutrition Division, University of Miami School of Medicine, Miami, Florida 33152, (305)547-5170. Dr. Christakis specializes in the treatment and prevention of medical problems caused by overeating, smoking, lack of exercise, and other factors associated with life-styles.

Barbara Fiedler Edelstein, Bloomfield, Connecticut, (203)242-4044. A psychiatrist and author of *The Woman Doctor's Diet for Women* (Englewood Cliffs, N.J.: Prentice-Hall, 1977), Dr. Edelstein specializes in weight control. She is particularly interested in the metabolic aspects.

Morton Glenn, Dietetic Consultation Service, 121 East 60th Street, New York, New York 10022, (212)838-4040. Dr. Glenn, the author of *But I Don't Eat That Much* (New York: E. P. Dutton, 1974), specializes in the treatment of obesity.

Sigrid Nelius, director, Dietary Rehabilitation, Duke University, Durham, North Carolina 27706, (919)684-6331. Dr. Nelius specializes in the treatment of obesity, smoking, and other problems associated with life-styles.

Neal Solomon, Hilton Plaza, Pikesville, Baltimore, Maryland 21233, (301)484-3080. Dr. Solomon is assistant professor of medicine at Johns Hopkins University and author of *Dr. Solomon's Prudent Master Plan for Total Body Fitness* (New York: Berkeley Publishing Corporation, 1978). He is in private practice and specializes in weight control.

DIET GROUPS

Diet groups are based on the methods that worked for another addiction, alcohol. Alcoholics Anonymous developed the technique, in which members discuss their problems with each other and help each other overcome the compulsion to drink. AA has worked when psychotherapy, jail, and many other methods have failed. The group strength technique has also proved successful for many people who cannot lose weight on their own.

The authoratative *Medical Letter,* a publication produced by leading experts in the medical field, reported that about one-third of those participating in organized group weight reduction programs lose 20 pounds or more; another one-third stick with the programs but lose little weight; the remainder drop out. A few years later, most of those who lost weight have regained it. The statistics offered by the various groups show a much higher success rate. The truth probably lies somewhere in between. But if you can lose weight and maintain the weight loss with the aid of a group program, then for you, it is 100 percent successful. However, before you invest the time or money in a diet group, ask yourself whether you are the type of person who can get up in front of a group and discuss your eating habits.

Nonprofit diet clubs began with TOPS (see page 103). They are patterned almost exactly after Alcoholics Anonymous. Weight Watchers was the first big, successful commercial club. It developed not only a wide variety of techniques, including behavior modification, but has a magazine, food products, and other commercial ventures under its aegis. Many community organizations, health departments, and schools also run low-cost or free diet groups.

Almost without exception, the founders and leaders of the various groups were fat people who finally succeeded in losing weight. The big commercial organizations train speakers or leaders for franchised operations; these people are usually former clients who came and conquered their weight problem with the specific program.

When diet group is best for you? They all have different personalities. All those listed here are excellent and have been successful with scores of dieters. Remember, the best one is the one that works for *you*.

Weight Watchers International Inc., 800 Community Drive, Manhasset, New York 11030, (516)627-9200. Dynamic, blond Jean Nidetch proved that helping others lose weight could be a big business. She founded the company in May 1963, after she reduced from 214 to 142 pounds on a diet developed by the Obesity Clinic of the New York City Board of Health. More than 9 million people have joined Weight Watchers since its inception, and it is now a franchised organization. There are approximately 12,000 individual classes held weekly throughout the world. You have to be at least 10 pounds overweight to join.

The principal purpose of Weight Watchers classes is to help you lose weight and learn how to keep it off through a program that consists of a nutritionally sound, scientifically developed diet together with the Personal Action Plan, a behavior modification program that was added in 1975. The basic program, which has been widely imitated, involves a weight-reducing regimen, a plateau plan for those who temporarily stop losing weight as their bodies readjust, and a maintenance plan.

Weight Watchers has made many changes in the program during the years because its staff believes that the field of obesity research is dynamic, and they want to take advantage of all research developments. Albert Lippert, chairman of the board of Weight Watchers International, reported the changes instituted in 1977: The new Maintenance Plan for members who have reached their weight goal introduces a new concept, the reintroduction of formerly forbidden foods. All foods are now allowable. The Maintenance Plan is taught in a way that provides greater aid in furthering your success in maintaining normal body weight.

The Basic Maintenance Plan allows 300 foods within eight groups. Every week, those on the program receive a new group of foods, each of which contains approximately the same caloric value (about 50 calories). Thus, members find they are able to handle, on a permanent basis, anywhere from 50 to 400 additional calories a day and still maintain their desired weight. The weight reduction eating program provides many appetizing new foods that members can enjoy regardless of how much weight they must lose. Foods previously forbidden on the Basic Weight Reduction Program but now permitted include sardines, corn, yogurt, ketchup, cocoa, flour, cornstarch, arrowroot, tongue, smoked poultry, smoked meat, smoked fish, and cured meat. All can be eaten within limits.

The program has been markedly simplified, yet it continues to provide optimum nutrition. There are fewer rules to learn, and emphasis is on what the overweight can do, rather than on what they cannot do. The original fourteen food categories have been trimmed to eight groups: fruit; eggs and cheese; bread, cereal, and starches; milk; poultry, meat, fish, and legumes; vegetables; fat; and optional. The optional group includes a category of specialty foods such as some low-calorie gelatins, jams and jellies, salad dressings, and syrups and toppings. Foods from all eight groups may be used within the program's guidelines.

For some foods, there is now a range in terms of quantity, rather than a specific amount. For example, there is a range of three to four ounces of poultry, meat, or fish for the midday meal and four to six ounces of poultry, meat, or fish for women and youths (six to eight ounces for men) for the evening meal. This flexibility still permits members to obtain the proper nutrients.

Before the program was reshaped, fifty-six species were listed in the fish category. Members can now select any fish for their "at least three to five times weekly" consumption. In addition, shellfish, once limited to once a week, are no longer limited.

Weight Watchers experts noted that a variety of tastes, textures, and other characteristics are needed to meet the general need for variety in food choices and for the opportunity to use the process of biting, chewing, and swallowing satisfactorily. Mr. Lippert says this is especially noteworthy because failure to provide variety in a food plan often leads to boredom and the urge to deviate from the plan.

The initial registration fee for Weight Watchers classes varies from $3 to $7, and there is a weekly attendance fee that varies from $2 to $5, depending on the locale. There are no contracts, and you can drop out at any time.

Two food licensees of Weight Watchers International distribute products such as Weight Watchers frozen luncheons and dinners, artificial sweeteners, broths and seasonings, frozen desserts, soft drinks, fruit snacks, and margarine. Weight Watchers has licensed summer camps for overweight boys and girls.

Weight Watchers Magazine is published monthly and costs $.75 on newstands; it has a circulation of more than 1,750,000. The *Weight Watchers Program Cookbook* has sold more than 1 million copies since its publication in 1973, and the *Weight Watchers Cookbook*, by Jean Nidetch, first published in 1968, has passed the 1.5 million mark.

TOPS Club Inc., International Headquarters, 4575 South Fifth Street, P.O. Box 07489, Milwaukee, Wisconsin 53207, (414)482-4620. TOPS (which stands for Take Off Pounds Sensibly) is the popular name for this nonprofit, noncommercial weight control organization, which was the first major weight control club. Founded in 1948 by Esther S. Manz, a Milwaukee homemaker, it has its own building, which includes a complete printshop for producing *TOPS News*, the members' monthly magazine, and a computer center for handling the extensive weight data on members.

TOPS currently has 338,600 members in 12,500 chapters in the United States, Canada, and twenty-eight other countries. In one year, these chapters had a documented weight loss of 1,166 tons, or 2,331,228.75 pounds.

Here are the five facets of TOPS:

1. *Medical orientation:* All TOPS members are required to obtain their individual weight goals from their personal physicians. They are also required to use diets approved by their own physicians. Medical supervision is encouraged during the entire term of weight loss. The organization feels that all diets should be individually prescribed and medically supervised because no one standard diet could possibly be optimal and safe for all persons, particularly persons with the allied health conditions that so often accompany obesity.

2. *Group therapy:* Unlike commercial groups that call for weekly weigh-ins and listening to a paid lecturer, TOPS charges no fee and elects its volunteer leaders from its membership. TOPS members remain in contact with each other all week long, not just at meetings, along lines similar to the Alcoholics Anonymous program. Phone calls, cards, letters, and personal visits all play a part in the battle against the common problem, obesity. Programs at chapter meetings vary but have one thing in common: They contribute in some way to weight control goals. Often, a noncommercial professional speaker will talk on some phase of obesity or its allied problems. Sometimes, the program is quite social, involving games, contests, sing-alongs, skits, and other entertainment, all related to weight control.

A special facet of the ongoing therapy are the TOPS retreats, which offer members a time apart from their ordinary environments and responsibilities during which they can give and receive each other's help. Retreats are held in different locations throughout the United States and Canada. Specially planned low-calorie meals are served. Costs are held as low as possible so that all members can enjoy this time for renewed inspiration.

3. *Competition:* Among the unique facets of TOPS is the keen competition in weight loss that goes on the year round on the local and international levels. Contests are held for the greatest weight loss, greatest improvement, and charm and beauty after weight loss. The competitions culminate in the announcement of the international winners each year.

4. *Recognition:* Those who have achieved outstanding weight loss are literally crowned king and queen in their various areas. Other forms of recognition include trophies, charms for TOPS charm bracelets, Century Club medallions for those who lose 100 pounds and KOPS (Keep Off Pounds Sensibly) diplomas for those who reach and maintain the weight goals set for them by their doctors. Rallies and recognition days at all levels honor the "best losers" each year.

5. *Obesity Research:* In 1966, a longtime dream of founder Esther Manz came true when a fund for a research program was established. Dr. Ronald Kalkhoff, professor of medicine at the Medical College of Wisconsin, is director of TOPS research program. More than $1.5 million dollars in TOPS earnings and the voluntary contributions of its members has been given to the fund.

In calling for his colleagues in medicine to support the organization, Dr. Albert Stunkard, well-known University of Pennsylvania nutrition researcher, said that TOPS "represents a uniquely successful self-help approach to obesity, with results apparently superior to those of routine medical management." If you are interested in joining TOPS, write to international headquarters for information; a TOPS member near you will get in touch with you.

As a nonprofit organization that does no advertising, TOPS is able to keep its fees low. In the United States and Canada, the fee is $9 annually for the first two years and $7 annually thereafter. Unlike some commercial weight control groups, TOPS does not charge a weekly weigh-in fee.

Diet Control Centers, Inc., 1021 Stuyvesant Avenue, Union, New Jersey 07083, (201)687-0007. Organized in 1968 by Jacqueline Greenspan, Ruth Lipp, and Ruth Landesberg, three formerly overweight New Jersey residents, this organization has grown rapidly throughout the United States. Using the original Obesity Clinic Diet developed by the New York City Board of Health as their basis, they put together a formula that they consider the perfect diet. They explain that "any diet will allow you to lose weight, but how do you *stay thin* . . . if you are

Jewish and happiness is eating a bagel and lox and cream cheese? . . . if you're Italian and happiness is eating spaghetti and meatballs with salad and garlic bread and having a glass of wine?" They have successfully designed a diet regimen that includes ethnic foods. They also allow members to eat peanut butter, chocolate, pasta, bacon, wine, and alcoholic beverages while they are losing weight, thus taking the boredom out of dieting. Fish and liver are not requirements of this diet. Creative recipes for exotic and ethnic foods are given, and members have three proven-successful formulas to choose from. Mild isometric exercises that are performed while one is seated are part of the routine at each meeting, and a behavioral awareness system is monitored by trained personnel. Weigh-ins are private to avoid embarrassment, and a friendly, social atmosphere prevails at weekly meetings.

The registration fee, which includes the cost of the first meeting, is $8.50. There is a $3.50 fee for each weekly meeting after that. Diet Control Centers also offers a book of tickets to weekly meetings at a cost of $30 for ten weeks, a savings of $5 over the regular fee.

PUBLICATIONS

Diet Control Centers, Inc., offers the following publications:

DCC Formula Handbook. The price is $7. This book presents an easy to follow program with good and easy menus.

DCC Recipes	*Snacks and Sides*	*Slim Chef*
Gourmet Recipes	*Poultry Power*	*Single Servings*

Each of these books contains kitchen-tested DCC gourmet recipes. The price is $1.50 for each book. Add $.50 to cover postage and handling.

Lean Line, Inc., 151 New World Way, South Plainfield, New Jersey 07080, (201)757-6446. Two believers in mind over matter, Lorraine Wurtzel and Antonia Marotta, former overweight members of another weight-reducing group, founded their own organization in 1968. They conjured up a reducing diet that lets you eat spaghetti and meatballs, bagels and lox, cheesecake, chopped liver, and baked potatoes with sour cream. Using a combination of behavior modification techniques and scientific food selection, they developed a program that stresses ethnic food in moderate amounts. Lean Line members do not count calories; they just eat according to directions.

Behavior modification plays a major roll in the success of Lean Line members. Paper placemats with behavioral reminders printed on them help to reinforce the Lean Liner's new habits. A circle for your plate says, "Think small." There are outlines for your hands that say, "Hands down. Place hands here between bites. It'll keep them from shoveling food you know where."

When a member reaches his or her goal weight (which is determined on the first visit), he/she is permitted to go on Lean Line's Tailor-Made Maintenance Program, which is designed to fit into any life-style. A Lean Line charm is issued when a member has successfully maintained his/her goal weight for six weeks. The member is then awarded lifetime membership. Lifetime members have the privilege of attending Lean Line meetings at no charge as long as they stay within 2 pounds of their goal.

Cassette tapes featuring Lolly Wurtzel and Toni Marotta, directing you through the steps of two extremely effective relaxation techniques.

The tape begins with a countdown—50 to 0. With each count, you learn how to relax each part of your body, how to lose the physical grip of tension. It is recommended that the tape be used twice a day in the comfort of your home. The cost is $7.80 from Lean Line.

Lean Line has developed a full line of frozen foods (including lasagna, shrimp chow mein, stuffed shells, pizza, cheesecake, and frozen dietary desserts). Lean Line 100 percent veal sausage has been endorsed by the American Heart Association because of its low cholesterol content.

In addition to classes in its home state of New Jersey, Lean Line offers classes in New York, Connecticut, Pennsylvania, Florida, Texas, and Arizona. The first class costs $7.50. Subsequent weekly classes cost $3.25, and special discount coupon books are available.

Diet Workshop, 111 Washington Street, Brookline, Massachusetts 02146 (617)739-2222. Diet Workshop is the largest privately owned national chain of franchised group weight control programs. It was founded in Boston in 1965 by Lois L. Lindauer, who finally decided to do something about her weight when her bridge partners told her she looked like she had been blown up by a tire pump. The workshop's medical consultant is Dr. Morton B. Glenn, (see page 100), past president of the American College of Nutrition and former nutritional consultant to the United Nations.

In January 1979, Diet Workshop instituted a new program designed to meet the demand for rapid weight loss. The progressive Six Super Cycles Program is dedicated to maximum weight loss in minimum time while carefully meeting daily nutritional needs. It retains elements of the workshop's former programs, including nutrition facts, simple isotonic exercise, behavior modification techniques (Diet Workshop was the first to use behavior modification as part of a complete weight control program), shopping and cooking hints, and complete menu plans (including recipes). Activity goals that reinforce good dieting behavior and a record-keeping method of recording successes are also included in the new program.

Under the Six Super Cycles Program, the dieter begins with Super Starter, a 650-calorie cycle of set menus with no substitutes allowed. The dieter remains on this diet for at least one week and then has the option of remaining on this restrictive diet for another week or progressing to

Cycle 2, Super Slimmer. This is a 900-calorie diet that allows a choice of certain proteins, vegetables, fruits, and grain products. After a week, the dieter progresses to Cycle 3, Super Mini, a 1,000-calorie diet with wider food choices. Cycle 4, Super Maxi, which consists of 1,200 calories, is followed until the member comes within 5 pounds of his or her weight goal. This cycle allows for three bonuses per week, consisting of one ounce of liquor or three ounces of dry wine, rice, or pasta or an extra dinner roll. Cycle 5, Super Leveler, is a 900-calorie diet that is followed until the member reaches his/her goal. Cycle 6, Super Maintainer, is Diet Workshop's all-inclusive maintenance program.

At the discretion of the instructor, a member may elect to stay on one cycle longer than two weeks or not to follow a particular cycle at all. Lois Lindauer feels that flexibility is often the key to successful dieting.

In test-marketing the additions, Ms. Lindauer found that weight losses improved. She says, "I feel that people to whom having a drink at a social occasion is important responded to the lifting of the ban by being even better dieters."

What is a Diet Workshop meeting like? There is a private weigh-in for each member, followed by instructor-led discussion of a diet problem or nutritional information. Because group participation is encouraged, the weekly recipe is read, rather than posted. Weight losses are announced and applauded. Simple isotonic exercises to firm the body give a relaxing change of pace to each meeting. New members receive an intensive briefing on the entire program once the meeting is over. All members strive to reach the weight goal set for them at the first weigh-in.

Diet Workshop believes that a significant change in eating habits is necessary to lose excess weight and keep it off. Weight loss on fad or crash programs is usually only temporary. Few people can tolerate the boredom of foods eaten on such programs for long. Furthermore, such limited diets could result in serious nutritional deficiencies if continued for a long time. The workshop recognizes that medications may be necessary to help the overweight person attain his or her weight objectives and to treat associated conditions. Nevertheless, Diet Workshop firmly believes that there is no substitute for sensible eating, which is absolutely essential for long-term successful weight loss.

The workshop charges $8.00 to join and $3.50 each week until a member reaches the desired weight. After the workshop there are four weeks of maintenance training. Lifetime membership is free as long as a member stays within two pounds of the desired weight. If they go above this goal, they have to pay a fee of $3.50 to attend the sessions.

PUBLICATION

Calorie Counts of Foods Found in Vending Machines. Diet Workshop will send you this booklet free. Simply enclose a stamped, self-addressed envelope with your request.

WEIGHT REDUCTION BY MAIL

Duke University Diet Kit, Duke Medical Center Bookstore, Box 3102, Durham, North Carolina 27710. Dr. Susan Schiffman, a medical psychologist at Duke, developed this dietary companion kit for those who are losing weight. It includes a cassette narrated by a man with a soft but authoritative British accent, scratch-and-sniff cards for desensitizing the sense of smell to food odors, a clicker counter for counting the number of times food is chewed, a plate that limits portion sizes, and a booklet that guides the user through the program. The kit, based on a successful behavior modification program at Duke, is designed to take the place of diet groups and the support that such groups give the individual dieter. One of its techniques involves assertiveness training that allows you to successfully counteract would-be diet-destroyers with responses such as: "Thank you for your concern, but my weight is my business." The kit has been medically and scientifically tested with good results. The price is $9.95 plus $1.00 for postage and handling. North Carolina residents should add 4 percent sales tax.

Correspondence Weight Reduction Course, 734 West Adams Boulevard, Los Angeles, California 90007. This weight loss program based on behavior modification techniques that can be carried out by mail was devised by Albert Marston, Ph.D., a professor of psychology at the University of Southern California, and his wife, Marlene Marston, Ph.D., an educator with specialized experience in teaching weight control. The course is geared to those who have tried and failed in group sessions and those who have been unsuccessful at losing weight through other methods. The course runs for thirteen weeks, with a new session beginning each month. Anyone in the United States or in foreign countries is eligible, but the material is in English only. Participants are sent weekly assignments and are asked to record their eating habits in daily journals. The journals and completed assignments are mailed back for evaluation and further instructions. The course is aimed at a slow, steady weight loss because weight lost on crash diets is quickly regained. The goal is to learn self-control skills and to eat in a natural, comfortable way. Follow-up shows excellent results. The price of the course is $225.

PUBLICATIONS

Are You Robbing Your Body of Vitamins, Bronson Pharmaceuticals, 4526 Rinetti Lane, La Canada, California 91011, (213)790-2646. This booklet discusses the need for various vitamins, the foods they are in, and how we miss out on some of them. It is free.

Calories and Weight: The U.S. Department of Agriculture Pocket Guide, Agriculture Information Bulletin No. 364, Superintendent of Documents, U.S. Government Printing Office, Washington, D.C. 20402. This ninety-nine-page book gives you all the basic information about calories and weight that you need to know. Foods are listed according to usual servings: for example, "roasted leg of lamb without bone, lean and fat, 3 ounces, 235 calories; lean only, 160 calories" and "apples, 2¾-inch diameter, 80 calories." The book is about the size of a wallet. The price is $1.

Healthy Approach to Slimming, American Medical Association Department of Foods and Nutrition, P.O. Box 821, Monroe, Wisconsin 53566. The American Medical Association's new guide to health has some fresh pointers on how to take off the pounds and keep them off. The AMA shifts its approach from emphasis on weight consciousness to stress on overall health consciousness. Exercise may be equally as important as diet and nutrition. There is new stress on the importance of exercise in the overall improvement of health and in burning up the calories that otherwise would go to fat. Tables of suggested weights for men and women according to height and build are included to assist dieters in setting goals. The price of the booklet is $1.

Reducing salons and health clubs are fine if you can afford them, but you can exercise just as well at home. Write for another AMA booklet, *Basic Bodyworks for Fitness and Health*, which offers a simple home exercise program (see pages 16-17).

Exercise and Weight Control, President's Council on Physical Fitness and Sports, Superintendent of Documents, U.S. Government Printing Office, Washington, D.C., 1976, No. 0-221-117. For years, physicians have talked about the varying caloric needs of differing occupations and physical recreations. Yet, in their attempts to lose excess fat, people who wish to lose weight have neglected the role of exercise. For those who are too fat, increasing physical activity can be just as important as decreasing food intake. This booklet gives you the energy expenditure of a 150-pound person in various activities. The booklet also points out some weight control fallacies. The cost is $.35.

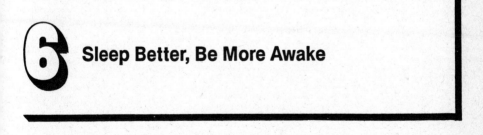

6 Sleep Better, Be More Awake

The wings of night do not always bring rest. All of us suffer from insomnia occasionally, and for an estimated 20 million of us, the torment of not being able to fall asleep easily is chronic.

People with sleep disorders who seek medical help are often given a pat on the shoulder and some pills and told to "go home and relax." But within the past two decades, sleep researchers have found that how we sleep is one of the best indicators of our physical as well as mental health. Insomnia has many origins, some of which are strictly psychological and at least one of which, sleep apnea, is life-threatening.

Temporary insomnia is usually caused by a stressful situation, such as the loss of a loved one or financial worries or exciting plans. The sleep system cannot inhibit the arousal system. You are so wide awake and your muscles are so tense that you cannot relax and fall asleep. Chronic insomniacs, on the other hand, falls into three general categories: those who cannot seem to fall asleep, those who wake up during the night and have a hard time falling back to sleep, and those who awaken too early in the morning.

Not all who claim they have insomnia really do. Dr. William Dement, director of the Stanford University's Sleep Laboratory (which is nicknamed Hotel Insomnia) says that insomniacs' descriptions of their own sleep are poor indicators of the situation. He reported that in one study, fifty self-proclaimed insomniacs observed for four consecutive nights actually had from 6½ to 7½ hours of uninterrupted sleep.

How much sleep must you miss before you are considered a true insomniac? Dr. Dement points out that there are no ironclad rules. In his laboratory, they use less than six hours as the cutoff for most patients. If they average more than that each night, they are not considered true insomniacs unless they take an excessively long time to fall asleep or they awaken often for long periods during the night.

What are the causes of insomnia? Dr. Dement's laboratory has found a number of conditions that have been missed by many physicians as causes of sleeplessness.

Sleep apnea: The patient stops breathing and must awaken to catch his or her breath.

Restless leg syndrome: This is so bizarre, Dr. Dement says, that "the patients often have difficulty describing it. They usually say they feel as if something were crawling inside their legs." Moving about banishes the symptoms, so that victims may be forced to get out of bed in the night.

Nocturnal myoclonus: This may occur alone or with restless leg syndrome. Patients have a pronounced jerk in both legs simultaneously, with a tendency for flexion to occur at the ankle and knee. It may be highly rhythmic. The Stanford group is working with a new drug, gamma amino butric acid, a neurotransmitter that works at the spinal cord level and that seems to relieve the myoclonus.

But a great number of patients, perhaps the majority, who suffer from sleeplessness are depressed. In fact, antidepressant drugs are prescribed by most sleep clinics. The researchers know antidepressants work to allow insomniacs to sleep but are not sure whether the result is because of the antidepressant effect or because some brain chemicals that cause insomnia are affected by the chemicals in the drug.

What about sleeping pills? The consensus among sleep researchers is that current prescription sleeping medications—with the exception of flurazepam (brand name Dalmane, manufactured by Hoffmann-LaRoche)—work for about two weeks and then create, rather than cure, insomnia. If these drugs are withdrawn suddenly, they cause greatly disturbed sleep with intense dreams. The nonprescription sleep drugs are rated useless by most sleep researchers. They have the same affect as antihistamines, which is what most of them contain.

How much sleep do you really need? In the past, the health books have always advised eight hours, but sleep researchers now know that this is not true for everyone. Some people need no more than three hours of sleep; others require ten or more. It depends on your physical and emotional state. The average adult sleeps about 7½ hours, according to Dr. Dement, and about 2 percent of the population habitually sleeps more than 10 hours.

According to Dr. Ernest Hartmann, director of the Sleep Laboratory at Boston State Hospital and a faculty member of Tufts University School of Medicine, if you are a short sleeper (less than six hours a night) you are likely to be energetic, ambitious, decisive, socially adept, and satisfied with life. If you are a long sleeper (nine hours or more), you are likely to be anxious, often mildly depressed, a complainer of minor aches and pains, and not very sure of yourself. Dr. Hartmann says your pattern is usually set in high school or college and continues throughout life. The short sleepers are more extroverted and have a high energy level and fewer complaints about the world. They seldom leave themselves time to think about problems. Long sleepers, on the other hand, tend to be nonconformists, critical of social and political views, introverted, and mildly neurotic.

How can you determine how much sleep you really need? The simplest way is to get up in the morning unaided by another person or an alarm clock. If you find yourself waking up at approximately the same time or even earlier each day and you do not feel tired or listless, you are obviously satisfying your sleep requirements. If you tend to sleep past the hour, you probably need to go to bed earlier.

If you have a minor sleep problem, there are a number of techniques being used to induce sweet sleep that you can adopt.

Learn to relax as soon as you feel fatigued; that is the advice of the American Medical Association experts. If you wait until you are exhausted, it is much harder to fall asleep. Stretch out, if possible, just before lunch, in the evening, and when going to bed. Let yourself go limp. If you learn to relax the different parts of your body, starting with your toes and gradually moving up to your neck and eyes, you can become a skillful relaxer.

If you have difficulty relaxing, you can learn with the aid of biofeedback. Dr. Johann Stoyva and Dr. Thomas Budzinski of the University of Colorado at Denver, under a grant from the National Institute of Mental Health, have been using biofeedback specifically to train insomniacs to relax. They concentrate on the forehead muscle, which is unwittingly tensed by anxious people. Electrodes are attached to the area, and the person attempts to relax the forehead while watching his or her success on a machine that measures the electrical activity of the muscle. Once the insomniacs learn how to relax the forehead muscle, they begin to relax their minds. The subjects find it possible to coax themselves into a twilight state in which they float gently into sleep.

Dr. Richard Bootzin of Northwestern University is using reconditioning to enable insomniacs to fall asleep. He instructs subjects to go to bed only when they can fall asleep immediately. They cannot get into bed and worry about business or personal problems. If they do, they must get out of bed and go into another room. They must repeat this procedure, no matter how late it is, until they can fall right to sleep in bed.

Dr. Maxie Maultsby, Jr., of the University of Kentucky has carried this behavior technique even further. He calls it "rational emotive imagery." The first step is to set a relatively constant time to go to bed. Before turning in, the insomniac must sit for fifteen minutes picturing himself/herself sleeping peacefully. No activities must be attempted in bed except sleep and sex. Reading, talking, planning, eating, and watching television are all forbidden.

Once in bed, the insomniac must consciously slow his/her respirations to about four to six a minute and must consciously think relaxing thoughts. If the subject senses or sees on the clock that twenty minutes have gone by, he/she must get out of bed and perform twenty-five push-ups (fifteen for women). If, while the subject was in bed, he/she had troublesome thoughts, he/she must think those same thoughts during the push-ups. This associates the sleep-preventing thoughts with the self-inflicted punishment. Once the insomniac has finished the push-ups, he/she can return to bed. If he/she again cannot fall asleep within twenty minutes, he/she must repeat the cycle.

"Success is almost guaranteed," Dr. Maultsby said. "I have never had a patient who required more than six sets of push-ups. Often the subjects wake up on the floor, which is fine. It means they have reached their therapeutic goal. After the third or fourth night of this routine, the mere thought of push-ups is enough to inhibit the sleep-preventing thoughts."

If nothing works and you really have a serious sleep disorder, such as chronic insomnia, narcolepsy, muscular weakness with fits of over-whelming sleepiness, or continuous daytime fatigue, you should get a complete medical evaluation, including, if necessary, a diagnosis at one of the sleep research centers.

Association of Sleep Disorders Centers

This is a list of members of the Association of Sleep Disorders Centers. Please note, however, that this is not an exhaustive list of institutions where sleep disorders medicine is being practiced. These centers have various procedures for accepting patients. Some accept patients only through referral from a primary-care physician; others will see patients on a self-referral basis. Information on the nature and treatment of the many and varied sleep disorders is usually available from individual centers.

Sleep Disorders Center
Baltimore City Hospital
Baltimore, Maryland 21224
Attention: Richard Allen, M.D.
(301)396-5859

Sleep Disorders Clinic
Boston Children's Hospital
300 Longwood Avenue
Boston, Massachusetts 02115
Attention: Myron Belfer, M.D.
(617)734-6000

*Sleep-Wake Disorders Unit
Montefiore Hospital
111 East 210th Street
Bronx, New York 10467
Attention: Charles Pollak, M.D.
(212)920-4841
Sleep Disorders Center
Department of Neurology
Crozer Chester Medical Center
Chester, Pennsylvania 19013
Attention: Calvin Stafford, M.D.
(215)874-1184

Sleep Disorders Center
Rush–Presbyterian–St. Luke's
1753 West Congress Parkway
Chicago, Illinois 60612
Attention: Rosalind Cartwright, Ph.D.
(312)942-5000

*Fully accredited centers

Sleep Disorders Center
Suite 214
Wesley Pavilion
Northwestern University Medical
    Center
Chicago, Illinois 60611
Attention: John Cayaffa, M.D.
(312)649-8649

*Sleep Disorders Center
Cincinnati General Hospital
Cincinnati, Ohio 45267
Attention: Milton Kramer, M.D.
(513)861-3100

Sleep Disorders Center
Psychiatry Department
St. Luke's Hospital
Cleveland, Ohio 44118
Attention: Joel Steinberg, M.D.
(216)368-7000

Sleep Disorders Center
Mt. Sinai Hospital
University Circle
Cleveland, Ohio 44106
Attention: Herbert Weiss, M.D.
(216) 795-6000, ext. 531

*Sleep Clinic
Department of Psychiatry
Ohio State University
Columbus, Ohio 43210
Attention: Helmut Schmidt, M.D.
(614)422-5982

Sleep Laboratory
National Jewish Hospital
3800 East Colfax Avenue
Denver, Colorado 80206
Attention: David Shucard, Ph.D.
(303)388-4461

Sleep Disorders Center
Henry Ford Hospital
2799 West Grand Boulevard
Detroit, Michigan 48202
Attention: Thomas Roth, Ph.D.
(313)876-2233

Sleep Disorders Clinic
Department of Psychiatry
Dartmouth Medical School
Hanover, New Hampshire 03755
Attention: Peter Hauri, Ph.D.
(603)646-2213

*Sleep Clinic
Baylor College of Medicine
Houston, Texas 77030
Attention: Ismet Karacan, M.D.
(713)790-4886

Sleep Laboratory
Department of Anatomy
University of Arkansas Medical
  Center
Little Rock, Arkansas 72201
Attention: Edgar Lucas, Ph.D.
(501)661-5272

BMH Sleep Disorders Center
Baptist Memorial Hospital
Memphis, Tennessee 38146
Attention: Helio Lemmi, M.D.
(901)522-5651

Sleep Disorders Center
Mt. Sinai Medical Center
4300 Alton Road
Miami Beach, Florida 33140
Attention: Martin A. Cohn, M.D.
(305)674-2613

Sleep Laboratory
Department of Psychiatry
State University of New York, Stony
  Brook

Stony Brook, New York 11794
Attention: Merrill M. Mitler, Ph.D.
(516)444-2563

Sleep Laboratory
Department of Neurology
University of Massachusetts Medical
  Center
Worcester, Massachusetts 01605
Attention: Sheldon Kapen, M.D.
(617)856-3081

Sleep Disorders Center
Neurology Department
Hennepin County Medical Center
Minneapolis, Minnesota 55415
Attention: Milton Ettinger, M.D.
(612)347-2430

Sleep Disorders Clinic
Hopital du Sacre-Coeur
5400 ouest, Boulevard Gouin
Montreal, Quebec, Canada H4J 1C5
Attention: Jacques Montplaisir, M.D.
(514)333-2070

Sleep Disorders Center
Medical Sciences Building
New Jersey Medical School
Newark, New Jersey 07103
Attention: James Minard, Ph.D.
(201)456-4300

Sleep Disorders Center
Psychiatry and Neurology
Tulane Medical School
New Orleans, Louisiana 70118
Attention: John Goethe, M.D.
(504)588-5236

Sleep Disorders Center
Presbyterian Hospital
Northeast 13th at Lincoln Boulevard
Oklahoma City, Oklahoma 73104
Attention: William Orr, Ph.D.
(405)271-6312

Sleep Disorders Center
University of California, Irvine
  Medical Center
101 City Drive South
Orange, California 92688
Attention: Jon Sassin, M.D.
(714)634-5777

Sleep Disorders Center
Ottawa General Hospital
43 Bruyere
Ottawa, Ontario, Canada K1N 4C8
Attention: Roger Broughton, M.D.
(613)231-4738

Sleep Disorders Center
Suite 1402
1260 15th Street
Santa Monica, California 90404
Attention: John Beck, M.D.
(213)451-8828

Sleep Disorders Center
Western Psychiatric Institute
3811 O'Hara Street
Pittsburgh, Pennsylvania 15261
Attention: David Kupfer, M.D.
(412)624-2246

*Sleep Disorders Program
Stanford University Medical Center
Stanford, California 94305
Attention: Laughton Miles, M.D.
(415)497-7458

A description of the most respected treatment and research facilities follows. Those centers listed offer similar services.

Sleep Disorder Clinic, Peter Bent Brigham Hospital, 721 Huntington Avenue, Boston, Massachusetts 02115, (617)732-6750, Quentin R. Regestein, M.D., director. This facility provides clinicians with a particular interest in sleep disorders, a polysomnographic laboratory especially for patients with serious medical difficulties, such as irregular heartbeat and nocturnal epilepsy, and the ancillary services that a well-developed teaching hospital can offer. The patient's vital functions are measured and recorded electronically during sleep. The approach is flexible and clinically oriented, rather than standardized or primarily devoted to research. Usually, a patient is seen for one or two 50-minute interviews. On the basis of the interview(s) and some homework done by the patient, a diagnostic assessment is made, and a treatment plan is formulated. A trial of treatment is then begun. In the majority of cases, relief is obtained. Periodic half-hour follow-up visits may be necessary occasionally in the next few months. More cumbersome, expensive investigations are undertaken when diagnosis remains unclear, when serious medical problems are suspected, or when little relief is obtained. Sleep recordings, polysomnography, and hospital admission may be prescribed as needed. After further diagnosis and refinement of treatment, frequent follow-ups are scheduled. There are particular facilities for the continuing assessment and refinement of treatment for difficult cases of narcolepsy, subwakefulness syndromes, and sleep apnea (brief respiratory arrest during sleep).

The clinic's patients are adults suffering from the entire range of sleep disorders, including insomnia, excessive daytime sleepiness, and problems related to sleep, such as nightmares, sleepwalking. Most are experiencing chronic, severe, or intractable sleep disturbances. Children are referred to the Children's Hospital.

A wide range of treatments are prescribed. The clinic has found that rather sober, unglamorous prescriptions, such as discontinuing drugs and instituting regular bedtimes and wake-up times for insomnia patients, have often proved effective. But new and novel treatments are available as needed, occasionally on an investigatory basis.

At present, most outpatient visits are covered by medical insurance. Inpatient procedures are also covered, and coverage of outpatient polysomnography is becoming more common. Patients who are not adequately covered by insurance are seen in the regular clinics of the hospital. Patients who come to the clinic from great distances are first prepared by means of correspondence to make their evaluation visits maximally efficient, and they are followed up by telephone.

Stanford University Sleep Disorders Center and Laboratory, Room R 303, Stanford University Medical Center, Stanford, California 94305, (415)497-6601. The center, which was founded in 1970, is staffed by neurologists, psychiatrists, psychologists, and technicians who are constantly involved in the most recent developments in the field of sleep-wake disorders. They diagnose and treat excessive daytime sleepiness, insomnia, and other sleep-related disorders.

If you suffer from uncontrollable daytime sleepiness—that is, if you fall asleep at times when you should normally be able to stay awake and if you never feel fully alert or experience sudden sensations of muscular weakness when surprised, angered, or amused—you may be diagnosed as suffering from excessive daytime sleepiness, and you may have respiratory problems during sleep that have been unrecognized.

Insomnia may be caused by some job conditions, such as working night shifts, or by frequent travel across time zones, as well as by those reasons cited earlier in this chapter. The Stanford experts believe that a frequent cause of insomnia may be chronic use of sleeping pills.

Sleepwalking, sleep talking, bed-wetting, frequent nightmares, and night terror attacks are all sleep-related disorders that affect both children and adults. These conditions may be caused by an underlying psychiatric or neurological disturbance.

According to Stanford's Sleep Disorders Center, most sleep-wake problems can be treated or managed effectively once they are accurately diagnosed. Some conditions may require treatment with medications over a period of years; others may require a change of working hours. For still others, psychiatric treatment, including medication, counseling, or psychotherapy, may be the best solution. Occasionally, an operation is advised to relieve severe respiratory problems during sleep.

On your first visit, you will be interviewed and examined by a staff physician. As a routine part of the initial evaluation, you will be asked to fill out extensive questionnaires. You may be asked to spend one or two nights at the hospital so that all-night recordings of your sleep can be made. You will have a comfortable private room equipped with monitors that record your sleep patterns, breathing, heart activity, and body movements throughout the night. After all information is gathered and evaluated by the staff, they will discuss your entire case with you, and a written report and recommendations will be sent to your physician. Fees are $125 for the consultation, $300 to $500 for night recordings, and $50 for return visits.

PUBLICATION

Some Must Watch While Some Must Sleep, William C. Dement, New York: W.W. Norton Co., 1978, $5.95. Dr. Dement is the director of the clinic and a pioneer in sleep research. The book describes Dr. Dements' research at Stanford University and describes the many facets of what is commonly lumped together as "insomnia."

MERCHANDISE

Better Sleep, Inc., 57 Industrial Road, Berkeley Heights, New Jersey 07922. For mail orders, phone (201)464-2200. New Providence, New Jersey 07974. This company will send you a free catalog that contains not only products for sale but a number of pages of suggestions for greater comfort and better sleep. The company sells numerous pillows of different sizes and shapes with such names as Relax-n-Sleep Contoured Pillow ($7.99), Foam-Filled Relax-a-Pedic Head Pillow ($11.95), and Tranquilizing Bath Pillow ($3.49). Their antisnore mask ($5.00) will help you get to sleep if your partner snores, and their Sleep-Mate ($30.00) will produce a blend of rhythmic, tranquil sleep-inducing sounds that help block out noises and promote "beneficial deep sleep."

DO YOU NEED TO IMPROVE YOUR EYESIGHT?

A continuing awareness of the signs that might indicate a problem is the best way to care for your eyesight. The American Association of Ophthalmology thinks you should be on the lookout for the following signs* that may indicate eye trouble:
1. Eyes crossed (turning in or out) at any time
2. Frequent headaches, nausea, or dizziness
3. Body rigidity while looking at distant objects
4. Thrusting the head forward or backward while looking at distant objects
5. Avoiding close work
6. Short attention span or daydreaming
7. Turning the head in order to use only one eye
8. Tilting the head to one side
9. Placing the head close to a book or desk when reading or writing
10. Blurring of vision at any time

*Reprinted with permission of the American Association of Ophthalmology.

11. Frowning or scowling while reading or writing
12. Excessive blinking or frequent rubbing of the eyes
13. Closing or covering one eye
14. Dislike for tasks requiring sustained visual concentration
15. Nervousness, irritability, or restlessness after maintaining visual concentration
16. Unusual fatigue after completing a vision task
17. Losing the place while reading or difficulty in remembering what is read
18. Using a finger to keep one's place while reading
19. Persistent letter reversals after the second grade
20. Confusion of similar words
21. Poor eye-hand coordination or unusual awkwardness

All of these signs are good reasons to consult your ophthalmologist. He or she is a medical doctor who is trained to detect diseases or malfunctions of your visual system. In fact, an ophthalmologist is the only practitioner qualified to provide all aspects of eye care. He/she is the best source of accurate information about the health of your eyes.

PUBLICATIONS

Family Guide to Vision Care, American Optometric Association, P.O. Box 24643, Saint Louis, Missouri 63141. Many eye problems are very subtle and may be mistaken for other problems. This publication answers some commonly asked questions about eye examinations, glasses, contact lenses, vision therapy, and regular professional vision care. The booklet is free.

Facts about Contact Lenses, American Optometric Association, 243 North Lindbergh Boulevard, Saint Louis, Missouri 63141. Almost 14 million Americans wear contact lenses. It pays to get the facts before you decide whether or not to join their ranks. This booklet will give you tips on obtaining contacts and wearing them successfully. This booklet is free.

Total Health:
Health Clubs and Spas

CHOOSING A HEALTH CLUB

Just as there is no magic pill for weight loss, there is no easy, quick way to get physically fit if you are out of shape. Nevertheless, health clubs often promise miracles.

There are an estimated 2,000 health clubs in the country, and their services vary from excellent to dangerous. What has caused the boom in such facilities in recent years? Certainly, the medical studies which found that lack of exercise and overweight are harmful to health have been a prime factor. The media's emphasis on youth and slimness has also fueled the desire to improve the body, and advertisements for the health clubs played on this, showing attractive, shapely young people using their facilities. Of course, if most people looked like that, they wouldn't need the facilities; and if the facilities could change overweight, out-of-shape, middle-aged patrons into the slim young things of the ads, health clubs would indeed be performing miracles.

Even though they cannot perform miracles, health clubs are still popular because of something they *can* do. In our increasingly isolated society, these facilities provide a place for people to meet and enjoy themselves, just as the Roman baths did in the days of the Roman Empire. A health club can be a lot of fun, an excellent way of relaxing and obtaining physical fitness—*if* you choose the right one. How can you be sure that the facility near you is not a financial rip-off and/or a place that is potentially dangerous to your health?

The Federal Trade Commission (FTC) has found that many health clubs have misled consumers in their advertising and sales pitches by using high-pressure sales tactics; bait advertising and offers of fictitious bargains (in one case, a club offered a year at half price but did not say you first had to pay for two years); deceptive pricing; and misrepresentation of length of enrollment periods available, facilities available, qualifications of spa employees, results that can be expected through participation in spa program, and contract obligations of consumers who have joined a spa. In addition, FTC says many spas have closed their facilities or gone out of business without refunding money to consumers who have already paid for their services or have sold membership contracts to consumers who are not physically qualified to take part in the spa's activities. Clearly, the wrongdoers often hurt the legitimate health spas. In some cases, the established spas have even offered, as a public service, to fulfill the contracts of patrons who were taken by fly-by-night outfits.

Here are some steps you can take in order to choose a health club that will offer you the best in services.

Arrive unannounced at the time of day you would be most likely to use the club, and take a good look around. Is it crowded? Are there instructors available if you want them?

What's the background of the instructors? Are they informally trained, or do they have a degree in physical education, physical therapy, or some other profession that makes them qualified to teach their specialties?

Are there enough instructors for the number of members? Will they work on a step-by-step conditioning program with you?

Is the equipment the kind that really fosters physical fitness? Medical experts say you are wasting your time if you use a pulley-rope machine, wear a rubberized suit while exercising, or use a device that promises to take pounds off certain parts of your body (this includes heat and massage). Therefore, a club that offers trapeze bars, rings, and rowing machines is better than a club that offers vibrating machines and rollers. Furthermore, if exercises are done properly—that is, *without* equipment—you will receive more benefit.

Is the location convenient enough and do you really have sufficient time to attend to get your money's worth out of a club?

Is there a club pool? Swimming is one of the most effective overall fitness exercises, it is relaxing, and it can be a social asset.

Can you really afford to belong? Add up the *total* cost, not just the seemingly low monthly rate. Ask if there are extra charges for tips, saunas, massage, and so on. Most clubs range in price from $200 to $400, depending on where you live and how plush the club is. Divide the total fee by how often you think you will use the club. If, for example, you will attend only six times a year, that's a pretty steep price; whereas if you will go practically every day, it will be a great bargain.

Check to see if the company is liable for any injuries you may incur on the premises.

Be aware that your contract may not be cancelable or transferable to another party.

Ask if you will be able to get out of the contract if you suffer a serious disability for which you can provide medical proof. However, chances are that if you get bored, catch a virus, or find you are too busy to attend, you must still pay, and interest on installments may be 18 to 22 percent. The

FTC has ruled that after you sign a health club contract, you are allowed three days to change your mind and receive a full refund. If you cancel *after* the three-day period, you may still get a prorated refund, but the spa or club would be able to keep a 5 percent cancellation fee.

Clubs, like people, have personalities and attract certain types of clients. If you just want to use the facilities and do not care who else uses them, then this will not matter to you. But if you want to be with people with whom you feel comfortable, visit the club when it is in full operation *before* you sign up.

Many Ys offer health club facilities. They are not so elaborate as the commercial clubs, but their staff members are usually well trained. Some of the Y programs specialize in coronary prevention and postcoronary exercise programs.

So, you see, you *can* get your money's worth out of a health club and have a wonderful time *if* you proceed with caution in making your choice.

SPAS: IMMERSING YOURSELF IN TOTAL SELF-IMPROVEMENT

Did you ever feel as if you just wanted to get away from it all and be completely pampered? Have you looked in a three-way mirror lately and not liked the view? Bulges around the hips? Bags under the eyes? "I should really start a new diet and go in for some more exercise," you told yourself. But your life is so busy, and your willpower is rather weak, so you keep postponing such plans. And how about your last vacation? Didn't you come back more weary than you were when you went?

We all reach the point at which we feel as if we want to get away from it all, be completely pampered and renewed. We yearn for a starting place at which we can capture the self-discipline to begin putting ourselves and our lives in shape. The answer to such a quest is both very ancient and very modern: the health spa.

The word *spa* is believed to have been popularized after the resort town of Spa in the province of Liège, Belgium, became famous for its mineral water springs in the seventeenth century. The springs were said to be beneficial to victims of heart disease. Bathing for health is mentioned in the Bible, and a bath and drainage system more than 3,000 years old can be seen in the ruins of King Nestor's palace near Pylos, Greece. The Romans maintained warm public baths for the benefit of their citizens. Facilities were established at natural mineral springs. Two of the more famous were on the outskirts of Naples and at Thermopylae. One of the largest was the Baths of Caracalla, where 16,000 people could take a dip together.

In the Middle Ages, barbers were often bath keepers as well as surgeons, specialists in both health and beauty. They sometimes prescribed immersions in water for as long as 124 hours to cure bodily ailments. The Belgians made the most of mineral waters and named an entire town Spa in the province of Liège. They claim that is where the word and concept of a modern health spa originated. Spa's world-famous springs were said to benefit victims of heart disease.

North America is not without such natural resources; it has more than 800 hot springs. If you visit the Palm Springs Spa in California, you can bathe in the same waters in which the Agua Caliente (literally "hot water") Indians dipped themselves hundreds of years ago. The curative power of American hot springs was widely touted in the 1800s, but by the early twentieth century, with the advent of modern medicine, the lure was not as great. Just before World War II, however, when the visits of President Roosevelt to Warm Springs, Georgia, were publicized, there was a renewed interest in the therapeutic waters. Taking advantage of the situation, many spas advertised facilities and water products in ways that made the claims of nineteenth-century barkers with traveling medicine shows seem conservative. The American Medical Association felt compelled to establish the American Health Resorts Treatment Committee to educate the public and to work for better controls over outlandish claims and treatments. The committee placed emphasis on medical supervision and the separation of spa treatments from the commercial sale and exploitation of mineral waters with unproven medical claims.

Despite such problems, doctors do not deny the benefits of hydrotherapy. Medicinal bathing involves the use of mineral waters in tub baths with still water, gently flowing water, or vigorously moving water, often in whirlpools. Alternating hot and cold high-force water sprays are invigorating and therapeutic.

You can, of course, buy mineral water in your supermarket and hot tubs and saunas in appliance stores. But spa treatments do not depend entirely on bathing and drinking the waters, although many of the resorts, such as California's Palms Springs Spa and the Greenbrier in White Sulphur Springs, West Virginia, are built close to natural hot springs. All the resorts described in this section are in scenic areas, and they offer good, calorie-controlled food; relief from responsibilities; and exercise, massage, and entertainment. They are places to be relaxed, refreshed, and reborn. They vary in facilities and in personality, but they are all excellent.

Whichever spa you choose, if you expend a little effort, you will drop some weight, firm up, and perhaps get the inspiration that may lead you to a healthier existence when you get home. Most spas will give you recipes to encourage your continued diet awareness, and some have even produced big, glossy books detailing their routines and giving culinary advice. They are all relatively expensive, but the very cost may be therapeutic. Your willpower is increased when you realize you are paying for the health and beauty routines.

Nineteenth-century author and philosopher Jeremy Bentham wrote in *An Introduction to the Principles of Morals and Legislation,* 1789, that "Nature has placed mankind under the governance of two sovereign masters—pain and pleasure. It is for them alone to point out what we ought to do as well as to determine what we shall do."

Today's health spas can take the pain out of controlling your indulgences and turn it into a real pleasure.

Arizona

Maine Chance, Phoenix, Arizona 85018, (602)947-6365. Elizabeth Arden believed that each woman could be beautiful in her own way. She promoted the idea of beauty as a combination of health, individual charm, and grooming, not just a matter of birth, and pioneered the concept of a posh health and beauty spa where women could go to be renewed. In 1945, Arden established the main house, guest houses, and treatment areas on 105 acres nestled at the foot of Phoenix's Camelback Mountain. According to her design, each building is located to afford the best view of the magnificent "camel." The scent of many roses and the sight of exotic tropical palms, paloverde trees, and giant cacti feed the soul as well as the eye. That is why Maine Chance has been called "the most exquisitely appointed beauty oasis in the world." The ambience is continued inside with Chagalls and Georgia O'Keeffes gracing the walls, priceless china on the tables, and polished marble on the floors.

You are greeted at the Phoenix Airport by the Maine Chance chauffeur and turned over to your personal maid at your luxury quarters. She helps you unpack, serves you breakfast in bed, and generally pampers you.

The health and beauty regimen is designed to make the most of your natural assets and to concentrate on areas where you need improvement. Thus, the daily diet and beauty programs that you follow are worked out especially for you. They take into consideration the need to lose or gain weight, the desire to firm up the body or sagging spirits. The Main Chance Diet is only 900 calories per day, but it includes a well-balanced selection of garden-fresh vegetables and fruits, lean meats, and fish, all prepared with special seasonings and the culinary secrets of the chef. Just a few of his skillful contributions to the famous Maine Chance Diet include his special cheesecake, apricot mousse, baked Alaska, creamy salad dressings, and a variety of soufflés. During classes, two refreshing snack breaks—a vitamin-filled potassium broth in the morning and fresh fruit juice in the afternoon—are served near the pool.

At 9:00 A.M., there are exercises to warm up, limber up, and shape up. These are followed by steam cabinet, sauna, Ardena wax bath, or whirlpool. At 10:00 A.M., there is a soothing massage and then an exercise session, followed by face, hair, and nail treatments. After lunch, there are makeup classes, then rest and relaxation. Curfew is 10:00 P.M., but evening programs include movies, trips to the repertory theater in Phoenix, and games of backgammon, bridge, canasta, or bingo.

A doctor is on call for emergencies, but the emphasis here is on health and beauty, not medical problems (the focus of many European spas). Reservations are booked Sunday to Sunday. The season runs from the last Sunday in September to the end of May. Rates vary according to accommodations, from $1,050 to $1,300 for a single room and $900 to $1,000 for double occupancy.

California

Ashram, P.O. Box 8, Calabsas, California 91302, (213)888-0232. This spa offers a poem to explain itself:

> *When your body's gone to flab and your emotions jingle-jangle,*
> *You're bursting in the seams and your fat goes dingle-dangle,*
> *Then it's time to get together your swimwear, shoes and sox,*
> *A book to read, a toothbrush and put them in a box.*
> *And come Sunday evening you tell the world goodbye.*
> *You're on your way to Ashram, the health resort in the sky.*

The retreat is located thirty minutes west of Los Angeles and ten minutes inland from the Pacific Ocean in a secluded valley surrounded by mountains and running streams. It consists of one large building with a gymnasium and exercise areas. A geodesic dome for yoga classes and meditation is located on a hilltop close by.

There is a resident doctor who gives you a thorough checkup. The diet consists mostly of raw foods, and the attire—sweat suit, T-shirts, robes, kaftans—is furnished by the Ashram. The Ashram's reputation is a vigorously spartan one. Barbra Streisand chose it to train her mind and body before filming *A Star Is Born,* and she continues to go there for one-day visits each month or two. Other Hollywood celebrities who shape up there include Zsa Zsa Gabor, Esther Williams, and Racquel Welch. Catharina Hedberg, associate director, signs her letters, "Peace be with you."

The program is limited to six to eight guests at a time and runs from Sunday afternoon to the following Saturday. The charge for the week is $800. There is an additional charge of $200 when a single accommodation is reserved. A $300 deposit per person sent within ten days of making a reservation confirms your stay.

The Golden Door, P.O. Box 1567, Escondido, California 92025, (714)744-5777. Located in the quiet southern California countryside, the

Golden Door is perhaps the most luxurious spa in the world. This facility has room for only thirty-two guests. It has a staff of ninety-seven and caters to a clientele from around the world.

Set in a wooded area with a natural running stream, the Golden Door has its own orchards and vegetable gardens. Hens pick their way about a red farmhouse. Guests, clad in black-and-white cotton kimonos, stroll beneath covered walkways that connect varied Japanese formal gardens. The spa buildings take their inspiration from a traditional Japanese inn. The ambiance of gardens designed for contemplation and the poet's deck on each individual guest accommodation (which also has its own private garden) imbued writer Thomas Whittingslow with a sense of balance between "an elevated state of physical well-being and an elevated aesthetic awareness." In summary, he wrote, "The Golden Door can only be described as a Japanese transcendental experience."

The facilities are open to men eight weeks of the year. Men start the day at 6:30 A.M. and women at 7:00 A.M., but both begin their activities with a mountain hike. Women return to luxuriate with breakfast in bed. Then begins the nonstop daily schedule: stretch exercises, exercises, steam bath, massage, gym work, pool volleyball (during men's weeks, this boisterous sport can get rough). Lunch consists of just-picked strawberries, pineapple, and homegrown vegetables. Afterward, there are spot-reducing exercises, a hair treatment, manicure, pedicure, facial, dance exercises, and end-of-day relaxation. In the evening, low-calorie hors d'oeuvres and an exquisitely served dinner are followed by a class in anything from biofeedback to dietetic haute cuisine.

For women, in particular, the Golden Door means extraordinary peace built into a program that is bound to banish some pounds and more inches. For men, it is no male beauty parlor. Instead, during men's weeks, the spa exudes a robust atmoshpere of hearty good fellowship and sport. Six times a year the Golden Door offers couples weeks. For couples, it is a time to readjust, to reacquaint themselves with each other, to realign themselves with the world. For everyone, it is a week or two out of the year to step back, find sources of true vitality, get in touch with their inner currents, and seek new directions. Rates are $1,850 per week. Couples should double that amount.

La Costa Hotel & Spa, Rancho La Costa, Carlsbad, California 92008, (714)438-9111. Many say this is the ultimate modern spa. Nestled between the tawny hills and the deep blue sea in the sunniest part of southern California, it boasts 5,600 acres stretched out under a clear sky. The temperature averages 74 degrees in summer and 68 degrees in winter. There are his and hers spas, each with complete facilities. If you choose the spa's plan, you meet first with the medical director and staff and with the dietician. The result will be a personal program specifically designed to meet your individual objectives.

Classes range from water exercises to yoga, from isometrics to visual poise, beauty, and makeup. For women, the services of a beauty salon are part of the plan, along with courses in makeup and hair styling. There is also golf on the course on which the annual PGA Tournament of Champions is played. The Saddle Club features twenty-one miles of protected riding trails that meander through spectacular country. You can swim and sunbathe; there are four sparkling freshwater pools. There are twenty-five championship tennis courts and the Pancho Segura Tennis Institute. You can enroll in the institute and may have the master himself for an instructor. And at night, you can dance to the music of a variety of orchestras and groups.

If you still want more to do, there's the nearby San Diego Zoo, Sea World, and Mexico for the color and excitement of jai alai, thoroughbred and greyhound racing, and the bullfights. Even Disneyland is only forty-five minutes away.

You can't be bored with the food, either. There are five restaurants: the main dining room for gourmets, the Seville Room for Italian cuisine, the Pisces for delicacies of the sea, the Steak House for great beef, and the Spa Dining Room for diet menus.

Whatever accommodations you choose, they are sure to be luxurious and expensive. Rooms are $70 to $88 per day double occupancy without meals. Suites are $95 to $206, and villas are $120 to $150. It is often difficult to obtain a reservation, so book well in advance.

Palm Springs Spa Hotel and Mineral Springs, Indian Avenue and Tahquitz Drive, Palm Springs, California 92262, (714)325-1461. Right in the heart of presidential and celebrity vacationland, this facility has outdoor natural hot mineral water pools, masseurs and masseuses, a rock steam room, Roman whirlpool baths, a complete gymnasium, and an infrared inhalation room. The hot mineral springs were discovered centuries ago by the Agua Caliente Indians, who made the spot sacred, believing the waters possessed miraculous healing powers. At the turn of the century, a primitive wooden shack was built over the springs. As the spot grew in popularity, the facilities became more and more lush, until today, the bathhouse of the Palm Springs Spa has pink settees, free-form sculptures, and sparkling terrazzo floors. The springs are now a state historical site.

Pampering at the spa begins with five to ten minutes in the infrared heat of the eucalyptus vapor–inhalation room, followed by five or more minutes in the three-level rock steam room. It continues with a hot mineral water whirlpool bath for muscle toning and massage. Then it's into the cooling room for a rest, with a brisk wake-up afterward under multiple showers. A private massage follows. There are forty-five-minute toning facials that are popular with both men and women, a complete gymnasium for workouts either solo or with an instructor, and just outside the bathhouse are three mineral pools (immersion, 106-degree whirlpool, and exercise).

Women are treated in luxurious surroundings. Men, on the other side of the bathhouse, enjoy the benefits of vigorous, strenuous weight lifting in the gym.

Rates per night for a twin-bedded room, double occupancy, from September 15 to December 14, range from $65 to $100. From December 15 through March 1, rates are $85 to $100 per night. There are beauty and barber shops on the premises.

Use of the spa facility that includes a mineral bath, rock steam inhalation and cooling rooms, and the use of a gym is $6 per day. With a 30-minute massage, it is $15 and with a 45-minute, complete body massage, it is $19.50 (For a series of six, it is $32.50.) A single massage with steam is $10 for 30 minutes or $15 for 45 minutes. Facials are $20 and use of the outdoor pool is $5. The mineral baths are included in the room rate for registered guests.

Colorado

Ilona of Hungary, 3201 East Second Avenue, Denver, Colorado 80206, (303)322-4212. Also 1800 South Post Oak Road, Houston, Texas 77056, (713)961-4844. How about a Budapest cocktail or sea algae therapy? They are available at Ilona's Human Improvement Center. This elegant new center offers extensive programs, featuring European-style skin care and head-to-toe health and beauty treatments. Mineral- and magnesium-rich water is shipped in bottles from an artesian well on the outskirts of Budapest, Hungary, for use at the center. Both Ilona and her husband, George, were trained in skin, scalp, and body care in Europe. Ilona studied skin care in Budapest under Dr. Imre Papp and Dr. Erzabet Nemesh, two of Europe's famed skin-care specialists. They opened their salon in Denver in 1971.

Facilities also include a Hungarian mineral water whirlpool bath for "improved organic circulation, relaxation and skin conditioning," "acupressure point" massage to alleviate tension, a special ionized mist room for adding moisture and removing toxins from the skin, quiet rooms for relaxation after treatment, and a lounge area. There are two treatments believed to be unique to the United States: the sea algae bath for relaxation and weight reduction and aroma therapy, which uses the aromatic oils in herbs, flowers, and fruits as moisturizers, emollients, and relaxers.

The center offers complete skin-care services for all skin types. If you have a problem with your skin, muscle tone, weight, hair, or scalp, you can obtain help under one roof.

Clients can also choose from Ilona's Day of Beauty Program ($125) or Mini Day of Beauty ($75). Programs run from 9:00 A.M. till 5:00 P.M. and include such things as herbal wraps, massage, scalp therapy, exercises, aroma therapy, and ionized mist room therapy. A one-week program, Monday to Friday, costs $625, not including hotel accommodations.

The new center in Houston is devoted to skin care only. If you are unable to visit one of Ilona's centers, you can purchase her skin-care products, which have the Hungarian mineral water base, by mail.

Florida

The Spa at Palm-Aire, 2501 Palm-Aire Drive North, Pompano Beach, Florida 33060, (800)327-4960. Men and women have separate but equal facilities at this glorious, 2,500-acre monument to health, physical fitness, and beauty. The $2 million resort, one of the newer luxury spas in the world, is located between Palm Beach and Miami. Twin pavillions for men and women include showers, gymnasiums, massage rooms, saunas and steam rooms, outdoor Roman baths, exercise pools, warm and cool contrast pools, facial treatment rooms, and indoor private whirlpools. The more athletic guests may plan their programs to include time for tennis and golf. There are twenty-five tennis courts on the grounds, some lighted for night play, and five 18-hole golf courses. Sports facilities such as racquet ball courts, a mini par course, and a swimming pool to attract younger male executives will be added this summer.

Spa director Lisa Dobloug admits that most spas offer similar services, but she points out that at hers, it is the philosophy that counts. Within the time limitations (two weeks if possible, but a weekend if necessary, and in season only a one-, two-, or three-week stay), they try to teach guests that better diet and exercise habits have long-lasting benefits for the mind and body: "It goes far beyond vanity, although certainly anyone whose body is healthy and in control and whose mind is serene is much better-looking. Confidence and pride are extremely glamorizing."

What are Palm-Aire's specialities? Your program begins with a physical examination by the spa's resident doctor. And when they say exercise, they mean it. In addition to body movement classes, there are water exercises that are especially good for back problems and arthritis. Your body is more buoyant in water, and working against the resistance of the water increases the value of the exercises.

Personal services include massage, facial massage, salt-glow/loofah-scrub, and herbal wrap. The salt-glow/loofah-scrub includes a combination of salt and avocado oil applied and then followed by a brisk scrubbing with the natural loofah gourd and a rinsing with a high-pressure spray. This treatment removes dead skin cells, moisturizes, and increases circulation. The herbal wrap consists of wrapping the body in linen sheets that have been steamed in a combination of herbs including chamomile, eucalyptus, spearmint, and peppermint. Over the steaming sheets go a rubber sheet and a wool blanket. You remain mummified for twenty to thirty minutes while an attendant applies cold compresses to your forehead. The treatment begins with a few minutes in the Turkish bath and is followed by a warm shower to bring the body temperature down to normal. The object is to relax the body and to draw out excess fluids.

Other services included in the week's program are manicure, pedicure, makeup consultation, and a coiffure.

The diet for most guests consists of three balanced, high-protein meals limited to 600 to 1,000 calories a day, attractively prepared and served at the private dining room. Meals are planned and supervised by a trained dietitian. No alcholic beverages are served, and coffee and tea are used sparingly. Guests are urged to substitute herb teas, juices, and low-calorie soft drinks. No smoking is permitted in the spa or in the dining room.

A full-time social director plans activities for the resort, in which many of the spa's guests participate, such as theater parties, backgammon and bridge lessons, art shows, lectures, movies, and shopping tours. Here is a typical day for an adult guest: 9:10 A.M., warm-up exercises; 9:40 A.M., body movement class to music; 10:20 A.M., steam cabinet; 10:40 A.M., whirlpool bath; 11:00 A.M., body massage; 11:40 A.M., swim and rest time; 12:20 P.M., water exercises in the pool; 1:00 P.M., lunch; 2:00 P.M., salt-glow/loofah-scrub; 2:40 P.M., conditioning class; 3:30 P.M., herbal wrap; 4:00 P.M., yoga class; 4:30 P.M., facial treatment.

The cost of the full spa program is $980 per week per person single occupancy and $1,540 per week double occupancy, plus 4 percent tax and 15 percent gratuities. This includes all services and facilities, diet meals, medical examination, and a room at the spa hotel. All rooms are extra large, furnished as junior suites, with two double beds, and each room has two bathrooms and two dressing rooms. Greens fees and tennis fees are waived for spa guests. The age limit for guests is sixteen.

New York

New Age Health Farm, Neversink, New York 12765, (914)985-2221, Elza and Graeme Graydon, directors. The Graydons believe that a health farm should be "more than just a place to get rid of those excess pounds you want to lose, more than a daily massage, more than a luxurious pampering of cleansing creams and powder puffs. It should be the beginning of a whole new way of life."

The farm, nestled at an 1,800-foot elevation, has spacious lawns that slope gently around colonial guest buildings. Great trees dot the landscape, and flagstones surround the pool, making it seem as if it was natural. The 142-acre property looks like the set of *The Sound of Music,* and, indeed, Elza arrived from Salzburg, Austria, in 1951, to bring her ideas about health and beauty to the land of the free. She considers herself a metaphysician, and although she has formal training in music, psychology, cosmetology (she holds a diploma from a Viennese cosmetic school), and yoga, she believes that all her knowledge comes from within herself. She was administrator of the Group Therapy Consultation Center in New York City from 1968 to 1970 and obtained a New York state degree in group leadership in 1970. At present, she is working on her doctorate in metaphysics. Graeme Graydon, her husband, is a native New Zealander, a former dairy farmer, and as down-to-earth as Elza is.

Elza, a vegetarian, supplies a diet of natural foods that "nourishes the body and the spirit," with special emphasis on fresh juices and water fasting, which she calls "the ultimate diet." She studied nutrition and herbology for eight years, and much of the food served to visitors is grown organically on the farm.

"We have tried to create something unique in the eastern United States and perhaps in the whole world," Elza says. A day in the life of a New Age "juicer" begins with an 8:00 A.M. weigh-in "so I can tell if they're cheating" when it comes to the dining room, and ends with a lecture on any one of a variety of subjects, from herbal medicine to astrology to nutrition to meditation. In between, there is a lot of activity—enemas "for detoxification," yoga, calisthenics, hiking, swimming, sauna, hot tubs—and total liquid or calorie restricted diets.

Both juicers and eaters report to the dining room for meals, and there are flowers and candles on the tables, even if there is nothing to chew. It is good discipline, Graeme believes, for the juicers to watch the eaters eat, although—perhaps to avoid tempting them beyond endurance—they are seated at separate tables.

Most guests stay one to two weeks; some stay longer. A lot of theater people and models come for a long weekend when they have to lose 5 pounds. One guest who stayed at New Age for four months lost 120 pounds. However, not all guests come to reduce. For those who want to relax in the beautiful, natural setting, there are lactovegetarian menus of organically grown food, chicken and fish, and home-baked bread.

The cosmetics used at the farm are made from natural ingredients such as fruits, cucumbers, and honey. Elza follows a strict regimen of exercise and massage and expects her guests at the farm to do the same. She leads awareness sessions and meditation groups.

New Age Health Farm is open all year. Accommodations are limited to seventy. Weekend rates for deluxe accommodations are $65 double occupancy and $84 single occupancy. Weekly rates are $185 double and $240 single. Monthly rates are $700 double and $750 single. Miniweek rates (Monday to Friday) are $106 double and $137 single if available. All rooms have private baths. All activities are included except massages, herbal beauty treatments, and some special guest workshops. No children and no pets are allowed.

Pawling Health Manor, Box 401, Hyde Park, New York 12538, (914)889-4141, Joy Gross, director, Dr. Robert Gross, professional consultant. This is the place where many of the beautiful people, as well as the newspaper and magazine editors who write about them, go to fast. Open all year round, it has been in existence for twenty years. The grounds are well kept, and the area is beautiful. Consultant Dr. Gross says, "Only the agents of nature are used to maintain and restore vigor and vitality. We employ no treatments; only nature's requisites for vital living are used. These include sunshine, fresh air, exercise, natural foods, and rational fasting. Our living program includes the factors that should reduce nervous tension, develop emotional equilibrium, and improve general physical well-being. Special attention is given to people who want to reduce and regain a more youthful appearance. Fasting, exercise, and natural nutrition are used." There are beauty and barber shops, of course.

Smoking is not permitted, and they offer an effective method of overcoming the smoking habit very quickly and easily.

Director Gross, who has attended universities in this country and in Europe, assists you in devising a plan of exercise to tone up muscles and acquire that slim look. A modern gymnasium is available. "Pawling Health Manor is not a milk farm nor a spa nor a posh resort nor a maximum service hotel," Dr. Gross emphasizes. "It is a clean and attractive professional weight-reducing retreat. You will lose weight if you are a serious and cooperative patient. We have no gadgets, gimmicks, short-cuts, tricks, or miracles." Weekly group discussions relevant to weight problems are conducted by a biochemist and nutritionist.

It is suggested that you bring a radio, personal stationery, and ample reading material. Dress is extremely informal. In the immediate area, there are many historical sites to visit: Franklin D. Roosevelt's home; the Vanderbilt, Ogden Mills, and Astor estates; Vassar and Bard College; and even Woodstock. Antique shops are numerous. A public golf course, swimming lakes, and horseback riding facilities are located in the vicinity. The minimum stay is one week, and rates are $175 and up, plus tax, depending on accommodations. Rooms are assigned as available. All rooms are clean, airy, and comfortable. The grounds are well kept and the area is beautiful.

Prices begin at $6.00 for a single treatment, including a mineral bath, rock steam, inhalation and cooling rooms, and gym. The rate is $15.00 with a thirty-minute massage and $19.50 with a forty-five-minute complete body massage. A series of six treatments is $32.50. A single massage with steam is $10.00 for thirty minutes and $15.00 for forty-five minutes. Facials are $20.00. Use of the outdoor pools is $5.00; use of the mineral baths is included in the room rate for registered guests.

PUBLICATION

The 30-Day Way to a Born-Again Body, Joy Gross. New York: Rawson, Wade Publishers, 1978. The price is $10.95. The book contains the program and philosophy practiced at Pawling Health Manor with easy to follow directions.

Oregon

Great Oaks School of Health, 82644 North Howe Lane, Creswell, Oregon 97426, (503)895-4967. This holistic healing center aims the individual toward the restoration of health by returning to a "simpler, more natural way of life." The emphasis is on hard work, exercise, nutrition, fasting, and positive thinking. Kinesiology, acupressure, reflexology, massage, color therapy, herbs, homeopathy, vitamins, minerals, clay, colonics, live foods, wheatgrass, sensory deprivation tanks, and saunas are incorporated into their program. Through individual counseling and the group process, people "become aware of their insecurities and attachments and move through them to new levels of awareness." Here is a rundown on the services offered at the school:

Fasting program: Water and juice fasts are supervised.

Self-healing program: Many guests arrive in various states of dis-ease, including terminal cancer, overweight, arthritis, hypoglycemia, and diabetes. A warm, supportive atmosphere is provided for the healing process to take place. A program is established for each individual based on his or her particular health needs.

Holistic health program: People learn about health. They ingest fresh vegetables, fruit juices, and live foods and learn about organic gardening. They are given nutritional counseling and allergy testing; participate in group exercise, jogging, and yoga; and enjoy the benefits of the clean country air.

Work-study program: In this experimental program, the individual takes part in community life; goes through his or her own cleansing, healing process and learning; and then shares his/her skills and energy.

The fee for fasting room and board is $30 per day; for nonfasting room and board, $25 per day; for camping, $5 per night. A nutritional counseling session is $30. A body work session is $15. Colon cleansing is $15 per session. Five 1-hour sessions in the sensory deprivation tank cost $50. The fee for a foot massage and reflexology followed by a footbath is $10. An organic facial and massage cost $10. Psychological counseling is $30 per session.

Texas

The Greenhouse, P.O. Box 1144, Arlington, Texas 76010, (817)640-4000, Jill Cury, director. Over 100 specialists serve a maximum of thirty-eight guests in this luxurious facility halfway between Dallas and Fort Worth, which was established by Neiman-Marcus and Charles of the Ritz. If you need to get away from it all and be pampered, the Greenhouse is the place for you. You are given a luxurious room with a private telephone, lighted closets and makeup mirrors, sunken marble tubs, television, and radio. Sunlight streams into the solarium to highlight masses of tropical plants and growing flowers. And you can follow your complete health and beauty program without ever leaving the building. The staff of experts, assembled from Europe and the United States, guide you through a complete program designed to reshape and tone your body.

Guests arrive on Sunday in time for the buffet dinner at 6:30, which is followed by the director's welcome. The program schedule begins on Monday morning. From Monday to Saturday, you don your blue exercise suit and yellow terry robe and follow your prescribed schedule. Your individual care schedule arrives on your breakfast tray each morning. The enjoyable exercise sessions are interspersed with relaxing facials, massages, sauna baths, and the powerful whirlpool to ease and tone your muscles. Toni Beck, exercise authority and author, directs the exercise program. There are daily visits to the Charles of the Ritz Center, where makeup artists guide you in mastering the most flattering makeup techniques for day and evening. Daily facial, manicure, pedicure, and corrective hair treatments are included in the program. Because most women want to lose a few pounds, well-balanced diet menus are planned. These are based on menus that were created by Helen Corbitt, who was an author and consultant for Neiman-Marcus food services. From breakfast in bed to informal lunch by the indoor pool to formal dinner service in the dining room, every meal is special, with foods that please the eye as well as the palate. Quiet Night is a once-a-week special treat; each guest has a dinner tray in her room. You may spend your leisure time sunbathing at an outdoor pool or playing tennis. Swimming and tennis lessons are available. Cocktails, which may be iced soup or hors d'oeuvres or crisp vegetables, are served at 6:30. After dinner, there may be a lecture by an astrologer, a yogi, or an expert on jewels, travel, or fashion. If you wish, you can go on an excursion to Neiman-Marcus one afternoon each week. Once there, a fashion advisor will smooth your way.

The minimum reservation is for one week, and the rooms are reserved from Sunday noon to Sunday noon. The required deposit is $100, and reservations must be made at least three months in advance. The minimum charge is $1,620 per week for a single room.

West Virginia

Greenbrier, White Sulphur Springs, West Virginia 24986, (800)624-6070. If you want to step into life as it was lived in the grand manner, visit Greenbrier, one of the last repositories of true Southern hotel hospitality. It looks like the White House when you first arrive, but it is more elegant. There are three 18-hole golf courses, fifteen outdoor tennis courts, five indoor courts (with a complete spectators' gallery), pro shop, indoor and outdoor swimming, and horseback riding over 200 miles of woodland and mountain trails. You can practice your skeet shooting on a lookout point or your bowling right in the hotel's own bowling alley. Ice skating and platform tennis are available outside the indoor pool. Each room in the hotel is decorated differently and with great taste. If you don't experience a renaissance from the facilities alone, there is a mineral bath and massage for $16 that includes a steam bath, scotch spray (hard needle hose), sauna, and whirlpool.

Delicious meals are available in several dining rooms, including the elegant Tavern Room. Meals are also served at the stunning Golf Club. In keeping with Greenbrier's grand style, black tie is the custom on Saturday nights, and jackets and ties are required every night after 7:00 P.M. in the dining room, the Old White Club, and the upper lobby. For women, tennis dresses, shorts, or jeans are not permitted after seven.

Prices, which vary according to the season, range from $55 per person for a double- or twin-bedded room to $70 per person, MAP. (Modified American Plan, two meals a day.)

See Greenbrier Clinic, page 75.

Mexico

Hotel Ixtapan, Neuva Ixtapan, Paseo de la Reforma 132, Mexico 6, D.F., (903)532-7622, or for reservations, Robert F. Warner, Inc., 630 Fifth Avenue, New York, New York 10017, (212)687-5750. Known as the Resort Spa of the Flowers in the Motherland of Aztec Emperors, this luxurious modern resort, located seventy-five miles from Mexico City, offers a breathtaking view of mountains and valleys. The average daily temperature is 70 degrees; it is eternally spring. It has 250 junior, master, presidential, and chalet suites; a modern water purifying plant; a private theater; a night club; a golf course; riding stables; three purified and filtered swimming pools; ten thermal swimming pools; and every other resort feature. It claims to offer the most completely equipped ladies' beauty institute and men's health club on this side of the Atlantic, featuring six types of rejuvenating baths, electrotherapy, massage, gymnasium, diet, facials, and beauty and barber services.

To feed your soul, there are eleven dancing, colored fountains that display the story of ancient and modern Mexico, 146 Italian mosaic murals, a folklore ballet, and Aztec and Mariachi musical groups that play in the evening; there is a nightly entertainment.

The daily rate in the winter on the American plan (with three meals) ranges from $42.00 per person for a chalet bedroom with terrace to $57.00 per person for a master suite with two baths and a terrace. Doubles are priced from $63.50 to $77.00. There is no extra charge for the Diet Dining Room, a miniature railway ride through the park, with its thirteen lakes, swimming, riding horses and horse drawn carriages, the gymnasium, and the entertainment. Rates for the Health and Beauty Institute are $33.50 per day or $192.00 for a week. The golf course fee is $6.10. Use of the Roman private pools is $3.15, and use of the thermal swimming pool is $.90 (no kidding). A massage costs $3.20.

Spain

Incosol, Los Monteros Estate, Marbella, Spain. Contact Robert F. Warner Inc., 630 Fifth Ave., New York, New York 10017 for reservations, or call your travel agent. How about a castle in Spain, on the coast of the sun, where you can tend to your health and beauty? The nine-story hotel on the crest of the hill on the renowned Los Monteros Estate takes full advantage of the glorious views of the Mediterranean Sea and the Sierra Blanca range. There are lush gardens, Spanish art and furnishings, and private terraces. It has a complete medical clinic, a dental clinic, a beauty salon and barber shop, saunas, massage, heated pools, a gymnasium, an 18-hole golf course, seven tennis courts, stables, a beach club, and heated indoor and outdoor swimming pools, all supervised by a professional staff. If you can tear yourself away, you can explore the delightful town of Marbella, filled with shops, restaurants, and the activities of a busy resort marina. It is still to be discovered by many Americans, but it is a favorite of European sophisticates.

Prices for a single room with bath are 6,300 pesetas on the American Plan and 5,800 pesetas on the Modified American Plan. A twin-bedded room with bath and terrace is 8,300 pesetas on the American plan and 7,800 pesetas on the modified American plan.

PART II

Beauty

What is beauty? Can you describe a handsome man or an attractive woman?

The truth is that there is no single, permanent standard of beauty. There are fashions in features and figures, just as there are fashions in clothes and cars. And fortunately, what looks good to some people, does not look good to others. After all, if everyone loved blondes, what would we redheads and brunettes do? Every culture values beauty and endows its owners with status and sometimes with riches. But each culture has its own concept of beauty, which often differs greatly from place to place and time to time. Remember Twiggy, as thin as a stick? Voluptuous Marilyn Monroe? Barbra Streisand? Jackie Kennedy? Catherine Deneuve? How about Robert Taylor? Robert Redford? Dustin Hoffman? Henry Winkler?

The factors that determine beauty at one time and in one place are intriguing and probably have a lot to do with survival. The Eskimos, for instance, prized fat females; well-insulated women survived the freezing cold better. At one time, wealthy men also wanted fat wives to prove they were good providers; today, rich men in America prize svelte women. Thin wives have the option of selecting nonfattening foods and have the leisure to follow fashion.

Do blondes really have more fun? The answer has to be yes in countries where blond hair is prized as beautiful. But to a Ubangi man who thinks lips unstretched by plates are unattractive, the answer would probably be no. Beauty is certainly not constant, even in the movies and on Madison Avenue. The curvaceous, sex-kitten types such as Sophia Loren and Marilyn Monroe have been replaced as the ideal image by the slim, athletic, independent "Charlie" type of career woman on the go. The hairy chested cowboy has given way to the father doing the laundry.

If you are lucky enough to have universal appeal or to fit the current style of beauty exactly, then status and ease will be yours without effort. For most of us, however, keeping ourselves attractive and good-looking takes a little effort. But with today's facilities and products, no one need be unattractive.

The most important question to ask yourself is: Why bother? Why should you care about how you look or try to improve yourself when the most important thing is how you feel inside?

It is certainly true that you cannot judge a book by its cover any more than you can judge a person by his or her looks. But then why do publishers spend a lot of money on cover designs? So that you will be sufficiently attracted to the book to discover what is inside. How do you behave when a panhandler approaches you on the street or when a person you meet is sloppy about his or her appearance? You consciously or unconsciously shy away from them. How do you feel inside when you know you look your best? You have more confidence in yourself; you feel better.

Doctors have found that when a sick woman begins to comb her hair and put on lipstick or when a sick man wants to shave and comb his hair, he or she is on the road to recovery. That is why in modern mental institutions and old-age homes, beauty parlors and barbershops have been installed: to make residents look better and consequently feel better about themselves. When you are depressed, you tend to let your appearance show the world how you feel. Conversely, if you are depressed but you make an effort to improve your looks, your mood lifts.

Embarking on a self-improvement program for your appearance can change your whole outlook on life. It can be a new beginning after some landmark such as a milestone birthday, a divorce, children leaving home, a new job, or boredom, or it can just be a treat. But caution and common sense must also come into play. There are a lot of false promises made in the beauty business, and there is even fraud. Often, all that is offered is hope, which can, of course, be priceless in itself. But do not expect miracles. You cannot remove or prevent wrinkles with treatments, short of plastic surgery. You cannot turn back the clock; no one can. But you can look your best.

It is never too late to improve your looks. You have many opportunities today to change your appearance and make yourself more attractive to others and, more importantly, to yourself.

Skin

Your skin is your largest, most visible organ. It mirrors your emotions, responds to the environment, and reflects your mental and physical state.

Dermatology is the science concerned with the diagnosis and management of skin problems. Physicians who specialize in this field actually practice one of the most general medical specialties, a broad field that touches on the activities of other medical disciplines and on the natural, physical, and cosmetic sciences. Dermatologists use a variety of therapeutic tools, from antibiotics to the scalpel; they perform more minor surgery than a surgeon does.

Skin problems affect all age-groups and all economic levels of society. According to a survey of dermatologists, acne is the most often treated disease, accounting for nearly 20 percent of all cases seen in practice. This was followed by treatment for contact dermatitis, an umbrella term for skin diseases resulting from external causes such as poison ivy or industrial chemicals. Other frequent skin conditions seen by dermatologists are skin cancer, warts, fungal infections, and psoriasis, a skin disorder that affects from 2 to 8 million persons in the United States.

When should you go to a dermatologist? Many people continue to treat skin problems themselves until a minor annoyance becomes a serious ailment. When symptoms of a skin disease appear, it is best to seek medical advice as soon as possible. Your local medical society, hospital, or medical center can give you the names of physicians in your area who have had specialized advanced training in dermatology. You can also write to the American Academy of Dermatology, requesting the names of academy members in your area.

American Academy of Dermatology
2250 Northwest Flanders Street
Portland, Oregon 97210

PUBLICATIONS

The academy will also send you booklets containing solid information on common skin problems. You can request any of the following publications:

Psoriasis. This booklet describes the symptoms of the reddish, silvery lesions that characterize the condition and provides information about current therapies.

Acne. The booklet describes this acute inflammatory condition involving those areas of the skin where the oil glands are most prominent. The wide choice of available treatments is described.

Warts. The booklet discusses whether warts are dangerous and who is likely to have them. It describes the different kinds of warts and what can be done about them.

Allergy. This booklet explains how allergies develop, how a doctor finds the sensitizer, and how skin allergies are treated.

Vitiligo. The booklet describes this disorder, in which patients have a characteristic loss of pigment or skin color. It goes on to explain who gets vitiligo and what can be done about the condition.

Cancer. Cancers of the skin are the most common cancers, accounting for more than one-sixth of all new malignancies diagnosed. About 95 percent of all skin cancers can be cured. The booklet describes the various forms, explains how to eliminate primary causes, and tells you when to seek medical help.

Poison Plant Rashes. Plants of the poison ivy family cause the most universally encountered skin disease in this country, poison ivy dermatitis. This booklet discusses treatment, prevention, and plant eradication.

All these publications are free for the asking. Simply send a large, stamped, self-addressed envelope along with your request.

The following booklets can be ordered from the American Medical Association, AMA Publications, P. O. Box 821, Monroe, Wisconsin 53566.

Soap: Its Use and Abuse (OP 271), $.35
Understanding Hair Coloring (OP 060), $.75
The Hair You Can Do Without (OP 396), $.50.
The Housewife and Her Hands (OP 106), $.45.
Something Can Be Done About Acne (OP 035), $.45.
Allergic Contact Rashes (OP 239), $.35.
The Aging Skin (OP 333), $.35.

2

What Kind of Skin Do You Have?

Skin comes not only in varied colors, but in various degrees of dryness. How can you tell what type you really have?

Dry skin: More inclined to wrinkle. Flakes easily. Soaks up moisturizers, rarely breaks out and is finely textured.

Oily skin: This type is always shiny, has enlarged pores and tends to break out. Wrinkles much later than dry skin.

Combination skin: Usually developed by oily skinned persons as they age. It is shiny on the forehead, nose and chin and dry on the cheeks and under the eyes.

If you can afford the time or money for a professional makeup expert's advice, check with your local department store and find out when a representative from one of the major cosmetic companies will be demonstrating the products. If you visit the store during this time, you can have a free makeup lesson. You do *not* have to buy anything. But remember, the whole purpose of the makeup application is to lure you into buying the company's products. Use restraint and, if possible, try to obtain the services of more than one makeup representative. Then you can decide which products are best suited to your needs.

BEAUTY CENTERS

California

Aida Grey, 9549 Wilshire Boulevard, Beverly Hills, California 90212, (213)276-4681. Aida Grey, high priestess of Hollywood beauty seekers, maintains that "beauty is an arresting quality developed by the woman who has had the intelligence and foresight to acquire the skill and good taste necessary to accentuate the best facets of her physical being." Grey has developed cosmetics containing herbs, flowers, fruits, seafoods, and all manner of natural substances.

The salon offers a variety of services. The $100.00 Day of Beauty includes cleansing facial; body massage; shampoo, styling, and set; manicure; pedicure; makeup lesson, including eyebrow arch; and $25.00 worth of cosmetics. The special hair care services include a consultation, treatment ($7.50), color ($12.50 and up), styling ($11.00), and permanents. Hand treatments include removal of brown spots, manicures, sculptured nails, hot oil treatment with vitamin E, and shiatsu massage ($15.00), which relaxes fingers, decongests veins, and stimulates circulation. Foot treatments include whirlpool pedicures ($10.00) and foot reflexology (see page 225). Body treatments include contour exercises with Ron Fletcher (see page 21, series of 10 for $140, an individual, 2-hour consultation $75), special therapeutic massage, shiatsu massage, ginsu massage, cellulite sauna treatments. A special makeup lesson includes skin care, contour, eyebrow arching, and styling.

Some three hundred women a day pass through Aida Grey's salon doors. She also has a big mail-order business. Her Peach Cleansing Milk, for instance, is $5.50, and her Sensi-Lotion is $5.00. The Red Herbal Lotion is $5.00, and the Gin Seng Eye Masque is $7.75. You can write for a free catalogue.

Here is some makeup advice from Aida Grey. First of all, she emphasizes that "only when your skin is cleansed, lubricated or moisturized, and stimulated are you ready for makeup."

Foundations: Always have at least two shades, darker for daytime and a lighter one for evening. When applying foundation, don't forget to cover the tips of the ears and behind the ears, too, if you have a short haircut, and don't forget your neck. Remove the general excess with a damp towel. Use a cotton-tipped orange stick to remove excess from stubborn areas.

Face powder: Powder gives a well-groomed finish to your makeup. Apply with puff or cotton; remove surplus with brush.

Eye Makeup: It lends sparkle to the eyes and brightens the face. Eyeliner makes the lashes look more dense. Apply it right to the lash root. Mascara should be applied with an almost dry brush. When the lashes are quite dry, stroke them with a brush to separate them. Apply two or three coats. A little blue pencil under the lower lashes works wonders to brighten the eyes. Blur the line with a cotton-wrapped orange stick. Use brown or plum eye shadow to contour the eye. Shadow will make bulging eyes seem to recede. For well-set eyes, apply shadow only in fold. For sunken eyes, apply white shadow on the eyelid close to the lashes, brown shadow above, and white again under the eyebrow.

Aida Grey will send you a questionnaire. Fill it in, mail it, and you will receive your own makeup chart with shades and products selected just for you. You will also receive a catalogue of Aida Grey products.

Illinois

Syd Simons Studios, 2 East Oak Street (main office), Chicago, Illinois 60611, (312)943-2333. There are five studios in the Chicago area and studios in Kansas City and San Francisco. Syd Simons offers a complete private course in corrective and fashion makeup designed for the individual. It consists of three 1½-hour lessons, and you receive charts, diagrams, and written instructions with each lesson. The cost is $50. Makeup applications, individual lessons, and facials are also available.

The Syd Simons professional makeup artists and estheticians offer the midwesterner the same kind of makeup and skin care that are found in Beverly Hills, California, and in New York City.

Massachusetts

Elizabeth Grady Face First, 39 Newberry Street, Boston, Massachusetts 02116, (617)536-4447. Also 200 Boylston Street, Chestnut Hill, Massachusetts 02167, (617)964-6470. One of the oldest and largest skin-care facilities in the country, Elizabeth Grady Face First employs only graduate estheticians and an American refinement of the European science of esthetics. As authors of the Grady Bill, corporate principals were instrumental in making Massachusetts the first state in the nation to pass a law recognizing esthetics as separate and distinct from the hairdressing industry and to set standards for skin-care services and the licensing of estheticians. Because of this law, schools for the training of American estheticians (such schools were formerly found only in Europe and Canada) were established in this country. In February 1979, the Elizabeth Grady First National School of Esthetics was opened. It offers the first in-depth education of American estheticians, as well as the first text on the adaptation of European techniques for American skin types and skin-care needs.

The corporate philosophy is to "clean up problem skin, and help keep nice skin problem free." This is accomplished through deep, pore-cleansing facials and other specialized treatments in the salons and through educating clients about skin care and teaching them to carry out personalized programs for at-home maintenance.

The salons offer services for both men and women. These include makeup application and instruction, lash and brow tinting, and waxing. A full line of unique skin-care products and makeup is available. Another area of specialization is postsurgical skin care and corrective makeup for burn and scar victims; this work is done in close association with area hospitals.

Lash tinting $8.50. One hour full facial $17.50. Half-hour maintenance $10.00; 2½ hour facial treatment and makeup application $35.00; makeup application alone $25.00; leg waxing $30.00. Offer men's makeup and application instruction. Each service includes complete do-it-yourself instructions.

New York

Adrien Arpel, 666 Fifth Avenue, New York, New York 10019, (212) 397-6710. Arpel's facial services are available at many leading department stores—including Lord & Taylor, Saks, Macy's, Neiman-Marcus, Bloomingdales, and Burdines (in Florida)—and in just about every state in the Union and in England and Canada. For the regular treatment at an Arpel Skin Health Spa, an esthetician analyzes and prescribes an individual program to satisfy your personal skin needs. First, the Oxygenator dispenses a fine mist "to moisten your skin and intensify blood circulation." Then an Electric Brush briskly removes accumulations of surface dirt, dead skin cells, and pollutants that clog pores. A Skin Activator "bombards the skin with natural lemon and lime to stimulate the motor nerves and moisten dry skin cells." Finally, an Electric Vacuum that resembles a facial vacuum cleaner draws oils and dirt from the skin's surface and removes blackheads with a gentle, firm suction. A Heating Masque of either orange or spearmint gel closes the pores. A complimentary makeup provides the finishing touch. This full-hour treatment is $20.00; a series of six treatments costs $100. The minifacial, a shorter version that lasts fifteen minutes, is for the woman on the go. Minifacials cost $12.50 for one treatment and $45 for a series of four. Also available is a forty-five-minute deep-cleansing facial using products from the sea. Sea kelp is believed to have healing properties; the Electromechanical Sponge forces the kelp cleanser into the pores for cleansing efficiency. Then mildly abrasive salt crystals (imported from the Dead Sea) are hand-massaged into the skin to remove dead skin cells. An oxygenated Sea-Spray Vapor prepares your pores for further treatment. A manual Sea-Herb facial massage stimulates the skin with algae and seaweed. This is followed by the Heatless Heat Skin Penetration Treatment, which uses infrared rollers to "aid in the rapid penetration of specifically prescribed treatments for common skin disorders such as oiliness or acne." Finally, natural sea mud minerals are brushed onto your face in the Sea Mud Pack, which is adapted from the treatment given at the spa at Marienbad, Czechoslovakia. A volcanic ash masks absorbs dirt and oil from the pores and picks up cellular debris from the skin. The complete treatment is $17.50, including complimentary makeup.

Adrien Arpel recently introduced the Hot Paraffin Hand Treatment that softens and soothes the skin on your hands. The cost is $5 and up.

To check the location of stores that feature Adrien Arpel's treatments, contact the national headquarters in New York.

Beauty Checkers, Inc., Henri Bendel, 10 West 57th Street, New York, New York 10019, (212)CI7-2829. What do you have in common with Gloria Steinem, Candice Bergen, Ali McGraw, and Tuesday Weld? "Beauty problems," according to Amy Greene; and as their beauty consultant, she ought to know. "There isn't a woman alive who doesn't feel she has a beauty problem," says the former model and *Glamour* magazine beauty editor. She cites as an example Princess Grace, who requested advice on what to do about her "awful" hair during one of Amy's trips to Monaco on assignment with husband, photographer Milton Greene. Amy Greene is the originator of Beauty Checkers at Henri Bendel, where you can receive a makeup consultation and lesson for $15 for one hour ($25 for a session with Mrs. Greene in person). You can bring your own makeup from home or purchase makeup products (none of which is over $4) at Beauty Checkers. The service has been in existence since 1970, and 85 percent of its customers are repeats.

Beauty Checkers is geared to the needs of *all* women who, cosmetically speaking, have been "oversold and undertaught until they are in a total state of brand confusion—and confused or not, they keep buying more in the eternal hope of looking better." That is why Beauty Checkers ask clients to bring in the products they already have and give clients straightforward, clear instructions. They participate in doing the makeup and leave with a personal, diagrammed instruction sheet.

In addition to makeup, Beauty Checkers will give observations and suggestions on hairstyling, exercise, diet, hair removal, plastic surgery, clothing, and referral to other experts. Hours are 10:00 A.M. to 4:00 P.M., Monday to Friday and every other Saturday, by appointment only. Beauty Checkers is expanding internationally.

Elizabeth Arden Salon, 691 Fifth Avenue, New York, New York 10022, (212)486-7900. Also in Southhampton, New York; Beverly Hills and San Francisco, California; Chevy Chase, Maryland; Chicago, Illinois; Coral Gables, Fort Lauderdale, Palm Beach, and Surfside, Florida; Phoenix, Arizona; Washington, D.C.; London, England; Milan, Italy. If you want to make a new beginning for any reason—the winter blahs, a divorce, a marker birthday, or just for a treat, sign up for Maine Chance Day at the New York salon. This package deal includes exercise (three people and an instructor), steam cabinet, massage, hairstyling, manicure, pedicure, face treatment, daytime makeup, and a light lunch. The exercises are Marjorie Craig's (of the Mrs. Craig's 21-Day Shape-Up for Men and Women Program). I went in at 9:00 A.M. and was out by 3:30 P.M. Everything was arranged on a schedule. Everyone was polite and helpful. There was even a constant fashion show, with slim models showing off designer dresses. The cost of the Maine Chance Day is $90, plus tax, and 15 to 20 percent for tips. Another package, Miracle Morning, includes massage, shampoo, hairstyling, manicure, face treatment, and daytime makeup. The price is $70, plus tax and tips. The Visible Difference Day concentrates on the beauty services; it includes hair consultation, face treatment, shampoo, hairstyling, manicure, and an hour-long makeup lesson. The price is $75, plus tax and tips.

Not all salons have the complete range of services, so check with the manager in advance. At the New York salon, there are also two floors of fashions and two makeup sales counters

See Maine Chance, page 123.

"i" Natural Cosmetics, 737 Madison Avenue, New York, New York 10022, (212)734-0664. Lois Muller is founder and president of "i" Natural Cosmetics and a pioneer in the field of promoting real strawberries, oranges, papayas, and other of nature's products for modern beauty purposes. It was through Lois Muller's interest in nutrition and good, healthy things that "i" Natural Cosmetics was created. One day, she found cosmetics hidden on a back shelf of a health food store. Although the packaging was not very attractive, she opened the bottles and was bowled over by the fresh, fruity, wonderful fragrances.

Muller's idea that other women would like to use skin-care and makeup products based on natural, fruity oils and other natural ingredients was right. Her tiny, spring green shop opened in New York City in the early 1970s and was an immediate success. Today, there are some 90 franchise and company-owned shops across the country and in Europe.

Every "i" Natural Cosmetics Shop has a policy of offering customers a free makeup styling so that they can try everything before buying. Among the most popular products are Strawberry Cleanser ($6.50 for four ounces), Grapefruit Skin Freshener ($9.50 for eight ounces), and Orange Moisturizer ($6.50 for four ounces). In addition, "i" gives you a personal chart to take home.

Georgette Klinger, 501 Madison Avenue, New York, New York 10022, (212)838-3200. Also Bal Harbour Shops, 9700 Collins Avenue, Bal Harbour, Florida 33154, (305)868-7516; 312 North Rodeo Drive, Beverly Hills, California 90210, (213)274-6347; Water Tower Place, 835 North Michigan Avenue, Chicago, Illinois 60611, (312)787-4300. If an eighteen-year-old beauty contest winner hadn't suddenly developed a case of acne, one of the most successful skin-care chains for both men and women might never have been born. Seeking remedies for her problem, Georgette Klinger became fascinated by the field of skin care and skin analysis. She worked with professors of dermatology; took courses in cosmetic chemistry and cosmetology in Budapest, Vienna, Paris, and

London; and in 1938, opened her first salon in Brno, Czechoslovakia, with her own formulations and methods. She moved to London, opened a skin-care salon there, and finally came to New York, where she opened the first of the Klinger Centers.

After your makeup is removed by one of the Klinger-trained technicians, a special light is used to examine and diagnose your skin problems. Then a herbal massage of the neck, shoulders, and face is performed. A Turkish towel is then draped over your head to trap steam from a heated pot of herbal tea to moisturize your face and prepare your pores for cleaning; this part of the treatment lasts for ten minutes. The pores are then cleansed manually, removing impurities. Application of various facial masks, chosen according to your skin type, to tighten the pores and to soften the skin round out the treatment process. There are also longer, highly specialized treatments such as the Protein Treatment (for under-nourished skin), the Instant Softening Treatment (for sun-damaged skin), and the Ice Treatment (for postsurgery and chemotherapy patients).

After the treatment, the client is given written instructions and a booklet for an at-home skin-care program. Recommendations are made for the individualized products. For instance, there are twenty-eight cleansing lotions, seven makeup removers, twenty-one moisturizers, fifteen masks, and a dozen lubricating creams.

A complimentary makeup climaxes the visit. Although Miss Klinger says she would prefer no makeup except around the eyes, she has developed specialized makeup for each skin type. There are five different types of foundations. The makeup artist is trained to emphasize the good features of each client with the colors most flattering to her.

Because she has found that so many skin problems are caused by scalp problems, she also offers complete scalp treatments and products for the scalp and hair. Both skin and scalp consultations are complimentary.

Until recently, men have been more reluctant to admit interest in skin, hair, and scalp care. A man's skin can be categorized, just as a woman's can, and is sensitive and in need of care. So in 1972, Klinger for Men opened on Madison Avenue in New York. It has been expanded to all the salons.

There is a Salon Package for $95, which includes a facial, scalp treatment, body massage, makeup lesson, manicure, pedicure, and hairstyling. A woman's facial costs $32, $160 for a series of six. A man's facial costs $30, $150 for a series of six. Skin peelings are $15, and revitalizing facials are $42. A body massage for women is $25 for an hour; a scalp treatment is $25. A man's haircut is $20, and a woman's is $22.

The Georgette Klinger At-Home Care Program for both men and women offers personalized service for those who cannot visit one of the salons. The Georgette Klinger Skin Examination Chart contains a detailed questionnaire designed by Miss Klinger to give you a complete picture of your skin's condition. Once you have evaluated your skin, recorded your observations, and returned your chart to Georgette Klinger, a specially trained home-care expert will analyze it and prescribe a course of at-home treatments and a selection of Klinger products designed to solve your individual problem. You will also receive your own at-home skin-care booklet. The starter kit is $8.25.

Here are Georgette Klinger's guidelines for good skin care.

DO'S

Do use protection against sun and wind.
Do use only makeup formulated for your skin type.
Do be sure your scalp is in good condition.
Do cleanse your face several times a day.
Do use a pure shampoo.
Do get lots of rest.
Do cleanse your skin thoroughly before retiring.
Do drink lots of water and eat well-balanced meals that include fruits and
  vegetables.

DON'TS

Don't smother your skin problems with makeup.
Don't use hair spray, it's harmful to the skin.
Don't apply overnight creams (except in rare cases of extreme dryness).
  Allow the skin to "breathe freely" while you sleep.
Don't try to squeeze your own blemishes; you can bruise the skin and
  cause infection and scars.
Don't use cake makeup or powder in any form.
Don't scrub your face, but rub it gently.

Remember, although skin type is inherited, skin condition is created. Georgette Klinger firmly believes that "there is no true beauty without a beautiful skin."

Caroline Leonetti. See pp. 188-190 on beauty and dressing better.

Make-Up Center, Ltd., 150 West 55th Street, New York, New York 10019, (212)977-9494. Also Washington, D.C.; Columbia, South Carolina; Beverly Hills, California; Portland, Oregon; Ontario, Canada; and Paris, France. Beautiful Naomi Sims and Diana Ross get their eyelashes here; Barbra Streisand, her iridescent translucent powder; Catherine Deneuve, pearl dust highlighter; and Appolonia von Ravenstein, gold powder shadow. The list goes on and on. The Supremes, for instance, like the mint pack facial masks; Bette Midler, the shimmer liquid highlighters; and Cher, the honey and almond paste. Make-Up Center makes its own special things and supplies almost every model and actress around with at least part of her cosmetics. The shop in New York is small, nonscented, plain, and known the world over as the cosmetic "in spot" for models and actresses, whose autographed pictures adorn the walls.

All the brands in the center were originally theatrical products. The center also carries its own private brand, On Stage, and a complete line of cosmetics for the black woman. Today, purely professional colors are kept in a separate section, but there is a large selection of stage makeup that has been adapted for everyday wear by the ordinary woman. There is no longer any difference between the techniques of professional and everyday makeup, except that models know what products to use and how to use them, and many other women do not. That is why many of the professional's tricks are taught to women at the Make-Up Center. Here are a few: Use rouge for cheek highlight but not for color. Never use anything but a beige base. It's softer to use brown eyeliner instead of black. Muted colors in eye shadows are also softer. Don't intermingle colors on your face any more than you would on clothes. Structure your face as the models do; use contour and highlight. Touch, a concealing cream, used under the eyes will keep the shadows from showing and will draw attention to the eyes.

Hours at the Make-Up Center are 10:00 A.M. to 6:00 P.M., Monday to Friday, and noon to 6:00 P.M. on Saturday. Makeup lessons and application cost $12.50 a session. The products used are included in the fee.

Performers Make-Up Inc., 13 East 47th Street, New York, New York 10017, (212)752-6800. Not only can you learn how performers cover up defects and create beautiful illusions, you can obtain the actual makeup by mail. Professor Herman Buchman teaches stage makeup at the State University of New York at Purchase and at the Juilliard Theater Center and film makeup at the School of Visual Arts in New York City. After years of opening dozens of greasepaint containers to get even small effects, he decided to design a kit that would contain everything, be without opening jar tops, and be, in effect, a palette for painting on the face. The kit holds enough for an average year of stage performances and has all the basic colors needed for even the most elaborate makeup creations. It is small enough to fit into a handbag or a coat pocket. The women's kit contains mascara and eyelashes; the men's kit contains spirit gum and crepe wool for beards. Each kit sells for $28.00, plus $1.50 for postage and handling.

In addition to the kit, Professor Buchman has written *Stage Makeup* (New York: Watson-Guptill Publications, 1978), $19.95 and *Film and Television Makeup* (New York: Watson-Guptill Publications, 1977), $19.95. Each book has over 500 photographs and a step-by-step photographic breakdown of each task, as well as a section of special effects. Include $1.50 for postage and handling for each book.

Natural Face Lifting by Exercise, P.O. Box 23, Lenox Hill Station, New York, New York 10021, (212)752-4195. M. J. Saffon, director. You can look younger and have a glowing complexion in just fifteen minutes a day. Saffon claims that this program, a combination of massage and exercise, firms and fills your facial contours without plastic surgery, no matter what your age, sex, or skin condition. He says it can take years off your face. He also maintains that exercising muscles and skin brings a vigorous supply of blood to the surface of the skin and that by tightening and flexing, you make the muscles grow again. Results can usually be seen after three months. Saffon also has a skin-care program that teaches you how to cleanse and moisturize.

The methods are taught in two-day sessions which are held from 10 A.M. to 4 P.M. and cost $30. Check scheduling by writing to the above address since there are no set dates.

PUBLICATIONS

Fifteen Minute A Day Natural Face Lift, by M. J. Saffon, $7.95, was published by Prentice Hall, Inc. in 1979 and gives the complete program.

WRINKLES, How to Erase Them, How to Prevent Them, by Lida Livingston and Constance Schrader, $7.95, was published by Prentice-Hall in 1978, the paperback edition was published by Ballantine Books in 1979. It provides a complete program of face-lifting exercises and a unique method of pressing wrinkles away.

Makeovers, by Constance Schrader, $10.00, published in 1979 by Prentice-Hall, will provide a complete program course in applying makeup for every situation in professional and private life, from sports events to evening galas.

Sandy O' Faces by Mail, 123 Main Street, Cold Spring Harbor, New York 11724, (516)367-4664. "Send me your face," says Sandy. She has a questionnaire that you fill out including such questions as: "Your makeup tends to change color? If so, on skin or on mouth?" "Your working clothes are formal? Casual? Anything goes?" "Would you like the color on your face to appear totally natural? Showing a bit of color? Showing a lot of color?" Send her a color photo and a check or money order for $20.00, plus $1.50 for postage and handling; she will send you your personal color pattern (applied with actual makeup) on a eight-by-ten blowup of your photograph; swatches of flattering colors to use on your face; simple, exact instructions that tell you how to apply the color to your face; and special suggestions for hair design, eyebrow shape, and eyeglasses frame shape. She also sells natural cosmetics.

Stan Place, Beauty Bookings, New York, New York. A licensed cosmetologist with a master's degree in fine arts, Place has taught makeup in colleges, theatrical schools, and beauty clinics. He has been on many television shows and written advice for magazines such as *Town and*

Country, Woman's Day, and *Good Housekeeping*. His subjects include such personalities as Cher, Marissa Berenson, and Olivia Newton-John. He charges $100.00 and up for personal consultation but has available a fifteen-minute cassette, *The Beauty Place*, for $5.98. He gives clear instructions every step of the way. You can replay it every time you apply your makeup. The tape can be ordered from Powers Professional Artists, 55 West 42d Street, New York, New York 10036, (212)594-2807.

Lenore D. Valery, Ltd., 119 West 57th Street, New York, New York 10019, (212)757-6585. Valery calls herself an "esthetician," and she says she is able to correct beauty problems and help prevent other problems from occurring. Lenore Valery holds diplomas in fashion designing and illustration from Traphagen Institute, two diplomas in electrolysis, two diplomas from the Wilfred Academy of Hair and Beauty Culture in cosmetology, a diploma in skin care, a diploma in makeup, and two diplomas in waxing. She offers services in skin care, permanent and temporary hair removal, scalp treatments, and hair reconditioning.

Valery believes that hers is the only salon that offers an analysis of skin, hair, and scalp and outlines a home-care program as part of the first treatment and at no additional cost. Her miniseries to prepare you for home care of your skin, hair, and scalp consists of one 1½ hour treatment and two 1-hour treatments for $65.00. Her treatment series for skin that is losing its elasticity and becoming dry consists of two weekly treatments (one for an hour and fifteen minutes and one for fifteen minutes) that stimulate and nourish the skin. The treatment costs $34.00 each session or $204.00 for the six-week series. For hands that are in need of care, there is a half-hour treatment that removes roughness and "penetrates" with rich oils that are massaged into the hands with special equipment. The cost is $9.50.

Electrolysis costs $28.00 per hour. IB probe method of permanent hair removal costs $33.00 per hour. (*IB* means "insulated bulbous"; the probe is insulated, and the tip is rounded out. This concentrates the energy below the surface of the skin. There is less sensation, less regrowth, less skin reaction.) Waxing is available for all parts of the body from the lip ($3.60) to the legs ($18.50). Skin-care treatment costs $21.00 an hour; for more resistant acnes, oily, or dry skins, the cost is $26.50 for an hour and fifteen minutes. A complete line of makeup products is also available.

Here are some of Lenore Valery's hints for home care:

Avoid detergent shampoos.
Don't use a blow drier or electric curlers too often.
Don't wash oily hair too often.
Avoid "instant" hair conditioners; they attract dirt to the hair and cause skin problems.

Don't apply too much pressure when washing hair. Pressure stimulates the oil glands.

Hair loss is normal for a short time when you stop taking the birth control pill.

The salon hours are 10:00 A.M. to 8:00 P.M., Monday, Wednesday, Thursday, and Friday; 5:00 to 8:00 P.M., Tuesday; and 10:00 A.M. to 6:00 P.M., Saturday.

Diane Von Furstenberg Salon, 681 Madison Avenue, New York, New York 10021, (212)759-2303. The sloe-eyed genius of fashion, Diane now has a posh salon offering makeup lessons for $30.00 per hour, facials for $30.00, and waxing for $6.00 to $40.00. The shop carries her complete line of cosmetics and Tatiana fragrances, as well as some accessories, such as sunglasses and scarves. There is a complete mail-order service for cosmetics, ranging from a $2.50 eye shadow applicator to a $12.00 Tatiana eau de parfum spray. Salon hours are 10 A.M. to 6 P.M.

Texas

The Beauty Terrace, Neiman-Marcus, Main and Ervay Streets, Dallas, Texas 75201, (214)741-6911. The department store that offers such things as a his and hers Rolls Royces for Christmas has created as extravagant a beauty parlor as can be found anywhere. The floors are white and gleaming; the decor, the wallpaper, and the matching fabric cushions on the bamboo chairs all have an exotic cast. There are the usual beauty services, with, of course, a Texas touch. There is an entire color studio and staff of colorists devoted exclusively to tinting. There are manicures that include hot oil treatments, nail sculpturing, and nail wrapping. Pedicures are done in little private rooms. There are numerous types of facials, false eyelash application, and various methods of removing facial and body hair. The Beauty Terrace also has a trained masseuse, sunlamp treatments, steam cabinet, and complimentary makeup.

As if that wasn't enough, you can have a gourmet-catered lunch, and a style director will consult with you about your overall appearance so that, if you wish, you can have a totally new look from head to toe.

There is a Day of Pampering series, ranging from three hours for a minifacial, shampoo, set, manicure, luncheon, and makeup lessons, to a full seven-hour plan. This all-day plan includes a gourmet lunch and the services of a personal shopper who shops for you while you grow more beautiful. The cost for the total day is $100.

There is even a Beauty Terrace Goodlooks Plan for Men. Men can have approximately two hours of skin treatment, hair analysis and conditioning, hairstyling, and manicure, all for $35. Of course, they have their treatments in absolute privacy.

3 Hair and Nails

COMBING THE COUNTRY FOR HAIRSTYLISTS

We Americans spend millions each year on hair care products and at beauty salons and yet the hair on our heads is dead. It cannot be revitalized or reborn. Although it is made of protein, it cannot have protein added to it. Hair can be damaged, however. Bleaching, coloring, having a permanent, straightening it, can all cause it to break, dry out, or shrivel and split. Some of the products used on hair can be hazardous to the rest of the body as well, and therefore you should patronize a hairdresser who is well trained and licensed. He or she should also be talented. Some hair stylists can take a scissors or rollers and, like artists, create a style that is both flattering and easy to care for. Others can make a mess.

The hair salons listed in this book are among the world's most famous. With fame, of course, prices go up. But just as in the world of high fashion, the styles filter down to the mass market where they are less extreme and less costly. If you wish to obtain a new hair style, look at photographs in the fashion magazines and in advertisements. When you see a style that you would like, take the picture to your hairdresser.

When you travel, consider, as part of your tour, making an appointment at one of the hair salons listed in the book. It may be not only a refreshing experience but a rewarding one. Since most beauticians engage in conversation with a great many customers, they usually learn the best places to shop and eat in the area.

HAIR SALONS

California

Beverly Hills Hotel Salon, 9641 Sunset Boulevard, Beverly Hills, California 90210, (213)278-2011. Jim Curtis, of this celebrity haven hotel, gave Suzanne Pleshette her award-winning coiffure; it "opens and frames the head, but doesn't distract from her face." Suzanne is a three-time winner of the annual Ten Best Coiffured Women award. Haircuts at the

Beverly Hills Hotel Salon are $15.00; a shampoo and set is $10.75; a permanent is $36.50 and up; coloring is $14.50 and up; a frosting is $20.00 to $25.00, and a manicure is $5.25.

Menage A Trois, 447 North Bedford, Beverly Hills, California 90210, (213)278-4430. Joel Israel is the man who gave Mary Tyler Moore her distinctive blunt haircut. For the past seven years or so, Mary has been coming to the salon for a set with hot rollers and a weekly conditioning; her hair is blow dried. Guy Richard of this studio gave Sandy Duncan, another TV star, her distinctive and functional hairstyle. This shop is a favorite of fashion magazine editors. A haircut costs $20.00; a shampoo and set, $20.00 with one of the owners and $12.50 with other operators; permanents, $35.00 to $80.00; coloring, $20.00 to $25.00; frosting, $60.00; and manicure, $5.00.

Jon Peters Salon, 1560 Ventura Boulevard, Encino, California 91316, (213) 981-7711. Also in Beverly Hills and Woodland Hills. Jon Peters is more of a romantic star than some of the famous Hollywood celebrities he has coiffed. Friend of Barbra Streisand and supposedly the model for the Warren Beatty character in the movie *Shampoo,* he is not so active in the hairdressing business right now, and he has sold the three salons bearing his name to Allen Edwards, the talented hair designer responsible for Farrah Fawcett's trend-setting hairstyle. Allen also tames the locks of such stars as Racquel Welch and Diana Ross. Allen Edwards maintains that "no two faces are alike; therefore, no two hairdos can be exactly alike," and every woman who walks into the salon expects—and gets— just what she wants: a pampered, unique experience, with a one-of-a-kind look.

Cuts by Allen are $30 the first time and $25 after that. Manicures are $5; pedicures, $12; and manicures with Juliette's paper wrap, $12. Porcelain nails are $45 a set. Regular hairstyling, wash, and blow dry prices range from $12 to $15, and color and tinting prices range from $20 to $50. A makeup lesson with Bobbe Joy, including eyebrow shaping, is $25; a makeup application is $20. The salon is always booked to full capacity. The spacious Beverly Hills salon has everything from a small coffee shop to a jewelry bar (with prices ranging from $17 to $1,000).

Vidal Sassoon, 405 North Rodeo, Beverly Hills, California 90210, (213)274-8791. Angelo of this smart salon is credited with the "long Isadora" for Toni Tennille. Before designing her haircut, he studied her bone structure, then scissor-cut "into her wavy hair" to add movement. A haircut is $25 to $36 at this shop. A shampoo and set ranges from $13 to $14, and permanents are $40 and up. Highlighting hair is $40 and up, and a pedicure is $12.

New York

Free Hairstyling by Experts, Hair Fashion Development Center, 666 Fifth Avenue, New York, New York 10019, (212)397-6580. This advanced hairstyling school uses about 300 models a week when in session. This makes it possible for you to have your hair restyled by top stylists for only a $3 service charge. Only licensed hairstylists attend the school to update their techniques and learn new fashion trends. The school is operated by Seligman and Latz, managers of beauty salons in fine department stores across the country.

Kenneth, 19 East 54th Street, New York, New York 10022, (212) PL2-1800. Kenneth burst into the headlines as Jackie Kennedy's hairdresser, but he has long been a favorite of the media. He is articulate and always quotable, as well as a skilled hairdresser. He has his own elegant town house between Fifth Avenue and Madison. He does not advertise his salon, but it is constantly filled with the world's most famous women, including Jackie Kennedy Onassis, the *Washington Post*'s Katherine Graham, Happy Rockefeller, Ethel Kennedy, and celebrities from fashion to front page. Mary Farr, one of Kenneth's top hairdressers, is very much in demand, and you cannot get an appointment with her unless you've had one before and have "influence."

Kenneth believes that his success comes from the fact that he has never been involved with any one specific look in hair. "Though I know I've been credited with creating the bouffant hairdo, I don't think I invented it or that anybody else did. It was merely an evolution of style." He says his favorite look for hair is clean, shiny, bouncy, soft, free, and healthy. It must look natural. Hair is basically a beautiful fabric, a marvelous material that can be glorious if it is treated with respect. But if it is forced to do something it was never meant to do, it is no longer hair, it is a mess. Hair should look like hair. It should be comfortable, something you can take care of yourself after you have left the salon. That is why Kenneth does not respond when he asks a woman how she wants her hair cut and she answers, "You do it." He wants to know about your life, your ability to take care of your hair, your image of yourself.

A haircut is $60 by Kenneth and $30 by his other stylists. Sets and blow drys are $10; straightening, $60 and up; scalp treatments, $35. Shading, frosting, streaking, and highlighting for a full head start at $70. A facial costs $30; makeup instruction and application costs $35.

Kenneth also offers a make-over day for $150. It includes scalp treatment, facial, shampoo, Kenneth's salon formula hair conditioner, cut, set or blow dry, cream manicure, pedicure, makeup instruction, brow arch, and lunch.

PUBLICATION

Kenneth's Complete Book on Hair, edited by Joan Rattner Heilman, editor. New York: Dell Publishing, 1974. The price is $1.25. Tells you how to set your own hair and how to care for your own hair.

Pierre-Michel Salon, 6 West 57th Street, New York, New York 10019, (212)753-3995. Co-owners Pierre Ouaknine and Michel Obadia are known for their excellent cutting and styling as well as their emphasis on "healthy hair." They feature the Rene Furterer System of organic hair products. Thomas of this salon often does the hair of sportscaster Phyllis George; he gives her an "unselfconscious, unlacquered creation." A haircut at this salon is $20.00; shampoo, $3.50; and blow dry, $10.00. Permanents are $35.00 to $60.00; frostings, $45.00 to $70.00; and coloring, $25.00 to $125.00. An hour's full-face makeup lesson is $20.00. The salon offers the Beauty Bash for $100.00; it includes the Rene Furterer hair treatments, restyling of hair, a facial and makeup with instructions, and a choice of ten Sculp-Nails or a manicure and pedicure.

Pennsylvania

Pierre and Carlo Di Roma, 106 South 13th Street, Philadelphia, Pennsylvania 19104, (215)735-0164. Carlo Cutrufello is co-owner with his brother, Pierre. According to one local newspaper, he has so much charm that "he could reduce the most dragonlike customer to pliant putty." He visits Paris twice a year, admires Sassoon greatly, but believes that Alexandre of Paris is the best. The two-level salon underwent a $20,000 renovation and is extremely popular with local models and ballet dancers. The price of a basic wash, cut, and blow dry is $20 to $25 if done by either Pierre or Carlo on a first visit and $18 after that. If another staff stylist does your hair, the price is $15.

Thunder, 110 South 19th Street, Philadelphia, Pennsylvania 19104, (215)563-2665. Bill Tomaccio named his shop after a beauty shop in Paris. There's a mirrored ceiling that reflects the natural wood floor, green plants soften the gleam of chrome, and it's generally a stunning place. Thunder provides, without charge, a glass of wine, neck massage, whirlpool foot bath, facial mask, and use of the selection of expensive perfumes on display at the receptionist's desk. As one newspaperwoman said, "About the only thing which isn't offered is a Nubian slave to wave a fan over your fevered brow, but if you mentioned it, they'd probably locate one somewhere." Tomaccio comes from a long line of barbers and hairdressers who emigrated from Foggia, in southern Italy. Among his customers are one of the nation's leading dermatologists, a famous male opera singer, and many female models. Men's haircuts are $14.00; women's, $16.00. All haircut prices include shampoo and blow dry. Permanents are $35.00; coloring, $12.50; frostings, $30.00 and up; and manicures, $3.50.

GETTING MORE HAIR

Hair has always had a great deal of psychological significance. First of all, it is highly visible and the only feature that we can easily change. It can be cut, curled, straightened, and dyed. For men, hairiness has long been associated with virility and strength. Remember what happened to Samson? It is not too different from what happens to a man today when he becomes bald. According to Dr. Robert Stolar, clinical professor of dermatology at Georgetown University in Washington, D.C., a man's image changes socially and professionally when he loses his hair. In order to compete in business, he is often forced to buy a wig or get a hair transplant.

The loss of hair can be even more devastating to a woman. It connotes desexualization. In fact, in the past, Orthodox Jewish women and nuns have had their heads shaved to demonstrate subservience and to put themselves sexually "off limits" to others. In modern times, some women's heads have been shaved as punishment for fraternizing with enemy soldiers.

The first known written medical record of a cure for baldness is the 4,000-year-old papyrus which recommended: "Take equal parts of the fat of a lion, a hippopotamus, a crocodile, a goose, a serpent and an ibex and apply liberally to the bald pate."

The average adult scalp has about 120,000 hairs. Blondes have about 140,000; redheads, about 90,000; and brunettes, about 110,000. Hair grows at a tremendous rate. The cells in the hair roots reproduce every twenty-four hours, sending forth a hair shaft that grows half an inch a month. Certain influences are known to slow down hair growth: radiation, very cold weather, certain diseases and infections, and various chemicals (among which are some used in treating cancer). During a lifetime (providing you don't become bald), you will produce about fifteen pounds of hair.

Hair grows in cycles. Many hairs grow for four or five years, enter a resting phase for about three months, and then fall out. After this, a completely new hair shaft is formed. Ordinarily, about 90 percent of the hairs are in the growing phase, and 10 percent are in the resting phase. Normally, about 25 to 100 hairs fall out each day. These are shed from follicles, the skin depressions containing hair roots. Such hairs are less firmly attached and are lost from combing, brushing, and shampooing. They are quickly replaced because the scalp grows new hairs every day. The rate of loss and replacement varies from person to person and from time to time in the same person. Only when the rate of hair loss exceeds the rate of new growth are thinness and balding a problem.

What upsets this careful balance? For the most common form of baldness, male-pattern baldness, there are three factors: sex, age, and heredity. For other forms of baldness, there are many causes. If the cause can be corrected, the hair may regrow.

"Hair today! Hair tomorrow, too!" is the cry of America's balding. They are rushing to barbershops and specialty salons to purchase hairpieces to replace their lost locks. Because most people associate balding with growing older, loss of hair can have a tremendous impact emotionally and financially because we live in a youth-oriented society. A man in his mid-thirties who wants to change jobs has a tough time. He must prove he is youthful and vigorous. Wearing a hairpiece or coloring gray hair is a practical way for a person to appear and feel young.

Fortunately, there are many things that can be done about baldness today. Before you do anything, you must have a dermatologist make an exact diagnosis of which of the many forms of baldness you have. Of course, if your father, grandfather, and uncles were all bald, you probably don't need someone to tell you the reason.

Here are some practical hints about taking care of your hair when you detect the beginning of baldness:

Don't brush too vigorously. Brushing is helpful up to a point, but too much can pull out even healthy hairs. Choose a brush that does not rip or tear out hairs with stiff bristles.

Massage stimulates circulation. Spread your fingers over your scalp with the thumbs above your ears. Rotate the fingers again and again. Then change the position of the hands, and repeat.

For thinness on top of the head, men can get away with a lower part and hair combed over the thinning area for a few years, and women can try an upswept hairdo.

For a widening part, change to a pompadour or change the location of the part.

Women can cover a receding forehead hairline with bangs.

If your head becomes shiny, you'll have to look for other ways of covering your scalp. If you still have some fine down (called *lanugo*), it may be possible in some cases to revive active hair growth.

See "Medical Treatment of Baldness" (see below) and "Hair Transplants" (page 164). If all else fails, a good hairpiece or wig that is properly fitted will serve as an excellent substitute for the missing hair.

Medical Treatment of Baldness

Edward Settel, M.D., Pilo-Genic Research Associates, Inc., 250 West 57th Street, New York, New York 10019, (212)246-2224. Dr. Settel has presented reports to national medical meetings about his pioneering work in treating baldness in thousands of persons. The key factor is the well-accepted dictum that *pattern baldness*, the most common kind, is inherited and caused by an imbalance in the male-female hormonal balance with an excess of androgen (male hormone). In his early work, this respected researcher utilized estrogen (female hormone) to counterbalance the male excess; however, because of the side effect that was encountered in 2 to 5 percent of the men (swelling of the breasts), Dr. Settel changed to a totally safe substitute, biotin. This coenzyme is a member of the vitamin B complex family and is totally safe. Dr. Settel has supplied his material to other doctors not only for their own hair but also for their patients who were beginning to go bald.

His preparations are known as Pilo-Genic cream, lotion, and shampoo; they are unique in that they utilize a miniemulsion, which is a vehicle that carries the biotin through the skin and delivers it to the dormant hair follicle, where it stimulates rapid and more luxuriant hair growth. It also stimulates dormant roots to revert to a growth stage again. The products are dispensed by doctors and trichologists who have been trained by Dr. Settel and are then qualified to dispense the products in their own cities.

The newest versions of the Pilo-Genic products contain from 0.125 to 1.0 percent biotin, amino acids, polymers, mild surfactants and detergents, and distilled water. Amino acids and nicotinic acid are added for special effects where advisable. Conditioners are utilized in the shampoo to prevent postshampoo tangling of the hair. They also add beauty, luster, and elasticity to the longer hairs. If the cream and/or lotion is applied daily by gentle massage, 90 percent of the men and women under treatment reported control of the excessive hair loss within six to eight weeks. Not only was the balding process stopped, but within four to five months new hairs were visible, and the texture of the thinner hairs improved, taking on a heavier appearance. (In a control group of fifty men who used a popular shampoo, there was no effect on hair loss after three months.) The shampoo is used three to seven times weekly.

With regard to new hair growth, researchers say that the younger the patient, the better the chance for success. The more live rootlets that are available, the more hairs can be stimulated to grow. Once the root atrophies, regrowth is impossible.

Pilo-Genic Research Associates, the parent company that sponsors the program worldwide, charges $60 for the first visit, which includes an indoctrination program, detailed history, closeup photography, and in-depth examination of the hair and scalp. The patient is taught the technique of administration, and a full month's supply given. Refills are available at $30. The refill plus a visit, which includes examination and closeup photography, is $40. Other listed treatment centers have their own fee schedule, but it is comparable to Pilo-Genic's.

Pilo-Genic Treatment Centers are now established in major communities across the United States, Canada, Australia, and London, England. In addition to the parent clinic in New York, these clinics are available.

ALABAMA
Pilo-Genic of Birmingham
Suite 116
1675 Montclair Road
Birmingham, Alabama 35210
(205)956-4430
Carmel Renda

ARIZONA
Dr. Abram Ber
Suite A
3134 North 7th Street
Phoenix, Arizona 85012
(602)279-3795

AUSTRALIA
Pilo-Genic of Australia
60 Kings Park Road
West Perth, Western Australia 6005
Jenny Burston, administrator

CALIFORNIA
Dr. Y. Y. Tang
345 West Portal Avenue
San Francisco, California 94127
(415)566-1000

Dr. J. La Barber
700 West Parr Avenue
Los Gatos, California 95030
(408)374-3303

Dr. Fred Kollwitz
1125 East 17th Street
Santa Ana, California 92705
(714)835-6767
      or
Suite 107
204 South Beverly Drive
Beverly Hills, California 90212
(213)274-1006

Dr. Robert Tantleff
Suite 215
9730 Wilshire Boulevard
Beverly Hills, California 90212
(213)274-8293

      or
6100 Ventura Boulevard
Encino, California 91436
(213)995-8995

Pilo-Genic of San Rafael
2400 Las Gallinas Avenue
San Rafael, California 94903
(415)479-7400
Dr. Eugene Pudberry

COLORADO
Dr. J. T. McGarry
501 West 5th Street
Florence, Colorado 81226
(303)784-6349

FLORIDA
Hair Health Centers
13957 N. W. 67th Avenue
Miami Lakes, Florida 33014
(305)558-5410
Dr. Alan Graubert
Dr. Edward Goldman

Dr. Jay Reese
5202 Busch Boulevard
Tampa, Florida 33617
(813)988-1171

GEORGIA
Pilo-Genic of Georgia
5640 Peachtree Ind. Boulevard
Atlanta, Georgia 30341
(404)455-6212
Dr. Hugh A. Hatfield

ILLINOIS
Pilo-Genic of Chicago
Suite 1628
30 North Michigan Avenue
Chicago, Illinois 60607
(312)346-1330
Joe Ollinger, Director

INDIANA
Dr. Louis Cusco

5506 E. 16th Street
Indianapolis, Indiana 46218
(317)356-7258

KENTUCKY
Pilo-Genic of Kentucky
Suite 1114
4010 Dupont Circle
Louisville, Kentucky 40207
(502)896-2446
Richard Tacon

MINNESOTA
Frommes of Minneapolis Co.
Suite 715
512 Nicollett Mall
Minneapolis, Minnesota 55402
(612)336-8236
Michael Cuniff, Jr.

MISSISSIPPI
Dr. H. G. McGehee
Highway 90 and Arnold Street
P.O. Box 48
Waveland, Mississippi 39576
(601)467-9281

MISSOURI
Pilo-Genic of St. Louis
Suite 102
Medical West Building
950 Francis Place
Saint Louis, Missouri 63117
(314)725-3055
Vernon Rose

MONTANA
Dr. James Kiley
Medical Arts Building
Kallispell, Montana 59901
(406)755-7700

NEVADA
Dr. Larry Robbins
3121 South Maryland Parkway
Las Vegas, Nevada 89109
(702)733-9800

NEW YORK
Pilo-Genic of Brooklyn
1924 East 29th Street
Brooklyn, New York 11229

(212)375-0678
Donald Hoyt

OHIO
Pilo-Genic of Columbus
2685 Sullivan Avenue
Columbus, Ohio 40204
(614)274-3483 or 274-3484
Braun Tacon

OKLAHOMA
Dr. Donald Graves
Cherokee Street
Wakita, Oklahoma 73771
(405)594-2292

OREGON
Dr. Andrew Slaski
3404 19th Avenue
Forest Grove, Oregon 97116
(503)357-4886

PENNSYLVANIA
Pilo-Genic of Philadelphia
Suite 500
1422 Chestnut Street
Philadelphia, Pennsylvania 19102
(215)568-0582
George Whiting

Professional Nutrients Inc.
R.D. #1 Overbrook Road
Valencia, Pennsylvania 16059
(412)963-8315
Dr. Murray Susser

George Whiting
406 Scranton Life Building
538 Spruce Street
Scranton, Pennsylvania 18503
(717)344-8537

PUERTO RICO
Jorge Perez, Director
B.S., M.S. Radio-biology
Santurce, Puerto Rice

RHODE ISLAND
Pilo-Genic of Providence
34 Arcade Building
Providence, Rhode Island 02903
(401)421-5589
George Hall

Dr. Neil Toback
33 School Street
Pawtucket, Rhode Island 02860
(401)728-6990

TEXAS

Dr. John McMasters
403 Madison Square Building
San Antonio, Texas 78215
(512)222-2147

Pilo-Genic of Dallas
1005 18th Street
Plano, Texas 75074
(214) 423-5660
Dr. Anna Bhuket

UTAH

Dr. Gary Crocker
2022 S. 1300 East
Salt Lake City, Utah 84105
(801)278-3152

WASHINGTON

Dr. Matthew White
Lakewood Professional Village
Suite 14
5900 100th St. S.W.
Tacoma, Washington 98499
(206)582-2141
(206)272-3166 (answering service)

WASHINGTON, D.C.

Donald Hoyt
3000 Connecticut Ave. N.W.
Washington, D.C. 20008
(202)234-0008

WEST VIRGINIA

Dr. A. Joseph Berlow
909 Central Union Building
Wheeling, West Virginia 26003
(304)233-1177

WISCONSIN

Pilo-Genic Hairworks
161 W. Wisconsin Ave.
Milwaukee, Wisconsin 53203
(414)271-7693
Dr. Herschel M. Schwartz

CANADA

Dr. Paul Desruisseau
1270 C.H. Ste. Foy
Quebec, GIS-2M6
(418)527-6267

Sandford Greenberg
Montreal, H3G-1W7
(514)488-3183

Pilo-Genic of Toronto
Suite 213
229 Younge Street
Toronto, Ontario
(416)362-3201
Floyd Orr

ENGLAND

Pilo-Genic of England
2 Pickwick Place
Harrow on the Hill
Middlesex, England
Ivan Graubert

ISRAEL

Dr. Elton Kilchevsky
2 Hanoter St.
Ramat-Hasharon, Israel

Hair Transplants

Should you have a hair transplant? The ideal time to begin the procedure is when you are just developing a bald spot. Then the doctor can take the plugs from where your hair is thick and cover the bare area. As you continue to bald, you can go back for repeated transplants so that no one will ever know you are balding.

Light-colored hair seems to blend better with the scalp, and fine hair lends itself best to the creation of a natural hairline. You also have to consider whether you can take the discomfort and the time to go through this long and tedious procedure.

Fees vary from $2 to $35 per plug; most doctors charge between $10 and $15. The complete hair transplant may involve several hundred plugs.

WHERE TO GO

Orentreich Medical Group, 909 Fifth Avenue, New York, New York 10021, (212)794-0800. Dr. Norman Orentreich, clinical associate professor of dermatology at New York University School of Medicine and the inventor of hair transplantation, compares the current situation in baldness to the state of astronautics five years before Neil Armstrong took his "giant step for mankind." He believes the medical world is on the brink of finding a way to prevent male pattern baldness and to reverse the condition where it exists.

The technique of transplanting full-thickness scalp punch grafts from the hairy area at the back of the individual's head to the bald area on the top of the head was first used for the treatment of baldness in 1954. Since then, millions of grafts have been transplanted and the donor hair has continued to grow in the recipient sites on the head of the original patient.

How is it done? The donor and recipient sites are cleaned with alcohol. The hair in the donor area is clipped with surgical scissors to the length of about 2 millimeters above the scalp surface. The donor and recipient areas are anesthetized. A special instrument removes a plug of hair-bearing skin from the donor site; this is then inserted in a similarily made hole in the bald area. The number of plugs cut during each treatment depends on the degree of baldness, the amount of tolerable cosmetic incapacitation, the amount of time available to complete the entire process, the time since the last procedure, and the number of grafts that can be successfully transplanted to any given area in one procedure. Ten to fifty plugs are usually transplanted at each visit. The site is allowed to heal for at least two weeks before additional grafting is performed in the same area. Other sites may be grafted the next day if care is taken not to disturb the previous grafts.

Dr. Orentreich tells his patients that it is impossible to predict in advance precisely how many hairs will appear in any given graft. The average is between six to twelve hairs per 4-millimeter graft, but a few patients average as few as three to four hairs, and some patients as many as fifteen to sixteen. He says that he and his colleagues have never encountered a patient who showed no growth whatsoever. Hair growth will not be seen for three months. The skin surface of the grafts usually blends with the surrounding scalp after a period of three to four months.

In some patients, however, the grafts may be a shade lighter than the sun-exposed bald scalp. The grafts are usually level with the surrounding scalp; occasionally, they are slightly elevated after healing. If that happens, they can be flattened with an electric needle without interfering with hair growth.

Dr. Orentreich says that hair redistribution with the punch graft technique is much more natural-looking than redistribution with the flap procedure or strip grafts because strip graft hair grows in backward. However, the doctors who use the strip graft technique claim this problem is easily overcome by styling.

See also "Medical Treatments of Baldness" (page 160), and "Wigs and Hairpieces" (see below.)

Strip Hair Transplants

Dr. Jose Juri, a plastic surgeon in Buenos Aires, devised the strip transplant operation ten years ago. A flap of scalp 3 to 4 centimeters wide and about 23 centimeters long is transplanted from the hairy part at the back of the head to the bald spot on top. As many as three flaps may be raised from the side and back of the head. The main benefits of the operation are its speed and the density of hair obtained. One flap is the equivalent of more than 300 punch grafts. The hair can be styled ten to fourteen days after the flap operation; whereas at least six months must elapse before hair grows long enough to be combed and styled after a punch graft procedure. The strip graft is done in three stages, the first two in the surgeon's office under local anesthesia, a week apart. The third stage of the procedure requires major surgery, with the patient under general anesthesia.

There are a handful of surgeons in Europe and the United States doing this procedure. Among the U.S. practioners, according to the *Journal of the American Medical Association* are Clyde Litton, M.D., D.D.S., a plastic surgeon in Washington, D.C., and Sheldon S. Kabaker, M.D., an otolaryngolgist in Oakland, California. Both surgeons visited Argentina to learn Dr. Juri's techniques. The cost of this surgery is high and includes hospitalization. To find the names of surgeons who may perform this operation near you, contact the American Academy of Facial Plastic and Reconstructive Surgery (see page 172).

Wigs and Hairpieces

Edith Imre Beauty Salon, 20 West 57th Street, New York, New York 10019, (212)247-4022. Edith Imre, a Hungarian cosmetologist, has contributed greatly to the design of fine-quality wigs and hairpieces. She worked with the classic wigmakers in France and Italy and applied

American methods, material, and ideas to the ancient art. She still makes regular trips to Europe, working with her suppliers on new designs and quality control. The Edith Imre line of wigs and fashion hairpieces is distributed through beauty salons in department stores throughout the country. She is continually researching new ways to help both men and women with their hair problems. She has developed a new technique for hair weaving and offers a specialized service for people who have lost their hair because of medical treatments. For whatever reason you buy a hairpiece, she advises that if you want a good match, purchase a wig or hairpiece at a salon where a trained consultant can give you professional advice. Your final selection should be observed both in direct sunlight and under indoor lighting, but the true color is the one seen in the daylight. Look at your hairpiece or wig not only from the front but also from the side and back. Full wigs can be of an entirely different color for fun or for a completely different appearance. Hairpieces must match as closely as possible because the natural hair is usually combed over them.

Mrs. Imre advises that if you buy a wig and do not like it or get sick of it, do not just put it in the closet, even if it was inexpensive. It can be taken back and adjusted. Wigs can be cut, restyled, and made larger or smaller.

How did Mrs. Imre specialize in hairpieces? She started in the depression, taking a job in a dress factory where she earned $12.50 a week. But in the evenings she made house calls in various boroughs of New York to give private skin treatments with her own concoctions. When she and her husband had saved enough money, they opened a small beauty parlor in mid-Manhattan. Before long, Hattie Carnegie, Fannie Hurst, Mary Livingston, and Princess Anne Bourbon, the grand duchess of Luxembourg, became their clients.

Today, she uses her New York salon as a laboratory for developing new wig designs for the older woman, and for men who need to improve their appearance. Unlike most salons, the Edith Imre salon does not have a policy against hiring older beauty operators. Mrs. Imre believes that "there is nothing like the gift of experience." She quotes the adage, "You can take no credit for beauty at sixteen, but if you are beautiful at sixty, it will be your own soul's doing."

Mrs. Imre feels that most men's hairpieces are badly executed. She said that even many TV performers have poorly done hairpieces that are obviously false. She buys real hair in Italy and still prefers it for falls and for the graying woman. However, she also uses a new synthetic she calls Imrelon that "rivals human hair for bounce and touch."

Here is Edith Imre's advice about choosing a wig: "Wigs are now available in more than twenty-four basic colors and can be subtly blended to suit your complexion. Consider the shape of your face. Is it oval, square, or pear-shaped? Do you have high cheekbones? The wig should take on the shape of your head and be comfortable. The wig should not be elaborate. It should have natural simplicity and be easy to manage. Some women look best with their own hair and need only a wiglet or hairpiece. The color should be matched very carefully to your own natural hair."

The Imre salon offers hair weaving. The piece consists of a base that is put over the bald spot and acts as a bridge. The hair is then woven into the true hair. Nothing goes through the scalp. With this method, hairpieces for both men and women can be washed, set, permanented, or colored without being removed from the head. This is of great psychological benefit to some customers.

The House of Anthony Izzo, 16 Ayers Lane, Little Silver, New Jersey 07739, (201)747-0004. Services in this hair replacement salon start with a short history of hair goods and a brief discussion of the pros and cons on all methods of hair replacement. They specialize in the designing of the lifelike hair replacement, and the piece is individually designed and fitted for the client. The designs range from a small filler-type replacement for the man or woman whose hair is just starting to fall out to the full replacement for the bald individual. They also make prosthetic replacements for someone with surgical or accidental scar tissue. Prices range from $200 to $900.

Upon request, Anthony will send you literature on his salon's services and a map showing you how to get to the salon. Services in the unisex facility cover a complete range of hair care for a wide range of ages, from a basic haircut to today's precision cut. Haircuts are from $7 to $30. Hair analysis and hair conditioning are priced from $7 to $20. Hair coloring and style-support permanents cost from $25 to $45. The charge for consultations on styles and appearance is $10, which can be applied toward services. Anthony's staff also services hair replacement clients, their haircuts, and care of their replacements. All consultations and services are performed in completely private rooms by appointment only.

GETTING RID OF TOO MUCH HAIR

For every person who wants more hair, there are probably ten who want to get rid of hair. In our culture, men are expected to be moderately hairy to demonstrate virility. But if they have a five o'clock shadow or are extremely hairy on their shoulders or have eyebrows that are too bushy, they often feel the need for hair removal. However, it is more common for women to try to get rid of the unwanted follicles. In our culture, females are not supposed to have hair on their face—except, of course, eyebrows and eyelashes—under their arms, or on their legs. Despite the exhortations of feminists to be natural, which includes hairy, women spend lots of money each year tweezing, scraping, bleaching, creaming, waxing, and electrocuting hair in an effort to defuzz themselves.

There is still only one permanent method of hair removal:

Electrolysis: In this method, a single electrified needle is inserted next to the hair follicle to kill the root. The electrocuted hair is then removed with a tweezer. This has to be done for each hair and can be very painful on certain areas, particularly on the lip just below the nose. It is a tedious procedure and expensive (from $6 to $18 for fifteen minutes). But it is also a permanent method of removal and has corrected many serious hair problems that were very damaging psychologically.

TEN TIPS FOR BEAUTIFUL DO-IT-YOURSELF NAILS

1. Do nail exercises daily: Tap nails gently on plastic countertops to stimulate the cuticle area and encourage growth. Typing on an electric typewriter is excellent for the nails.

2. Buff nails once a week with the heel of the hand or a buffer. Buffing is to nails what brushing is to hair; it increases circulation and stimulates growth. Buff in one direction (not back and forth) and for ten strokes *only*. Excess friction is not necessary.

3. Dry nails thoroughly before filing. Just as water dries out the skin, it contributes to brittle nails and breakage. Wear rubber gloves when cleaning with harsh detergents.

4. To keep nails and cuticles pliable, massage warm olive oil into the hands and nails once a week, and wear washable cotton gloves to bed.

5. Never peel off nail polish because doing that tears off the nails' natural layers. Remove polish gently, and try to give the oil treatment (tip 5) before reapplying polish the next day.

6. Apply a top coat to nails at least twice a week, especially across nail tips.

7. Dairy products (milk, yogurt, cheeses) are great nail strengtheners.

8. File nails in one direction only, not in a seesaw motion.

9. Nonprofessionals should use emery boards. Steel instruments can cause hangnails and injury if used incorrectly.

10. Never file into the side or corners of the nails. It weakens the entire nail surface.

Always remember that stress and tension (along with poor diet and excessive medication) can affect the appearance of one's nails. So relax, and take care of your nails.

4

Improving Your Appearance with Cosmetic Surgery

Why would you consider cosmetic surgery? Do you think changing a feature will automatically make you happier? Will it make you better-looking? Do you believe it could recement a relationship that is falling apart or save your job?

If the answer to any of those questions is yes, you may be disappointed with the results. Plastic surgeons cannot take a knife and turn back the clock, nor can they transform a wallflower into the belle of the ball. But, they *can* make you look better.

Cosmetic surgery was once looked on as vain and unnecessary. People who took advantage of it usually kept the fact a deep dark secret. Now Phyllis Diller and other celebrities have publicly proclaimed their face-lifts, and some individuals in the public eye undergo cosmetic surgery almost as routinely as they have their hair colored. And it is true that such operations may be a vocational and/or emotional necessity. As a matter of fact, in a study conducted by Johns Hopkins School of Medicine, psychiatrists and plastic surgeons found that a face-lift could actually improve a person's health. It was concluded that 70 percent of the patients who had undergone the procedure improved their life situations whether in terms of a job, a promotion or a raise, more harmonious marital relations, or new friendships. The psychiatrists concluded that these patients would not have bettered their situations to the same extent without surgery. Even the Internal Revenue Service has recognized the importance of such surgery. In 1976, it allowed cosmetic surgery to be deducted as a medical expense for the first time.

What is the definition of cosmetic surgery? According to the American Medical Association, it is "that surgery which is done to revise or change the texture, configuration, or relationship with contiguous structures of any feature of the human body which would be considered by the average, prudent observer to be within the broad range of 'normal' and acceptable variation for age and ethnic origin; and, in addition, is performed for a condition which is judged by competent medical opinion to be without potential for jeopardy to physical or mental health." What is your definition?

"If we could see ourselves as others see us," a plastic surgeon once said, "we plastic surgeons would be out of business." He explained that we don't really pay attention to how other people look. We are really concerned with how we look to ourselves. If we are satisfied with how we look, we are happy. If we are disatisfied, we are unhappy.

Most plastic surgery patients today are middle-aged and middle class. They find themselves caught in the trap of the youth culture and want to make themselves more acceptable at work and at play. They are not wrong in their quest. The fact is that in today's competitive marketplace, many salespeople and others who have to sell to the public, including show business personalities, must look young, even when they are not.

But there are some misconceptions about plastic surgery. Dr. James Stallings, director of the Plastic Surgery Institute of Des Moines, Iowa, corrects some of the myths.

There is a lot of pain involved. This is wrong. The nerves leading to the skin are temporarily interrupted during surgery.

All breast implants are alike. False. Dr. Stallings does not use the much-publicized silicone-filled implants; rather, he uses those inflated with saline solution. He believes the saline implants look and feel more natural.

Cosmetic surgery is just for women. Dr. Stallings says that the ratio of women to men is fifty-fifty in some regions and 30 percent men and 70 percent women in most.

A face-lift unnaturally changes facial features. This is not true when the lift is done with skill. It makes a person look eight to ten years younger.

Age is a barrier to plastic surgery. Dr. Stallings said he rebuilt the nose of a ninety-one-year-old cancer victim and has done breast implants on women in their sixties.

Prices for plastic surgery vary from area to area, and medical insurance may or may not pay for a procedure. But, as Dr. Stalling points out, saving for a face-lift is no different from saving for a car or something else you want.

Outside the United States, the place that has become legendary among the beautiful people who jet around the world and appear in the columns of *Vogue* and *Women's Wear Daily* and *Town and Country* is the clinic of Dr. Ivo Pitaguy in Rio de Janeiro. He performs half a dozen operations a day and is credited with making plastic surgery a badge of public honor among the smart set. Dr. Pitaguy says of his work, "Plastic surgery is the most creative branch of surgery. The plastic surgeon takes on a total committment to the patient. He combines physical surgery with the human soul in an effort to help the patient achieve his intimate well-being." There is an out-of-the-States place for the less wealthy who seek rebeautification in England.

In the United States, the centers of plastic surgery are mainly New York, Los Angeles, and Miami, although it is performed in every state in the Union. As Dr. Stallings points out, he has many patients from other cities who do not want their friends to know they underwent cosmetic surgery. "After all, who are you going to meet walking down a main street in downtown Des Moines?"

How should you select a plastic surgeon? First of all, proceed with extreme caution when you see advertisements. In the past year, a rash of cosmetic surgery centers blossomed when the government allowed plastic surgeons to advertise. These commercial centers, many of them not owned by physicians, are flourishing in California and spreading East. If your own family doctor or local medical society cannot recommend a plastic surgeon, or if you do not wish to ask them for a recommendation, write to either of the two professional societies that maintain strict rules for membership:

American Academy of Facial Plastic and Reconstructive Surgery, Inc.
Suite 4008
2800 Lake Shore Drive
Chicago, Illinois 60657
(312)644-2622

American Society of Plastic and Reconstructive Surgeons, Inc.
Suite 807
29 East Madison Street
Chicago, Illinois 60602
(312)641-0593

FACE-LIFT

In this procedure, incisions are made in the hairline at the temples and extended down in front of the ear, around the lobe, and up behind the ear, ending in the hair at the back of the head. The type of incision varies according to the surgeon's preference and the problem presented by the individual case. The skin of the face and neck is then undercut forward into the cheeks and downward and backward into the neck, thereby freeing it so that it can be drawn up, tightened, and smoothed. The excess is cut away. The skin edges are carefully tailored to fit smoothly into the scalp and around the ear. Local anesthesia is usually used because it is safer and causes less bleeding.

Face-lifting is a major dissecting of the skin and should be undertaken only by plastic surgeons or other individuals who have had specific training and experience in this procedure and have demonstrated their ability to perform with skill and safety. The operation takes about two hours on the table and costs from $3,000 to $4,000.

The so-called mini face-lift is done in a physician's office. Under local anesthesia, a triangle of skin is cut out above the temple hairline on both sides of the head. The edges of the skin are then sewn together, "lifting" the upper part of the face. The results may be more gratifying psychologically than physically because the skin can be only slightly tightened in the middle and upper thirds of the face.

WRINKLE REMOVAL

This procedure involves the use of a chemical face peel or dermabrasion and should be done only by a physician, although there are other operators in the field. A combination of chemical peel and dermabrasion or either procedure alone may be used with a face-lift.

Face Peel

A liquid chemical is applied, and the entire face is covered with a waterproof adhesive tape, leaving only the eyes, mouth, and nose exposed. After forty-eight hours the tape is peeled off under anesthetic, and the burned skin comes with it. The patient returns home in five to seven days, and in about twenty-eight days new skin is regenerated. The elasticity of the skin may be improved, with a decrease in freckles and in fine and moderate wrinkles. In the early weeks after treatment, improvement is dramatic because of the residual swelling of the skin. However, after three or four months, improvement is less marked, although still apparent. The best candidates are light-skinned people; those with darker skin tend to show the lines between their natural skin and the area bleached. There are also potential side effects such as scarring and dark spots. The average fee is $750 to $1,000.

Dermabrasion

The skin is frozen, and a rapidly rotating brush is stroked across the face to remove the upper layers of skin down to the level of the wrinkles. The procedure can also be done by hand, using sandpaper. Swelling and extensive crusting develop in the first twenty-four to forty hours; the crusts are shed in about two weeks, leaving the skin underneath a little more pink than before. The skin returns to a normal color within a few weeks.

Dermabrasion can be done in several sessions in a physician's office. The cost depends on several factors, including the size of the area to be treated. Generally, the price ranges from $500 to $2,000, depending on severity.

BREAST SURGERY

We are a nation of breast worshipers. If these containers of the mammary glands meant for breast-feeding babies are too large or too small or missing, a deep psychological problem may develop. These secondary sexual organs have come to mean femininity, thanks to modern advertising and magazines such as *Playboy* and *Penthouse*.

Breast Enlargement

This procedure is rapidly becoming one of the most requested plastic surgery procedures in the United States. It is estimated that more than 100,000 procedures have been performed within the past decade, and the number is increasing by 25 percent each year, despite the women's movement.

Safe surgical augmentation procedures have been developed that involve placing a plastic material filled with gelatinlike material or saline solution between the wall of the chest and the breast capsule. The surgery is performed under local or general anesthesia, frequently on an outpatient basis, and requires approximately one hour. There are three basic surgical approaches: In one approach, an inframammary incision is placed up from the crease approximately one inch to avoid detection of the scar on the breast when the woman is wearing a bikini. There is also the perioareolar approach, utilizing the junction of the skin and the nipple tissue from 3 o'clock to 9 o'clock on the bottom half. The newer transaxillary approach utilizes an under the arm incision with a pocket developed over the front rim of the chest muscle. This procedure leaves no scar on the breast and entails a very minimal recuperative period. Breast augmentation costs $500 to $2,500.

None of these three procedures impairs the ability to breast-feed. Should a tumor or cyst develop, it can be readily palpated by a physician and operated on as if there were no implant. Studies have shown that implants do not cause breast cancer. The implantation of the prosthesis does not produce the complications that resulted from the old liquid silicone injections such as migration of the plastic, cysts, tumors, pigmentations, and gangrene.

Despite the development and success of safe methods of implantation, there are still thousands of women who receive liquid silicone injections illegally. Why should this be the case? Some physicians are reluctant to refer women for breast augmentation; and unscrupulous persons may offer inexpensive, quick breast building with plastic injections (see page 175).

Breast Reconstruction

Some women feel they need breast augmentation for vocational or social reasons. If the implants make them happier, the procedure is valuable. In one case, however, implants are a miracle of modern medicine that may, unfortunately, be ignored. That is in the case where the breast has to be removed because of cancer.

Nearly 90,000 women a year lose breasts to mastectomy because of cancer, yet only a handful benefit from breast reconstruction. To have an almost perfect reconstruction, the surgeon doing the breast removal must save the nipple for later use, usually by implanting it in another part of the body. Then, after the tissue has healed, the plastic inserts are put in place, and the nipple is set in a normal setting. The woman's body image is restored. But this is more than merely a cosmetic measure. Many patients refuse surgery rather than face life "disfigured." Breast reconstruction has been done as early as four days after mastectomy and as late as twenty-five years after mastectomy. The ideal time seems to be four months after surgery, to give the tissue time to heal.

Breast Reduction

For breasts too large or sagging, the nipple is removed, the breast is partially amputated and contoured, and a new site is made for the nipple. The grafted nipple regains sensitivity and has a normal appearance, but the possibility of breast-feeding a child is, of course, eliminated. The cost ranges from $2,000 to $3,000, and there may be a visible scar.

SILICONE INJECTIONS

The injection of silicone under the skin to fill out wrinkles is done with a thin needle. There have been some poor results, including plastic floating around the body. These procedures are now being done on an experimental basis only by a few doctors with the permission of the U.S. Food and Drug Administration.

BIRTHMARKS

For vascular birthmarks (purplish discolorations) or small marks around the eyes or mouth, makeup is probably the best solution. If you have a prominent hairy wart or mark, a skin graft or excision may be possible, you will be left with a scar, but at least the color will be closer to your natural skin tone.

NASAL RECONSTRUCTION (Rhinoplasty)

In this procedure, the nose is reshaped, usually to improve appearance and sometimes to correct deformities from injury or to relieve nasal obstruction and sinus congestion. A rhinoplasty is a controlled fracture of the nose. The nose operation itself takes about one to two hours. Splints and a dressing are placed over the nose, and you are encouraged to be up and around soon after the operation to reduce swelling and promote healing. But real life is not like the movies; when the bandages come off, you do not see a brand-new, beautiful feature. It takes six to twelve months of healing to develop the new nose. In most cases, scarring takes place inside and is not visible; but in operations to narrow wide nostrils, it is necessary to leave tiny external scars at the base of the nostrils.

You will want to be sure not only that your surgeon is skilled but also that he does not give everyone the same nose. What looks good on someone else may look ridiculous on you. Your nose should literally fit your face. Ask to see photographs of former patients.

A rhinoplasty today costs from $500 to $2,500. If you have just the tip done the cost is $750 to $1,000.

EYELIDS

The operation called a *blepharoplasty* corrects excessive wrinkling and bagginess of the eyelids. The tendency to wrinkling and bagginess is usually hereditary and may occur quite early. Ordinarily, the scars of this operation are almost invisible because of the natural configuration of the area. The bags represent excess fat around the eye socket, bulging forward into the eyelids. These are corrected at the same time that the skin is tightened. Wrinkling and bagginess may be corrected independently of a face-lift or at the same time.

The skin around the eye is marked before surgery so that the surgeon knows exactly how much skin to remove. The procedure is performed at the hospital under local anesthesia and takes about an hour. An incision is made through the muscles around the eyes, and underlying excess fat is removed. An S-shaped section of skin is removed, and the remaining skin is pulled tight. Dressings are applied, and four days after surgery, they are removed, the stitches are taken out, and the patient is sent home. The cost ranges from $500 to $2,500.

EAR PINNING

Protruding or large, elephantlike ears can be pinned back. The plastic surgeon will carefully examine the ear and decide which of its components is giving it a protuberant look. Very often, the cause is an overgrowth of cartilage. Once this is removed, the ear will fall back closer to the head. The cost is $900 to $1,750.

CHIN IMPLANTS

The chin can accept foreign implants more readily than other parts of the body because softness is not required and the chin's covering is ample. Plastic surgery for a receding chin is called a *mentoplasty*. It is often combined with a nose operation to perfect the profile. The cost is from $250 to $1,000.

BUTTOCK REDUCTION

Having your seat reshaped will cost you about $2,000 to $3,000.

NECK-LIFT

Having your neck made svelte will cost you about $1,500.

TATTOO REMOVAL

Most tattoos were done when the individual was influenced by alcohol or youth. Tattoos are very difficult to remove. There are several available techniques. The cost is $800 to $2,000 depending upon size and location.

SCARS

Every operation leaves a scar, even a plastic surgery procedure. Sometimes, however, a large scar can be reduced or a depressed scar can be brought up to skin level, where it will be less noticeable. The direction of a scar can be changed so that it will fall in an existing wrinkle, and occasionally, a scar can be moved up into a hairy area, where it will not be noticed. The cost is $600 to $2,000 depending on size and location.

TOTAL BODY-LIFT OR BODY CONTOURING

You can have this radical procedure for about $10,000 to $20,000. You will have to spend about six hours on the operating table and take several weeks off from work, but it could be worth it. Body contouring is done by a few cosmetic surgeons who believe that people who want extensive plastic surgery purely for cosmetic reasons should have it—barring severe psychiatric problems, of course.

One forty-five-year-old widow who underwent body contouring not long ago had let herself go. She was very overweight and had a sagging chin, sagging breasts, and a large belly. During the operation, she had her face and breasts lifted, her abdominal muscles tightened, and the flab cut away. She had her thighs shaped, her buttocks sculptured, and her wrinkles smoothed. She was literally surgically reshaped. Did she benefit? Well, she is happily remarried.

If you want a breakdown of prices or just certain parts corrected, here is the current price range: arm-lift, $500 to $2,000; elbow-lift, $500 to $1,000; thigh-lift, $2,000 to $5,000; abdominoplasty, $2,000 to $4,500.

PUBLICATIONS

Plastic Surgery, American Academy of Facial Plastic and Reconstructive Surgery, Inc., Suite 4008, 2800 Lake Shore Drive, Chicago, Illinois 60657. This booklet explains the key elements of the art and answers the frequently asked questions. You can obtain a copy from one of the 1,400 physicians who belong to the academy or by writing to the address above.

Aesthetic-Cosmetic Surgery: What It Can and Cannot Do, American Medical Association Booklet, No. OP 208. AMA Publications 0006, P.O. Box 821, Monroe, Wisconsin 53566. The price is $.55. This booklet defines the various procedures and tells you what to expect from a plastic surgeon.

5 How to Improve Your Smile, Your Face, Your Personality, and Your Health by Having Your Teeth Fixed

The definition of a beautiful smile, according to a poetic Italian professor of dentistry, is when "the lips open like a curtain and reveal two rows of perfect teeth—the true expression of health, strength, and beauty." Your smile can be a wonderful gift, both for you and for those to whom you give it. But ill-shaped, rotted, or missing teeth can undermine not only your smile but also your self-confidence and can give others the wrong impression of your character. For example, if you self-consciously hide your mouth as you speak, people may think you are either untrustworthy or sarcastic. Remember Edgar Bergen's dumb dummy, Mortimer Snerd? And what does Jerry Lewis do when he wants to appear stupid? Buck teeth and/or crooked teeth make people think the possessor is unintelligent and unreliable.

Yet, how your teeth and mouth impress other people is still not so important as how you yourself feel about them. When you were a child, your oral cavity was your very center of being. You gained your first satisfaction with it; you learned to talk with it. When our teeth first erupted, they hurt. Nevertheless, you were soon pleased by what you could do with those new, built-in knives and forks. You could bite and chew and defend yourself. As an adult, you use your mouth for communicating, eating, and expressing affection. Is it any wonder, then, that your teeth and facial structure are vital to your emotional health? They are also important to your physical well-being and your social and business relationships.

ORTHODONTICS

How do you feel about your teeth? Are they straight? Do you have an overbite?

Of course, not everyone sees the need for having "abnormal" teeth fixed, according to orthodontist and author Dr. Jay Weiss of Caldwell, New Jersey. He points out that actress Ali McGraw stoutly refuses to have her "severely rotated upper incisors" straightened. She likes them that way. He says that actress Sandy Dennis (like Gene Tierney before her) is afflicted with buck teeth, which evidently haven't hurt her career. Eleanor Roosevelt, the former First Lady, had a classical protrusion of both jaws, which didn't stop her from being one of the most popular personalities of her day. And yet, one can't help wondering whether Mrs. Roosevelt would have been saved a lot of pain if she had been provided with orthodontic care as a child.

Dr. Weiss points out that for many people, even more minor problems prove to be emotionally crippling. When such defects are corrected, there may be a startling rise in self-esteem, with a corresponding weight loss, a new interest in clothes and general appearance, and improvement in grades in school or achievement at work.

Fortunately, it is never too late to have your teeth and associated facial structures improved. Although it is best to have early treatment, more and more adults are having dental irregularities corrected with highly satisfactory results. In fact, one out of every ten orthodontic patients today is an adult. Adults who seek the services of an orthodontist are highly motivated and thus are most likely to cooperate and to complete their treatment rapidly.

Orthodontics is the special area of dentistry that involves the diagnosis, prevention, and treatment of dental and facial irregularities. The American Association of Orthodontists maintains that no adult is too old for orthodontia as long as there is sufficient bone for tooth movement. In fact, recent findings show that the upper jaw does not completely unite with the frontal bone of the skull until after the age of seventy. Therefore, it is possible to treat patients with protrusion of the upper jaw (maxilla) and other related disfigurements well into the upper decades.

It has been estimated that as many as 50 percent of American children either require or will require orthodontic care. Unfortunately, a lot of them will not get it, although more are receiving treatment today than ever before. Untreated orthodontic problems may result in harmful effects on the general health of the patient, including speech defects, psychological and emotional disorders, and often undetermined personality influences that result in the failure of the individual to reach otherwise attainable social or vocational goals. If left untreated, malocclusion may cause tooth decay, loss of teeth, diseased gums, bone destruction, and jaw joint problems. Therefore, the increased cost of dental care for the untreated malocclusion, whether for a child or for an adult, may far exceed the cost of orthodontic treatment.

What causes irregular teeth or facial disharmonies? Many orthodontic problems are inherited. These include crowding, spacing, protrusion, retrusion, extra teeth, and missing teeth. Acquired causes include thumb-sucking or finger sucking, lip habits, mouth breathing, abnormal swallowing, dental neglect resulting in the loss of teeth, enlarged tonsils and adenoids, early loss or prolonged retention of baby teeth, loss of permanent teeth, accidents, and certain diseases and dietary deficiencies.

Selecting an Orthodontist

Usually, a family dentist will refer you to a local specialist. Membership in the American Association of Orthodontists assures you that an orthodontist has met certain minimal standards of training, education, and experience. If you cannot find an orthodontist near you, write to

American Association of Orthodontists
7477 Delmar Boulevard, Saint Louis, Missouri 61630

You will be referred to a local orthodontic society or to several orthodontists near you.

Initial Appointments

The orthdontist usually charges a consultation fee for the initial examination. At this appointment, he or she will advise you about the severity of the malocclusion and the needed treatment.

If you agree to begin treatment, additional diagnostic records will be required, including X rays, photographs, and plaster models of your teeth. This may be part of the initial appointment, or it may be done at a second appointment specifically for this purpose. Following a thorough study of the diagnostic data, the orthodontist will give his/her recommendations to you. This evaluation will include an assessment of the length of treatment, a description of the techniques to be used, and the cooperation required in following instructions. There is usually a separate fee for diagnosis, which includes the case presentation.

Fees

Factors that enter into the fee consideration include the complexity of the problem, the estimated treatment time, the type of appliance to be used, the frequency of appliance changes, and the finishing and retention procedures. Fees vary from minimal for simple procedures to $1,500 or more for complex full-treatment programs. Generally, an initial amount is due when treatment is started, and the balance is divided into installments.

Treatment Time

The length of treatment required for the average full-treatment case will vary considerably depending on your body's response to orthodontic procedures, your cooperation, and the complexity of your problem. In general, it takes fifteen to thirty months. Difficult cases will require more time; simple procedures, less time.

Extraction

In some cases, it is necessary to remove certain teeth as part of treatment. This may be necessary to assure sufficient space for the remaining teeth or to permit desirable changes in facial appearance.

Surgical Orthodontics

In cases of extreme facial disharmony, which are rare, it is sometimes necessary to combine surgery with orthodontics to produce an acceptable result. Usually, the orthodontist will make the diagnostic recommendations and develop the treatment plan in conjunction with an oral or plastic surgeon.

New Devices

Recent aesthetic breakthroughs have eliminated the need for unattractive metal bands and, with them, much of the discomfort associated with aligning and straightening teeth. New tooth-colored plastic appliances and tooth-colored wires make it possible for adult patients to wear practically unnoticeable appliances. Some appliances may be removable, so that they can be taken out on important business or social occasions.

PUBLICATION

There's Still Time, American Association of Orthodontists, 7477 Delmar Boulevard, Saint Louis, Missouri 63130. This booklet gives you information about orthodontics for adults. It is free upon request.

COSMETIC DENTISTRY

All dentistry is cosmetic because it improves your appearance as well as your health. But sometimes there is a strictly psychological need to improve the appearance of the mouth and smile. A variety of dentists practice the art of aesthetic dentistry. Once, only women were concerned with such procedures; but today, men are equally interested in the cosmetic improvement of their natural teeth.

Here are some of the things dentistry can do to improve the way your teeth look.

Aesthetic Recontouring

A dramatic and instant change can be made with this technique. A dentist can file and shape your teeth if they are uneven. He or she can put a veneer on the teeth, filling in wide spaces, thickening or lengthening teeth. The veneer is painted on the teeth and then permanently hardened with an ultraviolet light. It can be used for chipped and broken teeth or for patients with irregular or malaligned and crowded teeth.

Diagnostic casts and X rays of all teeth become necessary when there is extensive work to be done. Teeth may be marked with colored pencils, and anesthesia may or may not be necessary. Diamond stones with a water-spray attachment are used for gross tooth restructuring. The patient is handed a mirror, and his/her opinion is solicited throughout the procedure. Moving from one tooth to another while reshaping prevents irritation to any one tooth as a result of friction heat. Teeth may feel different to your tongue when changed, but this soon goes away.

Versatile new dental materials called *composite resins* are used in a variety of cosmetic restorative procedures. They can match the color and restore the function and appearance of damaged, decayed, or accidentally fractured teeth. They can fill in gaps or patch chipped teeth. They are best suited for use in the front of the mouth, where appearance is most important and where the teeth are not subjected to the tremendous wearing forces sustained by teeth in the rear of the mouth. Metals are sturdier for use on rear teeth. The composite resins have a great advantage because they can be applied instantly, they do not disturb the gum tissues around the tooth, and they do not require anesthesia. They can also be used on children and on adults whose physical health might preclude other procedures. The resins are mixed in a puttylike solution and painted on with a brush, shaped with a sculpting tool, and then hardened with an ultraviolet-light ray gun.

Whiteners

Sometimes a tooth turns dark or yellow. This may be the result of injury, root canal work, cigarettes, or antibiotic-produced or other stains, or just too many brushings with an abrasive toothpaste. There are bleaches that can be applied through a tiny hole drilled in the tooth. The strong solution is injected into the structure and bleaches it to a lighter color. Another technique involves painting the tooth with the new composite resins; an appropriate shade can be selected and applied as a veneer.

PREVENTIVE DENTISTRY

Today's dentists can show you how to take care of your teeth and gums so that tooth decay and gum disease can be nearly eliminated. Therefore, it is important for you to make a preventive appointment with your dentist *now*.

If you want the name of a qualified dentist, or if you want to know what you should expect from your dentist, write:

American Dental Association
211 East Chicago Avenue.
Chicago, Illinois 60611

If you cannot find your local dental society in the phone book or through the county health department, contact the association for referral to a qualified dentist near you.

Even with the best of care, problems sometimes occur. But even in serious situations, the loss of a tooth can be prevented. Here are some common problems with their solutions.

Root Canal

The pulp, or "nerve" of your tooth may be dead or dying as a result of an infection caused by deep decay or because of a bump you may not even have noticed. The death of the pulp can occur without a twinge, or it can be excruciatingly painful. An abcess may form around the tooth's root.

In the past, teeth that were infected were immediately removed. Today, endodontists can save most teeth if you visit them in time. They will use X rays and an electrical tester (if necessary) to locate the exact cause of the problem. Then they remove the dead or inflamed pulp and fill the resulting cavity with a permanent filler. Even when the root of the tooth and the surrounding gum become damaged because of the death of the tooth, the tooth can still be saved by a surgical procedure called *root resection* or *amputation*. There will still be a sufficient supply of blood from the gum to keep the tooth firmly anchored, but it may be more brittle than a normal tooth, and it may change color, necessitating capping (see page 184), or painting (see above). The cost for endodontic work ranges from $75 to $200 per tooth, depending on the procedures necessary.

Fractures

In the past, failure to diagnose and treat a tooth with a tiny fracture of the dentin resulted in loss of the tooth as the crack extended into the pulp or root of the tooth. A careful examination with X rays, plus a thorough history, now makes it possible to make an early diagnosis and to save the tooth. Successful treatment depends on locating the fracture before it is irreversible and by tying the entire crown of the tooth into a single unit so that pressure on one area of the tooth will not allow the crown to flex, causing an extension of the fracture.

Prosthodontics

Prosthodontics is the special area of dentistry concerned with the replacement of missing natural teeth and other mouth and jaw structures. The loss of teeth gives humans a feeling of helplessness, and with good reason. When teeth are not replaced, it is impossible to chew properly, and the face is disfigured. Therefore, everything should be done to save the teeth. Replacements are never as good as the real thing. However, new dental restorative material can provide fast, temporary replacement for missing teeth.

Caps

A porcelain jacket, or crown, provides the ultimate in aesthetic restoration. Capping is an instant way of correcting an unsightly tooth. It is not so strong as the real tooth, but it may be more even and more beautiful. Most actors and actresses have their teeth capped to make their smiles bright and even. But not all caps should look alike. There has to be proper shade selection to match the other teeth and to look natural in the mouth. When a crown, or jacket, is put on a tooth, the enamel and dentin must be filed away, to be replaced with porcelain. The cost ranges from $200 to $500 per tooth, so it can be quite expensive to have all your teeth done.

Crooked Gums

There are a few dentists who specialize in recontouring gums. Some people who believe they need caps or extensive orthodontia really need a reshaping of their gum tissue into even arches of appropriate height. X rays are taken so that the dentist can determine just how much gum to take away. Then minute amounts of tissue are removed by electrosurgery each time. Local anesthesia is used. The patient experiences little pain and bleeding afterward, and the healing period takes about two weeks. Fees for electrosurgery range from $30 to $50 per tooth.

Tooth Implanting

Never throw away a tooth that has been knocked out. Pack it in ice, and hurry to a dentist. Often, the tooth can be reimplanted. Reimplantation of children's teeth is almost always successful; reimplantation of adult teeth is successful more than half the time. Teeth have been successfully reimplanted twenty-four hours after an accident, but the preferred time is twenty to thirty minutes. Current experiments are now going on with implanting plastic or real "bank" teeth with some success.

Total Dentures

Sometimes, usually because of gum disease, all an individual's teeth have to be removed, and he or she needs a full set of dentures. More than 20 million Americans wear complete upper and lower dentures. As in the case of a prosthesis, the set should mimic the real teeth as closely as possible. If you need complete dentures, your dentist should try to match the color, size, and shape of the teeth to your face.

Just because you have a full set of dentures, that does not mean that you will never need a dentist again. As you age, the shape of the bone in your mouth changes, and your dentures may need adjustment. The dentist will also watch for any underlying problem with the gum tissue.

Gritting and Grinding Your Teeth

If you grit or clench your teeth to relieve tension, you can damage them. Approximately one out of every five Americans suffers from some form of *bruxism*. Although some tooth grinders experience no adverse physical effects from their habit, others suffer severe damage to their teeth and supporting structures. Frequently, excruciating pain will radiate from the hinge joint of the jaw.

Treatments include splints and biofeedback to prevent clenching. An advantage of the biofeedback technique is that you learn to control muscle tension without medication or such prosthetic devices as tooth guards or splints. The biofeedback technique (see page 112) teaches you to relax the masticatory muscles that control jaw movement.

PUBLICATION

How to Become a Wise Dental Consumer, Bureau of Dental Health Education, American Dental Association, 211 East Chicago Avenue, Chicago, Illinois 60611. This booklet tells you how to choose a dentist and how to reduce your dental bill and gives advice about toothbrushes and cleaning aids.

6 Dress More Successfully

One of the easiest ways to improve the image you present to the world is to improve the way you dress. Your clothes reveal the way you feel about yourself and the world around you. Sometimes they are misread, but not often. For instance, picture a housewife, a farmer, a pimp, a top executive. Right away, you have a mental image of the way they dress.

But the reasons we choose our wardrobe styles are not quite that clear. Dr. Helen Wagenhiem, clinical associate professor in psychiatry at Temple University Medical Center in Philadelphia, observed in *Medical Aspects of Human Sexuality*, a medical magazine: "Women choose their style of dress for numerous, sometimes complex reasons. While many people view the question of women's dress exclusively in terms of pleasing men or other women, this is oversimplification." She pointed out, for instance, that women often unconsciously wear red at the time of their menstrual period. Some women choose their clothing primarily hoping to attract men, but such women are rarer than most people imagine. "There are women who deemphasize their sexual attributes by their manner of dress because of their fears of normal sexuality. There are some women who buy only the clothing that will meet with their husband's approval, but again there are fewer than one might imagine. There are some women who dress hoping to gain the approval of other women, because they are unsure of being accepted generally. However, these are specific surface manifestations of deeper, unconscious motivations that are also frequently reflected in other areas of the woman's behavior." Among those unconscious motivations in choosing clothes, Dr. Wagenhiem cites:

An identification with the infantile role. The woman wears clothing too young for her years.

A rejection of identification with her mother. A large number of women go to great lengths to deny or reject any identification with their mothers in the matter of dress.

Women with low self-esteem pay little attention to their clothing as well as to other aspects of their appearance and grooming.

Narcissistic women may invest inordinate amounts of time, energy, and thought and even one-third or more of their husbands' income in their attire. (Unconsciously, the careless dresser and the narcissist may be closely related, in effect showing the two sides of the same coin.)

As for men, Dr. John F. Cuber, professor of sociology at Ohio State University, Columbus, said in the same issue of *Medical Aspects of Human Sexuality* that today's young man is almost as free in his styles and choices as a woman is and that the question might just as well be put: "Do they dress to please each other?" And if they don't, does anybody care? In fact, their styles and colors are often interchangeable, leading to what has been called an *androgynous blending*. Dr. Cuber believes that there is a trend toward dressing to please oneself, to express one's own personality, to facilitate one's own activities and style of life.

One person who does not think that casual and similar dressing is good is Kenneth Battelle, who is known by his first name, Kenneth. Through the doors of his midtown salon pass some of the world's most famous and fabulous women: Happy Rockefeller, Jackie Onassis, Ethel Kennedy, Katherine Graham of the *Washington Post*, and the editors of most of the fashion magazines. He is widely quoted as a fashion authority. He believes we are in a transitional time and that it is being spearheaded by a kind of uniform. "I heard a man in a London hotel who was paying $125 a day arguing because they wouldn't let him have tea in his Levi's. There are no rules in fashion anymore. Business regulations about dress have been relaxed, and people can wear anything. But informal does not necessarily mean comfortable. Pants that are too tight are uncomfortable, and so are boots in the summertime."

Kenneth noted that some young people have never worn anything but jeans, even though they are now in the professional or business world. He concluded rather wistfully, "I don't want to live in a drip-dry world."

What led to the popularity of denim, formerly a workman's material? Woodstock and the 1960s brought it to the fore among young people. Then Nelson Rockefeller was photographed in blue jeans, then Bing Crosby, and soon it became acceptable for older people to wear them. The designers began to use denim in fashion, and now even bankers allow tellers to wear denim to work.

Fashion designers and fashion editors can indeed make many of us accept new ways of looking at styles, but whether we follow fashion or not, we project an image of ourselves with our clothes. Do your clothes project the image you *wish* to project? If not, what can you do to improve matters?

Here are some experts who can give you advice on clothing and your image.

Amelia Fatt, Personal Fashion Consultant, 16 West 16th Street, New York, New York 10011, (212)PL7-6300. A skilled image maker, Amelia can transform a college girl into a successful businesswoman or a suburban housewife into the very model of Madison Avenue. The first step in her service is an at-home consultation. Both of you weed through the clothes closet; you try on your favorites, and Amelia takes stock.

After discussing your color preferences, taking measurements, flipping through fashion magazines, and determining what your business or social life demands in the way of clothes, Amelia sets out for the stores, doing the legwork by having clothes put aside for you to see. Then she takes you on a shopping expedition to try on the clothes.

Amelia, who has a background in fashion editing and an eye for color and design, says she sometimes would like to start from scratch when she sees her clients' wardrobes but understands that most women are cautious about totally changing their looks. She sees many women who are insecure about their appearance, particularly about their taste in clothes, but she also sees many women with good taste who hate to shop or have no time. She will go so far as to chart everything in a wardrobe, specifying exactly what goes with what if a woman feels anxious about coordinating her clothes.

Most of Amelia Fatt's customers are well-to-do New Yorkers. Many are business or professional women working on Wall Street, in law offices, or on Madison Avenue, where appearance is important; others want to look their best for a more private life. All are seeking new, chic images.

The at-home consultation costs $50. If Amelia visits stores to select clothes for your approval, her fee is $75. Shopping tours with Amelia cost $30 per hour.

Caroline Leonetti, Ltd., 6526 Sunset Boulevard, Hollywood, California 90028, (213)462-2345. For more than thirty years, Caroline Leonetti and her staff have taught charm to thousands of women of all ages, including numerous Hollywood stars and many television personalities and high-fashion models. Today, Caroline Leonetti is actually a conglomerate of image services. The school is coeducational, and the original program, based on self-analysis and beauty care, has been expanded in concept while retaining its guiding philosophy of personal discovery and self-image. Courses and programs are individually tailored to fit your personal needs, budget, and time schedule. Your course can be as brief as eight weeks or as comprehensive as one year of various workshops.

To begin with, there is the Basic Course (for women only): Caroline believes that your face is a mirror that constantly reflects the inner you. Therefore, your personal instructor will teach you how to acquire and maintain this outer image. You will learn how to have a healthful skin through a simple but scientific skin-care program. An individual facial analysis is followed by a study in skin care and the art of applying the makeup that will cosmetically enhance your individual appearance to its fullest potential. Another important segment is devoted to learning how to key fashion trends to your individual needs and to get the most of your fashion dollars. The course also includes an introduction to charm, poise, inner beauty, personality projection, speech analysis, voice, diction, conversation, etiquette, entertaining, and interview techniques. This is a forty-eight-hour, twelve- to sixteen-week course; $330.

More specialized courses include Model's Workshops for Men and Women, Basic Radio/TV Workshops for Men and Women, and Advanced Radio/TV Workshops. Each twenty-four-hour course costs $165.

The Male Image Workshop teaches participants how to improve personal grooming, wardrobe, manners, speech, and written communications. This comprehensive course is designed for modern men who are spending more money on clothes and grooming aids than ever before and who recognize the importance of "total image" in today's competitive world. The course includes:

Personal grooming and skin care: You learn the basics of a vigorous, healthy-looking complexion and hairstyles created to fit your individual needs.

Wardrobe: Personal analysis is made of your stature and coloring. You learn how to select contemporary wardrobe choices and color coordination and how these factors affect your total look and wallet.

Body language: Your body coordination affects your poise and confidence. You learn how to develop a confident image through your body language, including how to stand, sit, walk, enter a room, and shake hands.

Etiquette: You study the everyday manners that are prerequisites for successful personal and business relationships.

Speech: You practice exercises that are designed to improve diction, to help soften regional accents, and to aid you in freeing yourself of affectation. At the same time you learn to develop the art of expressing yourself easily and clearly.

Letter communication: You learn the proper choice of stationery and preparation of your résumé. Your résumé offers an excellent opportunity for you to project your individual style and personality. You learn how your letter-writing techniques can create a right or wrong impression and how the right résumé can result in personal interviews.

The fee is $165 for twenty-four hours of instruction. This course is a prerequisite for modeling, photography, and TV workshops for men.

Upon completion of the Basic, Modeling, and Photography courses, the faculty recommends a select number of exceptional students, male and female, for the LTD training program, a system of graduate training to bridge the gap between student and professional and to promote and establish careers in all facets of the fashion world.

Basic boutique: Established in 1972 by Margo Leonetti, Caroline's daughter, this is an extra service for students and for you if you are interested in the business of beauty. The boutique was designed to be an extension of the school training, by offering individual guidance, analysis, and coordination advice by specially trained consultants in makeup, clothes and face design. Makeup and clothes are sold in the boutique.

Beauty clinic: You can visit the boutique's beauty clinic just for a complimentary half-hour individual clinic. A specially trained expert will teach you personalized skin-care and makeup techniques.

The Leonetti lecture program provides fashion and beauty career-oriented lectures by Leonetti staff for business, school, or club programming.

New Image, Emily Cho, 663 Fifth Ave., New York, New York 10022, (212) 757-3794. Emily Cho, one of the leading personal image consultants, began her service in 1971 and now has more than 300 clients. She has great empathy for today's women, who are going through many transitions in their lives and need a professional eye to clarify who they are image-wise—women from out of town, women who have become lazy and have lost their clothing identity, women executives who know the importance of presentation and yet just don't have the time to put themselves together.

After an initial consultation in which budget, personality, and life-style are discussed, Ms. Cho scouts the stores before your shopping date and reserves masses of specifically selected clothes for you to then choose from. The following day she acts as fashion advisor, confidante, and a firm but understanding friend, helping you to select an entire season's wardrobe, while discovering who you are and how you want the world to see you.

Her fees are $50 for the initial consultation, $75 for the research shopping, and $50 an hour for shopping with you.

BY MAIL

Emily Cho Inc., P.O. Box 1594, Cathedral Station, New York, New York 10025. You send in $24.95 and receive a questionnaire which you fill out and reveal your figure type, personality, and life-style. You send it back and then receive a kit with a personalized wardrobe plan totally illustrated just for you.

PUBLICATION

Looking Terrific, Emily Cho and Linda Grover. New York: G. P. Putnam, 1978. Hardcover, $10.95; softcover (Ballantine, 1979), $4.95. A book filled with advice about how to shop and put together a wardrobe without taking a loan from a bank or being untrue to your own style.

PART III

Improving Your Mental Health

If you are eager and willing to improve your body through dieting, health checkups, beauty treatments, and exercise, why should you be reluctant to improve your emotional functioning? In a physical checkup, a physician may find a physical condition early enough to prevent a serious disability. In a mental health checkup, a psychotherapist may find an emotional problem early enough to prevent a serious disability.

None of us feels at ease all the time. But how do you know when the way you cope with the world emotionally could use improvement?

The National Institute of Mental Health says that mental health has to do with the way you adjust to life, with your ability to stay on top of it, even when the going is rough. Good mental health involves both the way you think and act and your relationships with others. Of course, no one is entirely worry-free. Things happen that can cause you to become instantly angry, anxious, and/or fearful. But the important thing, according to the institute, is that the anger and fear and distrust are only temporary and that you do not become bogged down in such feelings.

If you are mentally at ease, you can cope with life, even when it isn't easy and you have to struggle. If you are mentally unhealthy, bad things are exaggerated and seen as bigger than life. You lose your grip; problems that can be conquered by a healthy person become too much for you. The joys that you should be experiencing are always replaced by grimness.

When should you seek help?

When you have undue, prolonged anxiety, an uneasiness out of proportion to any reason or cause you can identify.

When you are so depressed that you withdraw from friends, loved ones, your occupation, your hobby. Everyone gets depressed periodically, but when you are so down in the dumps that you lose your confidence and feel constantly pessimistic and helpless, you need help.

When you are so tense that you have physical symptoms such as headaches or nausea. When pains are exaggerated or you have a general feeling of illness, you need help.

When you habitually fall below your potential. If you are adequately equipped to do something well, but you are not doing so, the possibility of an emotional problem should be considered.

When you feel compelled to do things in a rigid, programmed way.

When you have developed a personality pattern that causes you to have poor judgment and that affects your relationships with others, you could use help.

It is *never* too late to change. Help *is* available.

If you have a problem that is so severe that you can no longer function socially or vocationally, you need expert referral. Ask your family physician, local medical society, or one of the agencies listed in this section for the name of a psychiatrist or psychiatric clinic. In the case of serious, incapacitating mental illness, you need the services of a psychiatrist, who can offer hospitalization and medications if necessary.

Unfortunately, there is still prejudice about seeking such help. As the late movie tycoon Samuel Goldwyn allegedly said, "Anyone who goes to a psychiatrist should have his head examined."

It is vital to look beyond such prejudice and evaluate the matter clearly. Ask yourself what the difference is between going to a physician and receiving therapy for an ulcer or a migraine or even a heart attack and going to a physician and receiving therapy for the underlying emotional disorder that caused the physical symptoms in the first place? Our society still believes it is all right to suffer a physical pain, but an emotional one means that you are weak and should be ashamed. Yet one way to improve your whole life greatly and perhaps even lengthen your life is to get rid of emotional pains.

There are many ways to do this. For the less serious emotional problems such as mild anxiety, shyness, mild depression, tension, or discontentment, you will find there are many coping techniques discussed here. Often, several techniques can be used effectively to deal with a given problem. Dr. Ernest Hilgard of Stanford University, an expert in the field of hypnosis research, explains that with transcendental meditation, biofeedback, or hypnosis, you can alter the temperature of your hands and make one warmer than the other. "The locus of control may be different. You may feed your body different signals, but the result is the same." Furthermore, he maintains, many of the techniques of treating emotional problems have two things in common: suggestibility and control.

Even method acting, Dr. Hilgard points out, involves an actor thinking about something in his or her past that made him/her happy or sad in order to put himself/herself in the appropriate mood for the part that he/she is playing. (Method acting is very similar to the mind trips used in behavior therapy. See page 94.) Biofeedback allows you to control previously uncontrollable body processes by observing visible records of the workings of internal organs. Transcendental meditation is a state of learned relaxation. Hypnosis involves tenacious concentration.

Some techniques work for one type of person, and some work for another. Dr. Hilgard points out that scientists, particularly engineers, are difficult to hypnotize because they are more in touch with reality; whereas humanistic persons such as actors and writers are very easy to hypnotize.

Hypnosis and transcendental meditation are actually ancient arts. Biofeedback and method acting are relatively new. Novel therapies are introduced all the time. They spring up like fast-food chains. Celebrities recount their great experiences with a particular technique, and the leader becomes a guru. Then the system fades from fashion, a new one takes its place, and the cycle is repeated. There are actually people who are pop psychotherapy freaks, going from one group to another, always looking for easy answers and comfort from someone who says, "Follow me!"

Clearly, many of us need someone to worship, someone we can believe will solve our problems for us or show us the one true way. Well, of course, there is no one true way to improving your emotional outlook on life. There are many equally valid ways. But there are also scores of charlatans in the field because people with emotional problems are so vulnerable.

Then what do you do if you are suffering and you want to improve your emotional functioning and general outlook on life? Read the descriptions of the various therapies listed in this section, and select those that you believe may suit you. But first, you must consider the following factors:

Your state of mental stability.
The reputation of the organization sponsoring the group.
The methods of screening participants. Do they take anyone? Do they ask
    for a real medical and psychological history?
Do they state the goals of the program?

Do they clear limits of acceptable behavior during the program?
Do they offer individual follow-up?

Group therapy is usually much less expensive and sometimes more effective than other forms of psychotherapy. But group therapy, even under expert guidance, can also be dangerous. In *Facts About Group Therapy* (see page 197) the National Institute for Mental Health defines group therapy this way: "The group is made up of people who aren't happy with their lives or doing as well as they could because of problems involving their thoughts and feelings. Their purpose is to learn to get along better with themselves and others and to develop healthier, more effective ways of coping with their life's difficulties and challenges." But the truth is that you don't need a college degree to lead a group therapy session. In fact, you don't even have to be sane. In a group in which there is an attempt to break through defenses to reality, there is always the danger of removing the needed defense, which then results in chaos and a breakdown of self-respect and of ability to deal with the world. Many psychiatrists and mental hospitals have received patients who were pushed over the edge by well-meaning but destructive therapy groups.

Before joining any group, you have to check the leader's credentials for yourself. Look at the person's affiliation. Is he or she associated with a university or mental health center? Be very wary of a leader who works alone and has built up a following because of charisma. This does not mean that a person who has a degree is better than one who does not, but it does give you an additional measure of the leader's personality. You should also find out a little about what kind of person he or she is. Is the leader going to push you or leave you alone? The bad results that partipants experience in a group, according to an authority on the subject, Canadian psychiatrist Dr. Thomas Verny, comes from leaders who push.

Dr. Verny says that there are some people who are better off in a group than in individual therapy. These are people who don't fit in. They unknowingly exceed the ordinary limits of socially acceptable thinking and behavior; they do not succeed in their attempts to understand other people; they are constantly disappointed in their social endeavors. Many have been isolated from their peers and/or society in general for one reason or another during critical periods of their lives.

In a group, such patients are not required to talk so much as they would be in individual treatment. They may challenge anything they wish. They may come late, miss sessions, or drop out without the consequences such behavior incurs in the individual treatment situation, such as having to pay for an expensive missed consultation and antagonizing the therapist whose time was wasted. They accept corrections of faulty thinking from other members of the group more easily than they would from a therapist. There are also people who are afraid that a therapist will assault them and therefore work better within a group.

There are many forms of group therapy. Here are the basic ones.

Encounter groups: These groups come in more varieties than Jello and are stronger stuff. A great deal of stress is laid upon becoming aware of the kind of person you are, how you come across to other people, why you are the way you are. Such groups often question your values, what you want to achieve in life, what is holding you back. They deal with the underlying dynamics and motivations of your behavior.

T-Groups (sensitivity training): Although these groups are no longer so popular as they were in the 1960s, many are still in existence. The objective of T-groups, like that of encounter groups, is to reduce unproductive defenses. According to the American Medical Association, you should not consider joining one unless you are well adjusted and emotionally stable and the group is led by a qualified professional—and even then you may be in for trouble. The AMA's Council on Mental Health found that both psychological benefit and psychological disaster can result from T-training. In some instances, depression, psychosis, and homosexual panic, and even physical injuries, have resulted.

Marathon: This is a form of encounter in which you get it all out at once over a period of several hours or days. It involves personal honesty and confrontation. The physical hardships involved help to break down defenses.

For more information about therapy groups, write to:

American Group Psychotherapy Association
1995 Broadway
New York, New York 10023
(212)787-2618

PUBLICATION

Facts about Group Therapy, National Institute of Mental Health Publication No. (HSM) 72-9155. This booklet can be obtained from the Superintendent of Documents, U.S. Government Printing Office, Washington D.C. 20402. The price is $.10. This booklet describes the various types of groups, their advantages, and what to expect.

The Grover B. Neurotics Anonymous Test

Honesty is the most important single item in taking this test. As you read the questions, it will be quite obvious what the best answers are; that is no secret. If everyone checked "Yes" to all the items, everyone would have a beautiful psychological profile on the test. But no one could *honestly* answer "Yes" to all the items. In other words, no one could *honestly* get 100 percent on this test.

Anyone can fake the test. But the individual who fakes it is, in fact, the one who loses out. The test is for fun and for your general information. No one else cares what your score is; in fact, no one else need know your score. Here is your chance to place yourself loosely on the scale (see page 201) if you want to do so. No one will be the wiser—except, of course, you yourself.

Here are the simple rules for taking the test:

1. Read each item.
2. Check "Yes" if the item is true for you. Check "No" if the item is false for you. Check "Sometimes" if the item is true for you sometimes.

Here is the test. Be honest if you are curious about your score and your subsequent placement on the scale.

	YES	NO	SOME-TIMES
1. I love people and enjoy being with them.	—	—	—
2. My life is rich, full, and rewarding.	—	—	—
3. I have a deep faith in the good life. (This can be God, a power greater than man, a general principle for good.)	—	—	—
4. I consider it a privilege to have been born and to be alive.	—	—	—

	YES	NO	SOME-TIMES
5. I look forward to each new day as a stimulating adventure.	—	—	—
6. I have peace of mind and a quiet joy.	—	—	—
7. I am doing the work I want to do.	—	—	—
8. I am content with my position in life.	—	—	—
9. My needs are met.	—	—	—
10. I consider all human beings to be my brothers and sisters.	—	—	—
11. I enjoy helping other people.	—	—	—
12. I feel I live to serve.	—	—	—
13. I believe that everything in creation is infinitely beautiful.	—	—	—
14. I feel that I am a minute but important part of all creation, as is everything else.	—	—	—
15. I enjoy being alone as well as being with people.	—	—	—
16. I am usually relaxed.	—	—	—
17. I usually feel good.	—	—	—
18. I sleep well.	—	—	—
19. I have a good appetite.	—	—	—
20. I have the energy for the things I do.	—	—	—
21. I seldom, if ever, take any drugs or medications.	—	—	—
22. I feel adequate to do the things I am capable of doing.	—	—	—
23. I am content to do what I can and to know that there are many things that I cannot do.	—	—	—
24. I have an active interest in many things.	—	—	—
25. I have a warm, rewarding emotional life: I love; I feel; I seek to understand; I have compassion.	—	—	—
26. I use calm, objective, intellectual thought, unencumbered by emotions.	—	—	—
27. I consider my emotions an asset, not a liability.	—	—	—
28. Depression that I hear discussed is an unknown feeling to me.	—	—	—
29. I know and accept myself and accept other people as they are.	—	—	—
30. I feel that my life runs on a smooth level, with only minor ups and downs.	—	—	—

	YES	NO	SOME-TIMES
31. I am content to do my part, then wait for things to work out.	—	—	—
32. I seek to learn more and consider this a lifetime quest.	—	—	—
33. I enjoy the so-called small things: a flower opening, a rain shower, a seashell.	—	—	—
34. I seldom, if ever, have physical complaints (headaches, backaches, upset stomach, nausea, and so on).	—	—	—
35. I know that I am responsible for my own actions and that other people are responsible for their actions.	—	—	—
36. I feel comfortable with people and situations.	—	—	—
37. I consider myself healthy.	—	—	—
38. I look forward to even better things.	—	—	—
39. I believe that the world is steadily and inevitably getting better in spite of many problems.	—	—	—
40. I appreciate the value of small detail work as well as great ideas and great projects.	—	—	—
41. I believe that people are good, that difficulties are caused by illness.	—	—	—
42. I believe that the way to the brotherhood of man and peace on earth is and has always been available to man; it is up to him to learn to use it.	—	—	—
43. I respect every person and his work. I consider the street sweeper who does his job as important as the physician who does his job.	—	—	—
44. I know that health (physical, mental, emotional, and spiritual) depends upon maintenance. It is not something that, once acquired, remains as such.	—	—	—
45. I feel that I am free.	—	—	—
46. I am happy to be just a human being, no better and no worse than any other.	—	—	—
47. I feel that I am of worth just being myself; I have no need to prove anything to anybody.	—	—	—
48. I accept the inevitable. Death is of no concern to me.	—	—	—
49. I forgive myself and others for mistakes made and hold no grudges.	—	—	—
50. I try to help others to achieve a richer, happier, healthier life.	—	—	—

SCORING

Count up the "Yes" answers and the "Sometimes" answers. Each "Yes" answer counts 2 points; each "Sometimes" answer counts 1 point. "No" answers have no value. Obtain your score as follows:

Number of "Yes" answers _____ times 2 equals _____

Number of "Sometimes" answers _____ times 1 equals _____

Total score _____

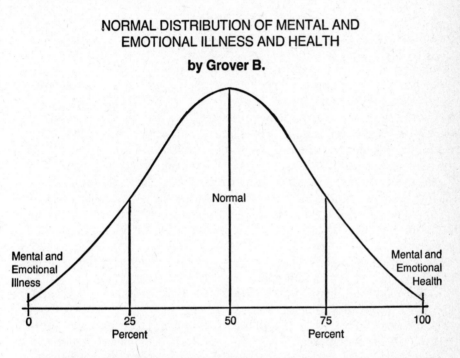

NORMAL DISTRIBUTION OF MENTAL AND EMOTIONAL ILLNESS AND HEALTH

by Grover B.

The scale on the distribution runs from 0 to 100. Locate your score on this scale, and find your placement under the curve. *Remember, you can always move up the scale as you improve your life.* Scale placement is not a definite, unchangeable thing. You can change and move up the scale. Indeed, that is the purpose: to move up the scale and aim toward that 100 percent level.

1. Mental and emotional health and illness are on a continuum from health to lack of health, which is illness.

2. Mental and emotional health and illness are normally distributed in the population.

Reprinted by permission of Grover Boydston, Chairman, Neurotics Anonymous International Liason, Inc.

2 Self-Help for Neurotics

Neurotics Anonymous, 1341 G Street, N.W., Washington, D.C. 20005, (202)628-4379. This self-help organization operates on the principles of Alcoholics Anonymous and, in fact, adapted AA's twelve steps into its program. NA is composed of people who are banded together to solve their mental and emotional problems. It was started by Grover B., a former neurotic who overcame his problems. The organization exists for the single purpose of helping mentally and emotionally disturbed individuals to recover from their illness and to maintain their recovery. This group does not use the word *neurotic* in its scientific sense. Members define neurotics as "persons whose emotions interfere with their functioning in any way and to any degree whatsoever as recognized by them." Recovered individuals help those who are still suffering. Everyone is welcome at open meetings; everyone with mental and emotional problems is welcome at closed ones. At meetings, recovered individuals talk about their experiences, newcomers are made welcome and are introduced to the program and shown the way to recovery, and sympathetic understanding is offered. Anonymity is respected. No membership records are kept, and there are no dues or fees.

Neurotics Anonymous has been accepted by many psychiatrists, doctors, psychologists, ministers, and other professionals who refer patients.

Write to the Washington address for free introductory literature.

Recovery, Inc., 116 South Michigan Avenue, Chicago, Illinois 60603, (312)263-2292. Members are referred to this association of nervous and former mental patients by psychiatrists, psychologists, physicians, hospitals, and clinics. Their symptoms may include heart palpitations, dizziness, sweats, numbness, tremors, fatigue, depression, and chest pressure. Some have fears of being alone, of crowds, of closed spaces, of open spaces, of journeys, of people, and especially, of making mistakes. Underlying all these manifestations are the basic fears of mental and physical collapse. If the condition persists for some time, a third basic fear enters the picture: the fear of never recovering, of having a permanent handicap.

Recovery, Inc., was founded in Chicago in 1937 by the late Abraham A. Low, M.D., professor of psychiatry and neurology at the University of Illinois. Because of his wide experience as a psychiatrist and neurologist, he became convinced that nervous and former mental patients need training in self-leadership.

The purpose of the Recovery Method is to prevent relapses in former mental patients and to forestall chronic nervous behavior in people. Recovery does not supplant the physician; offer diagnosis, treatment, advice, or counseling; or make professional referrals. Each member is expected to follow the recommendations of his physician or other professionals. Leaders of the Recovery meetings are drawn from the group membership. They receive training before becoming a leader. Except for a small paid staff at Recovery headquarters, leaders and all other Recovery personnel are volunteers.

You should attend at least two meetings to obtain an idea of how the method works. Meetings last about two hours, and you may bring a friend or relative with you. You are given the number of a senior member of Recovery whom you may call if you wish help at any time.

Dr. Low emphasized two major principles:

No one should be held responsible for the ailment he or she suffers.

There is no hopeless case among nervous and former mental patients, regardless of the duration of the condition.

The following are among the techniques used by the group:

Spotting: This technique identifies and analyzes a disturbing symptom when it occurs or recognizes that such a symptom is imminent. It gives the symptom a name and acknowledges that the symptom is a response to special precipitating factors. This must be followed with coping action (exercise of willpower and muscle control) to prevent disruption of functioning. Any response that is nonadaptive is considered sabotage.

Endorsing: This technique emphasizes the positive, recognizing and accepting one's accomplishments. Endorsing focuses on small things that too often get overlooked such as getting up in the morning, bathing, making beds, keeping appointments on time, and relating in productive and useful ways to others. Persons with emotional problems too often tend to negate their accomplishments. Recovery members endorse themselves and encourage others to endorse themselves by pointing to specific instances in which control was obtained, in which coping worked.

Dr. Low believed that 95 percent of life's irritations are manageable trivialities and that at weekly group meetings members could help each other sidestep common annoyances and cope with stresses. Many psychotherapists consider this an excellent program, and it has helped thousands of nervous and former mental patients to improve their ability to enjoy life.

Recovery is a nonprofit, self-supporting organization. The concept of self-help is basic to its financial structure. Meeting places are provided by clinic and community establishments in recognition of Recovery's service in the field of mental health. There is no charge for attending meetings. Funds are obtained mainly by voluntary contribution at the group meetings and by voluntary annual memberships. A subscription to the *Recovery Reporter*, the organization's official bimonthly magazine, is included in each membership.

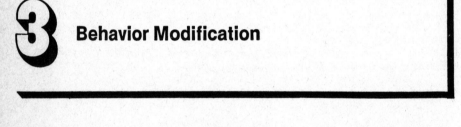

3 Behavior Modification

The term behavior modification is really a catchall for a number of down-to-earth, rapid techniques to alter the way you act. It is a relatively new concept, only about three decades old. It involves scientific, experimentally derived concepts to change behavior patterns in a systematic fashion.

The behavioral approach is affected by the environmental events that precede or follow it. In treatment, for instance, a thorough understanding of present conditions that make you tense or that force you to overeat or that make you an alcoholic would be sought, rather than what was in your past that caused you to react that way. Then prescribed actions are taken. For instance, Dr. John Paul Brady of the University of Pennsylvania, one of the foremost practitioners of behavior modification, uses a tiny electronic metronome to help you combat tension. The metronome, which he developed and which is designed to be worn in the ear, is very effective. His patients learn to relax and unwind to the rhythmic cadence of its beating. After the initial session, the metronome can be used at home, in the office, anywhere tension occurs.

Dr. Frances Stern, on the other hand, director of the Behavioral Awareness Institute in Springfield, New Jersey (see page 94), uses mind trips, or imagination, to help you overcome behavior patterns. Dr. Stern says that anyone can learn imagery or mind tripping. One way to become skilled at it is to watch your favorite TV program and then turn off the set and rerun the program in your mind. Imagery can combat phobias. Dr. Stern tells the story of one man who was afraid to fly. He developed the anxiety after declining a flight with a friend in a private plane that he frequently took; the plane crashed, and the friend was killed. The man who was afraid to fly was encouraged to picture himself in an airplane for ten minutes each night before he fell asleep. He was told to fasten his seat belt, feel the texture of the seat, smell the coffee brewing, and so forth. He did this every night for weeks. Then, when he actually entered a plane to fly, he was instructed to picture himself in bed picturing himself in a plane. This simple technique allowed the man to fly in a plane for the first time in years.

Whatever the clever technique employed, behavior modification, which is primarily the forte of the psychologist rather than the psychiatrist, works for many people in an amazingly short period of time, and it has often proved effective in cases where other methods have failed. It is recommended primarily for behavioral disorders such as anxiety neurosis or obsessive-compulsive reactions, rather than for schizophrenia or other very serious mental disorders.

4 Associations, Information, and Places to Write

The following are the national offices of associations in the mental health field. They offer referral services if you wish the name of therapists in your area and a wide variety of free material dealing with emotional disorders from "stress" to "schizophrenia."

American Psychiatric Association
1700 18th Street, N.W.
Washington, D.C. 20009

American Psychological Association
1200 17th Street, N.W.
Washington D.C. 20009

National Association for Mental Health
1800 North Kent Street
Arlington, Virginia 22209

National Institute of Mental Health
5600 Fishers Lane
Rockville, Maryland 20852

For the name of a behavior therapy program near you, write to

Association for Advancement of
   Behavior Therapy
420 Lexington Avenue
New York, New York 10017

PUBLICATIONS

Behavior Modification, Irving Dickman. Public Affairs Pamphlet No. 540, 381 Park Avenue South, New York, New York 10016. The price is 35 cents. A thorough discussion of the pros and cons of this form of therapy that is concerned with relearning behavior patterns.

Behavior Modification: Perspective on a Current Issue, National Institute of Mental Health, U.S. Department of Health, Education, and Welfare Publication No. (ADM) 75-202 (Washington, D.C.: U.S. Government Printing Office, 1975). Free.

It's Good to Know about Mental Health, National Institute of Mental Health. This booklet is free. It gives a simple, accurate explanation of what mental health is and where you can find help to maintain or achieve it.

Mental Health Information, National Institute of Mental Health, 5600 Fishers Lane, Rockville, Maryland 20852, (301)443-4513. The institute's public inquiries section maintains and continually updates publications, articles, and references on many aspects of mental health and mental illness. Topics include aging, alcoholism, autism, care and treatment of the mentally ill, children's mental health, death and grief, genetics, group therapy, juvenile deliquency, mental hospitals, religion and mental health, sleep and dreams, and suicide prevention. Most of these materials are available free on request. The staff also maintains a list of psychiatric facilities and of organizations that offer help to troubled persons.

Institutes and Mental Health Centers

There is emotional first aid just as there is physical first aid. The growth of community facilities during the 1960s and 1970s has made it possible to obtain expert counseling in or near your hometown. To find a location with the type of service you wish, you have merely to ask your local school office, hospital social worker, community fund office, clergyman, or Mental Health Association office. If you wish to go outside the area for help, there are national organizations listed who will refer you to someone in the area you specify.

The following are examples of the type of services available around the country:

Georgia

The following Crisis Centers in the state offer immediate help for anyone experiencing any type of emotional disturbance. All you need do is to pick up the phone. They are nonprofit and will charge whatever you can afford to pay. If you can't pay, you will not be denied treatment.

The Link
218 Hildebrand Avenue, N.E.
Atlanta, Georgia 30304
(404)256-9797

The Bridge Family Center
848 Peachtree Street, N.E.
Atlanta, Georgia 30304
(404)881-8344

The Hub Meditation Center
5115 La Vista Road
Tucker, Georgia 30084
(404)934-5600

Northside Community Mental Health Center
1000 Johnson Ferry Road
Atlanta, Georgia 30304
(404) 256-8950

Illinois

Fourth Presbyterian Church Counseling Center, Michigan Avenue between Delaware and Chestnut, Chicago, Illinois 60607, (312)787-8425. The counseling center has two counselors: an ordained minister with pastoral counseling experience, John Boyle, Ph.D., and Elizabeth Hutchens, Ph.D. Counseling areas here include vocation, career, life crises, family, marriage, divorce, death and dying, and religion. Both counselors can refer when appropriate those who need other types of counselors to Ys and medical organizations for help. This is a nondenominational center and therefore open to all. Fees are based on ability to pay.

Institute for Psychoanalysis, 180 North Michigan Avenue, Chicago, Illinois 60607, (312)726-6300. This is an outstanding research and teaching center, one of the few of its kind in the country. The institute offers a variety of services, including diagnosis, treatment, and referral. There is a low initial consultation fee. Treatment fees vary, based on the ability to pay.

Wexler Clinic, Michael Reese Hospital, 2960 South Lake Park, Chicago, Illinois 60607, (312)791-3900. The clinic offers individual, family, group, and child therapy in the milieu of a teaching hospital. Fees are on a sliding scale.

Neuropsychiatric Institute, University of Illinois Medical Center, 912 South Wood, Chicago, Illinois 60607, (312)996-7362. Group, individual, and family therapy is available for individuals of all ages. Fees are based on ability to pay.

North Shore Mental Health Association, Irene Josselyn Clinic, 405 Central, Northfield, Illinois 60607, (312)441-5600. This is a first-rate suburban clinic for North Shore community residents. The staff includes psychiatrists, psychologists, child therapists, and psychiatric and other social workers. Fees are based on ability to pay.

Oasis Center for Human Potential, 7463 Sheridan Road, Chicago, Illinois 60607, (312)274-6777. What the Oasis Center stands for is summed up in its name. It offers group therapy of various kinds, workshops, weekend experiences, and the like, all based on Gestalt therapy. Fees vary but are generally stiff.

Kentucky

Center for Rational Behavior Therapy Training and Emotional Self-Help, Office of Continuing Education, University of Kentucky Medical Center, Lexington, Kentucky 40536, (606)233-6009. The techniques developed by Dr. Maxie C. Maultsby, Jr., a psychiatrist and director of the training center at the University of Kentucky Medical School, involve no drugs and little or no additional physician time or patient expense. The patient's homework involves a description of the facts and events associated with an emotional problem, a summary of thoughts during the events (self-talk), a description of emotional reactions, and a rational analysis of the problem. Dr. Maultsby says that this technique for treating patients teaches people to increase their reasoning skills so that they will be better able to deal with the stresses of daily living. The method is based on the fact that the ability to think logically enables you to keep your emotions under better control, to see problems more clearly, and to solve them more effectively.

You write down the facts of the event that occurred at the time of emotional upset. You write only a concise version, just as it happened. Then you write down the feelings you had at the time of the event. Were you angry, sad, embarrassed? Next you write down why you think you felt that way. You are urged to be rational and objective about it. After the event has been pinpointed and the reaction and reason for it have been stated, imagine yourself in the situation again and think about behaving in a way you would have liked and the rational reason you should behave in this new way.

Another technique involves deliberately thinking about the situation that made you tense. Consciously observe the effects of that tension, such as rapid breathing, tight muscles, distress. You write down or say out loud how you feel. Then try one of the various relaxation techniques such as tensing and relaxing each set of muscles starting at your forehead and moving down to your toes or taking a deep breath, holding it to a count of 5, and exhaling through pursed lips. If you find you cannot relax, repeat the mental image of what made you tense, and again concentrate on the symptom of your tension (the tight muscles, the rapid breathing, perhaps the headache). Then relax again. Keep repeating this process until you are over the upset.

Still another technique, the easiest of all, involves lying in your bed and reviewing the events of the day, starting with the last ones, just before you go to sleep. When you come to something that made you tense, stop. Revise the scene; make the event happen in your mind as you would have wanted it to occur. Then resume your review. By doing this, you can defuse situations that play over and over again in your mind and make you tense.

RECORDING

The Create-Your-Own-Happiness Kit. Rational Behavior Therapy Center 00840-M.C. Room N-204A. University of Kentucky College of Medicine, Lexington, Kentucky 40536. (606)233-6166. $22.95. Maxie Maultsby, M.D., director, believes that we live in a do-it-yourself world where modern people are taking more and more direct control of the externals of their own lives. He believes you can increase your practical skills in mastering your own emotions as well as in controlling your physical actions. The kit he has designed gives step-by-step directions for using research tested techniques to help yourself to happiness. It includes audio cassettes and easy daily exercises for positive emotional practice.

New Jersey

Institute for Behavioral Awareness, 810 South Springfield Avenue, Springfield, New Jersey 07081, (201)376-8744, Frances Meritt Stern, Ph.D., director. The institute focuses on stress management training and personal effectiveness workshops. The ten-week Stress Management Workshop teaches you to identify, control, and/or eliminate destructive tension. You learn to make stress a valuable coping asset by mastering concrete stress management techniques that can be rapidly implemented and incorporated into your existing life-style. Your body, thoughts, and actions are all utilized in the workshop experience. Some of the areas dealt with are identifying your personal stress level, raising the tension threshold, low-tension responses to stress triggers, coping with stress carriers in your life, and developing a personal action plan for controlling destructive tension.

Personal effectiveness workshops are designed to help you learn how to make the maximum use of your potential. You can develop specific tools for increasing a positive self-image, for developing greater coping skills, and for increasing your effectiveness in dealing with others. The accent is on you as a totally functioning person. In the ten-week workshop, you can begin to develop the skills that can result in an increase in your ability to define, organize, and move toward goals that are personally meaningful and then fit these new skills into your way of life. Some of the areas dealt with in the workshop are creative problem solving, self-centeredness versus selfishness, increasing appropriate assertiveness, and learning to feel up to yourself.

The institute's goal is to introduce you to ideas and techniques that can help you reduce destructive tension, increase your awareness, and develop skills that allow you to perceive alternatives, identify, and make more meaningful personal choices. Both the personal effectiveness and the stress management programs consist of weekly sessions of approximately 1½ hours. These sessions are conducted by a skilled professional. You work with a small group of people who share similar problems. The fee for the ten-week course is $15 per week. The institute also works with business and industry.

See page 94 for the institute's Weight Control Program.

Rutgers University Graduate School of Applied and Professional Psychology, New Brunswick, New Jersey 08903, (201)932-2000. The school offers frequent behavioral science clinics for obesity, smoking, and other conditions that respond to this type of therapy. Fees are very low, there is no charge to those who cannot afford to pay. Check with the clinic for current schedules.

Women's Counseling and Psychotherapy Service, 270 State Street, Hackensack, New Jersey 07601, (201)487-5070; 185 South Livingston Avenue, Livingston, New Jersey 07039, (201)992-9190; 600 Valley Road, Wayne, New Jersey 07470, (201)628-0137. The Women's Counseling and Psychotherapy Service was formed to help women who are experiencing problems in their personal or family lives. The service is staffed by women therapists of various disciplines with advanced clinical training and experience. They provide a full range of psychological and vocational services. In addition to counseling, the staff offers workshops, community consultations, assertiveness training, career counseling, and psychological testing.

New York

Institute for Sociotherapy, 39 East 20th Street, New York, New York 10003, (212)260-3860. Founded in 1968, the institute offers psychotherapy and counseling services for adults and children. Courses in psychodrama, music therapy, and psychopoetry are available to the general public. Fees are moderate, and a sliding scale is in effect. For additional information, you can contact the institute between 1:00 and 10:00 P.M., Monday to Friday, and between 9:00 A.M. and 5:00 P.M. on Saturdays.

Behavioral Stress Clinic, University of Rochester Medical Center, Rochester, New York 14642, (716)275-3623, Nancy MacWhinney, R.N., technician, or Ronald F. Kokes, Ph.D., director. This clinic provides treatment for persons who react to stressful life situations by developing symptoms such as migraine or muscular tension headaches, anxieties, phobias, obsessions and/or compulsions, and certain other somatic complaints. By practicing relaxation skills and using biofeedback technology to monitor learning, a person is taught ways to control and express feelings, a progressive relaxation procedure and the rationale for its use, skills for refocusing thoughts and attention and the relationships of those skills to the reduction of effects of stress, and how feelings such as depression, anger, and guilt contribute to the continuation of symptoms. Courses begin approximately every six weeks. The treatment program includes six group sessions and five individual sessions. Charges are $24 per group session and $40 per individual session.

StressControl Center, 777 Third Avenue, New York, New York 10017, (212)486-8926. Sidney Lecker, M.D., director. Dr. Lecker is a psychiatrist specializing in organization and individual stress management. The staff includes other psychiatrists, psychologists, educational consultants and researchers, biofeedback therapists, registered nurses, and business executives from the health field. The center has developed a comprehensive program to deal with stress and stress-related symptoms. Programs are short term and are designed especially for people who deal successfully with many areas of their lives but who need to improve their ability to deal with stress.

StressControl provides services to corporations and individuals nationally through a network of certified psychologists and psychiatrists, employing these standardized, quality-controlled methods:

Preplacement screenings: The screenings are used to identify behavior problems in job applicants, particularly for security-sensitive positions.

Periodic preventive consultations: Long before stress immobilizes, this early-warning system discovers problems before they build up and gives employees the means to cope with them. Many client organizations now include this service as a routine part of their annual health checkup.

Employee retraining: This program helps valued executives and other employees to stablize their performance when it has declined because of life-change stress and retrains them with energy-freeing self-help techniques so that they can make a fresh start. Alcoholism in its early stages is generally best handled by this type of action-oriented retraining program.

Biofeedback training: StressControl is a pioneer in the use of biofeedback to train the relaxation response for coping with stress overload.

Disciplinary case evaluation: This program is designed to let personnel know whether the problem is an isolated, short-term one or whether it is probably chronic.

Pre-relocation assessment: This service provides management with an estimate of the probability that a major executive transfer will go through and helps the family to plan for life in a new culture, be it domestic or foreign.

Work-setting space planning: This service collects design information from the people who are going to be using new or redesigned space. It seeks to learn what employee needs are before costly design mistakes are made.

Emergency crisis support: If a mental health crisis occurs, registered corporate clinics have guaranteed access to a psychologist or psychiatrist through a twenty-four hour hot line.

The StressControl Examination is a two-session evaluation of a person's present ability to cope with stress in daily life. The first session includes two hours of written personality and attitude questionnaires and biofeedback assessment.

This is followed, ten days later, by a private consultation with a psychologist who is a specialist in stress management. At the second session, a detailed written report is provided that includes recommendations for improving your ability to cope with stress; this is your personal StressControl plan.

The center's Headache Relief Program incorporates the techniques developed by the Menninger Clinic, the Institute for Living (Connecticut), and other centers across the United States into its own medically supervised, biofeedback-based program. Through private sessions with a registered nurse specially trained in relaxation therapy and through home practice of relaxation techniques, significant relief from migraine and tension headaches can be achieved. The program lasts approximately five weeks, with six private lessons totaling eight hours.

Stress Seminars deal with such topics as emotional stress, success and failure, goal setting, assertiveness, authority relations, interpersonal and family life communications, stress and health, and the mid-life crisis. These small-group seminars are conducted over a weekend or in eight 2-hour weekly evening sessions. They include lectures, group discussions, small-group exercises, individual identification of self-development issues and problem areas, and development of individualized stress management programs.

The Relaxation Training Program emphasizes biofeedback training for stress reduction. Just as a thermostat can be set to a desired temperature, it is possible, through biofeedback relaxation training, to set the body's physiological responses to stress at an optimum level. This acquired ability can improve your feelings of well-being and help you resist the destructive potential of stress. This course lasts approximately five weeks, with six private sessions totaling eight hours.

The fees are $95 for the StressControl Examination, $245 for the Headache Relief Program, $95 for the Stress Seminar, and $245 for the Relaxation Training Program.

Pennsylvania

Center for Behavioral Medicine, Department of Psychiatry, Hospital of the University of Pennsylvania, 34th and Spruce Streets, Philadelphia, Pennsylvania 19104, (215)662-3503, Ovide F. Pomerleau, Ph.D., director. John Paul Brady, M.D., chairman of the Department of Psychiatry, is a pioneer in behavioral techniques; Ovide Pomerleau is one of the leading researchers and practitioners in the field of behavioral medicine, which is the application of the principles of experimental behavioral science to health-care problems. Several other prominent psychiatrists and psychologists in the department specialize in behavior modification. As practiced, behavior therapy largely involves techniques using positive reinforcements (rewards) rather than aversive techniques (punishments). Behavior therapy or treatment is available to individuals for neuroses; speech and learning disorders; marital, social, and occupational maladjustments; sexual disorders; problem drinking; and various other behavioral problems. See also "Diet," page 92 and "Smoking," page 79. The fee for individual treatment ranges from $25 to $50 per session. Under special circumstances, a fee reduction may be arranged.

Psychological Clinic of the Pennsylvania State University, Suite 314, Moore Building, University Park, Pennsylvania 16802, (814)865-2191. The clinic's psychological services may be requested by an interested person. Individuals may contact the clinic directly or may be referred by physicians, parents, teachers, counselors, social workers, legal authorities, and so on. University students and all residents of the state of Pennsylvania are entitled to the services offered by the clinic. Clients may walk in during clinic hours or phone for an appointment and be seen immediately by an intake supervisor. If it is determined that services are needed, assignment to a clinician is usually made, with a waiting period of one to three weeks; otherwise, the client is referred to an appropriate alternative facility. The professional staff includes the faculty and advanced graduate students in clinical psychology. All information is confidential. No information is released without the written consent of the client or, in the case of a child, without the written consent of a parent or guardian.

Because this is a training clinic, fees are kept low and are based on a sliding scale, depending on income. Students are charged a flat rate for a one-hour session. Anyone who earns under $5,000 and is a nonstudent is helped free of charge. The highest rate, $15, is charged to those making over $17,000 who have no dependents. An average fee is about $4.80 a session. The clinic is open from 9:00 A.M. to 4:00 P.M., Monday to Friday.

The clinic offers the following services:

Individual therapy: Individual psychotherapy is available to individuals who are motivated and able to work closely with a psychologist to work through their personal problems. Individual psychotherapy is usually scheduled for one or two hours per week.

Group therapy: Group psychotherapy is sometimes available to individuals who find it most helpful to approach their problems within a small group with the help of a group therapist. Clients in group therapy may also be involved in individual therapy. A group usually meets once or twice a week.

Child treatment and parental guidance: Parents who feel that their child has a problem may bring the child for observation and/or assessment and may discuss the situation with a therapist. Resolution of the problem may involve play therapy or other treatment for the child, parental guidance sessions, or both.

Marital and family counseling: Sometimes the nature of the problem is such that married couples or families are counseled as a unit. Individual members of the family may also be involved in other therapy programs.

Behavior modification: Techniques that involve direct intervention with life problems and coping skills training are offered by the clinic. Such services are available for both children and adults.

Special programs: From time to time, special programs may be offered for such things as training to increase assertiveness or helping people to lose weight or stop smoking.

See "Empathic Communication and Interpersonal Negotiation," page 262. Psychotherapy through speech and communication improvement.

6 Parenthood Problems

Most of us start the most important job in the world with no experience and a great deal of anxiety. Who among us does not regret something we did or did not do when raising our children?

Because of the pattern of American mobility, many young parents are far away from family members who could give them the benefit of their own experience in dealing with the many crises of parenthood. To fill in the gap and sometimes to make up for the poor parenting that new parents themselves had, there are organizations that offer expert advice and help.

Early Childhood Development Center (ECDC), Center for Comprehensive Health Practice, New York Medical College, 163 East 97th Street, New York, New York 10029, (212)860-7403, Nina K. Lief, M.D., director.

Do you want to enjoy being a parent more? Do you want to know how to deal with the problems of parenthood? The purpose of ECDC is to enhance the intellectual, emotional, and social development of children through enhancing the parent-child relationship in the crucial period from infancy to three years of age. The center also aims at early detection of any physical or emotional problems. The ECDC, which was founded and maintained with aid from the Junior League, is a prototype for other centers that could be established across the country as the need for such development centers is being recognized. The center believes that "Mothers need help in understanding their children today. They should be enjoying their role as parents. Women have to be helped to realize that motherhood is an important profession . . . and needs society's support and recognition."

The center holds weekly sessions for small groups of parents and their babies. The sessions, which are conducted by trained group leaders, are designed to impart knowledge and understanding of children's developmental processes and of child-rearing techniques that can improve each child's progress. There are eleven groups of mothers and children meeting and additional groups of addicted mothers and their children. The eleven groups consist of about 25 percent upper-class families, 50 percent middle-class families, and 25 percent lower-economic-class families.

Some of the problems with which ECDC deals are physical care of the child, patterning and scheduling, input of motor and sensory stimulation, understanding crying as a baby's language, input of language and communication, permitting exploration, how to encourage fathers' participation in child rearing, guiding social relations with others, interest in achievement and mastery, enjoyment of child as a person, misinterpretation of children's normal needs as "spoiled" behavior, maternal self-concept and role, fostering trust and personal relations, dealing with separation, establishing autonomy, discipline versus punishment, and learning to assess baby-sitters.

Parent Effectiveness Training, 531 Stevens Avenue, Solana Beach, California 92075, (714)481-8121, Dr. Thomas Gordon, director. Parent Effectiveness Training (P.E.T.) classes are sponsored by a variety of community organizations, including schools, Ys, churches, social agencies, mental health centers, and probation departments. Its principles have also been incorporated into many federally funded experimental educational programs. Trainers conduct workshops throughout the country and train and certify new P.E.T. instructors. Dr. Gordon has trained 14,000 instructors.

Dr. Gordon has devised a concrete, easily understood course of study to teach specific child-rearing methods. At the heart of the program is a simple approach to teaching parents communications skills and a democratic method of conflict resolution. Dr. Gordon believes that with his methods, parents can give up using power in disciplining children except in an emergency involving danger to the child. P.E.T. teaches parents how to confront children honestly when their behavior bothers the parent.

Tuition for the course varies greatly, depending on locale. Part of the fee is paid to Gordon's organization to cover participant materials (text, workbook, and so on).

PUBLICATION

P.E.T.: Parent Effectiveness Training: The Tested New Way to Raise Responsible Children, Thomas Gordon. New York: Wyden, 1970. The hard-cover edition costs $9.95; the paperback edition costs $4.95. This best seller gives down to earth, specific advice on how to deal with everyday problems in the home.

7 Hypnosis

Less traditional but sometimes more effective psychotherapeutic methods are available. Hypnosis is one such technique. Of course, you should proceed with caution.

Hypnosis—the technique has fascinated people for ages. Although it faded after Sigmund Freud decided psychoanalysis worked better without it, hypnosis has aroused renewed interest in the 1970s. Dr. Ernest Hilgard of Stanford University, one of the foremost researchers in the field, says that hypnosis is simply suggestion; if anyone has power over you, that person is *you*. As far back as 150 years ago, Abbé Faria recognized that the responsibility for entering into a hypnotic state rests more on the subject's ability than on the hypnotist's skill. This is not to say, however, that hypnosis should be taken lightly, nor is it denigrating the ability of hypnosis to work wonders. Some people can be hypnotized and some cannot. The difference is in suggestibility and in defenses.

Many hypnosis programs are available. Here are some of them:

Herbert Spiegel, M.D., P.C., 19 East 88th Street, New York, New York 10028, (212)LE4-8877. Dr. Spiegel, associate clinical professor of psychiatry at Columbia University's College of Physicians and Surgeons, is one of the outstanding medical hypnotherapists. He conducts many classes on the subject for physicians. In general, he can help patients control "simple" problems such as smoking in one 45-minute hypnotherapy session. Other habit control and pain problems may require more than one session.

Here, reprinted with Dr. Spiegel's permission are 10 myths about hypnosis:

1. *Hypnosis is going to sleep.* Hypnosis is a waking state; it is intense concentration. Often, people who are hypnotized appear to be sleeping, but the physiological signs of sleep are different. Sleep and hypnosis are, in fact, polar opposites.

2. *The hypnotist has some mysterious power of the patient.* This is not true. The hypnotist merely taps the patient's capacity for concentration.

3. *Only mentally weak or sick people can be hypnotized.* Actually, it is the mentally healthy person who has the ability to concentrate and enter a trance. If a person is mentally disturbed or unable to concentrate, he or she probably will not be able to be hypnotized.

4. *Trances can be induced only by hypnotists.* In fact, roughly 15 percent of the population can put themselves into trances without any previous training, and one of the prime objectives of the hypnotist is to teach patients how to hypnotize themselves.

5. *Removing pain through hypnosis means another symptom will take its place.* This idea was first postulated by Freud. There is no evidence that removing a symptom will, by itself, cause another symptom unless the doctor tells the patient to expect one, in which case, the patient will usually fulfill the prophecy.

6. *Hypnosis is not dangerous.* Hypnosis is grounded in an atmosphere of trust. If somebody in a trusting state goes into a trance and the doctor violates that trust and exploits the patient, that, of course, is dangerous. But the practice of hypnosis is not intrinsically dangerous.

7. *Hypnosis is not therapy.* Hypnosis is the idiom in which a patient can learn to reprocess pain, but it is not, in itself, therapy.

8. *The hypnotist has to be extremely charismatic, mysterious, or magnetic.* Such behavior on the part of the physician does not, by itself, increase his or her ability to teach people how to enter trance states. Charisma may be helpful if the patient regards the doctor that way, but it is certainly not essential.

9. *One sex is more hypnotizable than the other.* Contrary to what many contend, women are not more hypnotizable than men. All the studies, including our own (Dr. Siegel's), show that the distribution of hypnotizability is the same for women and men.

10. *Hypnosis is a unique psychological phenomenon.* It is not simply an isolated psychological phenomenon that has no relationship to real physiology. The capacity to go into trance is a neurophysiological shift that enables a person to alter his or her psychological perception.

The following list includes hypnotists with doctorates who use the technique in therapy. They are well known in the field and well practiced in the art.

Russell Blanchard, M.D., President
International Society for Professional
  Hypnosis
2364A Vallego Street
San Francisco, California 94123
(415)346-2123

Don Eugene Gibbons, Ph.D.
Department of Psychology
West Georgia College
Carrollton, Georgia 30117
(404)834-1211

David A. Gouch, M.D., President
Association to Advance Ethical
  Hypnosis
4124 Blanding Boulevard
Jacksonville, Florida 32210
(904)771-8270 or if no answer
  (904)356-9461

Frank S. Caprio, M.D.
Suite 214
Lauderdale Beach Bank Building
221 Commercial Boulevard
Lauderdale-by-the-Sea, Florida 33308
(305)771-1050

Francis J. Cinelli, Doctor of
  Osteopathy
153 North 11th Street
Bangor, Pennsylvania 18013
(215)588-4502

Areed F. Barabasz, E.D.D.
Genesee Psychiatric Institute
2110 West Hill Road
P. O. 7179
Flint, Michigan 48507
(313)239-7691

Henry S. Tugender, Ph.D.
35 Wickatunk Village
Morganville, New Jersey 07751
(201)591-1932

CENTERS FOR LEARNING HYPNOSIS

Ethical Hypnosis Training Center, Inc., 60 Vose Avenue, South Orange, New Jersey 07079, (201)762-3132, Harry Arons, director. This school teaches many courses in hypnosis to physicians, dentists, psychologists, teachers, and individuals. Courses are repeated throughout the year and the staff members travel to present seminars around the country. A combination course, Scientific Hypnosis and Self-Hypnosis, is given once a week for ten weeks; sessions start in February, May, and September. The cost is $295. The Clinical Course for medical professionals is $325. For full information about the courses and schedules, call or write the institute.

PUBLICATIONS

Handbook of Self Hypnosis, Harry Arons. New Jersey: Power Publishers, 1964. The price of this paperback is $4.95.

New Master Course in Hypnosis: A Textbook, Harry Arons. New Jersey: Power Publishers, 1961. The price is $12.00.

Handbook of Professional Hypnosis, Harry Arons and Marne F. H. Bubeck, Ph.D. New Jersey: Power Publishers, 1971. The price is $15.00.

Hypnosis in Criminal Investigation, Harry Arons. New Jersey: Power Publishers, 1977. This paperback is $7.50.

Hypnosis Institute of Fort Worth, 3515 Blue Bonnet Circle, Fort Worth, Texas 76109, (817)926-4652, Frank Monaghan, director. Founded in 1960 by Frank Monaghan, the school at first operated on a part-time basis, offering courses to anyone interested in hypnosis as a tool for self-improvement. The school gradually expanded, giving courses to physicians, psychologists, and other professionals. In 1972, it was approved by the Texas Education Agency, Division of Proprietary Schools, becoming the first school of hypnosis in the United States to be regulated by a state board of education. Psychological testing of applicants for professional training is required, and an applicant whose profile indicates personality maladjustment or psychopathology is rejected. The school reserves the right to make an independent inquiry of the applicant's employers and of schools previously attended; the school also reserves the right to deny admission to any applicant who, in its judgment, fails to meet personal or academic standards.

The institute's undergraduate and graduate programs are designed to meet the needs of individuals planning to become professional therapists. Most (but not all) students have degrees in other specialties. The beginning course, An Introduction to Hypnosis, is open to anyone seeking a comprehensive background in, and application of, hypnosis for self-improvement or self-control through self-hypnosis. The course meets one night per week for fifteen weeks.

A personal counseling service is conducted in conjunction with the institute's academic program. This service employs the philosophy and technique of Frank Monaghan, described in his books *The Hypnotist in Criminal Investigation* (Iowa: Kimball/Hunt, 1980), $7.95, and *Analytic Relaxation Therapy* (Iowa: Kimball/Hunt, 1980), $8.95. Clients are taught to relate to the conditions that serve as causal factors to their maladjustments. Effective counseling should remove the client's "need" for the symptom or behavior. For example, if an overweight client recognizes that obesity helps him or her to avoid the attention of someone in the past by making himself/herself unattractive and then recognizes that the offending personality no longer poses a threat, his/her appetite should spontaneously diminish. The personality inventory and reassessment is normally completed in three to seven 1-hour sessions.

Neither the institute nor the counseling service advertises; they operate on referrals.

The fee for An Introduction to Hypnosis is $140; the fees for advanced courses range from $75 to $140. Students pay only for classes attended. If a student does not complete a course, refunds are made in accordance with the state's policies. There are no long-term contracts. Counseling sessions cost $40 for each hour-long session.

8 Institutes for Altered States of Consciousness

The great quest for self-understanding and nontraditional treatments has somewhat slowed but the popularity of some organizations remain. The following are examples of techniques that still have avid followers.

WORKSHOPS

Arica Institute, Inc., 235 Park Avenue South, New York, New York 10003, (212)673-5130. The institute has been called "the nearest thing we have to a university for altered states of consciousness." Arica (which rhymes with *Topeka*) was founded by Oscar Ichazo, a Bolivian, in 1956. He began teaching his principles to groups of students in Santiago, Chile; and by 1968, he had founded the Instituto de Gnoseologia in Arica, Chile, where he taught and developed techniques for "internal realization and processing." In 1971, the Arica Institute, Inc., was founded in New York City; it has offered training programs ever since.

Sam Keen, consulting editor of *Psychology Today*, once said that he could spot ego-reducing and consciousness-raising techniques borrowed by Arica from Zen, Sufism, Buddhism, psychoanalysis, encounter, the Gurdjieff work, and many other disciplines. Oscar Ichazo says, "The Arica method for self-realization is presented as trainings, courses, and workshops that follow the nine stages necessary for the total clarification of consciousness. In all its work, Arica emphasizes maintaining the student's energy at a constant peak while stimultaneously improving confidence and reducing stress. The method has been developed so that it is easy to learn and requires no previous knowledge. Although some of the programs are self-teaching, Arica is aware of the fact that working in a group necessarily accelerates the learning process. This method does away with the need for a personal guide in all but its final two stages."

Here are brief descriptions of three of the institute's most popular training courses.

Three Days to Kensho: Kensho is the recognition that the clarification of consciousness is the entire purpose of life. The three-day program induces the state of kensho by giving you a "full understanding of yourslef" as a human being. In ten hours of filmed lectures that form the core of training, Ichazo outlines the laws of consciousness and the structure of the psyche. The workshop meets approximately 10½ hours a day, including time for lunch and dinner. Between the lectures, each of which lasts approximately 1 hour, simple meditations and relaxation exercises provide variety and an opportunity to assimilate the lectures. The program also includes approximately 4½ hours of group discussion that help you remember and explore the occasions in your life when the various situations mentioned in the lectures occurred. $150.

Psychocalisthenics: This is a balanced sequence of twenty-six exercises that move the entire body as economically as possible under the control of the breath. No special apparatus is necessary, and once learned, Psychocalisthenics can be completed in about twenty minutes, leaving you with the security that you have received all the exercise you need for the day. The course consists of eight 1-hour lessons. The cost is $50.

The 40 Day Training: First offered in 1972, this course "radically acclerates the process of self-realization to match the speed of modern life, yet this method is easy to learn and requires no special knowledge." During the forty days, you share the energy of a group moving with speed and solidarity and with a sense of mutual support that allows you to probe deeper into yourself. The core of the training is a series of more than 1,000 questions that evoke memories of past events, thereby releasing repressed emotions. Other tools used in the training program include physical exercise and movement that reduce both physical and psychic stress as they strengthen the body, interpersonal exercises that awaken love for others, self-analysis that clarifies present situations, meditation that calms the psyche and stimulates awareness, and breathing and relaxation exercises that integrate the whole being. This is an intensive, tightly scheduled 320-hour program. There are two formats: an intensive format of five 8-hour days a week for six weeks and an extended format of 3 hours two evenings a week and 8 hours on four Sundays for fifteen weeks.

Prices vary according to where the courses are given. For further information, contact Arica Institute in New York. All the trainings are offered by program centers around the country and each sets its own price.

The New York training center is called *The 24 Company* and is located at 24 West 57th Street, New York, New York 10019 (212)489-7430. The headquarters estimates that the prices in New York may be slightly higher than elsewhere. Here they are: For *Three Days to Kensho*, $150; for Psychocalisthenics, $50; and for the Forty Day Training, $750.

PATTERNING

Aston-Patterning Consultants, Inc., P. O. Box 114, Tiburon, California

94920, (415)433-6299, Judith Aston, director. Judith Aston, who received her master's degree in fine arts from the University of California, trained in Rolfing with Dr. Ida Rolf (see page 225). As she began to do Rolfing, Judith observed the need for additional movement education. Combining her background as a teacher of movement with her ability to "see" movement, Judith developed Aston-Patterning, based on Dr. Rolf's concepts of alignment.

Aston-Patterning has now been developed into three forms based on the understanding that there are different types of holding patterns in the body and that each of these patterns needs to be released in an appropriately unique way.

Neuro-Kinetics (NK): This form of Aston-Patterning allows you to find more agreeable ways of sitting or walking, or performing sports, or dance.

Arthro-Kinetics (AK): This is a massagelike form through which the teacher assists you in releasing the stress patterns that have set themselves into the joints of your body. As these holding patterns are eased, you begin to experience more "harmonious movements."

Myo-Kinetics (MK): In this massagelike form, the teacher assists you in releasing chronic stress patterns that have set themselves into your body's soft tissues. When layers of unnecessary stress are unwrapped, the body can begin to organize itself more effectively, thus providing "easier balance and more resilient movement."

Teachers

Judith Aston, director
P. O. Box 114
Tiburon, California 94920
(415)435-0433

Michael Batliner (MK)
5917 Blairstone Drive
Culver City, California 90230
(213)838-3583

Lyn Blake (NK, AK)
P. O. Box 19528
New Orleans, Louisiana 70179
(504)891-4323

Susan Beauchamp (NK, AK)
22003 Pacific Coast Highway
Malibu, California 90265
(213)456-8105

Bob Braun (MK)
4107 Northeast Hazelfern Place
Portland, Oregon 97232
(503)238-6746

Christine Caldwell (NK)
8901 Hickory Hill
Lanham, Maryland 20801
(301)459-0119

Sophie Darbonne (NK)
1212 Fisher
Manhattan Beach, California 90266
(213)545-5830

Vickie Dodd (NK, AK)
1305 North Judson
Evanston, Illinois 60201
(312)492-0508

Bud Earley (MK)
1079 Sterling
Berkeley, California 94708
(415)841-7309

Anna Eichenberg (NK, AK)
320 Mesa Lane
Santa Barbara, California 93109
(805)962-7142 or (805)962-2700

Harriet Glass (NK)
2443 Pacific Heights Road
Honolulu, Hawaii 96813
(808)537-1684

Doug Hales (NK, AK)
805 Leavenworth, #705
San Francisco, California 94109
(415)673-8265

Faith Hornbacher (NK, AK)
240 Alta Vista
Los Altos, California 94022
(415)948-4988
also San Francisco

Joanna Johnson (NK)
392 Dune Circle
Kailua, Hawaii 96734
(808)261-6348

Jaison Kayn (MK)
Lee Hill Road
Boulder, Colorado 80302
(303)447-2739

Ron Kirkby (MK)
8434 Avenida de las Ondas
La Jolla, California 92037
(714)459-4735

Rachel Lahn (NK, AK)
220 Redwood Highway, #44
Mill Valley, California 94941
(415)332-5373 or (415)383-5420

John McConnell (MK)
1932 Shattuck Avenue
Berkeley, California 94704
(415)841-6500

Don McFarland (MK)
2928 Fourth Street
Santa Monica, California 90405
(213)396-7914

Elizabeth McIver (NK, AK)
507 Welch Street
Houston, Texas 77006
(713)522-3632

Michael McIver (MK)
507 Welch Street
Houston, Texas 77006
(713)522-3632

Marcia Michael (NK)
102 Lehman Lane
Mill Valley, California 94941
(415)388-3557
also Los Angeles, (213)451-0848

Peter Michael (MK, NK)
102 Lehman Lane
Mill Valley, California 94941
(415)388-3557
also Los Angeles, (213)451-0848

Hal Milton (MK)
Box 3341
Santa Barbara, California 93105
(805)687-4838

Ronnie Neufeld (NK, AK)
140 20th Avenue, #206
San Francisco, California 94121
(415)751-4771

John Parker (MK, AK)
531 Cowper Street
Palo Alto, California 94301
(415)326-0387

Pompe Strater (NK)
3939 Orchard Street
Boulder, Colorado 80302
(303)444-5595

Tim Stringari (NK, AK)
2124 Menalto Avenue
Menlo Park, California 94025
(415)325-1174

Dale Townsend (MK, AK)
1308 Casey Key Road
Nokomis, Florida 33555
(813)485-5555
also Cincinnati, (513)836-2063, and
    Indianapolis, (317)849-6470

REFLEXOLOGY

International Institute of Reflexology, P.O. Box 12642, Saint Petersburg, Florida 33733, (813)343-4811. Reflexology is a science that deals with "the principle that there are reflexes in the feet relative to each and every organ and all parts of the body. Stimulating these reflexes properly can help many health problems in a natural way just like preventative maintenance." Reflexology, which, like acupuncture, is an ancient art, received its modern boost from Eunice Ingham in her books, *Stories the Feet Can Tell* and *Stories the Feet Have Told.* Her nephew, Dwight C. Byers, who carries on her work, hastens to point out that they are not physicians and that reflexology is not a replacement for medical care. Reflexology is used primarily for relaxing tension, improving circulation, and normalizing the body. Because feet are the farthest part of the body away from the heart and must carry the weight of the body, improving circulation by manipulating them cannot hurt, and might help. Weekend seminars to train reflexologists are held by Beyers in major cities around the country during the year. Cost is $125. For referral to a reflexologist near you, write the institute.

PUBLICATIONS

Stories the Feet Can Tell and *Stories the Feet Have Told,* Eunice Ingham. These two books can be ordered from Ingham Publishing, P.O. Box 12642, Saint Petersburg, Florida 33733. The cost is $8, plus $1 for postage and handling for both. They describe the history and theory of reflexology with diagrams and text.

ROLFING

Rolf Institute, P. O. Box 1868, Boulder, Colorado 80306, (303)449-5903. The late Dr. Ida P. Rolf, once an organic chemist with the Rockefeller Institute, perfected her technique of Structural Integration over many years; that technique is now popularly called *Rolfing.* Rolfing is a technique for "reordering the body to bring its major segments—head, shoulders, thorax, pelvis and legs—toward a vertical alignment."

The Rolfers say that if we picture the body as a stack of partially independent weight segments, the least energy will be expended in rotational movement when the blocks are stacked directly above one another. The stacking will also result in the highest possible center of gravity because the spinal curves will be shallow and the body will consequently be longer. Rolfers claim that many of us have let our body weights slip out from the vertical axis. That is, we have shortened our bodies. Our heads are slumped forward, and our buttocks are probably carried up and back. Most likely our bodies have twisted as we have

slumped; one shoulder or one hip may lead the other as we walk. Knees may track out or in, and misaligned ankles may throw our weight to the outside of our feet. One foot probably carries more weight than the other. These distortions come not only from the remarkable plasticity of the body but also from accidents, Dr. Rolf maintained, and patterns of imbalance tend to reinforce themselves. As a result of these imbalances, our joints lose their ease of movement, circulation is restricted as the body tightens, and there is a general imbalance.

Rolfing balances the body by taking advantage of the body's tendency to hold the shapes induced by applied force. In a carefully worked out sequence of manipulations, the Rolfer "reverses the randomizing influence of the environment, moving tissue back toward the symmetry and balance that the architecture of the body so clearly calls for."

Dr. Rolf's theory is that because emotions are intimately involved with muscular tone, correcting the imbalance will help emotions. For instance, a child with a threatening mother may continually shrink away, lowering his head, raising his shoulders, and depressing his chest until the pattern becomes a norm for him; or like a racer, he may wait for the starting signal that never comes, building tension in his legs through an unfulfilled impulse to run away. The muscular tension and the emotions are two aspects of the same organic pattern.

Fascia is a sheet of fibrous tissue that envelopes the body beneath the skin and surrounds all the muscles and tendons. When a part of the body is injured or chronically held in a position out of the vertical alignment, the fascia thickens or sticks to itself at connecting points in order to support the increased load on the muscles. These thickened areas remain even after the injury has healed and thus prevent the body from totally regaining its previous freedom of movement. In addition, because the fascia is an interconnecting system, changes in one area may cause compensatory changes in other parts of the body.

Dr. Rolf recognized that if she could release the fascia in places where it was stuck, the body could return to its structurally optimal position. She learned to accomplish this by applying pressure to the tissue in the direction in which it was originally intended to move. Because fascia is interconnecting, she worked over the entire body, lest remaining problems pull the corrections out of line again. She evolved a system of ten sessions in which every part of the body was worked on and then integrated into the whole. The first seven Rolfing sessions concentrate primarily on individual parts of the body, such as the chest, legs, head, and neck. The remaining three sessions integrate the whole body along its new lines.

The Rolf method of releasing the knots appears to be similar to massage. At times, pressure is very strong along the muscles and tendons. The Rolfer can feel the tension areas in the normally smooth tissue and uses fingers, knuckles, or elbows to push them along the tissue according to the pattern prescribed. Sometimes, they do not smooth out easily. Depending on what emotional and physical problems are present in the tissue, this process can be very painful.

The Rolfer must apply sufficient force to stretch and move tissue; furthermore, he or she is frequently working on tissue whose chronic tension carries an emotional load. Even if pain is intense, it disappears immediately when the pressure is removed. Sometimes, there is also soreness of the kind felt when the muscles are overworked; this soreness usually lasts a few days. Pain frequently marks an emotional release and may be strongly colored by associated emotions. While being Rolfed, people often recall specific traumatic episodes as associated with particular parts of the body. But with or without such recall, the release of chronic contractions has an emotionally purgative effect.

The results of Rolfing are as varied and complex as the organisms being altered. Rolfers say that the body generally acquires "a lift or lightness as the head and chest go up and the trunk lengthens; the pelvis, in horizontalizing, brings the abdomen and buttocks in; the knees and feet track more nearly toward the soles of the feet, which meet the ground more squarely." As the joints and major segments of the body rotate and hinge more freely on one another, there is less pitching of the body from side to side in walking and less raising of the body weight with each step. Conserved energy is available for other purposes.

The idea of changing body structure for ease of movement and relaxation is not too far afield from what chiropractors and osteopathic physicians claim for their manipulations. It may seem difficult to accept the notion of permanent benefits from such a course of treatment, but research data developed at the Movement Behavior Laboratory at UCLA and at the California Department of Mental Hygiene seem to add weight to Rolfing claims.

According to Ida Rolf, "We are not interested in making a more adequate body for men and women so that they can disregard the problems of the body and stick to their job or their sports. We don't set out to cure a body. But we get the body to grow to a place of greater strength and greater adaptability, greater grace in movement and greater capacity for moving and adjusting." Rolfing and patterning are still relatively small movements. Some swimmers and athletes have been through it, and John Denver has been pictured with Dr. Ida Rolf.

There is a list of certified Rolfers. Some are willing to travel to areas where there are no resident practitioners. The usual arrangement is a guarantee of twenty sessions in a week at a suggested fee of $40 per session (the fee charged by most Rolfers) plus travel expenses. Write to the institute for a list of Rolfers near you.

MIND CONTROL

Silva Mind Control International, Inc., P.O. Box 1149, Laredo, Texas 78040, (512)722-6391. Since 1966, when the first Silva Mind Control lecture series was offered to the public, more than 1.5 million people have learned this method of mental training. Jose Silva, a Mexican American with no formal schooling, began his research into Mind Control in Laredo, Texas, in 1944. His purpose was to find means of increasing the IQ factor. As is often the case, his incidental findings proved more significant than his original goals; the results of those findings and continued research led to the Silva method.

Mr. Silva explains that there are four primary brain waves: the beta waves (associated with outer conscious levels, physical activity, anxiety, tension, and so on), the alpha waves (associated with inner levels of mental activity, tranquillity, inspiration, creativity, concentration, ESP, improved functioning in health matters, memory, learning, and recall capabilities), the theta waves (a low-keyed, significantly reduced frequency associated with drowsiness), and the delta waves (associated with deep sleep). In just forty to forty-eight hours of classroom lecturing and mental exercises, Silva maintains, participants learn how to function with awareness at inner levels of consciousness of mind. "When at these altered levels of mind, they can sense information with conscious awareness and controls, impressed upon the brains of others at a distance. This kind of sensing is called Subjective Communication or ESP." Mr. Silva explains that his present concept of the human mind is that it is a sensing faculty of human intelligence, much as sight is the sensing faculty of the eye and hearing is the sensing faculty of the ear. The mind appears to be "humanity's master sense." It can apparently sense information stored by other senses on brain neurons and is capable of impressing or detecting information on cell life.

Silva training is available all over the United States and in Mexico, Canada, Spain, South America, Central America, and Europe (a total of more than 37 nations), which is an indication of its wide appeal. Here is a brief description of the programs available.

Basic Lecture Series: In forty to forty-eight hours, participants learn how to start alpha and terminate alpha with eyes open and eyes closed. They develop a greater facility to enter sleep without drugs and to enter deep levels of relaxation. This, you are taught, is critical to the reduction of potentially damaging physical tension and psychological stress. If you practice the Silva principles for ten to fifteen minutes each day, you will achieve an extraordinary ability to control bodily vitality and energy and to solve problems without stress or strain. You will have increased efficiency, concentration, self-control, learning capacity, and better relations with others.

Graduate Series: This thirty- to thirty-five-hour course is designed to help Mind Control graduates advance themselves even more.

Relaxation Seminar: Many companies have brought in Silva Mind Control instructors to teach relaxation to high-powered executives. A single seminar lasts 3½ hours.

The cost of the Basic Lecture Series is $225. The Graduate Series costs $200, and a single Relaxation Seminar costs $20 per person.

RECORDING

Educator 2001 Learning Laboratory. This is a tape program for the chief executive, the key person, the leader of people, and/or the very busy person who cannot personally attend the sessions required to learn controlled relaxation and biofeedback. The cost is $495.

MERCHANDISE

Trainer. This is a biofeedback device that features an external jack earphone and a place for you to place your finger. It is about the size of a pack of cigarettes and picks up the degree of electrical skin resistance present. When you are relaxed, the electrical resistance is high; but when you are not relaxed, the resistance is low, and the Trainer will sound a faster rate of beeps than usual. Thus, by attempting to get the Trainer to sound a slow rate, which means you are relaxed, you *become* relaxed. The Trainer can be purchased from the institute for $45.

TRANSCENDENTAL MEDITATION

Transcendental Meditation, International Meditation Society, 11428 Santa Monica Boulevard, West Los Angeles, California 90025, (213)479-6505. There was a burgeoning following for the teachings of Maharishi Mahesh Yogi, who first came to the public view when Mia Farrow and the Beatles sought peace at his feet in India. TM, which he developed, is now being taught by hundreds of teachers affiliated with the International Meditation Society.

Once you learn to meditate, you usually go into a quiet environment and sit in a comfortable position. You try to shut out other stimuli and repeat a personal, secret word called a *mantra.* The repetition is supposed to free you from logical, externally oriented thought. Your eyes must remain closed throughout this "quiet time." It is recommended that the technique be practiced for twenty minutes twice a day, usually before breakfast and before dinner.

There is no doubt that TM is beneficial to many people. Meditators have been found to have improved memory and learning ability and to have increased emotional stability; it has physiological benefits as well. But it is also somewhat cultish, which disuades people from trying it. Meditation instructions that do not require the ceremony (ask your local librarian for a list) are available in book form. Prices for instruction in TM vary from $75 to $200.

YOGA

For the ancient Hindus, yoga was a system of self-discipline and psychic training, the aim of which was to unite the lower and higher selves. There are different systems of yoga. Hatha-yoga, the one practiced by most Westerners, is a regimen of physical training that is traditionally used to prepare the mind and body for meditation. It consists largely of practicing postures and breathing exercises that can help to increase physical fitness and flexibility. There is also raja-yoga, a type of meditation similar to Transcendental Meditation. For the best results, raja-yoga and hatha-yoga should be combined.

Yoga is among the most accessible, least expensive therapies for mental and physical conditioning. But doctors have reported patients who developed pinched nerves from yoga positions, so proceed with caution and make sure that your teacher is qualified. Yoga is taught in schools, health spas, and Ys and by commercial groups. However, yoga schools tend to disappear quickly, and even your *Yellow Pages* may be out of date. Here are two well-known yoga facilities.

Yoga Institute, 2168 Portsmouth, Houston, Texas 77098, (713)526-6674. The purpose of the institute is "awakening a consciousness through physical, mental or spiritual development." Classical Indian yoga is the technique used to accomplish this. The institute conducts classes in six-week sessions and has seven different grade levels. No new students are permitted to enroll after the first week of each new session, and enrollment is limited. Both hatha-yoga and raja-yoga are taught in each class. The fees are $26 for an individual and $42 for husband and wife or other member of the family. For advanced courses tuition is $16 per individual and $27 for husband and wife.

Temple of Kriya Yoga, 2414 N. Kedsey, Chicago, Illinois 60611, (312)342-4600; also 125 North Marion, Oak Park, Illinois 60302, (312)848-6688; Retreat House and Monastery, Route 3, Box 450, South Haven, Michigan 49090, (616)637-6171; 1209 Canyon Boulevard, Boulder, Colorado 80302. The temple offers classes in meditation and astrology and an extended range of Hinduistic, Buddhistic, Indic, and Yogic studies, emphasizing the science of Kriya Yoga. Hatha-yoga classes cost $3.50 per class or $18.00 for a six-class card.

PART IV

Improving Communication

Sexual Sensations, Sore Spots, and Successes

Sex is something a lot of people talk about but few people really understand. Where *can* you go when you love someone and yet you have a problem expressing that love biologically and emotionally?

The Family Services Association of America, the largest volunteer family-counseling organization in the United States, estimates that at least half of the 3,400 to 5,000 sex therapists reported to be operating in the United States today are charlatans. Some even have criminal records. Anybody can hang out a shingle in any state and call himself or herself a sex therapist. And even those with medical degrees and with the best intentions may not be qualified to offer help on the subject.

The World Health Organization reported that human sexuality is inadequately taught in the majority of the world's medical and nursing schools. "Students in many parts of the world grow up in cultures that evade direct confrontation with sexuality; sex acts are private and secret and are only referred to by indirect suggestion or by joking," the WHO experts maintain. "This may lead the health practitioner into defensive attitudes, blaming the patient for inadequacies or overemphasizing organ dysfunction and avoiding any reference to feeling.

"Handicapped by lack of formal training, the physician and nurses often find themselves personally embarrassed and professionally incompetent when faced with a patient's sexual problems. More often than not, the patient is turned away with nothing but a superficial reply."

The problem of sexual dysfunction is not an easy one, and certainly no one type of treatment will work for everyone. There are a number of physiological causes for impotence and frigidity; diabetes and vascular complications are among the most common. Therefore, a thorough physical evaluation should be a part of every sex therapy program. Male sexual dysfunctions include the inability to obtain an erection, inability to maintain an erection, inability to delay ejaculation, and inability to achieve orgasm. Female sexual dysfunctions include the inability to become sexually aroused, inability to become aroused to the point of orgasm, and inability to tolerate vaginal penetration.

In an article in *Annals of Internal Medicine*, April 1976, pp. 448-453, Dr. Stephen B. Levine of the Department of Psychiatry, Case Western Reserve University, Cleveland, Ohio, bases his definition of good sexual function on his work with recovering dysfunctional couples: "Both partners are willing to make love. Each is able to relax. Nonsexual concerns disappear from awareness. A special alteration of consciousness supervenes marked by exclusive attention to one's own and one's partner's pleasurable sensations. The concern for the partner's sensations inconspicuously results in the formation of a feedback system whereby clues from skin, breathing, posture, and utterances are used somewhat automatically to direct what happens next. The pleasure and excitement of each partner is infectious and augments the pleasure and excitement of the other. The rights of each partner to give and receive sexual pleasure, if not equal, are fully acceptable to both. Sex is completed with a high degree of personal pleasure and also with a sense of having shared a meaningful experience."

Dr. Levine points out that a person's sexual problems invariably have profound effects on his or her partner. These effects are the basis for the generalization that there is no such thing as an uninvolved sexual partner.

Dr. William H. Masters and his wife, Dr. Virginia Johnson Masters, pioneers in the field, claim that probably half of U.S. marriages are either sexually dysfunctional now or in danger of becoming so. A problem of this magnitude, which adversely affects millions and exacts so heavy a toll in human misery, deserves a therapy with realistic goals, one that produces results quickly and inexpensively and whose technique can be taught to other professionals.

Many sources of legitimate sex therapy are available. Some people need no more than a book that describes various techniques; others need intensive therapy. Some prefer weekend seminars; still others can be helped by sex therapy tapes. For a few, the particular sexual relationship itself is so bad that not even the most expert sex therapist could help because the problem is not really sexual.

Sex therapy is a term that encompasses a wide range of techniques. Although there are standard procedures followed by qualified sex therapists for certain problems, each program should be adapted to a specific couple's needs. Qualified sex counselors have had a high rate of success in alleviating problems. Some report 98 percent success rate for males with premature ejaculations and 81 percent for women who could not achieve orgasm.

Masters and Johnson believe that treatment should always be conducted by a male-female therapy team. Many, but not all, programs do employ such teams.

The number of therapy sessions required varies. Some programs (e.g., the Masters Johnson Institute) are residential, requiring the couple to be away from home and jobs for a period of time. Others require weekly appointments at a clinic in the person's hometown. Some treatments take one or two consultations; others take weeks, months, and even years.

Most sex therapists do not require clients to remove clothing or perform any sexual acts under observation. Homework assignments are usually a necessary part of the treatment, and it is up to the persons involved to carry them out.

Fees vary from no fee at all to $1,500 and up.

There are two certifying groups for sex therapists, the American Association of Sex Educators (see page 236) and Eastern Academy of Sexual Therapy (see page 237), and although not all legitimate therapists belong, the standards set by these organizations are high and assure you that member therapists have met certain requirements. All the therapists listed in Chapter 2, "Resources for Information on Sex," are certified by one of these organizations or have a fine reputation among medical authorities. You can write to either group, or you can contact your local family service agency or medical society to obtain the names of sex therapists in your area.

Of course, you should remember that in sex therapy, as in any form of counseling, the counselor's qualifications are not the only important factor in the therapy process. It is also vital that you establish a good rapport with the therapist or therapy team.

The following list of organizations can provide you with the names of qualified sex therapists in your area. Since there are many poorly trained or outright charlatans in the field, check first with one or more of the resources listed here.

Resources for Information on Sex

American Association of Sex Educators, Counselors, and Therapists, Suite 304, 5010 Wisconsin Avenue, N.W., Washington, D.C. 20016, (202) 686-2523. This nonprofit organization was founded in 1967 by a group of professional people interested in developing competency and standards for sex educators, counselors, and therapists. Its membership is open to qualified family and sex educators, sex counselors, therapists, researchers, and practitioners. The association currently has two categories of certification: sex educator and sex therapist. The standards for certification are high; they include more than 1,000 hours of employment as a sex therapist and a master's degree or higher.

Here are some key stipulations from the association's code of ethics:

The therapist and/or sex educator shall not be judgmental in promoting or propagandizing a sexual point of view. It is essential that the therapist and/or educator create a climate of openness and trust concerning the sex value systems of the clients/patients and respect their right to express them and value them, irrespective of conflict between sex value systems.

Patient and/or sex therapist nudity in an alleged therapeutic situation is prohibited in a one-to-one therapy situation.

The therapist shall refrain from examining male or female patients for the purpose of stimulating the patient in order to elicit a sexual response. However, the therapist can familiarize the patient/client and his or her partner with the procedure for stimulating a response by suggesting ways in which the couple can experience various responses to sexual stimuli.

All personal information, records, and communications, received about the clients are considered confidential unless clients waive their right to confidentiality in writing.

The association publishes a directory listing more than 600 member therapists. For each listing, a code indicates the treatment format: whether there is an individual therapist or a team and the type of persons treated (heterosexuals, homosexuals, individuals, couples). The price of this publication is $3.

236

Community Sex Information Program, Inc., (212)677-3320. This free telephone information and referral service for sexual health problems is available Monday to Thursday from 6:00 to 8:00 P.M. Dr. Michael Carrera is president of the service, a past president of the American Association of Sex Educators, Counselors, and Therapists, and a professor at Hunter College School of Health Sciences. It is staffed by professionals who volunteer their time.

Eastern Academy of Sexual Therapy, 10 East 88th Street, New York, New York, (212)369-1777. This group, which was founded in 1976, includes both individual therapists and university-affiliated sex therapy programs. All its members have met high standards of practice, including postgraduate training and recognized standard counseling techniques.

Institute for Family Research and Education, 760 Ostrom Avenue, Syracuse, New York 13210, (315)423-4584, Dr. Sol Gordon, director. The institute publishes innovative sex education resource materials, articles, and journals and provides interdisciplinary training programs in family planning, sex education, sex counseling, communication, curriculum development, human relations, group leadership and strategizing skills for professionals and paraprofessionals. It also provides education training programs for religious, education and community service agency staff so that they can learn to help parents deal with the sexual education needs of their children. The institute also provides consultation services to schools, churches, clinics, agencies, and private groups.

PUBLICATIONS

Ten Heavy Facts About Sex. This publication uses a comic book format to tell kids what they want to know. The price is $.45.

Sex Education: The Parents Role. Sol Gordon and Irving Dickman. Public Affairs Pamphlet No. 549. A clear, concise explanation about how parents should approach and discuss sex with children of various ages. The price is $.50.

Sexuality Today and Tomorrow: Contemporary Issues in Human Sexuality, Sol Gordon and Roger Libby. Ed-U Press. This is a wide-ranging collection of original essays and selected pieces from classic and recent works. The price is $7.50.

Sex Information and Education Council of the United States (SIECUS), 84 Fifth Avenue, New York, New York 10011, (212)929-2300. This resource center and catalyst for change provides materials and information for professionals working in the field of human sexuality and sex education and for all individuals interested in increasing their knowledge and understanding of sexuality. SIECUS is a nonprofit, voluntary health organization financed by individual donations and foundations. It is not affiliated with the federal government. For a catalog of publications and to order books, write to Human Sciences Press, 72 Fifth Avenue, New York, New York 10011, or call (800)325-5900 toll free.

PUBLICATIONS

For a single copy of any of the following publications, send a stamped, self-addressed, legal-size (#10) envelope and $.25. Bulk rates are available upon request.

Human Sexuality: Books for Everyone. This is an annotated reading list for the lay public.

Family Life and Sex Education in the School, Church and Home. This United Methodist Church bulletin is a report by the Task Group of the General Committee on Family Life on the controversy over sex education.

Human Sexuality: A Selected Booklist for Professionals. The list was compiled by the SIECUS informational resources staff.

Human Sexuality: Spanish Language Resources. This list of resource organizations and publications on human sexuality and sex education available in Spanish was prepared by the SIECUS informational resources staff.

Sex Education: Position papers on sex education programs.

SIECUS Dispatch. This is an occasional newsletter. It describes new publications available and gives news of sex education programs in the United States.

These publications are available from SIECUS, 137-155 North Franklin Street, Hempstead, New York 11550.

LIST OF SOME CERTIFIED AND/OR WELL-KNOWN SEX THERAPISTS

Alabama

Patricia Travis, M.A., Marital Health Studies, Dept. of Psychiatry, University of Alabama in Birmingham, Birmingham, Alabama 35294. (205)934-3850

Arizona

Robert Cornelius, Ph.D., executive director, Casa Grande Counseling Service, 108 West 4th Street, Casa Grande, Arizona 85222, (602)836-0440.

Arkansas

Calvin Simmons, M.D., 1714 West 42d Street, Pine Bluff, Arkansas 71601. (501)535-3213.

California

Bernard Applebaum, Ph.D., Berkeley Group for Sexual Development, 2614 Telegraph Avenue, Berkeley, California 94704.

Mary Dreyer, M.A., 2369 Highland Avenue, Altadena, California 91001. (213)798-9445.

William Hartman, Ph.D., and Marilyn Fithian, B.A., Center for Marital and Sexual Studies, 5199 East Pacific Coast Highway, Long Beach, California 90815. (213)597-4425.

L. Jerome Oziel, Ph.D., University of Southern California School of Medicine, 1934 Hospital Place, Los Angeles, California 90003. (213)226-2622.

Wayne Schoenfeld, M.A., Los Angeles Guidance and Counseling Service, 924 Westwood Boulevard, Los Angeles, California 90024. (213)477-6017.

Connecticut

George M. Murphy, Ph.D., 45 Elm Street, Winstead, Connecticut 06098. (203)379-1215. (He has several offices.) Senior psychologist, West Hartford Health Department, Town Hall, West Hartford; Member, Counseling Affiliates of Greater Hartford, Suite 334, The Exchange, Farmington. Dr. Murphy is a certified hypnotist as well as a certified sex therapist; he uses hypnosis as the treatment of choice when warranted.

Robert Ryder, Ph.D., University of Connecticut, Storrs, Connecticut 06268. (203)486-3515

Alan J. Wabrek, M.D., Hartford Hospital, Hartford, Connecticut 06115. (203)524-3011.

Colorado

Warren G. Gadpaille, M.D., 3601 South Clarkson, Englewood, Colorado 80110. (303)761-3520.

Florida

Jon E. Mundorff, Ed.D., 3303 Santiago, Tampa, Florida 33609. (813)837-6596.

Libby A. Tanner, M.S.W., Department of Family Medicine, University of Miami Medical School, 1600 N.W. 10th Avenue, Miami, Florida 33152. (305)547-6604.

Georgia

James Kilgore, Rel.D., Northside Medical Center, 275 Carpenter Drive, N.E., Atlanta, Georgia 30328. (404)252-5224.

Frances Nagata, M.S., 3582 Columbia Parkway, Decatur, Georgia 30034. (404)289-4012.

Hawaii

Jack S. Annon, Ph.D., 680 Ainapo Street, Honolulu, Hawaii 96825. (808)395-5157.

Illinois

Sexual Dysfunction Clinic, Loyola University Stritch School of Medicine, 2160 South First Avenue, Maywood, Illinois 60153, (312)531-3000, Domena Renshaw, M.D., director. In addition to training sex therapists, this clinic offers services to persons suffering from sexual dysfunctions, including primary and secondary impotence, dyspareunia, premature or retarded ejaculation, and secondary impotence, dyspareunia, premature or retarded ejaculation, and lack of interest in sex. There is a waiting list both for couples needing sex therapy, and for trainee therapists. Loyola graduates receive first consideration. The innovative program has attracted physician and medical student trainees from out of state and abroad. In a national rating of U.S. Sex Clinics that appeared in *Psychology Today* (March 1976), the Loyola clinic was rated at the top of the list.

Indiana

Indiana University Institute for Sex Research, Alan Bell, Ph.D., sex therapist, Room 416, Morrison Hall, Bloomington, Indiana 47401. (812)332-0211.

Kentucky

Theresa J. Wood, M.S.W., 2266 Bradford Drive, Louisville, Kentucky 40218, (502)456-2203. Ms. Wood, a social worker, is a certified sex educator and sex therapist. She is a clinical member of the National Association of Social Workers and the American Association of Sex

Educators and Counselors and a board member of the American Group Psychotherapy Association.

Maryland

Leonard Derogatis, Ph.D., Johns Hopkins School of Medicine, Baltimore, Maryland 21205, (301)955-5000.

John K. Meyer, M.D., Sexual Behaviors Consultation Unit, Johns Hopkins University, Baltimore, Maryland 21205, (301)955-5000.

John Money, Ph.D., professor of Medical Psychiatry, Johns Hopkins University Hospital, Baltimore, Maryland 21205. Dr. Money, one of the world's leading experts on gender problems, deals with sex problems involving birth defects of the sex organs, psychoendocrinology, sex offenders, transsexualism, and children's sexology, (301)955-5000.

Harvey Resnik, M.D., and Audrey Resnik, R.N., Suite U-4, Science Park Medical Center, 6201 Greenbelt Road, College Park, Maryland 20741, (301)345-2323.

Massachusetts

Eleanor Hamilton, Ph.D., Hamilton School, Inc., Silver Street, Sheffield, Massachusetts 02157, (413)229-2149.

Richard Pigott, Ed.D., 6 Babson Park Avenue, Wellesley Hills, Massachusetts 02157, (617) 237-5992.

Michigan

Marshall Shearer, M.D., and Marguerite Shearer, M.A., East William St., Ann Arbor, Michigan 48106, (313)668-6341.

Loren G. Burt, M.D., 5878 Jerome Road, Alma, Michigan 48801, (517)463-4027.

Minnesota

James W. Maddock, Ph.D., licensed consulting psychologist, 1455 Grantham Street, Saint Paul, Minnesota 55108, (612)647-0062.

Program in Human Sexuality, University of Minnesota Medical School, 2630 University Avenue, S.E., Minneapolis, Minnesota 55514, (612)376-7520. This program offers therapy to individuals, couples, and groups. Clients are often referred by physicians or by various departments within the university. The program also offers Sexual Attitude Reassessment seminars, which are directed primarily to those in the helping professions. Costs vary, depending on the length of the seminar being offered. Therapy costs also vary, depending on the type of treatment offered, the length of treatment, and so forth.

Missouri

Masters and Johnson Institute, 4910 Forest Park Boulevard, Saint Louis, Missouri 63108, (314)361-2377, William Masters, M.D., Virginia Johnson Masters, D.Sc., codirectors. This is the team that taught many of the sex therapists listed in this section. For information about treatment at the institute, write or call the admissions director.

New Hampshire

Norman Tandy, M.A., P.O. Box 2, Winchester, New Hampshire 03470, (603)239-6024.

New Jersey

Center for Sexual and Relationship Enrichment, Teaneck Professional Building, 175 Cedar Lane, Teaneck, New Jersey 07666, (201)837-7200. Kenneth Harman, Ed.D., and Richard Samuels, Ph.D., both certified sex therapists, are the directors of the center, which is a division of the Psychological Service Center (founded in 1955) and the Sexual Enlightenment and Counseling Service (founded in 1974). The center's orientation is based on a psychosexual approach that utilizes current sex therapy techniques integrated within a psychotherapeutic framework. Three basic programs are offered: sex therapy, sexual enrichment, and relationship enhancement. An initial session is conducted to determine the appropriate program, and a medical examination is recommended when the need for one is indicated. Patients are seen regularly and are given assignments to be conducted in the privacy of their own homes. Films are often used to demonstrate the techniques of sex therapy and to guide the patient. Concurrent marital and/or individual psychotherapy is utilized when necessary.

Mona Devanesan, M.D., Mrs. Martha Calderwood, and Morton Sunshine, Sexual Guidance Clinic of the New Jersey College of Medicine, 100 Bergen Street, Newark, New Jersey 07107, (201)456-4300.

Sandra Leblum, Ph.D., clinical associate professor of psychiatry and codirector of sexual counseling, College of Medicine of New Jersey Rutgers Medical School, P.O. Box 101, Piscataway, New Jersey 08854, (201)463-4273 or (201)463-4485.

Dennis Massler, M.D., 1 Center Street, South Orange, New Jersey 07079, (201)763-8104. Dr. Massler is affiliated with the New Jersey College of Medicine.

Hirsch Silverman, Ph.D., 123 Gregory Avenue, West Orange, New Jersey 07052, (201)731-6646.

New York

Mary Ann Friderich, M.D., University of Rochester School of Medicine, 200 White Spruce Boulevard, Rochester, New York 14623, (716)473-3550.

Barbara Hariton, Ph.D., Leon Zussman, M.D., and Shirley Zussman, Ed.D., Long Island Jewish Hillside Medical Center, Hillside Long Island, New York 11040. (212)470-2000.

Sheila Jackman, Ph.D., and Lawrence Jackman, M.D., 12 Greenridge Avenue, White Plains, New York 10605 (914)946-7274, and Albert Einstein College of Medicine, Department of Obstetrics and Gynecology, Division of Human Sexuality, 1165 Morris Park Avenue, Bronx, New York 10461, (212)430-2655.

Helen Singer Kaplan, Ph.D., 30 East 76th Street, New York, New York 10021, (212)249-2914. Dr. Kaplan is a well-known sex therapist, author, and TV personality.

Alexander Levay, M.D., and Virginia Lozzi, M.D., Columbia Presbyterian Medical Center, New York, New York 10032, (212)694-2500.

Rebecca Liswood, M.D., 10 Plaza Street, Brooklyn, New York, (212)UL7-8881. Dr. Liswood, a well-known marriage and family counselor, author and professor, has taught human sexuality at Adelphi University, New York Medical College, and Sheepshead Bay Adult Education School. Her adult education course covers the need for accepting the disillusionment common in the first five years of marriage in such areas as communication, economics, in-law problems, sexual adjustment, contraceptives, venereal disease, and preparation for parenthood. She does private counseling, and her fee is $35 for a fifty-minute hour.

Virginia Lozzi, M.D., 65 East 76th Street, New York, New York, (212)879-7408. Dr. Lozzi is in private practice and on the staff of the Psychiatric Department, Columbia Presbyterian Medical Center, New York, New York 10032.

Avodah K. Offit, M.D., 23 East 69th Street, New York, New York 10031, (212)628-8538. A psychiatrist and author.

Clifford Sager, M.D., Jewish Family Services, 33 W. 60th Street, New York, New York 10023. (212)586-2900.

Paul C. Schiavi, M.D., Mount Sinai School of Medicine, City University of New York, Fifth Avenue at 100th Street, New York, New York 10029, (212)650-6500.

Lawrence Sharpe, M.D., New York State Department of Mental Hygiene, 2 World Trade Center, New York, New York 10047, (212)488-5886.

Don Sloan, M.D., New York Medical College, Flower and Fifth Avenues Hospitals, New York, New York, (212)369-1777.

Stanley Yolles, M.D., State University of New York at Stonybrook, Stonybrook, New York, (516)246-5000.

Arthur Zitrin, M.D., New York University School of Medicine, 550 First Avenue, New York, New York 10003, (212)679-3200.

North Carolina

John Reckless Clinic, 5504 Durham–Chapel Hill Boulevard, Durham, North Carolina, (919)383-1502, John Reckless, M.D., medical director. Dr. Reckless is a psychiatrist who trained with William H. Masters and his staff in Saint Louis in the treatment of sexual dysfunction. He is a member of the editorial board of the *Journal of Marriage and Family Counseling* and a lecturer in nursing at Duke University Medical Center.

Ohio

Robert W. Birch, Ph.D., 5780 Twinsville Drive, Zanesville, Ohio 43701. (614)453-9027.

Stephen B. Levine, M.D., Sex Thereapy Clinic, Case Western Reserve University, Cleveland, Ohio 44106. (216)368-2000.

Oklahoma

Becky Clouse, M.S.W., Family Planning Center, Pott County Health Department, P.O. Box 1487, Route 5, Shawnee, Oklahoma 74801. (405)273-2157.

John B. Nettles, M.D., Hillcrest Medical Center, 1120 South Utica Street, Tulsa, Oklahoma 74104, (918)749-5531.

Oregon

Department of Psychiatry, University of Oregon Medical School, Portland, Oregon 97401, (503)225-8145.

Pennsylvania

L. Michael Ascher, M.D., Temple University School of Medicine, Philadelphia, Pennsylvania 19104, (215)221-4046.

Marriage Council of Philadelphia, Inc., affiliated with the Division of Family Study, Department of Psychiatry, University of Pennsylvania School of Medicine, 4025 Chestnut Street, 2nd Floor, Philadelphia, Pennsylvania 19104, (215)382-6680, Harold Lief, M.D., director. The council's staff not only counsels individuals and couples but also teaches marriage and sex counseling and education to the health professionals, social workers, nurses, and others. Dr. Lief has a long waiting list, but there are about fifteen other staff members who may be able to accept new patients without too long a wait. All fees go to the support of the council, a nonprofit organization.

Gerald Melchrode, M.D., Hahnemann Medical College, Philadelphia, Pennsylvania 19104, (215)448-7000.

Martin Weisberg, M.D., Suite 1020, Jefferson Building, 1015 Chestnut Street, Philadelphia, Pennsylvania 19107, (215)923-5770.

South Carolina

Oliver J. W. Bjorksten, M.D., University of South Carolina, 80 Barre Street, Charleston, South Carolina 29401, (803)777-0411.

South Dakota

Wayne A. Dahl, M.S.W., 2421 South 3d, Sioux Falls, South Dakota 57105, (605)334-9171.

Tennessee

Embry A. McKee, M.D., Department of Psychiatry, Vanderbilt University Hospital, Nashville, Tennessee 37232, (615)322-2665.

Texas

Emma Lee Doyle, Ph.D., 6805 Willow Lane, Dallas, Texas 75230, (214) 386-8600.

Paul C. Weinberg, M.D., Department of Obstetrics and Gynecology, University of Texas Medical School, 7703 Floyd Curl Drive, San Antonio, Texas, (512)691-6181.

Virginia

Brian Campden-Main, M.D., Suite 4A, 3545 Chain Bridge Road, Fairfax, Virginia 22030, (703)385-0406.

Washington, D.C.

Robert A. Harper, Ph.D., MacArthur Medical Center, 4830 V Street, N.W., Washington, D.C. 20007, (202)337-4878.

Ruth Newman, Ph.D., 2761 Brandywine Street, N.W., Washington, D.C. 20008, (202)362-3865.

Patricia Schiller, M.D., J.D., executive director, American Association of Sex Educators and Sex Counselors, Howard University College of Medicine, Washington, D.C. 20016, (202)636-6270.

Washington

Richard B. Hartley, Ph.D., 802 North 12th Street, Tacoma, Washington 98403, (206)272-8223.

Wisconsin

Lloyd Sinclair, M.S.W., 3132 North Del Hill, Route 7, Verona, Wisconsin 53592, (608) 845-9338.

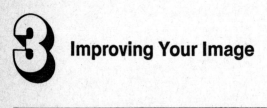

Improving Your Image

"I'm petrified when I have to speak in public."
"He never talks to me!"
"She never listens to what I'm saying."
"I hate to walk into a room full of strangers."

How many times have you heard such statements? How many times have you made them yourself? Communication—between husband and wife, between parent and child, between employee and employer, and between strangers—is a vital but complicated process. It is not just what you say but the way you say it that reveals who you really are and what you mean. Your appearance, the image you project, is also vital. The first impression that you make can prejudice those you meet before you even open your mouth.

Most of us could use help in learning to express ourselves better. The art of communication, both verbal and nonverbal, has become so important today that employers are actually hiring consultants to help employees improve themselves in this area. Dr. Gerald Phillips, professor of speech and communications at Penn State (see page 262) explains that top business leaders and government agencies regard communications skills as the number-one criterion for advancement. "Most people do not work silently anymore. People who are hired for corporate operations, even in steel mills, are required to talk with other people about the job."

Dr. Phillips teaches his pupils, who include steelworkers, that there are proper things to say at various times and places and that one ought to learn what they are and say them. Young people often tell him this concerns foolish small talk, but he informs them that the small talk is important. "When two dogs meet, they sniff each other in order to make a decision about what the relationship is going to be. People do their sniffing through some very highly structured communication exchanges. For instance, while I am going through the routine of "Hello, how are you? What's new?" I am also sizing up your face. I am looking at your responses. You are doing the same thing to me, and we both are making a decision about whether we want to go any farther."

Dr. Phillips identifies the following points about communication:

Communication situations are very complicated.

Communication is evocative. If you are getting a particular kind of response from other people, a response you don't like, then you are going to have to take a look at yourself and figure out what you are doing wrong.

You can't make excuses. You are responsible for the way the other person is affected by you. There is no way you can put more than 50 percent of the blame on your listener.

How can you change long-term habits of speech and body language? Your voice is still your most efficient tool of communication. It carries information about your personality, mood, and present state of functioning. It often tells more about what you are thinking and feeling than you want people to know. There are new techniques and prescribed routines that can change your voice, the way you speak, and even the way you feel when you are talking.

Doe Lang, president of Charismedia, Inc. (see page 254), who teaches private people public speaking and public people more private speaking, believes that the nonverbal is as important as the verbal. She points out that Jimmy Carter does not speak with impeccable elocution but that he comes across as sincere and as a man who genuinely likes people. That's charisma!

Why is it so difficult for so many of us to act and speak well in front of others? One of the first questions Doe Lang asks her pupils in a class is, "Who was the most critical person in your childhood? Was it your father, mother, brother, sister, friend, teacher?" Why does she ask that? Ms. Lang explains: "Because it is vital *you* know so that *you* are aware of who it was that gave you those messages that somehow you are not able to measure up to expectations. If you are petrified getting up to speak before an audience, if you can't carry your own in a conversation with other people, it is because you somehow have lost trust in yourself. As you speak, you hear self-criticism. You build up tension, and your throat tightens." Children, she points out, shout at each other in play all day long and do not become hoarse because they do not constrict their throats. They let their feelings out. When we are uneasy speaking, we constrict our throats, breathe shallowly, and stand awkwardly.

"Just as a dog responds to fear in a human, one human responds to the breathing pattern of another," Ms. Lang. "If you are breathing shallowly or uneasily, the subliminal message will get across to others in the room. Most people breathe shallowly and are unaware that they never really empty their lungs or get a full breath. Some get dizzy the first time they start breathing exercises because they are not used to that much oxygen."

This charismatic teacher of charisma maintains that if you don't know what to do with your hands while talking, you are not only breathing incorrectly, you are standing incorrectly. "If you stand as tall and as comfortably as a tree, you won't have to worry about your hands. You'll gesture naturally."

Ms. Lang feels that you have to be well prepared in order to have spontaneity in speaking. If someone yawns when you are talking, or if the person you most want to impress gets up and walks out, what do you do? How do you react when someone criticizes you or says outlandish things to you?

If you know the answers to these questions, if you are sure of yourself and prepared to handle what happens, you will have charisma, and you will improve your ability to communicate. Chapters 5, 6, and 7 deal with communication both from the lecture podium and face to face between any two humans. No matter what your profession or your position in life is, the ability to express yourself effectively will be of great benefit to you.

TEST YOUR SOCIAL AWARENESS LEVEL

The purpose of this quiz, which was developed by Penn State's College of Agriculture, is to start you thinking and to test your special awareness level. It is part of the first lesson of Course 159, Self-Improvement: A Common Sense Approach. If you wish to take the course and receive the correct answers to the quiz, send $3 to Correspondence Courses, Pennsylvania State University, 307 Agriculture Administration Building, University Park, Pennsylvania 16802.

NAME_____STREET, RFD_____

CITY_____STATE_____ZIP CODE_____

Choose one answer.

1. When giving a party the hostess shakes hands with
 a. those who offer to shake hands
 b. all the guests
 c. women only

2. Men always shake hands when
 a. being introduced to each other
 b. being introduced to women
 c. being introduced to men and women

3. Men rise when being introduced to
 a. another man
 b. a woman
 c. always—man or woman

4. You meet a couple at a friend's house and you have recently entertained the friends. Later, you invite the new couple to dinner at your house. Which of the following is correct?
 a. invite the new friends alone the first time
 b. invite your former host and hostess also
 c. if your former host and hostess cannot come, cancel the dinner until another time

5. The envelope containing your reply to an invitation is addressed
 a. to the host
 b. to the hostess
 c. as it appears in the invitation

6. Engraved invitations to a wedding reception require a formal answer
 a. always
 b. only if you plan to attend
 c. when you are sending your regrets

7. A written regret (to wedding invitation) gives the
 a. time
 b. date
 c. place

8. Midmorning socializing is called a
  a. reception
  b. coffee hour
  c. tea

9. In choosing becoming clothing, the least important item to consider is
  a. high fashion
  b. good taste
  c. figure type

10. Acknowledge an introduction correctly with
  a. "How do you do."
  b. "Pleased to meet you."
  c. "I am glad to make your acquaintance."

11. When dining in a restaurant or a home, married couples are seated, when possible
  a. next to each other
  b. together with wife to the right of her husband
  c. separated and next to other couples

12. When traveling, husband and wife sign the register as
  a. Henry and Nancy Brown
  b. Mr. Henry Brown and Wife
  c. Mr. and Mrs. Henry Brown

13. After being an overnight guest at a friend's home, you correctly show your appreciation by
  a. sending a gift for the house
  b. sending a note as soon as you return; gift is optional
  c. sending a printed thank-you card with your signature

14. When eating soup
  a. dip the soup spoon toward you
  b. dip the soup spoon away from you
  c. tip the bowl

15. When invited as a dinner guest, you properly arrive
  a. five minutes before the dinner hour
  b. fifteen minutes before the dinner hour, to help
  c. five minutes after the dinner hour

16. The correct way to hold a goblet is by
  a. holding the bowl near the top
  b. grasping the stem
  c. placing fingers on top of stem and bottom of bowl

17. To be a popular guest you must
  a. be prompt in accepting or regretting an invitation
  b. delay, and then call at least 24 hours before the party
  c. if you cannot go at the last minute, find someone to go in your place

18. When you are a houseguest don't
  a. keep your room in order
  b. tag along to parties with your host and hostess
  c. offer to help with household chores

19. It is good practice to
a. clean your plate with bread
b. stir foods together on your plate
c. cut one bite of meat at a time

20. When you are not using your knife and fork you may
a. hold them
b. place them across the right-hand side of your plate
c. rest the handles on the tablecloth

21. To consider entertaining you should
a. have sterling silver
b. have bone china
c. do the best you can with what you have

22. At a tea table, the person pouring
a. fills a cup before putting it on a plate
b. puts the cup on a plate and then fills it
c. allows guest to place cup on plate

23. A hostess can make it easier for guest who must hold a filled plate on his lap by using
a. salad plates
b. large plates
c. knives and stemmed glassware

24. Mother is served first when
a. guests are present
b. only the family is present
c. eating in a public dining room only

25. When serving a meal you place, pass, and remove all dishes to the left of the person sitting at the table and this is done with the left hand except for food placed to the right of a guest. The food usually placed and removed at the right side, by the right hand, is
a. salad
b. beverage
c. dessert

26. You can be well-dressed
a. on a small clothes budget
b. if you have lots of money to spend
c. if you have lots of jewelry to wear

27. Appropriate clothing for a woman at an informal buffet is
a. casual dress
b. socks
c. cocktail dress

28. When a death has occurred, you may express sympathy by
a. sending a printed sympathy card
b. calling on the telephone
c. sending a brief handwritten note

29. When a hotel quotes American Plan rates this includes
a. room with breakfast

b. room and all meals

c. room only

30. When visitors arrive unexpectedly, and you are about to leave the house, the proper thing to do is

a. invite them to stay to dinner

b. insist that they call first the next time

c. explain that you were leaving and invite them to come again soon

31. In selecting the silver for each course, begin from the

a. inside

b. outside

c. left side

32. When not seated at a table and you have finished with plate, glass, or cup, you may

a. take it to the kitchen

b. automatically hand it to the hostess

c. take your cue from what the hostess does

33. A good rule for women and men is

a. never lean against anything—walls or furnishings

b. lean only if you can maintain good posture

c. if tired, lean by placing your hand on the wall, not your body

34. To avoid talking too much, allow everyone in a social group to speak before you speak the

a. second time

b. third time

c. fourth time

35. The secret of conversation is to

a. speak at length if you are well informed

b. add something to every subject being discussed

c. be a good listener

36. At the dinner table, when ash trays are *provided*, it is permissible to smoke

a. after the dessert course

b. during the meal

c. between courses

37. It is correct to drink bottled drinks from the bottle *except*

a. when seated at a properly set table

b. standing around in a play room

c. at a picnic

38. When a plate or coaster is not placed under iced-tea glasses, the spoon is

a. left in the glass

b. placed on the dinner plate

c. placed on the table

39. When an intimate friend asks you, the day of an event, to fill a place

a. you are bound by the rules of good manners to accept if possible

b. you have a perfect right to decline the invitation saying you are busy

c. you may decline the invitation with no explanation

40. When you sit down at the table open your napkin
  a. immediately
  b. after the food is served
  c. when the hostess takes and opens hers

41. Whether a meal is correctly called dinner or supper depends upon
  a. the hour it is served
  b. what is served
  c. who is served

42. Hospitality depends more upon
  a. lavishness of provisions
  b. personality
  c. wealth

43. The following should not correctly give showers
  a. friends of honoree
  b. business associates of honoree
  c. families of honoree

44. At any event where gifts are displayed it is correct to
  a. remove the card with name of sender
  b. leave the card with gift
  c. display cards separately with gift described on each

45. If food is too hot,
  a. spit it out in your napkin
  b. take a swallow of water
  c. swallow it quickly

46. When you are the guest of honor, a speaker, or the older person in a group, and a courtesy is extended to you such as the best chair, or arm chair, you should
  a. accept graciously
  b. decline graciously
  c. feel insulted

47. Gum chewing is not frowned upon usually
  a. in church
  b. on the street
  c. at home

48. Develop the habit of thinking before you speak. Acceptable topics are
  a. your child or children
  b. your wealth
  c. civic affairs

49. When you have received a gift for any reason you may
  a. thank the giver in person
  b. thank the giver by telephone
  c. always write a personal note promptly

50. Social awareness is
  a. putting on airs
  b. knowing what to do and acting quickly
  c. showing off to let others know you know the correct thing to do

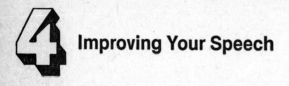

Improving Your Speech

Do you have difficulty saying what you mean?

Does your throat feel tight when you talk before strangers or when you are feeling strong emotions with a loved one?

Dr. Gerald Phillips, a professor of communications at Penn State University (see page 262) points out that most of us mistakenly believe that speech is spontaneous . . . that it just happens.

"You can't do something as important as getting another person to like and respect you by expecting that it will just happen. You have to deliberately plan how you want to be seen. You have to select general information and transmit it to other people. Nobody can see into your head. You can be warm, kind, gentle, but that may not be the impression you convey by your speech."

The following experts can help you speak better than you do now, no matter what your problem may be. You can learn to really *communicate*, whether before a large audience or in the privacy of your own home.

Georgia

Speakeasy Inc., Suite 1130, 400 Colony Square, Atlanta, Georgia 30361, (404)892-0889, Sandy Linver, president. Speakeasy's courses are aimed at middle-level and upper-level executives who need help in speech effectiveness. There is a three-day seminar, Seriously Speaking, for $495 per person; classes are limited to ten students. Speakeasy will also conduct seminars tailored to an individual firm's needs; the fee is $1,500 per day, plus travel expenses.

New York

Charismedia, Inc., 610 West End Avenue, New York, New York 10024, (212)362-6808, Doe Lang, director. Ms. Lang is a multitalented woman. A former Fulbright scholar, she studied opera in Italy and has been a pianist, opera singer, and performer on stage and television. She played nurse Karen Adams in "As the World Turns" and Maria in *West Side Story.* According to the dictionary, *charisma* is a personal magic of leadership, arousing special popular loyalty or enthusiasm. But according to Ms. Lang, it is a divine attribute within *each* of us. The trouble is that we are not always in touch with our personal charisma because we have become self-critical and blocked.

Ms. Lang teaches at the New School in New York City and at the American Management Association and gives classes for individuals and small groups in her own studio. She acts as a consultant to many corporations, making their executives more charismatic, and to authors, politicos, and people from every walk of life. Nothing pleases her more than to see one of her pupils on television expressing and defending his or her ideas effectively. She believes we are all "works in progress" and that anyone can learn to communicate charismatically.

Here are some of her techniques to help you look comfortable when you are really uptight, to make your speech more effective and spontaneous, and to prepare you to be at your best even when you feel less than your best.

Breathing properly can change how you feel and how you come across and can enable you to respond optimally to pressure. As you increase your intake of air, you greatly increase your stamina, stability, endurance under stress, and composure. Studies show that people who are composed are viewed as more authoritative.

Stand with your feet apart (at about shoulder width), and feel that the floor is there to support you. (It is.) Relax your shoulders, arms, and hands. If necessary, clench your fists hard for 5 counts, then relax them. Begin slow, deep breathing (your shoulders shouldn't rise). Think of the area from your ribs to your groin as a balloon that expands roundly as you slowly fill it with air. Make sure you exhale completely before inhaling again.

When you want to make an off-the-cuff remark, take a deep breath *first* (without raising your shoulders). The greater oxygen supply thus carried to the brain triggers alertness, fast response, and creative intuition.

Licking the lips is an undesirable nonverbal symptom of nervousness. To avoid dryness, put Vaseline on the inner portion of the lips. It won't show, but it will prevent discomfort because of dryness and thus eliminate lip licking.

To find best head position, drop your head to your chest as low as it will go, and very, very slowly unroll the back of the neck (not by lifting the chin, as usually happens) until you feel that your head is exactly poised at the end of your spine as a continuation of the spine. You will be able to feel when it is in this organic position. (It will probably seem to you that your head is slightly lower or higher than usual.) This position looks good, feels good, obviates tension, and helps keep the throat open, and your eyes will now be at intense-gaze level.

The throat tends to tighten under pressure. To keep it open, imagine a huge ball in the back of your mouth, and yawn with your mouth closed. (This requires practice to locate muscles at back of neck that expand, but it's worth it. It will be easier if you remember how you stifle a yawn when you are bored.) This is much more effective than throat clearing. In this closed-mouth, open-throated position, inhale and exhale slowly 5 times. Keep your jaw and shoulders relaxed throughout. Visualize air smoothing the frown lines between your brows.

To achieve the right preperformance look, hum until your head feels like a vibrating, empty cage of bones. Mentally surround your entire head with this hum. Think of something delightful that gives you a lot of pleasure. You will begin to smile, and as you do, your cheekbones will lift, your eyes will be open and alert, your face will look alive. Drop the smile from your mouth, but leave it on the rest of your face. Continue slow, steady breathing. The result of the open throat, relaxed mouth, lifted cheekbones, and alert eyes is excitement without tension.

To achieve natural pacing, breathe between phrases, articulate clearly, make eye contact, and pause after something important while holding eye contact.

Stick to simple words. Your audience must be able to understand, follow, and be interested in everything you say. Keep it human.

To conquer stagefright, clench your fists powerfully, stand with your feet wide apart, bend from the waist (dropping head and torso), and begin to inhale powerfully in quick breaths with mouth closed, coming up as you do. On the third part of the breath, your arms should be high over your head. Now, exhale and bring your arms down in a karate chop; at the same time, let out the deepest, most powerful "Hah!" you can summon from the depths of your gut, bending your knees and bringing your arms way down in one sweeping movement. Movement and sound should be simultaneous. Do this 5 times. (Obviously, you will need privacy for this exercise. Do it in the john if no other place is available.) You will emerge calm, refreshed, and ready for everything.

Doe Lang's fees vary depending on whether lessons are private or in a group and on how much instruction you need. Private lessons range from $100 to $175 per hour; some partial scholarships are available. Fees for workshops and classes are based on duration, group size, and location. TV playback is used for all classes.

PUBLICATION

The Charisma Book, Doe Lang. New York: Wyden Books, 1980.

Communispond, 485 Lexington Avenue, New York, New York 10017,

(212)687-8040; 1156 Fifteenth Street, N.W., Washington, D.C. 20005, (202)296-6450; 875 North Michigan Avenue, Chicago, Illinois 60611, (312)787-0484; 27 Central Avenue, Glen Rock, New Jersey 07452, (201)445-0050. This company has many different programs and communications services, ranging from techniques for running meetings (closed conferences, news briefings, general meetings) to the development of effective speaking in the individual. The motto of the company is "to speak as well as you think."

Communispond has developed a "simple, direct way that enables any speaker to remove the barriers and let the ideas come out naturally with all the force and impact intended." Their approach does not involve practiced behavior, tricks, or changes in outlook. It does, according to Communispond, involve a number of principles that are quickly learned and mastered and that enable you to become more relaxed, more yourself. You learn to use your nervousness to "free up your resources" and thereby come across with natural, human conviction.

On the first day of the General Program, you participate in the following sessions:

Benchmark: You take a good look at your current skills on videotape.

Physical control/nervousness: You learn fundamental skills to control nervousness and reduce audience pressure so that you can think more clearly.

Physical control/inhibitions: You expand your visual and vocal skills to project your message better and to overcome inhibitions so that you will be more natural.

Visual presentation: You develop and deliver a visual presentation for maximum attention and retention. This presentation is videotaped and reviewed.

On the second day of the General Program, you give a presentation to persuade. The assignment and format for this talk are given at the end of the first day. Your presentation is videotaped and reviewed. Your course concludes with lectern techniques and how to handle question-and-answer sessions.

Upon the completion of the two-day program, you will have learned how to overcome nervousness and inhibitions through understanding of their cause and an entirely new method for organizing and visualizing presentations that can be applied not only in the program but in all future meetings. You will also have learned how to maintain control and be most effective during a critical dialogue or question-and-answer session with a group, how to give yourself more time to think, and how to keep your listeners involved.

The General Program consists of two 8-hour days and 3 hours of preparation on the evening of the first day. Charges are $675 per participant and $9,500 for the corporate program (twenty participants at $475 each). The fee for private instruction is $1,500.

Alfred Dixon Speech Systems, 138 East 36th Street, New York, New York 10016, (212)MU5-6415. Alfred and Elizabeth Dixon have worked as voice coaches for a show business who's who: Julie Andrews, Lauren Bacall, Warren Beatty, Barbara Bel Geddes, Charles Boyer, Kirk Douglas, Michael Douglas, Peter Falk, Jane Fonda, Rex Harrison, Rod Steiger, Edwin Newman, Loretta Swit, Jon Voight, and many others. Ms. Dixon is also voice coach consultant to major businesses and presents executive training programs and seminars.

Among the subjects: Speech for Theatre, Dialect Accents and Regionalisms Removed and Taught, Dramatic Coaching, Delivery for Public Speaking, and Clinical Therapy.

Ms. Dixon offers these general hints about speech: Examine tempo, volume, and clarity of diction, the three important factors of your speech. You can do this by taping your voice on a recorder and then listening carefully. Are you too breathy, too squeaky, too fast? Ask people who will be honest in their criticism to help you evaluate your delivery. Solicit regular feedback as an important step in changing your speech. Slow your tempo (speaking too slowly is rarely a fault). You can do this by deliberately thinking in idea units and by holding pauses, which will give you a chance to gather your thoughts into units for the next phrase.

You can work a little on your voice each day. Using your tape recorder, practice reading lyrical poetry, such as that of Keats or Shelley, which contains rich, flowing vowel sounds. Good speakers, Ms. Dixon says, are like good singers: "They tend to emphasize the vowel sounds while they just touch on the consonants and run." Do you speak too softly? If everyone keeps saying they can't hear you, you probably do. But simply speaking louder won't always help. It may also be that you are not speaking clearly enough or that you are talking too fast.

Here are some of Ms. Dixon's tips for parties:

Sounding good begins with a relaxed mind-set, so above all, try to hang loose, both mentally and physically.

Don't try to scream over the music. You can sometimes make yourself heard merely by lowering the pitch of your voice.

Work on your timing. Observe people who hold everyone's attention; you'll notice that they have excellent timing. There is always a brief pause between the time one person finishes speaking and the time his or her words register in the minds of others. You have to allow for that brief conversational beat before you start to speak. Otherwise, you will be talking into people's thought processes, and what you have to say won't sink in because your listeners are still digesting what someone else has said.

If throat discomfort results from your efforts to change your speech, it could mean that the muscular coordination involved in speaking is faulty and needs the attention of a speech professional.

Private lessons are available by the hour and the half hour; classes are available by special arrangement. Rates are $35.00 per hour and $17.50 per half hour.

Dr. William Formaad, 903 Union Street, Brooklyn, New York 11215, (212)857-8794. A professor and director of Communication Sciences and Disorders at Seton Hall University, Dr. Formaad gives private lessons in speech, voice and diction, language improvement and refinement, and accent problems. He keeps the names of clients, who include executives, professionals, singers, actors, and announcers, strictly confidential. Dr. Formaad works with actual conversation rather than isolated exercises. Each session is tape-recorded, and the individual progresses as fast as he or she is willing to work. The preliminary course is ten sessions, $450. Individual sessions are $50 each. Workshops for organizations are arranged. Fee is negotiable. Dr. Formaad also trains speech therapists. He is past president of the New Jersey Speech and Hearing Association and is a fellow of the American Speech and Hearing Association.

'UBLICATION

Articulation Therapy Through Play: A Multiple Sensory Approach, William Formaad. Exceptional Press, Glen Ridge, New Jersey, 1974. The price of the book is $8.95 for the hardcover edition and $4.95 for the paperback edition. The book contains procedures for correcting speech problems through communication-centered games and other activities for children.

Henry Jacobi, 344 West 72d Street, New York, New York 10023, (212) 362-6311. When you teach voice to members of the American Shakespeare Festival at Stratford, Connecticut, to members of the Repertory Theater of Lincoln Center, and to the members of the Salzburg Opera Guild, you have to be an expert. Professor Jacobi, who became a certified voice teacher at the age of nineteen in Berlin, Germany, and who held a professorship at the International Music Conservatory in Havana, Cuba, has had his own studio in New York for many years. His client list includes Jean Arthur, Martin Balsam, Dyan Cannon, Faye Dunaway, Lee Grant, Jack Lord, Anthony Perkins, Tony Randall, Maureen Stapleton, Cicely Tyson, Brenda Vaccaro, and many other celebrities of the stage, screen, musical comedy, and opera, as well as executives in industry who are seeking to develop vocal techniques to improve their sales presentations.

Professor Jacobi says there are four essential qualities to be found in the human voice: freedom, flow, ring, and roundness. These are the seeds that can grow and become manifest if you know how to look for them and if the conditions for their development are right. Private lessons are $25.00 for a half hour; semiprivate, $12.50.

Speech Dynamics. A subsidiary of Ogilvy & Mather International, 111 W. 57th Street, New York, New York 10019, (212)759-3996. Dorothy Sarnoff, speech consultant to top executives of corporations, prime ministers, officials and television personalities, State Department officials and plain ordinary folk who can spend six hours to learn how to present themselves and their ideas persuasively, is almost as famous as some of her star pupils. Author of *Speech Can Change Your Life* (Doubleday, $6.95) and a former opera singer and actress and chairwoman of Speech Dynamics, a wholly owned subsidiary of Ogilvy & Mather International, she has personally taught more than 50,000 people. Dorothy Sarnoff maintains that everytime you speak to someone, you say something about yourself. "People often judge you on your communicating style alone. You want every word you say to help create a powerful, positive impression on your audience, be it an audience of only one . . . or 1,000." You can take her course either privately, a total of six hours, or in a two-day intensive course. First you are recorded on closed circuit television. Then you watch a playback. You see yourself objectively, the way others see you. Together with Dorothy Sanoff and her staff, you acknowledge positives, eliminate detracting elements from your speech and actions, then add the spice and style that may be missing.

There is, of course, more to communication than just words. So Speech Dynamics works toward improving your total image: the way you look, your clothes, and your overall grooming. You work diligently on the nonverbal impact of your appearance, your face, your eyes, your tone, and your demeanor. You learn how to command and hold the attention of your audience. You also learn how to give a speech without reading it. And you develop greater self-confidence.

Dorothy Sarnoff offers these hints to help you improve your communication:

Good posture is essential for good voice. Keep your chest up and your abdomen in.

Resonate in your chest rather than in your nose. Many people talk with nasal resonance and high pitch, which produces an abrasive sound. Try to support the voice strongly by exhaling with the rib cage held high, and try to use the low end of your pitch scale.

Variety of pacing and phrasing can improve your style. Speak in phrases as though you are gliding from word to word—smoothly, not choppily, as though starting and stopping with your foot on and off the gas pedal.

Go down in pitch more often, particularly at the end of phrases and on anything you wish to emphasize.

Keep a mirror near your telephone so you can see yourself talking, and watch your face. If you look happy, your voice will sound happy. But when your face droops, so does your voice.

Keep the tape recorder on when you are on the phone or at home with friends. Play it back; listen; then practice to improve on what you hear.

Here are two exercises to improve your voice:

1. Stand in front of the mirror. Put your hands in a steeple position in front of you, with your elbows up and out. Push your hands together, heel to heel, as hard as you can, so hard that you can feel the pressure under the armpits. While you do this, contract the muscles where your ribs start to separate above your abdomen, and say, "Shshshshshsh," exhaling so that you feel your stomach muscles contracting. This is good for projecting.

2. Walk short city blocks in long exhalations. You may need only three exhalations to a city block. That does not mean you take big breaths. Big breaths are not necessary, just long, long exhalations.

In giving talks or making presentations, remember these points:

Keep your speeches short. It should not be longer than twenty minutes.

Do not start out with "it's a privilege," "it's a pleasure," or the like.

Always begin with something that is attention-getting and that will relax you and your audience. Use a light touch. Start with something local and/or an anecdote or something unexpected.

In the body of the speech, ask questions, give illustrations, examples, things that involve the listeners and relate to their lives.

Be descriptive. Use images that the listener can see in the mind's eye.

End with something memorable—a quote, a startling fact, a call to action.

When you type or write your speech in longhand, capitalize all the letters and triple space the lines. Mark the phrases for emphasis, color, pauses, and pacing.

If you walk to the lectern saying, "I love that audience" to yourself and look directly into the eyes of the crowd, you can't help but win them over.

Ms. Sarnoff is in demand around the world, giving seminars or private courses, presenting her techniques for improving communication on company premises in England, France, Germany, Austria, and Denmark as well as in the United States. She was one of the first to use TV playback to show a person just how he or she acts while conversing. Her methods have been widely imitated, a sincere form of flattery.

She conducts an intensive two-day course with eight to ten people in a class twice a month as well as her individual lessons and seminars. Speech Dynamics, Inc. also makes video tapes for Intra Company executive messages.

Ms. Sarnoff did not wish to publicize prices.

RECORDINGS

Dorothy Sarnoff Speech Dynamics, Inc. has cassettes of her techniques for sale.

1. How to control nervousness
2. How to prepare a talk or presentation
3. How to rehearse and deliver a talk or presentation

The casettes are $29.95 each plus tax and $1 for postage and handling. You can ask for the list by writing to Speech Dynamics Cassettes, 111 West 57th Street, New York, New York 10019.

Pennsylvania

Empathic Communication and Interpersonal Negotiation, Individual and Family Consultation Center, Pennsylvania State University, College of Human Development, Catherine Beecher House, University Park, Pennsylvania 16802, (814)865-1751. The center offers training in interpersonal and emotional life skills. Empathic communication, interpersonal negotiation, conflict resolution, and other relationship-building skills are taught to small groups (usually no more than six people). The training is conducted by faculty and graduate students. Individuals or couples may be accepted for nongroup tutoring. Often, members of the same family are involved in the learning process together and practice the skills together. Group interaction is not freewheeling; rather, it is restricted to behavior that the center believes fosters the learning of communications skills.

The basic training program requires two to three hours a week for ten weeks for skill training and supervision, plus homework assignments that require another hour or so. After an interview in which the goals and methods of the program are explained, clients are asked to decide whether they wish to enter the program with a commitment to see it through or not to undertake it at all. (Very few people decline, and almost none indicate any serious dissatisfaction with the program once it is under way.)

After the completion of the basic training, clients may choose to continue in the same group or in another one that is at a similar stage of training. They may continue for another ten weeks or even for periods spanning a year or two. Those who continue beyond twenty weeks are often (but not necessarily) working to resolve seriously disturbing problems that have threatened the quality of an important interpersonal relationship; that is, they use the skills they have learned and the supervision provided to them by the center to work through these problems. No matter how long a group has been in existence, center personnel never participate as problem solvers or helpers *per se*; their role is always that of teacher and supervisor of the skills needed to resolve problems.

In the long-term groups, the goals are often no different from those of marital counseling, psychotherapy, child psychotherapy, or family therapy. However, the means to these ends differ. The clients have acquired skills to help them reach these goals, and they, *not* the instructor, accept the responsibility for using the relationship-enhancing, psychotherapeutic, and problem-solving skills they have acquired to reach the goals.

Certain programs at the center are almost always available:

Filial Relationship Enhancement and Enrichment: Children from two to ten years of age and one or both parents participate in this program together. In a series of courses, the instructor systematically teaches and supervises the parent, who acquires skills designed to improve communication, create a sense of mutual understanding and harmony, and use emotions constructively. The instructor teaches children effective personal and social skills.

Parent/Adolescent Relationship Development: This program covers the age range from eleven to young adulthood. It provides child-parent pairs with systematic training and supervision to develop skills designed to enhance communication, utilize emotions constructively, and resolve conflict successfully.

Relationship Enhancement and Conjugal Harmony: This program is for married couples. In a series of courses, they are systematically trained and supervised in skills designed to open up communication, utilize feelings constructively, and resolve conflict successfully.

Family-Life Improvement Program: Parents and children nine years old and older are taught communication and problem-resolution skills as a family, with goals similar to those described for the other programs. This program is also appropriate for family subgroupings, such as one parent and two children or two parents and some of the children.

Premarital Relationship Improvement via Maximizing Empathy and Self-Disclosure: Through teaching couples skills such as those described for the program for married couples, the program seeks to provide dating couples with a deep understanding of each other. This should help them make a more realistic choice about marriage and, if they marry, should provide them with skills that may increase their marital happiness. It is hoped that this program will also help a couple to provide a more stable and harmonious environment in which to raise a family.

Marital Enhancement Program for Wives. The goals of this program are the same as those of the Relationship Enhancement and Conjugal Harmony program. However, the program is modified to accomplish the more difficult task of doing this when the husband is unwilling or unable to participate in the program.

Marital Enhancement Program for Husbands. This program is similar to the Marital Enhancement Program for Wives except that it is designed to meet the problem of nonparticipating wives.

The center also can call upon professionals from the College of Human Development's services who offer guidance in financial management and nutrition for individuals and families. Fees on a sliding scale according to ability to pay.

Improved Communication Through Theater

Theater techniques are increasingly employed by psychotherapists, teachers, and other professionals to help people express their feelings. You can learn poise and grace as well as appropriate communication through playacting and mime.

Interplay Productions, Inc., 3430 North Abingdon Street, Arlington, Virginia 22207, (703)524-1616. Donn Murphy, professor of theater at Georgetown University, is president of this group, which creates environment participation theater pieces, in which the audience members become performers in the drama. These events are designed to encourage individuals who may have had no previous experience in any type of creative performance to express themselves through bodily movement in the presence of others. Carefully structured exercises in a spirit of fun enable all to lose their inhibitions and explore their creative potential.

Here is a sample exercise you can perform by yourself: Take the point of a pencil, and make a hole in a piece of paper. Look through the hole. What do you see? One tiny part of the environment with a new structure and beauty.

Dr. Murphy believes that the more carefully, completely, and honestly we can perceive what is happening in the environment, the more we can reflect it in our art and in our lives. He says that good conversationalists, for instance, are not people who store a lot of facts in their heads; rather, they are the ones who are more clearly able to perceive the person with whom they are talking. He cites as an example a party he attended in Washington. He told a woman there that he liked her dress very much. "I wouldn't have told her if I didn't mean it. She said I was the only one who noticed it, and she had bought the dress especially for the occasion." The professor says that if you learn to perceive people with a little more care, you will be able to deal with them more successfully.

Interplay Productions help college students, general audiences, and even hospitalized schizophrenics gain more control over their emotions and environments. Performances, which are often free, are given in the Washington, D.C., area under various sponsorships. The cost for a group wishing to sponsor a performance is $300.

Pocket Mime Theatre, P.O. Box 269, Boston, Massachusetts 02117, (617)266-1770. While touring throughout the United States, the Pocket Mime Theater offers classes, workshops, and lecture-demonstration programs in addition to its concerts. The introductory course is for beginning students or for those who wish to brush up on their technique. Each class is divided into three parts:

Movement for mime: These are mime, movement, and dance exercises designed to increase the strength, stretch, and control necessary for nonverbal theater.

Mime technique: Basic illusionary mime techniques in four major categories—isolation, force illusions, transportation illusions, and object illusions—are surveyed.

Acting for mime: This covers applications of acting technique to the special needs of the mime performer.

For the intermediate student, the class division is:

Movement for mime: vigorous, varied, and fun. The program calls for work on balance, coordination, basic tumbling, conditioning, and simple equipment work.

Mime technique: This session covers illusionary mime technique in theory and practice for the serious student, including principles of illusion, explanation, and demonstration. Attention is given to problem solving and details of performance.

Acting for mime: This session is devoted to creating the mime character. Basics of characterization are covered in terms of body communication, including yourself as a character, typical characters, atypical characters, caricatures, and everyman/clown characters.

St. Nicholas Theater Company, 2851 North Halsted, Chicago, Illinois 60657, (312)348-8415. This outstanding off-Broadway-type theater company offers professional evening and weekend classes in tap dancing, modern dancing, jazz dancing, and ballet, voice and speech, acting technique, scene study, directing, fencing, makeup, design, and creative dramatics for children (a mother and daughter might be able to attend at the same time). The cost of lessons ranges from $35 to $90 per session.

PART V

Getting and Keeping More Money

Employment and Career Counseling and Information

Do you want to find a job? Change jobs? Get promoted? There are many skilled career counselors in the field who can help. There are also others in the field whose job may be just to take your money and do nothing. The following services are well known and reputable. Some are free. Some are quite expensive. All provide brochures that describe what they have to offer.

John C. Crystal Center, 894 Plandome Road, Manhasset, New York 11040, (516)627-8802. John C. Crystal's Life/Work Planning Process has been widely imitated around the world. Before World War II, Crystal majored in economics at Columbia University and then became an interpreter and intelligence officer in the army because he loved languages and was a true cosmopolitan. After numerous careers, including that of counterspy, he developed a new approach to career development. He found, for instance, that "résumés are a farce, a waste of time," and "personnel departments don't hire anyone, except for other people to work in the personnel department." Crystal maintains that the good jobs are given by top executives who deal on a personal basis with the people they hire. They are not interested in résumés or the usual bureaucratic appurtenances of hiring.

At dozens of colleges and universities, students are getting credits for learning how to find a job. Most of these courses are based to one degree or another on Crystal's pioneering work. Bits and pieces of it are also being taught at churches, corporations, service organizations, and other institutions all over the nation.

The center offers a twelve-week course, 3½ hours per week, that involves the Life Planning Process. Crystal also offers a one-week intensive course for people who do not live in the area and who visit the center. Crystal also has a one-day workshop that gives an overview of the Crystal process. The workshop runs from 9:00 A.M. to 5:00 P.M. and is usually held in Manhattan. Under special circumstances, Crystal will offer courses at universities and other institutions.

The fee for the full course, which includes tuition, materials, and individual counseling, is $500. The fee for the one-week course is $500; room and board are extra. The one-day workshop is $75.

The Life Planning Process helps you answer the following basic questions:

What do I really know?
What do I really want to learn?
Who am I?
What is the truth about the realities of the world of work?
What do I most want to accomplish with my life?
How do I go about accomplishing my goals?
What activities do I like to do the most?
What skills are involved in them that I really enjoy and that seem to come to me naturally?
What are my strongest personal qualities?
What type of people do I like most?
What must a career offer, both professionally and personally, to make me truly happy?
Where would I like to live?
Having chosen a career, what are my ultimate lifetime goals?
What do I require in order to realize these ambitions?
How do I achieve them in a balanced life entirely under my own control?

In short, the process helps you to choose and obtain the satisfying job or career that you really want. The fees are $35 for the one-day workshop, $450 for the full course, $525 (including lodgings) for the intensive course, $200 for the advanced course, and $100 for the young adult course.

Crystal maintains that a satisfying career is designed and built, not found and exploited. He claims the basic mistake most job seekers make is the failure to understand that they can control their own lives and careers and he believes you can do what you really want to do and get paid for it. Crystal's process was first summarized nationally in the still best selling, *What Color Is Your Parachute?: A Practical Manual for Job-Hunters and Career Changers*, Richard Bolles. Berkeley, California: Ten Speed Press, 1972. The price is $4.95.

PUBLICATION

Where Do I Go From Here With My Life? John C. Crystal and Richard Bolles. New York: Seabury Press, 1974. The price is $7.95. This is a step-by-step manual that tells how and when to make changes in your career.

Federal Job Information Centers, U.S. Civil Service Commission, Washington Area Office, Washington, D.C. 20415. The U.S. Civil Service Commission offers employment information through a nationwide network of Job Information Centers. If you want to learn about federal employment, you can visit, write, or call the nearest center. The facilities offer information about jobs in other jurisdictions (city, county, or state). You can get a directory of centers that includes the toll-free telephone numbers by requesting it from the Washington office.

Flexible Careers, 37 South Wabash, Chicago, Illinois 60603, (312)236-6028. This is a volunteer, nonprofit organization providing career information for women. Its services include peer counseling, job-hunting techniques, group counseling, courses, workshops, and job placement. Volunteers and staff are researching and developing flexibly scheduled employment opportunities, as well as working toward improved employment opportunities in general for women. Hours are 9:00 A.M. to 3:00 P.M. Wednesday; 3:30 to 7:30 P.M., Thursday; and 9:00 A.M. to 3:00 P.M., Friday. Hours will be expanded in the future, so please check. The registration fee is $30 for two sessions and includes the help of the People Network, a resource for clients ready to investigate a career field. It provides clients with information direct from women and men who are knowledgeable and experienced in the working world.

Individual Development Center, 1020 East John, Seattle, Washington 98102, (206)329-0600, Alene H. Moris, director. The center's staff of professional counselors offers decision-making assistance to individuals who need to think through a career or personal problem as objectively as possible. Résumé writing and job-search techniques are covered, and there are sessions designed to assist in developing effective interpersonal communication skills. Staff members act as career consultants and workshop leaders for many groups in business, government, and education, offering individual counseling for employees and seminars designed for managers and supervisors emphasizing both awareness and practical career coaching techniques. They can also assist in designing seminars for conventions and conferences. The center also has a terminal to the Washington Occupational Information Service, a computerized program of regional data, that provides up-to-date information on job market conditions. Contact the center for further information. Fees for individual counseling, $35 per hour. Group session with five to ten people in a group, seven days for two and a half hours each day; one individual counseling session afterward and including a testing package, $240.

Job Opportunities Information Center, Mid-Manhattan Library of the New York Public Library, 8 East 40th Street, New York, New York 10017 (212)790-6588. This free service aims to simplify your problem in finding employment by gathering all job-related information in one place. It acts as an up-to-date clearinghouse information on public- and private-sector job opportunities in the metropolitan area. A specially trained librarian is available daily from 9:00 A.M. to 5:00 P.M. to offer you assistance, provide you with information about techniques for finding employment, make appropriate referrals, and assist you in utilizing the library's vast resources. The librarian will provide names and addresses of possible contacts in specialized areas. Directories such as the Public Relations Blue Book, *Shopping Center Directory*, and *Who's Who in Insurance*, as well as vocational pamphlets and appropriate periodicals, are available. The Mid-Manhattan Library, library centers, and some regional libraries have special materials relating to federal, state, and city civil service positions and examinations, including copies of past New York City civil service examinations.

PUBLICATION

Job Opportunities Bulletin, Division of Examinations, New Jersey Department of Civil Service, 209 East State Street, Trenton, New Jersey 08625.

Life Management Services, Inc., 6825 Redmond Drive, McLean, Virginia 22101, (703)356-2630. If you are unemployed, underemployed, hoping to change careers, unhappy with your work, stymied by the system, a housewife or widow facing the world of work with anxiety, a teen-ager, a student, or someone facing retirement, LMS offers a series of time-proven and highly successful career and life planning programs. The concept of these services had their genesis with John Crystal (see page 269), with whom LMS president, Hal Shook, worked closely for more than ten years. LMS courses now have their own flavor, a blend of the Crystal-Bolles Life/Work Planning Process and other innovations. The mission of LMS is described by one of the participants: "You ask me what I got out of your course. I had an opportunity to look at me in a very special way. Using the autobiography, and the quick Job Hunting Map, I found out who I am, where I really want to go and what strengths I have to get there."

LMS offers a variety of courses and services in the Washington, D.C., area. Arrangements can be made for 1 to 1½-hour presentations anywhere. There is a ten-session course and an intensive one-week complete course. There is also a recently packaged version of the complete course tailored especially for young adults. The course can be presented by secondary- and college-level career and guidance counselors and others who work with young people. All the current services, as well as specially tailored courses, are available on a contract basis to the private sector (organizations, government, and institutions) around the country.

The ten-week course costs $500, and the one-week intensive course costs $650, including lodgings.

National Association of Personnel Consultants, 1012 14th Street, N.W., Washington, D.C. 20005, (202)638-1721. There are 8,600 placement firms that function throughout the country. Not all are honorable. Some overcharge, promise jobs they don't have, and waste your time and money. Approximately 2,600 reputable firms belong to this association, which requires all members to adhere to a stringent code of ethics. Service charges for placement firms vary, so read any contract carefully before signing. Some employers will pay the entire fee, some will pay only part, and some won't pay at all. If you do not accept a position, you do not have to pay a reputable firm's fee. If you accept the job and then lose it, that situation may be covered by state or local laws and is usually spelled out in the contract. The organization puts out a directory that includes a listing of firm specialties; The cost is $3.50 prepaid. Write for it at the above address.

National Personnel Associates, 150 Fountain Street, Grand Rapids, Michigan 49503, (616)459-5816. This is a recruiting network of independent management-level personnel services with 200 offices in 130 cities; the members cooperate in filling jobs internationally by exchanging résumés and job listings. Membership is by invitation only and is based on high standards; therefore, you are assured that you are being represented by professionals. Many NPA offices are internationally known for their expertise in specific fields. As a client, you are provided with current and continuing information on where your major opportunities are based. An industry index is drawn up by staff members from the multiple offices. When your career objective is linked to a preference for a section of the country or a region of the world, NPA's offices are a distinct advantage. One contact places all of NPA's services and its entire organization at your disposal; it is not dissimilar to the way a house is multiple-listed by real estate firms.

Of course, agencies can do an excellent job of lining up potential jobs for you and arranging interviews, but if you don't take proper advantage of the opportunity, it's your fault. What are the reasons most people fail to obtain a job? Charles W. Marks, NPA's executive director, says that a survey of staff experts from the organization's offices came up with the twelve basic reasons (in descending order of frequency) why job applicants are turned down by employers. He/she who is forewarned is forearmed.

1. Too many jobs. (The cost of hiring an applicant who might soon leave is too high.)

2. Reluctance of an employee or spouse to relocate.

3. Having the wrong personality for the employer. (Highly subjective factors come into play here.)

4. Unrealistic salary requirements.

5. Candidate is judged not to have the needed background.

6. Poor employment record.

7. Candidate is unresponsive, disinterested, or unprepared during the interview.

8. Candidate handles negotiations with prospective employer improperly.

9. Candidate judged to have little growth potential.

10. Subsequent meetings or reference checks show personality is inappropriate for employer.

11. Long unemployment periods.

12. Candidate judged an ineffective supervisor.

Personalized Counseling: Career Development, Life Training, Personal Management, Counseling and Learning Center, 106 Washington Place, New York, New York 10014, (212)243-2346. Self-understanding, making changes, finding new directions, coping with change (in self and society), choosing a career path are courses taught by sociologist Barbara Mogulescu, M.A., to help a person create a better quality of life for himself or herself. Ms. Mogulescu has taught Creating the Multi-Career Life at New York University's School of Continuing Education, a course that has attracted people of all age-groups, from the very young to mid-life people to women emerging from home to the older workers facing retirement. They all are faced with the common problem: wondering which way to go. By defining life goals, identifying needs and wants, and determining skills, talents, and strengths, such people can develop workable procedures and resources to implement them. In addition to teaching, Ms. Mogulescu does private counseling, offering individuals special help in redirecting their work lives and personal situations.

Personnel Sciences Center, 341 Madison Avenue, New York, New York 10017, (212)661-1870, Bernard L. Rosenbaum, Ed.D., president, Arthur A. Witkin, Ph.D., chief psychologist. Founded in 1956 primarily to provide behavioral science services to business, the center has specialized in matching people and jobs on the basis of aptitude. Individual career counseling was undertaken earlier by the center in response to specific client requests, but it was in 1970 that the Testing and Counseling

Division was established. Planning for school and career decisions is available for adolescents of high school age, young adults in college, and adults who wish to resume or change careers.

Here is the procedure at Personnel Sciences Center:

Biographical data review: You complete a comprehensive questionnaire or case history relating to your background, experience, accomplishments, plans, and aspirations.

Interview: You are interviewed about your current thinking and the options or decisions presently confronting you. Your immediate questions are discussed.

Testing: You receive an intelligence, aptitude, achievement, interest, and personality test so that your needs and problems can be identified.

Conferences: You discuss with a counselor your test results, and then together you make out a feasible and practical plan of personal, vocational, or educational action. You receive a detailed program of training and objectives, including referral to schools, courses, and placement agencies if appropriate. Additional conferences may be scheduled when needed.

Fee is $225 for a career counseling.

Eugene B. Shea Associates, Division of Intromation Inc., Management Consultants in Executive Job Search and Career Advancement, 800 Enterprise Drive, Oak Brook, Illinois 60521, (312)654-4266, and 100 South Wacker Drive, Chicago, Illinois 60606, (312)726-6577. Eugene B. Shea is president of this firm, which has helped more than 900 executives and professionals change jobs. Shea provides a comprehensive, professional inventory of your abilities, interests, and accomplishments and gives you a frank, objective appraisal of your executive potential, along with advice for improvement. In addition, the organization develops effective professional contacts with decision-making executives in selected employing organizations in a concerted effort to identify *all* appropriate employment opportunities. You receive training, guidance, and assistance in interviewing more effectively, negotiating better offers, evaluating positions and employers thoroughly, and getting started successfully in your new position.

The organization also provides standby career consulting services on a continuing basis. If you make a salary of between $17,000 and $100,000 and they accept your qualifications, Shea Associates will work with you on a nonprofit retainer basis until you have obtained the position you want. Total fees range from 8 to 12 percent of your most recent annual salary, plus out-of-pocket expenses. In many cases, your new employer will reimburse you for your investment. Shea Associates guarantees your satisfaction with a new position obtained through their services for a period of two years or will make replacement services available at cost.

If you do not live in the area, a limousine will meet your flight at O'Hare Airport and whisk you to the Shea Associates offices in Oak Brook. The initial interview takes 1½ to 2 hours. If you are accepted as a client, you will do twenty-five to thirty hours of homework, consisting of reading, writing, recorded material, and tests. Upon completion of this material, you spend anywhere from five to fifteen hours in personal consultation with the staff, and an additional twenty to thirty hours of senior staff time is expended on your behalf when you are not there. Shea Associates helps only those individuals it feels it can help.

PUBLICATION

Directory of Counseling Services, International Association of Counseling Services, Inc., 1607 New Hampshire Avenue, N.W., Washington, D.C. 20009. Three million people seek the counseling services provided by educational institutions, placement agencies, manpower development programs, rehabilitation centers, social welfare agencies, mental health facilities, drug abuse centers, adoption agencies, family services, and many other public and private agencies concerned with helping to solve educational, vocational, or personal problems. There is no universally applied federal or state licensing or certification requirement for counselors outside the public school system. Therefore, the responsibility of protecting the public against counseling services of questionable background and performance has been assumed by the profession itself through the International Association of Counseling Services, the only accredited organization evaluating counseling services in the United States and Canada and approving those that meet its professional criteria. The accrediting program administered by the association calls for evaluation of counseling agencies and services by three national accrediting boards, each representing a particular area of counseling within the association's membership. One board is charged with evaluating university and college counseling centers; another, with community, junior, and technical college centers; and the third, with public and private agencies. You can find a counseling service in your area or check on one you have chosen, by sending for the directory.

FOR WOMEN

Business and Professional Women's Foundation, 2012 Massachusetts Avenue, N.W., Washington, D.C. 20036, (202)293-1200. The foundation is a nonprofit research and educational organization devoted to improving the quality of working life for women. Its integrated program of research, information, and education offers a bridge between working women and the employer community. In addition to providing guidance in management and leadership roles, the foundation provides educational scholarships and loans. Today, the combination of in-house research and the funding of external research efforts makes the foundation one of the nation's most fully informed organizations on women's issues.

BPW Foundation Research Grants and Lena Lake Forrest Fellowships are awarded to doctoral and postdoctoral scholars for research in educational, economic, political, social, or psychological factors affecting working women. One or more are awarded annually, ranging from $500 to $3,000 each. The foundation administers the following scholarships to mature women: the Career Advancement Scholarship®, awarded to women at least twenty-five years of age; the Clairol Loving Care Scholarship, awarded to women at least thirty years of age; and the Kelly Services Second Career Scholarship, awarded to women at least twenty-five years of age who have spent five or more years in full-time homemaking and are seeking employment in business because of the death of a spouse or dissolution of a marriage.

Scholarships are awarded for full-time or part-time study. They may cover academic or vocational, paraprofessional, or office skills training. Amounts may range from $100 to $1,000 for one-year periods, but the average award is between $200 and $500. Scholarships are awarded twice annually, in June and in November. Deadlines for all applications and support materials are May 1 and October 1, respectively.

The Business and Professional Women's Foundation Loan Fund for Women in Engineering Studies is open to women who have been accepted for undergraduate and graduate-level courses at schools accredited by the Engineers' Council for Professional Development. Women may qualify for individual loans of up to $10,000. Repayment is scheduled over a five-year period at 5 percent interest, beginning one year after graduation. All applicants must be citizens of the United States and must be carrying at least six semester hours or the equivalent during each semester for which a loan is requested. Study may be full or part time.

The BPW/Sears–Roebuck Loan Fund for Women in Graduate Business Studies is open to women of any age who have been accepted for graduate degree programs or graduate-level courses of study at schools accredited by the American Assembly of Collegiate Schools of Business. Women may qualify for loans of up to $2,000 per academic year. Repayment is scheduled over a five-year period at 5 percent interest, beginning one year after graduation. All applicants must be U.S. citizens and must be carrying at least six semester hours or the equivalent during each semester for which a loan is requested.

The foundation's library and information center provides a reference and referral service to anyone interested in issues of concern to women. Since 1956, the library has built an excellent collection of journals, books, and audio tapes devoted to working women and has developed a computerized file of biographical data on outstanding contemporary women.

The foundation sponsors seminars, throughout the country, for special training to advance careers, to prepare women for management opportunities, and to develop leadership capabilities. Recent programs have ranged from work force entry guidance for displaced homemakers to management training for midcareer women. The 1979–1980 series of seminars emphasizes economic issues. Fee per seminar, $25.

Catalyst, 14 East 60th Street, New York, New York 10022, (212)PL9-9700. This national nonprofit organization helps to expand career opportunities for women. Catalyst works directly with women, local resource centers, educators, and employers and seeks to open new channels of communication among them. Founded in 1962 by Felice N. Schwartz, president, with the assistance of five college presidents, the organization offers not only undergraduate career guidance but also assistance to women who are considering returning to college or work and various materials designed to help employers seek qualified women for their companies. Catalyst works with a national network of more than 200 local women's resource centers and education, career counseling, job referral, and placement services.

Here are some of Catalyst's offerings:

Career information and self-guidance material: Career Options publications for undergraduate women in this series offer information about new opportunities in traditionally male fields: accounting, engineering, finance, government and politics, industrial management, retail management, sales, restaurant management, insurance, and banking. Each booklet describes the variety of positions and the range of life-styles possible within a particular career. Educational requirements, salaries, employment outlook, job-hunting tips, and interviews with women who have achieved success in the field are also included. Sample titles are *Choosing Your Career Path* and *Have You Considered Restaurant Management.* Each booklet is $1.95.

Résumé Preparation Manual helps women who are seeking employment or advancement to condense a lifetime of skills and training into a concise statement of strengths and experience and enables them to examine their skills, achievements, education, and work experience. The price is $4.95.

Self-guidance and career opportunity booklets: There are forty booklets prepared for women who are considering returning to college or work, who are formulating or redefining career plans, and pursuing opportunities for upward mobility. These Career Opportunities Series booklets, which cost $1.50 each, cover everything from engineering to fund raising to urban planning. Other offerings are the Job Campaign booklet, $1.75 each, a self-guidance manual to help you find the job you want, and the Education Opportunity Services, $1.50 each, including General Information for the Returning Student (E1), Business Administration (E2), and Urban Planning (E27).

Information Center: This is a library, research, and information service that answers telephoned and written requests concerning women and careers from the general public and the business and professional communities.

Options For Women, Inc., 8419 Germantown Avenue, Philadelphia, Pennsylvania 19118, (215) CH2-4955. Marcia P. Kleiman, M.S., and Vicki W. Kramer, Ph.D., are cofounders of this organization which specializes in career advice for women of all ages, backgrounds, and economic levels who are employed and who are making career decisions involving job changes or strategies for advancement. Options for Women is an independent, nonprofit, tax-exempt corporation with a staff of ten and an advisory board of experts in a variety of fields. It is a fee-for-service organization. There is some grant money available that supports a sliding fee scale for those in need. Current services include group and individual career advising, testing, adult school, college, and high school programs, and consultation on affirmative action and career development to business, civic, educational, government, and professional groups. There is a free orientation session.

Options Workshops are for women who are making career decisions, thinking of going back for more education, or who have been out of work for a number of years and wish to return to the job market. Six sessions. 9:30 to 11:30 A.M. No more than eight in a group. $150. (Includes books and materials).

Career Development Workshop for women who are working, are interested in a career change or advancement. 6 to 8:30 P.M. Six sessions. $200. (Includes books and materials).

Individual counseling, $35 per hour.

Vocational and educational testing, $150.

Today's Woman Placement Service, 21 Charles Street, Westport, Connecticut 06880, (203)226-4451. This is a nationwide placement service for executive and professional women in the $10,000-to-$40,000 range. Since it was started in 1972, more than 10,000 women and 400 organizations have registered with the service. Based on a review of your background against job specifications and additional information obtained from you in conversations, they present your qualifications to organizations for appropriate openings. If interest is expressed by a client, they will contact the service to make the necessary interview arrangements. A partial listing of client organizations includes the American Broadcasting Company, American Cyanamid, American Express, Anaconda, AT&T, Johnson & Johnson, Mobil Oil, Mutual of New York, Sperry Rand, Stauffer Chemical, Union Camp, Warner-Lambert, and Xerox Corporation. If you wish to register with them, send a copy of your résumé, with information covering your present or last salary and your salary goal and geographic limitations. No fees are charged to women who register with, or are placed by, the service.

Women's Bureau, U.S. Department of Labor, Washington, D.C. 20402, (202)523-6611. The objective of the bureau is to advance the welfare and status of women as workers and citizens and to increase their contribution to the nation's civic, social, and economic welfare. A fact-finding and service agency, it advises and cooperates with federal, state and local government agencies as well as individuals. The bureau encourages girls in high school and college to prepare adequately for employment and points out where the best opportunities exist. It reports on employment opportunities for part-time workers and provides informational materials to encourage mature women job seekers to improve their skills by obtaining training. More than 450 informational booklets are available. For lists of educational programs, job information, and program schedules, write or call the bureau.

PUBLICATION

Adult Female Human Being, Fran Murray and Mildred Erickson, Michigan State University Lifelong Education Programs, East Lansing, Michigan 48824. This booklet takes a realistic look at the costs and benefits of careers, the educational opportunities available, the laws, and women's rights. It gives comparative figures on men's and women's wages and salaries and tells where the future may lie for women workers. *Adult Female Human Being* has been in great demand since it was first issued in 1975. Fran Murray is the senior information officer of the Department of Information at Michigan State University; Mildred Erickson is assistant dean of the university's Lifelong Education Programs. The price of the booklet is $1.00, plus $.25 for postage and handling; make checks payable to Michigan State University.

2 How to Ask for a Raise

When you want a raise, how do you ask for it without antagonizing your boss and without being refused?

Here is some expert advice.

First of all, do more than is expected of you before you make your request. Don't watch the clock and leave promptly at the end of the day.

Many have found it wise to ask when the boss is in the best mood of the week. That may be on a Friday afternoon or a Monday morning. You should make it your business to know your boss's moods.

Find out if your company has a set time for considering merit raises, so that you will know whether you were passed over or whether you have time to influence the decision.

Be ready to explain in concise fashion why you believe you deserve a raise. Think your reasons over carefully, and put yourself in your boss's place, trying to visualize the boss's viewpoint. Again, you should understand your boss's behavior.

Do not give need as the main reason for wanting a raise. You may be in debt and supporting twenty members of your family, but it is your work that interests your boss.

Don't put your boss on the defensive by asking why you haven't gotten a raise, implying that you have been treated unfairly. On the other hand, don't feel guilty about asking for a raise.

Skip the threats and ultimatums. You can imply tactfully that you might have to look elsewhere, but be subtle.

Do investigate the financial situation of your company. If things are bad and your boss has to give a report about why your department didn't make money in the past quarter, this is not the time to ask for a raise. On the other hand, if your boss or division just obtained a big assignment or made a spectacular advance, that's the time to request an increase in salary.

If your immediate boss doesn't have the authority to give a raise or has let your request slide, ask if it is all right to ask someone in a higher position.

If you haven't had an answer in a month after you requested the raise, ask politely if something is delaying the answer.

If the answer to your request is no, don't get angry and storm out of the office or become sarcastic. Say that you are disappointed and that you would like to know how you can change or improve your performance to merit a raise.

When you do get a raise, don't forget to thank your boss and everyone else responsible for it.

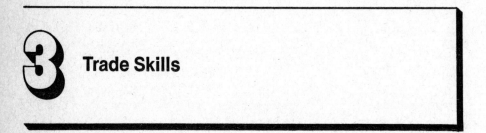

3 Trade Skills

If you are without skills, your opportunities on the job market are almost nil. If you are highly educated, even if you have a Ph.D., you may also find your opportunities lacking. Among the most secure and in-demand people in the job market are those who have trade and technical skills. As in other fields, it is practically never too late to learn a new trade.

National Association of Trade and Technical Schools, 2021 K Street, N.W., Washington, D.C. 20006, (202)296-8892. This voluntary organization of accredited private residence schools offers job-oriented specialty training in trade and technical occupations. As the standard-setting agency for private schools, NATTS admits those institutions that give evidence of subscribing to quality educational and administrative standards and ethical practices. Complete information on each member school has been placed on file at the national office. You can receive a national handbook, listing hundreds of accredited trade schools for everything from computer technicians to fashion design, free by writing to the association. You can also receive free information pamphlets such as *What's a Nice Girl Like You Doing in a Man's World?*, *Career Shortcuts*, *How to Choose a Career and a Career School*, and *College Plus: Put Your Degree to Work with Trade and Technical Skills.*

SECRETARIAL AND TYPING WORK

Typing as a Skill for Grads, Irene Cohen Personnel Services, 475 Fifth Avenue, New York, New York 10017, (212)725-1666, Irene Cohen, director. Without a graduate degree such as a Master of Business Administration, many liberal arts graduates find it hard to be chosen for management training programs. That is why Ms. Cohen recommends the secretarial approach to advancement. College graduates who started as secretaries have become administrative assistants, traffic managers, and production assistants. Once an individual has secured a position in a firm, there may be opportunities for continuing education sponsored by the company. Ms. Cohen insists that typing is just as important for a man as a woman. She suggests that college graduates not only sharpen up their typing and secretarial skills but also learn about computers and how they work. Today, most big companies are highly computerized.

Irene Cohen Personnel Services also offers career counseling, a résumé-writing service, skills evaluation, a refresher clinic, and an interview workshop for those looking for employment. For the company seeking help, it offers both a permanent and a temporary work force, testing facilities for applicants, and a professional placement service.

Zinman's Rapid Writing, EZ ABC Shorthand, Box Z, Point Lookout, New York 11569. This system of shorthand using the alphabet can be ordered through the mail for $12.25. It consists of a self-instruction book, an advanced test, and a workbook. Dictation records are also available for $6.50 a set (four extended play 45 rpm records). Zinman claims that students in adult education and college classes can learn Rapid Writing after a twelve- to fifteen-session course and be ready to take dictation in a business office. Academic high school seniors can learn the system in one term and take dictation at 70 to 90 words per minute. Commercial students can do it in one year at the same speed. Rapid writing materials by mail order are designed for self-instruction so that you can learn the theory at home in less than two weeks. Zinman said that surveys show that students can write 40 words per minute without using abbreviations. With Rapid Writing, they can easily double their speed: for example, *brought* (seven letters) becomes *brt* (three letters), and *opportunity* (eleven letters) becomes *op* (two letters.)

READING COURSES

Peter Kump, reading consultant, 333 East 69th Street, New York, New York 10021, (212)737-8669. Mr. Kump personally teaches all courses. For many years, he was the national director of education for Evelyn Wood Reading Dynamics Institute, the author of many of its courses, and in charge of training its teachers. He personally trained President Nixon's staff at the White House. Just think, if they had stuck to reading instead of tapes, history might have been different.

The cost of Kump's course is $175 for one person or $150 each for two persons registering together, payable in full prior to the first lesson. The average student can expect to triple his or her reading rate in most materials, learn how to improve comprehension, increase recall of the material, study better and faster, listen more effectively, take tests better, and much more. In addition to attending all the classes, you should plan to practice one hour each day that you are not in class if you wish to gain the full potential from the course.

PUBLICATION

Breakthrough Rapid Reading, Peter Kump. 1979. In his book, Kump reveals all the secrets of his method. The book is aimed at the good self-learner. The price is $14.95.

Evelyn Wood Reading Dynamics Institute, 72 West 45th Street, New York, New York 10036, (212)869-9440. If you are an average reader, your reading rate is 250 to 350 words per minute. The course is so education-ally sound that the institute guarantees to refund your entire tuition if you do not at least triple your reading efficiency (the measure of your reading speed *and* comprehension). There are more than 1 million gradu-ates. Ms. Wood, a soft-spoken former missionary, began to teach reading when she was five years old. She was so adept that she helped her fellow first grade students. She went on to obtain a master's degree in educa-tion. During six years of teaching remedial reading at Jordan High School in Salt Lake City, Ms. Wood developed a technique to improve poor reading skills. Her program was such a success that she was invited to teach it at the University of Utah. She taught her daughter, Carol, the technique; and when Carol enrolled in Columbia University, she amazed her political science professor by reading the entire year's textbooks and extracurricular material—thirty-five books—in three months. When she was tested on the material, she received an A.

President Kennedy was a naturally fast reader, but he was impatient with his staff members who read slowly, so he hired Ms. Wood to teach her method to the White House. She also taught reading to President Nixon's White House staff and to Jimmy Carter's.

Ms. Wood, whose commercial reading program has been a worldwide success, has met opposition from some educators, whom she claims have not changed reading instructions in the past sixty years.

The commercial course consists of seven weekly sessions of 2½ hours each. Prices vary greatly around the country, from $250 to $445, de-pending on location. The federal government and some state govern-ments allow you to deduct the cost of the course from your taxes if it enables you to improve skills necessary to your employment.

PUBLICATION

Evelyn Wood's At Home Reading Course. Consists of tapes, charts, and a workbook. Cost $195. Complete course for those who have the discipline to do-it-yourself at home.

School of Visual Arts, 209 East 23d Street, New York, New York 10010, (212)679-7350, Pernel Berkeley, director. Visual arts is one of the career fields that continues to grow and expand despite many changes in the economy. The definition of *art* has been expanded by the demands of our times, although that has not lessened either the importance or the significance of personal statements in painting, sculpture, drawing, or film. With new equipment on the market, videotape is expanding as a field. Photography has broadened its scope, and advertising continues to generate opportunities. Industry and government increasingly rely on visual material in both print and electronic media. Education has increased its use of films, slides, and videotapes.

The economic future for today's artist is a very positive one, but in art, perhaps more so than in other fields, success is dependent on personal talent and the way it is developed. The School of Visual Arts focuses on helping the artist understand how to continue generating new ideas and concepts throughout a lifetime, how to remain flexible and use talent in different ways, and how to adapt to changing technology.

PUBLICATION

Careers in the Visual Arts. In addition to career information, this publication answers questions frequently asked about the various art careers in photography, fine arts, media arts, film and videotape, and art therapy. Job descriptions are also given. A single copy is free.

FOR WOMEN

Apprenticeship: Skilled Women at Work, Women's Apprenticeship Outreach Service, Division of Apprenticeship and Training, Milwaukee, Wisconsin, Kathryn Lorrigan, director. Women are discovering the skilled trades and are seeking the higher wages and personal satisfaction that come from a skilled occupation. If you like to work with your hands, a career in this field may be for you. Of course, interest, desire, and ability are necessary for this work. But training is essential if you are to qualify as a skilled worker, and serving an apprenticeship is the best way to get that training. You will learn the trade both on the job and in the classroom. At the factory or job site, you will work under a skilled craftsperson; and in the classroom, you will take courses designed to familiarize you with the materials, tools, and basic principles of the trade.

You can become a construction worker, carpenter, electrician, painter, or heavy-equipment operator or work in the industrial trades as a machinist, toolmaker, millwright, or foundry worker. If you are interested in the service trades, there is training for dental technicians, auto mechanics, barbers, and so on.

Job opportunities in the skilled trades can be found in all parts of the country. To find out more about apprenticeship ask your school counselor, state apprenticeship agency, the U.S. Department of Labor (Bureau of Apprenticeship and Training), or the nearest Job Service Office or write to:

Department of Industry
Labor and Human Relations
Division of Apprenticeship and Training
P.O. Box 7946
Madison, Wisconsin 53707

PUBLICATIONS

Blue-collar Jobs for Women, Muriel Lederer. New York: E.P. Dutton, 1979. A Complete Guide to Getting Skilled & Getting a High-Paying Job in the Trades. $12.95 cloth, $7.95 paper.

What Apprenticeship Is All About. Free booklet that explains how and where to look for an apprenticeship. Write to: Wisconsin Department of Industry, Labor and Human Relations, Division of Apprenticeship and Training, P.O. Box 7946, Madison, Wisconsin 53707.

Part-Time and Temporary Employment

Not everyone can or wishes to work 9 to 5, five days a week for 50 weeks a year. Not everyone has to. There are part-time, temporary, and shared jobs that allow flexibility in working time. Here are examples of the opportunities available.

Job Sharers: Promoting Permanent Part-Time Employment, P. O. Box 1542, Arlington, Virginia 22210, (703)560-1117, (703)893-8916, or (703)533-9298, Judy L. Hodges, Carol Parker, counselors. Job sharing means two people dividing one permanent, full-time position. They share the responsibilities, the hours, and the salary. This simple idea has been a boon to people who cannot work full time or do not want to. Shared positions can be arranged in factory and clerical work and in the professions of education, management, engineering, and medicine.

Many employers and supervisors have resisted job sharing and other kinds of reduced-hours arrangements in higher-paying occupations because of concern about extra costs and administrative inconveniences. The main stumbling block is the per capita benefits required by law; state and federal unemployment contributions are usually higher for a job-sharing team than for a single person. Social security taxes are also higher when the combined salary of the job shares is more than $15,300 per year. Benefits such as vacations and insurance can be prorated. Carol Parker suggests that a "market basket" approach be used for those benefits that cannot be prorated; that is, the total benefits package should be offered to the team members, and they should be allowed to split the package to their satisfaction.

A big plus is higher employee morale. Job sharers are usually pleased with their jobs, not only because their schedules fit their life-styles but also because it is often easier to maintain a high level of enthusiasm in a part-time job. Absenteeism can be reduced when each worker has free time to conduct personal business. Also, one person can fill in for the other in cases of illness or emergency.

In jobs that involve creativity, the employers literally get two for the price of one: two people bringing two backgrounds and two sets of ideas to the job. Employers may find it advantageous to hire one receptionist for four hours in the morning and another for four hours in the afternoon and pay neither for a lunch hour. Firms with peak hours can plan their work schedules according to their needs, such as lunch time and dinnertime in restaurants, busy seasons, and so on.

In some areas, federally funded programs are under way that will provide research, training, and job development services. In one such program, Project Join, which is being implemented in Wisconsin, sixty employees share thirty jobs. When the study ends, its report should provide some hard data on the job-sharing concept. Legislatures of several states have either passed or are considering laws that would establish job-sharing programs or shared positions in state government. Clearly, the trend to break up the forty-hour workweek is gathering momentum.

For general information about job sharing:

New Ways to Work, 457 Kingsley Avenue, Palo Alto, California 94301, (415)321-9675.

National Council for Alternative Work Patterns, Inc. 1302 18th Street, N.W., Suite 203, Washington, D.C. 20036, (202)466-4467.

The following will counsel and in some cases help you find employers willing to hire job sharers:

Focus on Part-Time Careers, 509 Tenth Avenue East, Seattle, Washington 98102, (206)329-7918.

Project Join, Department of Administration, State of Wisconsin, 1 West Wilson Street, Room 290, Madison, Wisconsin 53702, (608)266-7964.

TEMPORARY EMPLOYMENT

For variety, spice, and a chance to test different kinds of jobs and different fields, you may want to consider the world of temporary employment.

Western Temporary Services, Inc., P.O. Box 773, San Francisco, California 94120, (415)981-8480. This organization has 185 offices throughout the United States and in Australia, England, Denmark, Germany, and Mexico. It makes more than 500,000 assignments yearly through five divisions: Western Girl, for office jobs; Western Industrial for jobs in plants and warehouses; Western Medical, for jobs in hospitals and other institutions; Marketing Services, for marketing support; and Santa Division, which provides department stores with Santas.

Temporary jobs are not all routine. For instance, here are some that you missed: a chicken chaser for a farmer whose barn roof blew off, an employee with an iron to iron out bills soaked when an office flooded, a witness for a hasty wedding, and a witch for a shopping center promotion. W. Robert Stover of San Francisco, president and founder of Western, points out there are assignments for which the only skill required is experience in homemaking, for instance, department store demonstrator or comparison shopper, poll taker, tour guide, inventory taker, gift wrapper, cashier, and convention hostess.

Stover explains that the salaries for temporary assignments are approximately equal to those for regular work at the same skills level. Unlike employment agencies, temporary firms do not charge a fee to the employee. They are paid only by the employer. Even in bad times, there is a good market for temporary help for both men and women because companies are thus able to hire help only when it is needed instead of keeping employees on the staff full time when there is no work to do.

According to Stover, many people use temporary assignments as a means of learning what kind of job they would like, whether they would prefer a large or small office or a downtown or a suburban job. They can learn what they are worth, whether they want to switch careers, whether there are opportunities in their hometown or whether they would be better off moving to a large city. Women whose children have grown find temporary assignments an ideal way to get back into the work force. They can work when they wish, and they can accept easy assignments at first and take harder ones as their skills sharpen. Furthermore, temporary help firms sometimes allow prospective employees whose office skills have gotten rusty to practice on their equipment. Stover also suggests that if you are a stenographer whose skills have been unused for a long time, you can practice by taking dictation from a favorite radio or television program. If a temporary employee likes the company to which he or she has been assigned—and that frequently happens—and would like to make the job permanent, that is fine with many temporary help firms. Stover says, "We allow employers to use our services to try out employees who might make good full-time staff. We also do not object to people taking temporary assignments in order to find a job or company they like."

PUBLICATION

Work When You Want to: A Guide to Employment Opportunities in Temporary Help. This brochure is available free upon request from Western Temporary Services.

Housework

Housework is work! And there are ways of improving your performance of this work, just as there are in any job. Remember, if you can do housework more efficiently, you will have more time to do other things. Dr. John M. Samuels, assistant professor of industrial and management systems engineering at Pennsylvania State University, believes that many of the efficiency methods used in industry can be adapted to reduce the time devoted to household tasks. The first thing you have to ask yourself is where you spend your time. In industry, this is called *placing the emphasis where it will do the most good.* Write down your chores; the order and emphasis of the list, of course, will depend on the size of your family, whether you have children, and how old they are.

How would you increase your efficiency in the kitchen, for instance? Dr. Samuels says that you must first consider the location of items. For example, what is the relationship between the range and the refrigerator, between the sink and the dishwasher? Where are the dishes and silverware kept? Look at each item, and try to minimize the number of steps it takes you to prepare and serve a meal and then clean up afterward.

The storage of items is another target. Those items that you use most often should be closest to your reach; whereas those items that you use less frequently should be kept in the higher places and toward the backs of cabinets.

Dr. Samuels points out that a well-arranged pantry allows you to organize your shopping list more quickly because it requires less work to determine what items need to be purchased. This could help to reduce the frequency with which you have to shop. How you store food is important, too. For example, cereals should be put into plastic containers, rather than kept in boxes. That will keep them fresh, and you won't have to shop for them as often. The next consideration depends on your personality. Some people have to have clear counters, with everything put away. But the most efficient way of doing things is to have various small appliances close at hand on the kitchen counter. One of the most time-consuming jobs is searching for something like a cookie cutter that has been put in some forgotten place.

As for the never-ending job of housecleaning, Dr. Samuels suggests that you place yourself on a schedule, just as hotel managers do with cleaning crews. Note the jobs that have to be done on a large calendar. Write down when to wax the floors and how often to do major housecleaning, and adhere to the schedule. In industry, a cleaning chart is used. He suggests that you use a basket for cleaning materials needed to clean the house or the room. That way, you won't have to waste time hunting for cleaning compounds or the proper broom or dustcloth.

You should use the proper tools. For example, use a wide broom rather than a narrow one if you are sweeping a large area; choose a floor mop that will reduce the number of motions required to clean the floor. When you select your cleaning utensils, test them out. That's what's done in industry. Do they feel good in your hands? Is the broom handle the right one for your height? Is the vacuum cleaner hose long enough to get into areas that you need to clean? Does it have an adequate cord?

What about doing the laundry? Keep materials together at the place they will be used. Have devices to measure exact quantities; that will save you time *and* money. Use a timer to tell you when a washer or dryer is done. That way, you won't have to keep checking. Have separate laundry baskets for storing clothes either by groups or by colors. This will minimize preparing clothes for the laundry. Use wash baskets that are the size of one washer load; you won't have to spend time counting laundry or dividing it into several piles.

6 Women's Organizations

When a woman over thirty-five loses her sole source of support, her husband, through death, desertion, or divorce, she may be in serious financial and emotional trouble. There are an estimated three million "displaced homemakers," former housewives with no current job market skills, in the United States today. State and federal agencies are just now beginning to recognize the special needs of these women, and centers have been established in eight states (as of this writing) to offer job training, placement services, counseling, and referral services for health care, legal problems, and financial management. The centers in Oakland, California, and Baltimore, Maryland, have already helped thousands of women become financially and emotionally self-supporting. The other states offering limited programs are Massachusetts, Minnesota, Nebraska, Ohio, Oregon, and Texas.

A guide to federal legislation that provides for a range of services for displaced homemakers is available from the Women's Bureau of the United States Department of Labor, Washington, D.C. 20210. This free publication, "A Guide to Coordinating CETA and Vocational Education Legislation Affecting Displaced Homemaker Programs," indicates possibilities for coordinating education, training, and support services. It is designed for planning personnel in the field but can be of help to individuals who wish to find services to fit their specific needs. To expedite a reply, write to Room S-3317, and enclose a self-addressed label.

The organizations below offer a wide range of services.

Hannah Harrison Career School of the YWCA, 4470 MacArthur Boulevard, N.W., Washington, D.C. 20007, (202)333-3500. Each year, this organization offers a limited number of mature women free board and tuition, full-time training programs in business skills, hotel and hospital housekeeping and practical nursing. These programs range in length from twelve weeks to twelve months. The school succesfully places 95 percent of its graduates.

The Women's Opportunities Center, University of California Extension at Irvine, California 92717, Rm. 148, (714)833-7128, Mary Moshy, director. This program offers vocation and educational counseling to women of all ages and backgrounds. Since the center opened in 1970, more than 8,000 women have utilized the services. The center is staffed by more than 40 volunteers. For a $10 membership fee, women can receive private counseling, a newsletter, follow-up sessions, reduced fees on workshops, awareness groups, and use of the center's library, which contains job listings, career descriptions, volunteer opportunities, educational information, and helpful ideas on the "how-to's" of job hunting. There is also a $12 vocational testing service that covers vocational interest, personality, and aptitude. Hours are Monday through Friday, 9 A.M. to 4 P.M. On the second and fourth Tuesday of each month, the center stays open until 8 P.M.

Hotline for New Jersey Women, (800)322-8092. The hotline, which is funded by a grant from the Community Affairs Division on Women to Together, Inc., Glassboro State College, gives women in need of advice a central source of information. The service covers all areas of information pertaining to women, including employment, health care, educational opportunities, legal and financial aid, services, and access to public programs.

Martha Movement, Suite 305, 1101 Arlington Boulevard, Arlington, Virginia 22209, (703)527-3334. This is a nonprofit, educational membership association that seeks to increase the status and recognition of homemakers and to address their needs. It is not a religious movement, a lobbying organization, or an antifeminist protest. Rather, it is an organization designed to help women seek fulfillment and identity through home and family. The $5 annual dues pays for a monthly newsletter of information for, by, and about homemakers and an 800 toll-free number that homemakers can call to receive or lend emotional support to help them through emergencies or to work together to reach compatible goals. There are seminars and programs on issues concerning homemakers and skills identification for homemakers who want to seek employment outside the home. Information is available on improving the quality of family life, on improving life skills, and on organizing skills that help you set up support groups and use your influence in the community.

7 How to Improve Your Financial Situation

Money really *does* talk. The way you spend it says a lot about how you feel about yourself, your mate, your children, your occupation.

Psychiatrists maintain that the emotionally well-balanced use of money requires that you plan realistically for your present and your future. But how can you plan realistically when you are constantly urged to buy now and pay later, when there are psychologists who design and market products so that you can't resist buying them? And what about those little pieces of plastic that enable you to purchase things for which you do not have the cash? Just how can you improve your finances, considering all these pressures *plus* the fact that inflation and the tax collectors keep taking more out of your pockets each year?

Actually, there is a wealth of solid advice about coping with all these problems, and much of it is free.

Everyone who is anyone in the field of finance recommends that you make up a budget. You can do this by taking your check book stubs for one year and categorizing how you spent your income. Or you can write down your major monthly obligations, such as rent or mortgage payments, taxes, food, clothing, car payments and maintenance, and so on, and then divide by four; that gives you your weekly estimate of expenses. You can even have your personal budget computed by a computer company that offers the service (see page 296). When you compare your expenses with your weekly income, then you have an idea of what your budget should be.

One way to stop going over your budget, according to Russ Jalbert, cofounder of the Oakland Financial Group of Charlottesville, Virginia is to destroy all but one or two of your credit cards. The next step is to put your affairs in order. "Getting your affairs in order is not the terrible experience that most people think it is," the financial advisor maintains. "It simply involves saying to yourself, 'I'm going to do it.'"

Jalbert admits that a person cannot really talk about financial planning if he or she has a total income of less than $8,000 a year. "Such people have severe problems just getting staples to survive. But actually, among the higher-income groups, there is a new set of money problems that are more acute during good times than bad. When money is tight, people are more realistic about their expenditures. But when there is money to spend, there is often a difference in priorities between husband and wife. The man may want to put the money into a sports car while his wife believes she needs it for necessary household furnishings." In fact, Jalbert thinks that money does not cause marital problems but just the reverse. "An extravagant man may earn $50,000 or $100,000 and still be broke. His problems are emotional rather than financial. The same with a wife who spends more than her husband earns."

Well, suppose you are happily married or happily single. What can you do to improve your financial situation? Jalbert advises that you first go to your bank's trust department and be very candid. "The bank, of course, will have a vested interest. The banker will want you to have a trust. But ask the banker to recommend other professionals such as a stockbroker and a legal expert."

Go to your library, and ask the librarian for current reports on companies and information about finances (see page 299). Read *Barron's*, *Forbes*, and *Business Week*, publications that report on what is happening in the world of business and on which companies are strong and which are weak. (You can subscribe to them or read them in the library.) Read the financial section of your daily newspaper. And, if you want to learn what the experts know, read one of the investment letters (see page 299).

Obtain free information from financial institutions. Most large stockbrokers' offices have a wealth of up-to-minute free reports available. For example, Merrill Lynch publishes *Investing in Municipal Bonds for Tax-Free Income,* an informative thirty-five-page booklet, and most banks have free investment advice material available (see page 301). In other words, gather all the information you can on your own, and then sit down and make your decisions about the following:

Your tax status: How can you protect your income? Is a tax shelter really a good investment for you?

Your insurance: Do you have too much cash value in your life insurance? Are your insurance policies adequate protection for you and your family in view of inflation?

Your investments: Is your stock portfolio too risky or too conservative in terms of your goals?

Your will: Is it current? Have you had another child since you wrote it? Did one of your children recently marry? Did a parent die within the past year?

Your retirement goals: Is early retirement possible? Are your goals realistic?

Your trusts: Laws change frequently. Have your trusts been reviewed in the past three years? Should a trust be restructured to care for a college student or aging parents?

Where it's at: Do you have a list of your assets and liabilities, your insurance policies, the names and addresses of your appropriate professionals such as your accountant and lawyer and insurance agent? Does your family know where that list is?

Don't put all your eggs in one basket: Executives who have become wealthy through the exercise of stock options frequently find themselves bankrupt on paper because of a precipitous drop in stock prices and large outstanding bank loans used to exercise options. Diversify!

Don't buy on tips: Do you have a portfolio cluttered with what were once hot tips, special-situation growth stocks? If you do, one problem you will have to deal with is how to sell a stock nobody else wants at any price, even to establish a capital loss.

Should you borrow? Sometimes the best investment is borrowing. You not only establish credit, but you can use the borrowed money to make a profit in addition to getting a tax advantage when you pay back the loan. For instance, as of this writing, many financial experts are advising clients to take a second mortage on property. The cash is then invested so that you have the advantage of making money on the borrowed money and still having the tax deduction of the interest payments on the loan. This type of borrowing should be done only with expert advice about your individual situation.

Match your investments and your emotions: You are a combination of reason and emotion. Unfortunately, many highly intellectual individuals make reasoned decisions about their financial affairs but still can't live with these decisions emotionally. The person who carefully selects an investment advisor and then constantly second-guesses that advisor is an example.

Once you have put your affairs in order and gathered all the information you can, you are well on the road to improving your financial situation. You may not believe, as George Bernard Shaw did, in *The Irrational Knot,* that money is indeed the most important thing in the world and all sound and successful personal and national morality should have this fact for its basis. However, money is important, and there are few of us who could not use more and who could not benefit from good advice about our finances. As Karl Marx's mother reportedly said, "If Karl, instead of writing about *Capital,* made a lot of *Capital,* it would have been much better."

FOR HOMEMAKERS WHO ARE THINKING OF GOING TO WORK

A job may have many intellectual rewards to offer the homemaker, but it does not always pay financially. Before you decide to seek employment outside your home, take a pencil and figure the following:

Your Potential Earnings		**Your Potential Expenses**	
Gross weekly salary	_____	*Average weekly expenses for:*	
Deductions:		Transportation	_____
Social security	_____	Lunches	_____
State income tax	_____	Child care	_____
Federal income tax	_____	Additional wardrobe	_____
State disability	_____	Additional personal	
Group life insurance	_____	grooming	_____
Group health insurance	_____	Increased household	
Pension deduction or		expenses (extra food	
union dues	_____	costs, cleaning help)	_____
Total deductions	_____	Office contributions	
Take-home pay	_____	and miscellaneous	
		expenses	_____

Your net weekly income is actually_____

BUDGETS

Budget Control Service, Inc., P.O. Box 105, Shelburne, Vermont 05482. This computer-based data processing service provides you with a monthly report to help you evaluate your spending habits and control your resources. Of course, the first step to effective budget control is to know where your money goes. The monthly report that BCS provides shows you all your expenditures on one sheet of paper. It is designed to fit anyone's budgeting needs, whether you already keep a simple account, an elaborate household journal, or no records at all. It can make keeping your household expenditures records easier and more meaningful and will build a historical file that can be very useful at tax time.

Most people know what they spend on a monthly basis, but they seldom have a real grasp of their month-to-month expenditures in all categories. To get that more complete picture, you must know the answers to these questions:

What did I spend *this month* on a given expense?

How much have I spent in *total* so far this year on the given expense?

Did I spend *more* or *less* than I did last month on this expense?

On an *average*, what have I been spending for this expense?

What *percent* of my total expenditures have I been spending on this expense?

BCS offers two versions of the household report. One utilizes a standard set of expense categories. The other is organized according to your exact expense categories. With the tailored report, you can name up to fifty expense categories that are meaningful to you or your household; you can add categories at any time as long as the total does not exceed fifty. BCS will supply you with an indexed notebook in which to file your tailored reports.

To get started, write for their brochure; then fill out and mail the application form or return card indicating the month you wish to start the service. When BCS receives the card or the application form, they will send you the necessary data sheets and return envelopes. You merely fill out a data sheet and at the end of the month mail it to BCS. Your report will be processed and returned promptly. BCS pays postage both ways. You can start at any time of the year. All information is held in the strictest confidence. The service charge is $3.50 per month for the standard data sheets and categories. If you wish the tailored report, there is a one-time programming charge of $15.00, and the monthly cost is $5.00.

CREDIT

Consumer Credit Counseling Services

There is a growing network of free communitywide services to give real help if you find yourself in credit difficulty. They operate under a national plan sponsored by the National Foundation for Consumer Credit and supported by funds donated by United Way Foundation and financial firms as a public service. These services have the cooperation of prominent local attorneys, the Legal Aid Societies, Better Business Bureaus, municipal offices, credit bureaus, and trade associations of the merchants, bankers, and consumer finance groups. They will give you special advice or help. They are usually welcomed by creditor groups in the community, and where the situation warrants, they are able to negotiate matters so that problems which seem mountainous may be ironed out for anyone honestly and cooperatively trying to keep his/her head up financially. If you cannot find a listing in your phone book, write to

National Foundation for Consumer Credit
1819 H Street, N.W.
Washington, D.C. 20006
(202)223-2040

PUBLICATIONS

The National Foundation for Consumer Credit publishes several excellent pamphlets. If you want to improve your budget and your credit rating, you may find them useful.

Measuring and Using Your Credit Capacity. How much can you really afford to spend? What should a down payment be? How long should you take to pay loans and accounts? What market conditions affect terms offered?

The Emergency Problem: What to Do About It. This booklet tells you your alternatives if you cannot meet a payment: what to do, what not to do, and what your rights are.

The Forms of Credit We Use. This publication describes the principal types of credit accounts, contracts, installment sales contracts, and installment loan contracts.

Consumer Credit. This is a general discussion of the types of consumer credit we normally use and how typical credit service charges and loan rates are figured and stated.

Establishing Good Credit. This pamphlet discusses how to establish a good credit rating.

These and other foundation materials are also available in Spanish. The cost ranges from $.10 to $.25.

Keep Your Credit History Up to Date

Most creditors periodically review their records and will drop any account that has not been used over a certain period of time. If you have several charge accounts, alternate from one to the other periodically, or charge minor purchases every so often. In this way, your credit will be there in case you need it in an emergency.

FOR MEN

Many provisions of the new Equal Credit Opportunity Act can benefit you directly, for example, the changes in mortgage lending practices, the counting of part-time work as income, and the prohibition against refusing credit because of a change in marital status.

If you are married, it is to your advantage to encourage your wife to establish credit in her own name and to maintain her accounts at a level of activity sufficient to sustain her record as a responsible credit user. The more chances she has to exercise her financial judgment, the better that record will become.

FOR WOMEN

Commercial Credit Corporation, 300 St. Paul Place, Baltimore, Maryland 21202, (301)332-3000. Many women are unaware of how credit works and what their rights are under the new consumer credit laws. The Commercial Credit Corporation, one of the nation's largest consumer finance institutions, has prepared a booklet, *Women to Your Credit*, in cooperation with the Maryland Commission for Women and the National Association of Commissions for Women. It explains consumers' rights in easy-to-understand language. Here is one of the many hints it contains: Establish credit in your own name. A married woman should establish credit as "Mary Smith," not as "Mrs. John Smith." If you have established credit while single and then marry, you may choose to change your last name, but you should continue to maintain your own credit record. This booklet is available free at Commercial Credit Corporation offices nationwide or upon request from the Maryland office.

Consumer Credit Project, Inc., 261 Kimberly, Barrington, Illinois 60010, (312)381-2113, Terri P. Tepper, executive director. The Consumer Credit Project, whose goal is to eliminate sex- and marital-based discrimination, is a not-for-profit consumer advocacy group. They have just published *New Credit Rights for Women*, which was underwritten by major creditors and credit reporting bureaus. The philosophy behind this book is that an educated consumer benefits all involved in a credit transaction.

Despite passage of the Equal Credit Opportunity Act and the Fair Credit Reporting Act and other laws, many women are not aware of the provisions of the acts and therefore not taking advantage of their rights. *New Credit Rights for Women* offers specific descriptions of how to identify discrimination and what steps to take to remedy unjust treatment, what to do if credit is rejected for reasons that the consumer feels are unjust, and how wives can establish their own credit rating. It also contains a complaint form that consumers can fill out and return to the Consumer Credit Project, Inc., for free assistance.

The book can be purchased at bookstores or from the Consumer Credit Project for $2.00, plus $.25 postage and handling.

INFORMATION ON INVESTMENTS, MARKETS, AND MONETARY TRENDS

You can gain insight and advance information by reading financial newsletters, books, and bulletins. The newsletters may, at first, seem expensive, but one good buying or selling tip can make them more than pay for themselves. They are considered business expenses and thus may be tax deductible for you.

Some of the publications provided by banks and brokerage firms and the government are free. You can and should be knowledgeable about investing your own money.

Bank Credit Analyst, Butterfield Building, Front Street, Hamilton, Bermuda. This publication discusses monetary trends and indicators that professionals consider when reaching decisions. It is not for the beginner. Issued monthly, $275.

Findings and Forecasts, 30 Rockefeller Plaza, New York, New York 10020. This is one of the most prestigious of the financial publications. Its editor, Edson Gould, has been successfully reporting for nearly half a century, so his record has to be pretty good. Issued twice a month, $150 quarterly or $50 annually.

Handbook of Small Business Finance, (1975) SBA 1.12:15/7 S/N 045-000-00139-3, Public Documents Distribution Center, Pueblo, Colorado 81009. If you own a business and want your financial management to be more than guesswork, you must have proper tools with which to work. This government booklet discusses such topics as good bookkeeping methods, profit and loss statements, balance sheets, and techniques (such as ratio analysis) for measuring the performance of your business. The handbook won't give you ready-made solutions to your financial problems, but it will give you tested facts and principles that can help you make sound decisions. The price is $.75.

Merrill Lynch Market Letter, 165 Broadway, New York, New York 10006, (212)766-1212. One of the world's large investment firms puts out this letter, which covers broad economic trends as well as recommendations of specific stocks and industry groups. The company also publishes many free brochures on specific subjects. Issued twice a month, $35 per year.

The Outlook, Standard & Poor's Corporation, 345 Hudson Street, New York, New York 10014 (212)924-6400. Published weekly. $125 per year. If you follow the Standard & Poor's averages, you will like this conservative newsletter. It offers a wide range of economic and stock market forecasts, as well as specific stock recommendations. It also provides a master list of recommended stocks that it monitors and updates regularly and publishes frequent special studies. Issued weekly, $125.

The Professional Tape Reader, P.O. Box 96, Wall Street Station, New York, New York 10005. Published semi-monthly. $90 per year. The eight-page letter analyzes the tape, charts, and other technical indicators. It concentrates on market timing, but it also follows groups of stocks and monitors specific recommendations.

Select Information Exchange, 2095 Broadway, New York, New York 10023. The exchange offers a free catalog of more than 800 different investment and business opportunity letters. You can choose twenty trial subscriptions (usually one issue, but in some cases up to five) for $11.95. You will also receive a copy of the large volume, *Guide to Business and Investment Books.*

MANAGEMENT AND FINANCIAL COUNSELING

Free Management and Financial Counseling, District of Columbia Chamber of Commerce, 1319 F Street, N.W., Washington, D.C. 20004, (202)347-7201. Counseling is available through the auspices of the D.C. Chamber of Commerce, the Service Corps of Retired Executives (SCORE), Chapter One, and the Small Business Administration, Washington, D.C. District Office. The chamber wants to help your business become more profitable. A qualified SCORE counselor is based in the office to assist you. Other Chambers of Commerce and local agencies have similar projects. Check with yours.

The Chamber of Commerce also provides information by mail or phone, with special emphasis in the following areas:

Relocation: Home and apartment guides, schools, churches, and shopping centers.

Federal agencies: Small business opportunities and information referral (useful no matter where you live).

Local government: Licenses and permits for business and general information about the history of Washington, D.C.

Urban business development in Washington, D.C.: Demography, geography, tax structure, city planning and development.

Tourism: Lodging, tours, maps and guides to the city, recreation and leisure activities, bilingual information on these items, historical sites, and lists of sights of special interest to various minority groups.

The Chamber of Commerce's Information Center has published *The Black Guide to Washington,* by Ron Powell and Bill Cunningham. The price is $2. It describes historical sights, restaurants, and hotels of interest to this special audience.

Federal Reserve banks provide a wealth of information, much of it free, on finances, both worldwide and individual. Here are a few of the publications available. (Where a charge is indicated, remittance should accompany request.)

Publications Services, Division of Administrative Services, Board of Governors of the Federal Reserve System, Washington, D.C. 20551.

Federal Reserve Bulletin. Issued monthly, $20 per year of $2 per issue.

Lending Functions of the Federal Reserve Banks. The price of this publication is $3.50.

Trading in Federal Funds. The price is $1.

Recent Developments in the International Finance Markets. This publication is free.

Boston Federal Reserve, Public Information Center, Boston, Massachusetts 02109.

New England Economic Almanac (1971). This publication is free.

New York Federal Reserve, Public Information Department, New York, New York 10045.

Federal Reserve Bank of New York Monthly Review. This publication is free.

Philadelphia Federal Reserve Bank, Public Services Department, Philadelphia, Pennsylvania 19150.

Federal Reserve Banks of Philadelphia Business Review. Issued monthly, free.

Cleveland Federal Reserve Bank, Publications Service, Cleveland, Ohio 44101. Write for information about available free booklets.

Richmond Federal Reserve Bank, Public Relations Department, Richmond, Virginia 23261.

Keys for Business Forecasting (1975). This publication is free.

Federal Reserve Bank of Richmond Economic Review. This publication is issued bimonthly and is free.

Atlanta Federal Reserve Bank, Research Department, Atlanta, Georgia 30303.

Fundamental Facts about United States Money (1971). This publication is free.

Federal Reserve Bank of Atlanta Monthly Review. The *Review* is free.

Chicago Federal Reserve Bank, Research Department, Chicago, Illinois 60690.

Business Conditions. This monthly publication is free.

Saint Louis Federal Reserve, Public Information Department, Saint Louis, Missouri 63166.

St. Louis Review. The monthly *Review* is free.

Minneapolis Federal Reserve Bank, Public Information Department, Minneapolis, Minnesota 55480.

Costs and Benefits of Inflation (1975) This booklet is free.

Ninth District Quarterly Review. The *Review* is free.

Kansas City Federal Reserve Bank, Public Information Department, Kansas City, Missouri 64198.

Federal Reserve Bank of Kansas City Monthly Review. This publication is free.

Dallas Federal Reserve Bank, Research Department, Dallas, Texas 75222.

Federal Reserve Bank of Dallas Business Review. This monthly publication is free.

San Francisco Federal Reserve Bank, Research Department, San Francisco, California 94120.

Silver: End of an Era (1974). This booklet is free.

Federal Reserve Bank of San Francisco Business Review. This monthly publication is free.

PUBLICATIONS

Some other publications offer excellent advice to consumers:

Changing Things: A Citizen's Guide, Donald G. Holtrop, Michigan State University Community Development Publications, 27 Kellogg Center for Continuing Education, East Lansing, Michigan 48824. Holtrop describes and illustrates with concrete examples a number of useful strategies (tools) for effective social change within a community. This is a practical guide for concerned citizens and citizens groups. The price is $1.

Consumer Views, Citibank, 399 Park Avenue, New York, New York 10043. This excellent four-page monthly newsletter gives solid hints on saving money. Recent issues discussed "How to Develop Your Personal Consumer Price Index" (June), "Inflation and Your Net Worth" (July), "How Other People Haggle" (September), "Cash Flow Budgeting" (October). The December 1978 issue gave an inflation-fighting sales calendar for each month of 1979. *Consumer Views* is available at all branches. It is free, and you do not have to be a Citibank depositor.

The Language of Investing, New York Stock Exchange, 11 Wall Street, New York, New York 10005. This free booklet explains the different terms used in the world of investment.

American Bankers Association in Washington, D.C. This organization has produced several excellent booklets. They *are not* available from the organization, but you can get copies from your local bank. If the bank does not stock the publications, request that it order copies for you. The booklets are free.

PUBLICATIONS

A Homebuyers Guide. This publication answers such questions as: "Can I afford a home?" "How will the home be financed?" "How do I select a house?" "How do I determine if the house is sound?" "What is the 'contract'?" "How do I apply for a bank mortgage?" "What are the settlement and closing costs?" "What should I know about moving?" "What about condominiums? Cooperatives?" "Should I buy or rent?"

How to Manage Your Money. "Money may answer all things, but it doesn't explain how to get enough to pay for the feast and the wine, let alone housing, clothing and insurance. For most of us, that's the real question." That is how this excellent American Bankers' Association booklet starts out. It provides you with a monthly budget chart, explains how a budget should be drawn, and gives you pages of hints about how to cut costs. It also lets you figure out "how much home" you can afford and explains the different types of life insurance, the variety of banking services available to you and what to do if you get into financial trouble. (A Spanish-language edition is also available.)

SHOPPING AND CONSUMER INFORMATION

Better Business Bureau, 257 Park Avenue South, New York, New York 10016, (212)533-6200. The bureau maintains more than 100,000 files on New York City business firms and adds more at the rate of about 150 each month. Thousands more are maintained by the bureau's unit offices in Harlem, Westbury, White Plains, and Fishkill, New York, and Newark and Paramus, New Jersey. The bureau's services are free to consumers and are as close as your telephone. If there is no bureau in your area, you can write or call the New York office and they will send a free directory of BB Bureaus. Any bureau will help you directly by providing information about a company before you do business with it, helping to resolve a complaint you might have against a firm, providing you with good consumer information to help you make intelligent buying decisions, and offering consumer arbitration to resolve disputes between buyer and seller if all other efforts toward solution fail. In addition, the bureau aids you by fostering ethical advertising and selling practices, monitoring advertising and selling practices, alerting consumers to bad business and advertising practices when the business in question will not cooperate with the bureau to eliminate the abuse, distributing consumer information through radio, television, and printed literature, and providing speakers for schools, civic groups, and business organizations.

The Better Business Bureau maintains that you can help yourself by being a smart shopper. It offers this advice:

Always shop in reputable stores and deal with reputable companies.

Don't look for something for nothing. It doesn't exist.

Shop around, comparing prices and values, before you make a major purchase. Buyer's remorse is a preventable disease.

Resist impulse buying, especially of higher-priced articles, and allow yourself a cooling-off period before reaching a decision on whether to buy.

Before doing business with a store or service firm unknown to you, check the experience of your friends, and call the bureau for its file report on the company.

If you cannot get satisfaction from a store, manufacturer, or service shop, write to the Better Business Bureau, giving the details of your problem. It will mediate, help clear up communications, and if a dispute persists, arrange for arbitration.

Better Business Bureaus offer hundreds of free one page reports on subjects such as "Moving Interstate" and "Technical Schools." Such reports give you questions to ask companies and warn you about pitfalls. The bureaus also will give you information about specific companies about whom there have been complaints. Staff will also refer you to the appropriate agency to help you deal with your particular situation.

Consumer Information Center, Pueblo, Colorado 81009. The U.S. government publishes a quarterly catalog of selected federal publications. This list includes many booklets to help you in every area of your life. The catalog is available free upon request.

PUBLICATION

Here is a sample of the kinds of publications available from the center.

In The Bank or Up The Chimney? Order No. 311D. This excellent booklet gives step-by-step illustrated help on weather stripping, caulking, insulating, and other energy-saving measures that the homeowner can take. The price is $1.70.

Shop by Mail

Mail-order shopping services are growing at a phenomenal annual rate, much faster than the total retail sales in the United States. The number of mail-order businesses is now estimated at 10,000 and is increasing rapidly.

Direct Mail Marketing Association, 6 East 43d Street, New York, New York 10017 (212)689-4977. The association points to the high price of gasoline and an increased female work force with little time to shop in stores as prime reasons for the mail-order boom. Shopping by mail allows a shopper to avoid the four Cs: cars, clerks, crowds, and crime. If you are an impulse buyer, mail-order shopping can save you money; if you are not in a store, you won't see that something you suddenly decide you *must* have. You also save time. How much is your time worth? You save money on gas, on shoe leather, on energy, and even on goods. Because they have small overhead, mail-order houses can afford to charge less. Furthermore, you may avoid state taxes if you buy something across state lines.

DMMA sponsors Mail-Order Action Line. This service is designed to help unsnarl problems that may occur. Consumer complaints are directed to the proper person at the mail-order company. If there is a serious problem of fraud, the organization has no legal clout but can nevertheless refer you to the proper agency, such as the postal inspectors or the Federal Trade Commission.

If you *hate* mail-order promotions, if you do not want to receive junk mail, you can have your name removed from all lists by filling out the association's Name Removal Form. Once you fill out this paper, DMMA's participating member firms will take your name off their mailing lists.

If you want to be put on particular lists because you are especially interested in particular things, you can have your name put on the Mail Preference List. Fill out the following:

Consumer Application Mail Preference Service

Mail to: Mail Preference Service
6 East 43rd Street
New York, NY 10017

From (print)_____

Street _____

City & State_____

I have checked the box to indicate by preference

□ I want less mail (removal) [OR] I want to shop by mail (add-on) □

□ Please add my name to the name-removal file. I understand that you will make the name-removal file available to direct mail advertisers for the sole purpose of removing from their mailing lists the name and addresses contained therein.

□ Others at my address who also want less mail (or variations of my own name by which mail is received) include:

_____

_____

I would like to receive information in the mail, especially on the subjects below (circle letter):

A. All Subjects
B. Automobiles, Parts and Accessories
C. Books and Magazines
D. Charities
E. Civic Organizations
F. Clothing
G. Foods and Cooking
H. Gifts
I. Grocery Bargains
J. Health Food and Vitamins
K. HiFi & Electronics
L. Home Furnishings
M. Insurance

N. Plants, Flowers	**R.** Sewing, Needlework Arts & Crafts	**U.** Stocks & Bonds
O. Photography	**S.** Sports,	**V.** Tools & Equipment
P. Real Estate	Camping	**W.** Travel
Q. Records & Tapes	**T.** Stamps & Coins	**X.** Office Supplies

Date_____ Signature _____

PUBLICATIONS

A Consumer's Shopping List of Inflation Fighting Ideas, 625G (1978). This booklet gives you tips for saving money on food, health, energy, and housing.

Be a Smart Shopper, Suave Smart Shopper, Dept. RW, 8th Floor, 150 East Huron, Chicago, Illinois 60611. A family of four can save more than $100 a year on personal-care products by becoming smart shoppers. Shari Bryant, consumer affairs advisor to the Chicago-based Suave Division of Helene Curtis, has put together a booklet instructing budget-conscious buyers across the country on how to get the most for their money. "There are so many products from which to choose," says Ms. Bryant, "and they come in a perplexing variety of sizes, shapes, packages, with numerous claims and costs. Personal care is an area in which impulse buying can get the best of even the smartest shopper. We tend to end up with lots of cosmetics and hair care products which we never use, or we pay more than we should for what we are buying." The booklet includes twelve steps to smart shopping. Send $.35 to cover postage and handling.

Budgeting for the Family, 069G (1978). This booklet outlines steps in developing a budget. It includes charts for estimating income, planning family spending, and recording expenses and a section on using credit. The price is $.90.

Consumer Credit Handbook, 659G (1978). This publication explains how consumer credit laws can help you shop for credit and apply for it. It tells you what creditors look for and what to do if you are denied credit. The booklet is free.

Shopping for Credit Can Save You Cash, 627G (1974). This booklet tells you how to compare the costs of buying with loans, credit cards, and revolving charge plans. It is free.

Where You Shop Is as Important as What You Buy, 628G (1974). This is a discussion of the pros and cons of shopping at different types of stores. The booklet is free.

Your Money's Worth in Foods, USDA Home and Garden Bulletin No. 183, Office of Governmental and Public Affairs, U.S. Department of Agriculture, Washington, D.C. 20250. This publication brings together information on meal planning and food shopping for consumers interested in economizing on food. Teachers and others helping families use their money wisely will also find this bulletin helpful. It includes estimates of family food costs, guides for planning meals, and tools for comparing food costs. These recommendations are supported by the continuing research of the Consumer and Food Economics Institute. It also contains daily food guides and sample meal plans and suggests how foods can be interchanged. The publication is free. You can also request a listing of other publications.

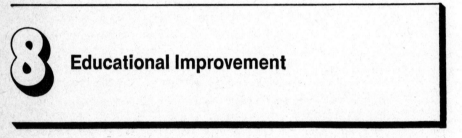

8 Educational Improvement

> The world is so full of a number of things, we should all be as happy as kings.
>
> Robert Louis Stevenson, *A Child's Garden of Verses*

Today, no matter what your age or geographic location, you can learn something new and useful. Formal education no longer need stop in a person's teens or early twenties; it can continue indefinitely.

You are literally never too old to learn. Dr. Paul B. Baltes, professor of human development at Pennsylvania State University, says, "Research by myself and others over the past ten years indicates that intelligence does not necessarily slide downhill from adulthood through old age; and in fact, by many measures, it increases as time goes by."

Dr. Nathan Shock, the National Institute of Health's pioneer in aging research, says, "Oftimes, what passes as aging is nothing more than atrophy or disuse. This is especially true within the sphere of mental activities. A good dictum would be to learn something new every day, even if it comes under the heading of useless information. We might well adopt the boy scout dictum of a 'good deed every day' to 'a new deed every day' for the maintenance of health and vigor." The only question, he says, is: What do you want to learn and where?

Plumbing? Witchcraft? Existentialism? Guitar playing? Chinese? Mushroom hunting? Citizenship journalism, such as writing letters to editors, journalists, and legislators? Whatever you want to learn or need to know, there is someone eager to teach you.

Dr. Baltes even suggests that the educational system be redesigned so that we do not obtain all of our education in a continuous, rigid fashion early in life but distribute it in different ways, perhaps in chunks throughout childhood, adolescence, adulthood, and old age, in order to achieve a greater balance between the needs of personal life and educational offerings. He sees people needing education for new tasks when jobs are changed, when a divorce occurs, when a spouse dies, when the nest empties of children, when a person is about to retire or has retired, and even when death must be faced.

And just as adults need education for change, changes in the population make it vital that institutions change and adapt to serving adults. The baby boom is over, and there are not enough young students around to fill the halls of ivy. The rapid advancement of technology makes it necessary for working people to update their knowledge constantly. A physician who learns nothing more after graduation from medical school will fail to practice good medicine, a computer technician who stops training after the end of the course will fall far behind, and an accountant who does not constantly keep up to date with the new tax laws will be doing clients a disservice. Retirement—soon expected to be at the age of 50 years—has also contributed to the need for adult education. Healthy adults who want to work or to achieve new things need retraining and new opportunities for expanding their horizons. The federal government has recognized the need for continuous education and has allowed tax deductions for the expenses involved, including registration fees, travel, meals, and lodgings when education is undertaken to improve professional skills.

Everyone is benefiting from these changes in the educational system. Young students and older students can intermingle in classes and give each other valuable insights from each end of the bridge.

Colleges and universities are not the only institutions offering educational opportunities for adults. Religious institutions, high schools, community recreational programs, professional associations, commercial enterprises—all are providing knowledge either free or at a nominal cost.

EDUCATION BY AUDIO CASSETTE, NEWSPAPER, AND TELEVISION

National Media Courses are college-level educational programs that utilize newspapers, television, radio, and cassettes (rather than the traditional classroom and teacher) as major course components. Developed by University Extension at the University of California at San Diego, they are available to any institution of higher education as educational packages, including texts, supplementary readers, and study guides written by leading scholars. To date, more than 400 colleges (over one-fifth of all four-year institutions in the nation) and universities have participated in the program. You can contact the people listed here or your local college to make arrangements to take the course for credit. The cost depends on tuition fees at the institution you choose.

Courses by Audio Cassette, National Media Courses, X-001. University of California, San Diego Extension, La Jolla, California 92093, (714)452-3422, Caleb Lewis, director. Three cassette courses are for use as independent study or for local radio broadcast. As in the case of Courses by Newspaper and Television, the cassette courses have been designed to be presented locally by any institution that wishes to do so. A local teacher/coordinator customarily conducts two on-campus sessions (at midterm and at the end of the course); otherwise, all instruction takes place off campus through radio (or cassette) and printed material. The three courses developed are Women's Studies: The Changing Role of Women in Contemporary Society, Introducing American Folk Music and Introduction to Eastern Religions. The total package will consist of audio tapes or audio cassettes, a book or reader, a study guide, and a teacher's manual. The books will be for sale, and the audio tapes or cassettes are now for sale or rent. If a radio station wishes to run the programs, the tapes will be available to them without charge. You can purchase the tapes yourself for about $35 each. Check with National Media Courses before ordering.

Courses by Newspaper, National Media Courses, X-002, University of California, San Diego Extension, La Jolla, California 92093, (714)452-3405, Goerge A. Colburn, director. You can receive college credit by taking a course that is offered cooperatively by newspapers and colleges and universities. By enrolling through a local participating college or university, doing additional readings, and taking tests, you can receive credit. More than 400 newspapers publish a series of fifteen weekly articles written by leading American scholars. There are cooperating colleges in forty-eight states and in Europe, Canada, Australia, and the Far East. You work independently but have to attend at least two class sessions on a campus near you and meet that college's requirements for course credit. Among the more than 200 educational institutions in the program are the City Colleges of Chicago, Delgado Community College in New Orleans, Louisiana, and the University of Washington in Seattle. To find out the names of cooperating institutions and newspapers near you, write to the above address. The University of California Extension at Berkeley also offers Courses by Newspapers with a completely independent study program that would make it possible to get University of Calfornia extension credit entirely through the mail.

Courses by Television, National Media Courses, X-001, University of California, San Diego Extension, La Jolla, California 92093, (714)452-3446, Jennie Chin, program representative. Begun in 1974 with a course on Jacob Bronowski's "The Ascent of Man," Courses by Television are offered by many colleges and universities and are built on selected national series aired on PBS. Students watch television programs, follow a study guide, and broaden their perspective with supplementary readings and contact sessions on a college or university campus. The programs are selected because they are of high quality, intellectually challenging, and interestingly produced. "The Adams Chronicles," "Classic Theatre: The Humanities in Drama," "The Growing Years," John Kenneth Galbraith's "The Age of Uncertainty," "Parent Effectiveness," and "The Shakespeare Plays" are examples of series for which courses have been developed.

PUBLICATIONS

Cassette Information Services, Box 9559W, Glendale, California 91206. The *Audio-Cassette Directory* provides a listing of all adult-level non-music, educational, and informational spoken-voice programs currently available on audio cassettes. Names and addresses of 516 producers and their charges for sale, rental, or loan of their programs are included. Professional education courses in motivation, medicine, sales, business, theology, management, banking, advertising, public relations, and many other subjects are available, as are cassettes of literature, drama, poetry, and language instruction. The directory includes descriptions of a variety of how-to-do-it programs for everything from bridge and astrology to cooking and marriage counseling. The cost is $12. The *Audio-Cassette Newsletter*, a quarterly report, supplements the directory, listing new producers of audio cassette programs and new titles, series, and services in this booming field. A year's subscription is $9.

FINANCING AN EDUCATION

No one, no matter how old, should be denied admission to college because of lack of funds. There are many foundations that will provide help. High school and college guidance offices will help you find the sources. And don't forget your local librarian; there are a number of books that list scholarships and grants. The Federal Guaranteed Student Loan Program offers loans to students; preference is given to families with incomes under $15,000 a year, but this figure is expected to be liberalized. Loans under this program are obtained through local banking institutions participating in the program.

The majority of banks also offer special loans for educational purposes. Rates vary from about 6 to 12 percent simple interest. If the loan is made directly to the student, rather than to the parents, interest charges and repayment usually do not begin until after graduation.

A number of private finance companies specialize in student loans; many of them are approved by colleges. Such firms pay the college bills as they come due, requiring the borrower to repay in forty-eight or sixty monthly installments. These are certainly more expensive than most bank and college loans, but they do provide a means of breaking up the usual two or three large bills per year into equal monthly payments. Proceed with caution so that the interest costs do not run way up.

Fellowships, Scholarships, and Loans

Danforth Graduate Fellowship Program, Danforth Foundation, 222 South Central Avenue, Saint Louis, Missouri 63105. Established in 1927, this foundation is a national educational and philanthropic organization. Its activities emphasize the theme of improving the quality of teaching and learning. If you are a college senior or a recent graduate, have not begun graduate study, are between twenty and thirty years of age, and are a citizen of the United States, you should contact the liaison officer at your undergraduate college. If you have already received a bachelor's degree and are between thirty and forty years of age and a citizen of the United States, write to Warren Bryan Martin, vice president and director, Danforth Graduate Fellowship Program, at the foundation. The fellowships are for one year and are renewable. The grants are from $2,500 for single persons to $3,900 for the head of a household with two children. The maximum grant will be increased by $400 for each additional child. The objectives of the fellowship program "are to help persons who receive these awards to go to graduate school for the purpose of completing the Ph.D. or an equivalent degree; to encourage people committed to careers in teaching to hold to their commitment in the presence of countervailing pressures and the sometimes difficult environment of the graduate school; to keep the theme of humane learning, learning infused with values, learning concerned for the ethical and moral dimensions of personal, social, and public life . . . before the Fellows to the end that they, as teachers, will share not only the skills of their profession but also a set of values that gives meaning to their work."

FOR WOMEN

Altrusa International Foundation, Founders Fund Vocational Aid Project, 332 South Michigan Avenue, Chicago, Illinois 60604. Awards of $50 to $500 are given to women of all ages, regardless of educational background, for training that will qualify them for employment, for retraining to move from a low-level job to a skilled occupation, to purchase equipment needed for self-employment, and for personal rehabilitation. In all instances, the applicant must have plans to move into the labor market, into a more skilled job, or become self-employed within twelve months. The emphasis is on vocational aid, not educational scholarships. Awards are designed for the woman who needs to earn but who, because of reverses in life, lacks the funds with which to learn a trade or the funds with which to become self-employed. Selection is based on aptitude and need. Preference is given to older women, but all ages may qualify. Among the women they help are the widow who suddenly has to reenter a changing job market without current skills, the mature woman who has never worked outside her home, the woman who is sole support of a family and who hopes to increase her income through training for a more advanced job, the deserted mother with dependent children who wants to be self-supporting, the handicapped woman who could lead a productive life if trained in an occupational skill, and the young woman from a disadvantaged family who needs vocational training beyond the high school level.

American Association of University Women Educational Foundation, 2401 Virginia Avenue, N.W., Washington, D.C. 20037. This organization offers grants and awards for women who want to improve their education and/or pursue areas of research. Approximately seventy dissertation fellowships are available for those who will have successfully completed all required course work and examinations for the doctorate except the defense of the dissertation. The fellowship can be used for the final year of the doctoral work. Several awards for postdoctoral research are also available. Stipends range from $3,500 up to $9,000 for postdoctoral fellowships. There are also fellowships for women who are in their final year of professional training in the fields of law, dentistry, medicine, veterinary medicine, and architecture. The awards, which may be used only for study in the United States, average about $4,000.

Business and Professional Women's Foundation, 2012 Massachusetts Avenue, N.W., Washington, D.C. 20036, (202)293-1200. The foundation exists to create greater career opportunities for women. They provide not only guidance in management and leadership roles but also educational scholarships and loans. Members and nonmembers, working women, full-time and part-time students, and young women seeking careers are all eligible.

Here are the services provided by the foundation:

Lena Lake Forrest Fellowships: These grants are awarded to doctoral and postdoctoral scholars for research in educational, economic, political, social, or psychological factors affecting business and professional women. One or more are awarded annually in amounts ranging from $500 to $3,000 each.

Research Fellow: This award is given for an ongoing, independent, in-house project for a woman investigating topics of emerging interest, such as hours of work when workers can choose and education and career interests.

Library and Information Center: This facility provides a public reference and referral service, including a computerized file of biographical data on outstanding contemporary women and oral histories.

Scholarships and loans: The foundation assists women at all stages of career development. Actual working experience weighs at least as heavily as academic records and financial need in selecting scholarship and loan recipients. Current programs include:

Career Advancement Scholarships for job-related training, academic training, or vocational training for women twenty-five and older; more than $85,000 awarded annually

Loan funds for business and engineering studies for women in graduage-level work; granted annually for study at accredited schools

Sally Butler International Scholarship for Latin American women who wish to study in the United States

BPW is the only organization in the United States devoted exclusively to working women. It holds seminars for special training to advance careers, to prepare women for management opportunities, and to develop leadership capabilities. These seminars are held throughout the country. The cost is $25.

Organizations

College Entrance Examination Board: Choosing and Financing Careers.

The College Entrance Examination Board is a nonprofit organization that provides tests and other educational services, including publications, for students, schools, and colleges; its membership is composed of more than 2,000 colleges, schools, school systems, and educational associations.

The following selection of the board's publications are produced on a nonprofit basis and reflect the organization's broad involvement in the education process.

PUBLICATIONS

Meeting College Costs in 1979-80: A Guide for Students and Parents, (1978), 236233m. This booklet offers general guidelines and gives specific examples to help students and parents estimate college expenses. It also gives information on sources of financial aid and how to apply for different grants and loans. The publication is free.

I Can Be Anything: Careers and Colleges for Young Women, Joyce Slayton Mitchell (1978), 219852. This is a detailed guide to a wide range of career opportunities open to today's women. For each of 108 different careers, the book tells what the work is like, what education and personal skills are needed, which colleges award the most degrees to women, how many women are employed and where, and their starting salaries and future prospects. The price of this paperback is $7.95.

Decisions and Outcomes, H. B. Gelatt, Barbara Varenhorst, Richard Carey, and Gordon P. Miller (1973), 221606. This booklet is intended to help anyone over sixteen who is facing important personal, educational, or career choices. Designed as a course of study in the development and application of decision-making skills, these materials are especially appropriate for use in group settings, as a major component in guidance and counseling programs, or as part of subject areas such as English, history, human relations, and drug and health education. The publication costs $2.50.

Free-Access Higher Education, Warren W. Willingham (1970), 237352. This book is a state-by-state study of the accessibility of higher education. The author defines a free-access college as one at which tuition is $400 per year or less, that accepts at least one-third of its freshmen from the lower half of their high school classes, that is within forty-five minutes commuting distance of the homes of students. Each state is profiled with concise date, supplemented by tabulated information showing the availability of free-access higher education and telling who can benefit from it. The price of this hardcover publication is $6.50.

Requests and payment for publications should be sent to:

College Board Publication Orders
Box 2815
Princeton, New Jersey 08541

Learn While You Earn

If you want to learn new job skills today, chances are you will have pay to be schooled in them. But in the Army Reserve, you are paid to learn. In recognition of the importance of career training in today's inflated economy and shrinking job market, the Army Reserve is offering on-the-job, part-time skill training in more than 400 civilian-related career fields, from electronics and communications to engineering and auto mechanics, as part of its "earn while you learn" program for qualified men and women. In 3,200 Army Reserve units throughout the United States, citizen-soldiers are augmenting their regular incomes and earning extra Army dollars while learning a job of their choice.

Through the Army Reserve's Civil Acquired Skill Program (CASP), men and women with no prior military service but with civilian work experience in such job areas as carpentry, construction engineering, heavy-equipment operation, welding, plumbing, or masonry can enlist in the Army Reserve at a higher rank and rate of pay than those individuals without similar job experience. In their first year in an Army Reserve uniform, privates first class can earn as much as $1,000 (and in some cases much more). This supplementary income is earned for just sixteen hours of training a month in their hometown unit (usually on a weekend) and two consecutive weeks of training a year. The rest of their time is their own. Under CASP, Army reservists draw starting salaries of $3.48 an hour, depending on prior skills and education, and with promotions, they earn more than $1,000 a year.

Army Reserve benefits and pay are also available to service veterans. Prior-service personnel can join an Army Reserve unit in or near the community in which they live; they may qualify to keep the same rank and proportionate rate of pay that they had when they left active duty. For example, a Specialist 5 with three years of military service can enlist in the Army Reserve and earn more than $68 a month for just sixteen hours work.

The job skills learned in the Army Reserve are readily adaptable to the civilian marketplace. In many instances, industry places a premium on those men and women with military experience, frequently advancing them to higher positions with better pay than employees without military experience. Army Reserve skill training lasts a lifetime and goes a long way toward building a rewarding civilian career. In an increasingly sophisticated job market, specialized training can mean higher pay and better job opportunities for those who have learned a skill. Although every skill training category may not always be available, a wide range of jobs are waiting to be filled at local Army Reserve units.

For a lot of men and women, Army Reserve membership helps open the doors to good employment opportunities. Many Army reservists hold high-level positions in civilian companies or run their own business. Companies are aware of the leadership skills and job training that Army reservists have been taught at local Reserve units, and they can often use those skills in enterprise. No matter what the rank or grade, Army Reserve pay and benefits are great equalizers in helping meet the problems of today's economy. Men and women in the Army Reserve not only earn extra income but also build up retirement credits, make valuable business and social contacts, and are eligible for PX and commissary privileges and up to $20,000 of low-cost group life insurance.

If on-the-job training is hard to find and training schools are too expensive, take a look at the opportunities available in the United States Army Reserve. You will find the center nearest you listed in the white pages under "U.S. Government."

If you wish to advance, you have to keep up and ahead of what is going on in your field. Every trade and profession has associations and firms that provide advanced training. Many of the courses are inexpensive and in some cases, you can be paid while you learn to earn more money.

Center for Professional Advancement, Box H, East Brunswick, New Jersey 08816, (201)249-1400. The center, which has been in business for twelve years, has conducted classes for approximately 40,000 scientists and engineers. It offers more short courses than almost any organization in the country. The catalog lists over 300 different technical courses that are offered on a varying schedule, from every three months to every eighteen months, with most courses being offered on an annual basis. The average course cost is $135 per course day; a three-day course costs $410. A small supplementary fee is added to pay for luncheons and coffee breaks.

The center is the world's largest private, nondegree educational institution offering graduate courses for scientists, engineers, and technical managers. Courses have been designed to help participants keep abreast of the latest advances in their specialties. Because most participants cannot be absent from their jobs for an extended period, courses follow an intensive two- to five-day schedule. Among the courses are Sensory Evaluation for Technologists in the Food, Beverage, Pharmaceutical and Cosmetic Industries; Solar Energy; Materials Management; Coal Mining Exploration; Minicomputers and Programmable Controllers for Progress Control; and Cement and Concrete Technology. The faculty members are drawn from the United States and foreign countries and are tops in their professions.

Wharton School, University of Pennsylvania Human Resources Center, New York Management Center, 360 Lexington Avenue, New York, New York 10017, information service manager (212)953-7272. Established in 1964 as part of the Management Department of the Wharton School, the center sponsors seminars in New York City, Houston, San Francisco, and Chicago. Experts speak on a variety of topics for both men and women executives and would-be executives, for example, organizational power and influence networks, group dynamics of effective decision making, and conflict management at the individual, group, and organizational levels. Certificates are awarded to all seminar participants by the Wharton School. The tuition fee is $495 per person, plus $65 registration fee per company; this includes all workbook and handout material. Each registration after the first is subject to the tuition fee only, a saving of $65 per person. Transfers or substitutions can be made at any time. If you cannot attend the entire session, the fee will be credited to any other program over the following twelve-month period. Seminars usually run two or three days.

PUBLICATION

The Levinson Letter, published twice monthly by The Levinson Institute, Inc., P. O. Box 95, Cambridge, Massachusetts 02138; (617)489-3040. $98 per year, U.S. and Canada; $125, foreign. A newsletter for managers dealing with the psychological aspects of leadership in organizations, including issues such as promotion, performance appraisal, rivalries, motivation, termination.

Continuing Professional Education, Drexel University, 32d and Chestnut Streets, Philadelphia, Pennsylvania 19104, (215)895-2154. The university sponsors seminars for the professional advancement of managers, engineers, and librarians. Each course emphasizes practical knowledge and focuses on state-of-the-art management science and technology. Most courses are offered in intensive two- to three-day sessions. Drexel presents a certificate upon completion of each course. Seminars are usually located on the Drexel University campus, but companies and groups can contract for in-house presentations of customized seminars and workshops. Fees vary from $25 to $475.

American Management Associations, American Management Associations Building, 135 West 50th Street, New York, New York 10020, (212)586-8100. This nonprofit educational membership organization derives its financial support from the fees charged for certain of its activities, products, and services. Its motto is: "We help your company grow by helping your people grow." It provides many seminars throughout the year for professional advancement in all fields of business.

EDUCATIONAL ALTERNATIVES

Free University And Learning Network, 1221 Thurston, Manhattan, Kansas 66502, (913)532-5866. A free university is an organization offering ungraded, unaccredited classes to the general public. Anyone can volunteer to teach a subject and the learning content and procedure are entirely up to the teacher and learners. The basic educational philosophy is, "Anyone can teach and anyone can learn." The free university seeks teachers, prints a brochure of classes, registers learners, and evaluates the session. Classes take place in homes and other informal settings. Courses may cover any topic, such as arts and crafts, scholarly subjects, practical skills, or societal issues. Free universities began in 1964 and today there are more than 200 in this country. Many are campus based while others exist as independent organizations in the community. A learning network is a telephone referral service for people who want to teach and people who want to learn. People call the network and register their needs and talents, which are recorded on file cards in an information bank. After referral, all teaching and learning arrangements are decided by the participants.

The Free University Network is headquartered at the University for Man in Manhattan, Kansas, where it maintains community education archives and publishes a newsletter. FUN is coordinated both from its central office and by its six regional coordinators in the Northeast, South, Great Lakes, Midwest, Rocky Mountain, and West regions. The Free University Network publishes *Free University News* monthly, $8 per year for individuals, $12 per year for institutions. It sends out an information packet, $2, to people interested in starting a free university or learning network. FUN also publishes the *Free University/Learning Network Directory*, $1. The network also has a sourcebook that covers to all aspects of free university organization and development, called *Free University Manual*, 442 pages, $25 for members; $35 for nonmembers. The network helps communities start education projects and promotes alternative education at the national level. The membership fee for an individual is $15 per year. Organizational members fees depend upon the size and character of the group but usually range from $15 to $35.

PUBLICATION

The Learning Exchange: An Alternative in Adult Education, Gregory D. Squires. Squires, one of the founders of the Learning Exchange in Chicago, examines and evaluates the operation, its successes, its failures, and its scope in this 50-page book. Squires' careful analysis of the data makes this publication useful to anyone seeking either to evaluate or duplicate the Learning Exchange. Write to Michigan State University Community Development Publications, 27 Kellogg Center for Continued Education, East Lansing, Michigan 48824, and include the number M55.

National Center for Educational Brokering, 1211 Connecticut Avenue, N.W., Washington, D.C. 20036, (202)466-5530, and 405 Oak Street, Syracuse, New York 13203, (315)425-5275. A new form of educational counseling emerged in the 1970s to meet the need of adults who want to continue their education. This network, with resources in forty-nine states, aims to open up all possible learning opportunities for adults. Educational brokers include formal and nonformal educational settings in their pool of alternatives for referrals, which may be to courses in colleges, schools, community centers, unions, or churches or to individuals or informal groups with particular knowledge or skills to share. The idea is to meet your needs with as many options as possible. Brokering services will also help local communities set up various programs to fill gaps in educational offerings.

If you don't know exactly what you want and need in the way of educational services, or if you would like a particular course but don't know where you can sign up for it, contact the center for referral to a counseling service in your area.

Yes Educational Society, 1035 31st Street, N.W., Washington, D.C. 20007, (202)338-6969. In a city of institutions, this institution manages to be unique. It offers a course in biomysticism, a workshop on Japanese vibrations, a seminar called "The Timetable for a Mass-Landing on Earth," a lecture called "Who or What Am I?" "Massage—Being in Touch," "Nutrition and Disease/Food and Consciousness," "The Science of Domesticating Peak Experiences," and numerology. Based in Georgetown, the Yes Educational Society (YES) is Washington's center for alternative education. It is an organization for those "who have found that traditional education, religion, and science have left some basic questions about who we are and what we are doing here unanswered." They talk about "harmony and balance in our relationships with others and with the planet we occupy, about reuniting religion and science, about Eastern philosophy, parapsychology, and ESP, about meditation and the universe within, about a revolution of consciousness."

YES is a small, nonprofit organization founded in 1974 by Ollie and Cris Popenoe, the husband-wife team who own and manage YES! Inc., a natural food store, restaurant, and bookshop in Georgetown. They offer a wide variety of courses, some held at Georgetown University, churches, and other locations.

PUBLICATION

Pathways is a free monthly guide to conscious living published by YES and available at YES!, health food stores, libraries, and many other points of distribution. For subscriptions, call (202)338-7675 or write to YES.

Extension Service, U.S. Department of Agriculture, Washington, D.C. 20250. Created in 1914, this unique system of education is designed to take knowledge directly to the people of America. The largest, most successful informal educational organization in the world, it is a nationwide system funded and guided by a partnership of federal, state, and local governments that delivers information to you through the land-grant university system (the land-grant college is usually your state university). There is an Extension Service in each state, the District of Columbia, Puerto Rico, the Virgin Islands, and Guam. Most people think of the Extension Service as an organization that helps farmers with their crop problems and that sponsors 4-H clubs for children, but it is much more than that, having turned a great deal of its attention to the problems of urban living. There is a wealth of free information and instruction available that you may be missing. First of all, there are the county agents, listed in your phone book under "County." They will answer questions by phone about almost any home problem from pests in the pantry to a water problem in the backyard. The thousands of home economists employed by the services will also answer questions about foods, homemaking, and children. They help advise on budgetary matters, food purchases, housing problems, and health matters. The Extension Service provides demonstrations, workshops, short courses, publications, and consultations. They even offer vocational courses. They are really a living encyclopedia of information and help, always trying to meet your needs. Take advantage of the Extension Service; call or write for a list of publications and a schedule of current events and workshops.

LIBRARIES: MORE THAN JUST BOOKS

Libraries have become more than places from which to borrow books. They are now vital, ever changing learning centers, true people's universities. Librarians will help you research any subject from a company's investment potential to how to fix a bathtub drain. Through interlibrary loans, they can obtain almost any book in or out of print.

Libraries are also offering a wide range of services to the public. For example, many libraries are offering programs that lead to college degrees, high school equivalency diplomas, or full literacy tests. For example, on Long Island, eight residents earned M.B.A. degrees through the Port Washington, New York, library. The master's program is a joint effort by the Manhasset, Port Washington, and Plainedge libraries and nearby Adelphi University.

College course credit is also offered by some libraries. Several in Maryland, for example, offer courses in conjunction with the University of Maryland. Patrons can earn a B.A. degree through this cooperative effort.

MUSEUMS

Like libraries, museums have become people's learning centers. They offer many unusual educational experiences for free or for nominal fees. Victor Danilov, Ph.D., director of the Museum of Science and Industry in Chicago, points out that there are now approximately thirty museums of contemporary science and technology in North America that have a number of common characteristics: They are concerned primarily with the physical sciences and engineering, and many have extensive exhibits in the life sciences. They make relatively little use of artifacts and collections; the emphasis is on constructed educational exhibits. They make extensive use of three-dimensional, interactive exhibit techniques designed to involve the spectator. They usually have extensive science education programs, often in cooperation with local schools and community groups. They frequently rely on industry and other outside groups for the preparation and funding of at least some of their exhibits and programs.

Dr. Danilov says that unlike their European counterparts, American museums of science and technology are concerned primarily with the present and the future, rather than the past. They seek to further public understanding of scientific principles, technological applications, and social consequences, and they do it in an enjoyable, participatory manner. In addition to furthering cultural enrichment, they are invaluable societal instruments because they help to develop an informed citizenry on matters affecting science, technology, and industry.

Here are descriptions of some outstanding science museums compiled by Dr. Danilov.

Lawrence Hall of Science, University of California, Berkeley, California 94704, (415)642-5132. This museum offers one of the most comprehensive museum science education programs in the nation. There are specialized lectures, workshops, and computerized information available for the public and a nationwide program of assisting minority students in entering college and majoring in math, science, and engineering.

Franklin Institute Science Museum, Philadelphia, Pennsylvania 19104, (215)448-1000. Among this museum's programs in science education is the Parkway Program, a school without walls that enables 800 high school pupils to use the resources of the Philadelphia Museum of Art, the Academy of Natural Science, the Free Library, and other cultural business and community organizations. Between 100 and 200 courses are available. Half the courses are taught by teachers from the public school system and the other half by the museum staff.

Oregon Museum of Science and Industry, Portland, Oregon 97208, (503)248-5900. The museum's student research center gives interested young people the opportunity to engage in independent research projects with the aid of museum equipment and personnel. Among some of the subjects covered are artificial intelligence, computers and other machines, rocket guidance, underwater breathing, and radio telescopes. A related program, the Independent Learner Program, is intended for individuals who have the maturity and ability to handle the freedom of an unstructured learning situation. Forty high school and college students spend two months working on individual research projects in the natural sciences at the museum's Camp Hancock in central Oregon. The museum and the Housing Authority of Portland have experimented with a drop-in learning center concept as a means of broadening the science experience of youngsters from low-income families.

Houston Museum of Natural Science, Herman Park, Houston, Texas 77002, (713)526-4273. There is a Hall of Petroleum Science and Technology in this museum, naturally, as well as a full range of science exhibits whose subjects range from the Texas marshes to the wilds of Africa. An adult education program, which is run in cooperation with the University of Houston, sponsors contemporary science seminars on subjects that include oceanography, energy alternatives, rocks and minerals, and nature photography. There are trips to the Atchafalaya swamp and to the Big Bend National Park. The museum also cosponsors trips such as an archaeology tour of the Bible lands. The museum also has a modern optical telescope with television capability; Night and Day Telescope Tours are available free of charge to the public. For information and reservations, contact the Houston Museum Planetarium. A one-year membership costs $15; a lifetime membership is $1,000.

Field Trips, Field Museum, Roosevelt Road at Lake Shore Drive, Chicago, Illinois 60605, (312)922-9410. The museum sponsors one-day trips to local areas of biological and ecological significance. Some trips are more strenuous than others and are so identified. A "strenuous" trip means participants should be in good physical shape; it involves rugged terrain and a lot of climbing. A "fairly strenuous" trip means you may get wet and/or dirty, hike long distances, or do some climbing. There are adult trips (minimum age, eighteen) and family trips for adults accompanied by children six years of age or older.

An example of a strenuous trip is the trip to Indiana Dunes–Warren Woods. Angela Gilhespie, of the Committee on Evolutionary Biology, University of Chicago, directs this excursion to the dunes at the southern end of Lake Michigan, which are characterized by successive zones of plant and animal communities. The trip includes a visit to a quaking bog that is rich in insectivorous plants.

Museum members are charged $6 per trip; nonmembers, $7.

Chicago Academy of Sciences, 2001 North Clark Street, Chicago, Illinois 60607, (312)LI9-0606. The academy offers Saturday environmental field trips and evening lecture series. Courses vary each season; phone to learn what's scheduled.

Cooper-Hewitt Museum, Smithsonian Institution's National Museum of Design, 2 East 91st Street, New York, New York 10028, (212)860-6868. The museum offers courses and tours for people interested in design and architecture. For instance, there is a tour called "Backstage on the Great White Way," in which you examine every aspect of theater design in a one-day tour of New York theaters. The tour includes on- and Off-

Broadway houses such as the Vivian Beaumont, the Mitzi Newhouse, and the Biltmore, and costume, stage, and/or lighting designers discuss their work. Lunch is at the famous Sardi's, with a talk by an internationally known stage designer. The price is $20 for members and $30 for nonmembers.

There are similar design tours of Washington, Philadelphia, the Southwest, and Charleston, as well as a course in New York architecture. A winter program is entitled "Do You Believe in Magic?" and for four Saturdays young people learn about rope tricks and amazing transformations and tabletop magic.

Fermi National Accelerator Lab, P.O. Box 500, Batavia, Illinois 60510, (312)840-3351. This is the laboratory where the atom bomb was developed; it houses the world's largest particle accelerator. There are self-guided tours from 8:00 A.M. to 5:00 P.M. weekdays and from 8:00 A.M. to 8:00 P.M. Regular tours for high school students and older adults are given Monday to Thursday between 8:30 A.M. and 5:00 P.M. Groups must have a minimum of ten people and a maximum of fifty.

Other Science Museums. Many science museums offer a wide range of exhibits, scientific demonstrations, supplemental courses, films, theater programs, speakers, and reference materials. Here are some outstanding examples:

American Museum of Atomic Energy, Oak Ridge, Tennessee 37830, (615)576-3200

Buhl Planetarium and Institute of Popular Science, Pittsburgh, Pennsylvania 15219, (412)321-4300

Cranbrook Institute of Science, Bloomfield Hills, Michigan 48013, (313) 645-3200

Dallas Health and Science Museum, Dallas, Texas 75221, (214)428-8351

Des Moines Center of Science and Industry, Des Moines, Iowa 50318, (515)274-4138

Exploratorium, San Francisco, California 94101, (415)563-3200

Hall of Science of the City of New York, Flushing, New York 11351, (212)699-9400

Milwaukee Public Museum, Milwaukee, Wisconsin 53202, (414)278-2732

Ontario Science Centre, Toronto, Canada (416)429-4423

Pacific Science Center, Seattle, Washington 98101, (206)625-9333

Rochester Museum and Science Center, Rochester, New York 14603, (716)271-4320

Science Museum of Minnesota, Saint Paul, Minnesota 55101, (612)221-9488

"What was any art but a mold in which to imprison for a moment the shining, elusive element which is life itself—life hurrying past us and running away, too strong to stop, too sweet to lose," wrote Willa Cather in *The Song of the Lark*. Before life hurries past you, take time to appreciate art.

Metropolitan Museum of Art, 83rd Street and Fifth Avenue, New York, New York 10028, (212)535-7710. This great museum offers outstanding concerts and lectures at reasonable prices, but they are in such great demand, that admission is on a first-come, first-served basis. Concert tickets are available in series subscriptions for the yearly season until September 7; tickets for individual concerts may be ordered by mail after that date. The box office opens one hour before each performance for the sale of any remaining tickets or standing room. Lecture tickets are available in advance by subscription only. For series that are not sold out, individual tickets are $3.00 and go on sale at the box office one hour before each lecture. Among the concert series in a recent season were Baroque Music (four evenings for $26.00, single admissions $7.50) and Music of the Renaissance (three evenings for $19.00, single admissions $7.50). A number of the concerts such as three Evenings of Music by the Guarneri Quartet for $22.00 were practically sold out as soon as they were announced, and only standing room was available.

LEARN A LANGUAGE

As the world shrinks, it behooves all of us to know more than one language and, besides, learning a new one is good for the brain. You don't even have to leave your home. You can learn by tape or by telephone.

Phone Lab Inc., 200 Park Avenue, New York, New York 10017, (212) 557-0919. Want to learn a language while lying in bed or taking a coffee break at the office? Phone Lab will call you at your convenience and put a native French, Spanish, Italian, German, Portuguese, Russian, Hebrew, Arabic, Japanese, or Chinese language instructor on the line for twenty-five minutes. If you make an error, you need not be embarrassed by having others listening to you. The teacher merely corrects you, and you continue your progress. A six-week course, by Phone Lab's patented method, is claimed to be the equivalent of two years of school lessons. All the teachers are natives of the country whose language they teach. Although you are being taught privately, Phone Lab's prices are not prohibitive. In fact, they are lower than most other group programs. Also, each phone call goes on Phone Lab's bill, not yours, with the exception of those outside of New York. You have your lessons every day, or at least three times per week. Phone Lab invites you to a free wine and cheese international soiree every month so that you can use what you have learned in a relaxed atmosphere. You meet native speakers of the language you are studying, your teachers, and other students. If you call Phone Lab Inc., they will arrange to give you a free sample lesson. Costs range from $10 to $70, depending on the length of the course.

Phone Lab's creator, Michael Lahlou, is a linguist researcher. He graduated from Ecole Normale Superieure de St. Cloud, Paris, and he has been a professor at United Nations and French Institute, Alliance Francaise, New York.

Educational Services, 1730 Eye Street, N.W., Washington, D.C. 20006, (202)298-8424. The international traveler can prepare for that big vacation or business trip abroad with a quick, effective, do-it-yourself taped course in one of the world's twenty major languages. Command of basic words and phrases in French, Spanish, Arabic, Russian, Chinese, and fifteen other languages can be the reward after a few hours of study. A leader in the foreign language field for more than twenty-five years, Educational Services has developed this language series jointly with the Dun-Donnelley Publishing Corporation. Language/30 is now available commercially. It first underwent exclusive testing and use in preparing U.S. government personnel for overseas duties. These courses cost $14.95 each plus shipping. They are available through bookstores and public libraries and directly from Educational Services.

Berlitz School of Languages, Research Park, Building O, 1101 State Road, Princeton, New Jersey 08540, (609)924-8500. Czar Nicholas of Russia, Gypsy Rose Lee, the Duke of Windsor, Sarah Bernhardt, and Princess Anne of Great Britain studied there; so did Nelson Rockefeller, John F. Kennedy, and James Joyce. Leon Trotsky taught there. Since 1878, more than 30 million people have studied every language from Arabic to Zulu at Berlitz schools throughout the world.

The Berlitz® system of instruction practiced by the schools is known not only for teaching people languages but also for helping them to understand the people whose languages they are learning. Unlike traditional techniques, Berlitz instruction utilizes direct conversation instruction from the very first lesson. Student and teacher communicate exclusively in the language being taught. There are no tedious grammar drills; emphasis is on comprehension, speaking, reading, and writing, in that order.

The direct conversational approach was developed by Maximillian D. Berlitz, a German immigrant to the United States, who founded his first school in 1878 in Providence, Rhode Island. Finding that grammar drills often hindered his students in actually speaking the language they were studying, he evolved his own method. Today, Berlitz schools continue to emphasize speech and understanding of the spoken word, constantly updating both vocabulary and teaching techniques to keep pace with each tongue's changes in word meaning and usage.

Berlitz schools offer private, semiprivate (two to four students), and group (five to ten students) programs. A Berlitz specialist interviews each prospective student, evaluating his or her linguistic abilities and background, as well as his/her purpose for learning a new language. These factors are weighed carefully in developing a program of instruction that will best meet the student's personal needs. Prices for thirty lessons—(the minimum that Berlitz recommends) range from $210 to $525.

The Berlitz Total Immersion® program is designed for those who do not have the time to approach another language at leisure. It employs a successful technique of saturation instruction to give the student a basic command of a new language in from two to six weeks. Students are involved with the language for nine hours a day, in a series of forty-five-minute classroom sessions. Instructors are rotated so that students are exposed to different voices. There's no escape in this program; instructors accompany students during class breaks and at mealtimes, continuing to speak with them in the language being taught. The program is particularly popular with businesspeople, ministers, and others going abroad on permanent assignments.

RECORDINGS

Berlitz Publications Cassettes, 866 Third Avenue, New York, New York 10022, (212)935-2000. There are two types of cassette programs in French, German, Italian, and Spanish. One consists of three cassettes with various voices and sound effects ($39.95); the other includes six cassettes with more difficult words ($95.00).

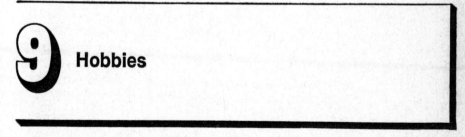

9 Hobbies

Hobbies can increase satisfaction. The ability to do something yourself from start to finish or to do something you particularly enjoy is good for your ego, providing, of course, that your hobby does not become an obsession. Here are some popular pastimes.

HOBBY CLUBS

Camera Club of New York, Inc., 37 East 60th Street, New York, New York 10022, (212)223-9751. The club offers instruction in photography for the hobbyist and the serious amateur. All courses are open to the public. The club was founded in 1884 to provide a congenial meeting place where photographers could enjoy each other's company, exchange information, discuss photographic technique and aesthetics, and further the contemporary art and science of photography. Through its programs and activities, including photographic courses, the club has pursued these goals. The courses are offered not only to increase the photographer's knowledge of the medium but also to enhance his or her enjoyment and appreciation of photography in its many aspects.

Here is a sample of the courses offered:

Available Light Photography: The purpose of this course is to provide the student with both the technical information and an attitude toward problem light situations indoors and outdoors that will enable him/her to approach previously avoided shooting situations intelligently. The course will cover necessary technical aspects of available light photography, uses of cameras, lenses, choice of films, and special films and their development in both color and black and white. Classroom discussion will include assigned work as well as evaluations of published photographs from various sources. Prerequisite, Basic Photographic Competence. The course, which is taught by Ed Rathaus, runs for eight weeks and costs $75.

American Contract Bridge League, 2200 Democrat Road, Memphis, Tennessee 38131, (901)332-5586. This is an organization of some 200,000 bridge fans of all degrees of skill; included among them are all the leading American bridge players and writers. Whether you play bridge for fun or for the competitiveness, for a pastime or for points, $6 will give you an annual membership, which includes a subscription to a monthly magazine that brings you tournament news and notes and features instructional articles by leading authorities of the game. You can send for a booklet listing affiliated duplicate bridge clubs to find a club in your area and for the *Easy Guide to Duplicate Bridge; How to Play, How to Win Law & Ethics* by writing to the League. Both are free.

National Backgammon League, 1102 Pratt, Chicago, Illinois 60607 (312)338-9216. This is the headquarters of an organization of clubs that compete against each other; it promotes this ancient but popular game, sets rules, and supplies news bulletins. Write for further information.

Mystery Library, University of California, San Diego Extension, Drawer P., Del Mar, California 92014. The library was developed by UC San Diego Extension. The classics will be republished in a numbered series of clothbound volumes and made available to the widest possible audience at moderate prices. Each book will contain not only a complete and authoritative version of the original text but a new introduction by an acknowledged expert on the book, the author, and the author's works. Each volume will be annotated. Many volumes will contain articles on the work and its author from *The Armchair Detective,* the leading critical journal of the mystery story.

If you enroll in the book club, you can cancel your membership at any time, and you are under no obligation to accept any minimum number of additional books beyond an initial purchase of *The New Shoe,* by Arthur Upfield for $5.95. Future volumes are sent for approval at two-month intervals, but you can return any you do not wish to buy.

In addition to the book club, a credit course, The World of Mystery Fiction, is offered. This independent-study course is coauthored by famed mystery writer Ellery Queen and Professor Elliot Gilbert of the Literature Department, University of California at Davis. Information on this course is available from Jennie Chin, program representative, National Media Courses, UC San Diego Extension, X-001, La Jolla, California 92093, (714)452-3446.

See National Media Courses, page 309.

WINESMANSHIP

Once you have had a taste of a foreign language, why not develop a taste for a foreign wine or an American one? Good wine is one of the great pleasures in life, and it doesn't have to be expensive to be good.

Most Americans feel insecure about ordering wine in a restaurant, or matching the proper product of the grape with a dinner served at home. Wine makes a meal more enjoyable. It is good for digestion, and it is relaxing. Therefore, it should be a source of comfort and pleasure.

According to Les Amis du Vin, a national organization and the largest, most successful national wine-tasting society, the secret to knowing about wine is simple: It lies in education. Americans have access to a greater variety of wines at a greater variety of prices than any other people in the world. All you have to do is develop your own tastes and learn to have confidence in them. Once, that was a lonely struggle, accomplished only with the aid of thick technical books and through repeated trips to many wine shops and restaurants. And it could be very expensive. Now, through wine clubs such as Les Amis du Vin, it can be a pressure-free, inexpensive process full of fun and social benefits.

Les Amis du Vin, 2302 Perkins Place, Silver Spring, Maryland 20910, (301)588-0980. Group wine tastings are held regularly throughout the year by local chapters all over the nation. This not only allows members to taste a wide variety of wines from all over the world but also promotes the fellowship of wine lovers at gourmet dinners and other wine-related events. There are special travel excursions such as champagne weekends and wine tours of France, Italy, Spain, and Portugal at considerable savings. Members tour vineyards and meet international wine and food authorities. There is a "wines of the month" service that makes special selections available to members at exceptional prices, but members are under no obligation to purchase the monthly wines. *Friends of Wine*, the bimonthly magazine, provides consumer-oriented information. Recent issues carried articles entitled "What Makes Cognac Unique" and "Wine Appreciation: Some Basic Concepts"; there are also regular features such as "Wine Opinion," "News for the Wine Consumer," and "Aperitif and Liqueur of the Month." A one-year membership is $20 ($10 for full-time students). A subscription to the magazine only is $9 a year.

Wine Information Course, Wine Institute, 165 Post Street, San Francisco, California 94108, (415)986-0878. More than 1 million people have taken advantage of this free course, which is administered by mail. Here is a test developed by the Wine Institute. (Answers are on page 334). If you can answer nineteen out of twenty-five questions correctly, you are already knowledgeable about wine. If you can't, take heart. Everyone can learn more about the drink of which Benjamin Franklin said, "Wine is constant proof that God loves us and loves to see us happy."

TRIPS, TOURS, AND HOSTELING

There is nothing like having an expert tour guide who really knows the history and significance of what you are seeing. In many cases, some of the museum trip guides have made the scientific discoveries that are in the literature. What makes these excursions really exciting is that you can ask questions and pursue subjects in depth.

Wilderness Institute, 333 Fairfax Street, Denver, Colorado 80220, (303)393-0400, Polly Lankford, director. This nine-year-old organization offers full-time professional backcountry instructor-guides. Expeditions are taken to the remote mountain and wilderness areas of the United States, Canada, Mexico, Africa, and Europe. Mountaineering and survival, backpacking expedition, climbing seminars, ski touring, and canoe trips are some of the kinds of trips conducted by experts in each field. Some trips are for beginners; others require some previous experience and expertise. Participants must be in good health and physical condition to participate. Contact the institute for information concerning schedules and fees.

Discovery Tours, American Museum of Natural History, Central Park West at 79th Street, New York, New York 10024, (212)873-4225, David D. Ryus, vice president. The museum plans these trips, selects the staff of lecturers, and arranges the special programs. It reaches beyond the well-traveled paths, more often than not substituting the mountaintop, the barrier reef, or the archaeological dig for the bustling metropolis or the overcrowded beach.

Wherever it takes you—from Chichén Itzá to Marrakech to Corinth, form Karnak to Juneau to Easter Island or Pompeii—it takes you differently. Museum experts accompany you throughout each trip. Shrines, excavations, and private collections not ordinarily open to tourists welcome you; lectures and seminars prepare you for each stop; your questions are answered, and your enthusiasm is shared.

Travel logistics themselves are supervised and executed by outstanding professional agencies. You need never concern yourself with luggage, transfers, schedules, or any such time-consuming details. Contact the museum for details and brochures.

Gallery Passport Ltd., 1170 Broadway, New York, New York 10001, (212)686-2244, Bunny Mautner, president. This art tour service, the first in America, specialized in trips, mostly on Saturdays, to out-of-town art museums and galleries, some not open to the general public. Guided visits to current New York exhibitions during the week and a Saturday series in the city are also offered. Lecturing by Gallery Passport's expert staff is provided on all tours, along with deluxe motor coach service and luncheon arrangements in famous country spots on all-day tours. Ms. Mautner employs eight or nine art students and writers as lecturers for both city and out-of-town tours. They spend a good deal of time scouting new tour possibilities. No trip is offered until the staff has been over the ground thoroughly, checking artworks, buildings, and restaurants.

All the scheduled tours and many additional ones are suggested for clubs or organizations at special group rates. Gift certificates are available for all in-town and out-of-town tours. Call or write for a brochure describing the tours and a current calendar of events. Prices vary according to the trip but average from $42 to $55 including lunch.

Earthwatch, Box 127SG, 10 Juniper Road, Belmont, Massachusetts 02178, (617)489-3030, David Pike, director. Excavating ruins in Scotland, exploring· shipwrecks off Florida, protecting endangered wildlife in Hawaii—these are among the many research expeditions "not for scientists" only. Participants actually become a vital part of research projects, working side by side with professionals in the field.

This year, Earthwatch is sponsoring sixty expeditions on six continents to explore such areas as archaeology, anthropology, botany, and oceanography. Participants must pay for their own transportation to the research site and make a contribution to help cover the costs of the expedition. Contributions can range from $500 for three weeks of radio-tracking raccoons in Georgia to $1,525 for a twenty-day study of spotted hyenas in Kenya.

There may be one or more wrong or right answers for each question —
Check all the right ones.

1 Wines used most often with meals:
- ☐ red dinner wines
- ☐ white dinner wines
- ☐ Champagnes
- ☐ Port

2 The requirements for proper wine storage are:
- ☐ an elaborate wine cellar
- ☐ a good deal of light
- ☐ even temperature 55° to 60° F.

3 The most popular white dinner wine types are:
- ☐ Chablis
- ☐ Rosé
- ☐ Rhine Wines
- ☐ Sherry
- ☐ Sauterne

4 Three of these are red dinner wine types:
- ☐ Zinfandel
- ☐ Chablis
- ☐ Cabernet Sauvignon
- ☐ Pinot Chardonnay
- ☐ Pinot Noir

5 Two of these are varietal wines:
- ☐ Burgundy
- ☐ Cabernet Sauvignon
- ☐ Claret
- ☐ Pinot Chardonnay

6 Two of the primary appetizer wines are:
- ☐ Sherry
- ☐ Tokay
- ☐ Rosé
- ☐ Vermouth

7 The grapes of California are of the
- ☐ Vitis vinifera family
- ☐ Vitis labrusca species

8 The California wine industry
- ☐ produces more than 82% of all wine consumed in the United States
- ☐ ranks number one in wine production among all countries
- ☐ represents the largest and most valuable fruit crop in California

9 Wine growing came directly to California from
- ☐ the Rocky Mountains
- ☐ Mexico
- ☐ Canada

☐ Leland Stanford   ☐ General Mariano Vallejo   ☐ Senator George Hearst

11   Aroma is best described as

    ☐ fragance of the grapes   ☐ fragrance of the wine   ☐ fragrance in a tasting room

Answer Yes or No — Look up the answers if in doubt:

	YES	NO
12 In cooking the alcoholic content of wine is lost with only the aroma and flavor imparted to food.	☐	☐
13 Sparkling wines are wines which have been made naturally effervescent.	☐	☐
14 Barbera is a Claret type wine.	☐	☐
15 Complete fermentation would result in a dry (not sweet) wine.	☐	☐
16 The color in red wine comes from the pigment in grape skins.	☐	☐
17 A major reason for blending most wines is to insure the consumer uniformity in a particular wine each time he buys it.	☐	☐
18 Cool temperature is essential in making Sherry and is one reason for Sherry's *nutty* flavor.	☐	☐
19 Because white wine is drawn off its skins after crushing it lacks the astringency of red wines.	☐	☐
20 California wines can be made only from grapes grown in California.	☐	☐
21 Wine is the only beverage that continues to improve after bottling.	☐	☐
22 One reason for wine's popularity in ancient civilization was that the juice of the grape naturally preserved itself through fermentation.	☐	☐
23 A Hungarian nobleman, Agoston Haraszthy, has been called the Father of Modern California Viticulture.	☐	☐
24 The present viticulture and enology department of the University of California developed from an experimental grape growing station established by UC in 1887.	☐	☐
25 The quality standards for California wine set in 1934 are higher in many respects than any comparable standards in the world.	☐	☐

ANSWERS TO TEST QUESTIONS

1 Wines used most often with meals:
   ☒ red dinner wines   ☒ white dinner wines   ☐ Champagnes   ☐ Port

2 The requirements for proper wine storage are:
   ☐ an elaborate wine cellar   ☐ a good deal of light   ☒ even temperature 55° to 60° F.

3 The most popular white dinner wine types are:
   ☒ Chablis   ☐ Rosé   ☒ Rhine Wines   ☐ Sherry   ☒ Sauterne

4 Three of these are red dinner wine types:
   ☒ Zinfandel   ☐ Chablis   ☒ Cabernet Sauvignon   ☐ Pinot Chardonnay   ☒ Pinot Noir

5 Two of these are varietal wines:
   ☐ Burgundy   ☒ Cabernet Sauvignon   ☐ Claret   ☒ Pinot Chardonnay

6 Two of the primary appetizer wines are:
   ☒ Sherry   ☐ Tokay   ☐ Rosé   ☒ Vermouth

7 The grapes of California are of the
   ☒ Vitis vinifera family   ☐ Vitis labrusca species

8 The California wine industry
   ☒ produces more than 82% of all wine consumed in the United States
   ☐ ranks number one in wine production among all countries
   ☒ represents the largest and most valuable fruit crop in California

9 Wine growing came directly to California from
   ☐ the Rocky Mountains   ☒ Mexico   ☐ Canada

10 Prominent California wine pioneers were
   ☒ Leland Stanford   ☒ General Mariano Vallejo   ☒ Senator George Hearst

11 Aroma is best described as
   ☒ fragrance of the grapes   ☐ fragrance of the wine   ☐ fragrance in a tasting room

ANSWERS TO YES OR NO QUESTIONS

		YES	NO
12	In cooking the alcoholic content of wine is lost with only the aroma and flavor imparted to food.	☒	☐
13	Sparkling wines are wines which have been made naturally effervescent.	☒	☐
14	Barbera is a Claret type wine.	☐	☒
15	Complete fermentation would result in a dry (not sweet) wine.	☒	☐
16	The color in red wine comes from the pigment in grape skins.	☒	☐
17	A major reason for blending most wines is to insure the consumer uniformity in a particular wine each time he buys it.	☒	☐
18	Cool temperature is essential in making Sherry and is one reason for Sherry's *nutty* flavor.	☐	☒
19	Because white wine is drawn off its skins after crushing it lacks the astringency of red wines.	☒	☐
20	California wines can be made only from grapes grown in California.	☒	☐
21	Wine is the only beverage that continues to improve after bottling.	☒	☐
22	One reason for wine's popularity in ancient civilization was that the juice of the grape naturally preserved itself through fermentation.	☒	☐
23	A Hungarian nobleman, Agoston Haraszthy, has been called the Father of Modern California Viticulture.	☒	☐
24	The present viticulture and enology department of the University of California developed from an experimental grape growing station established by UC in 1887.	☒	☐
25	The quality standards for California wine set in 1934 are higher in many respects than any comparable standards in the world.	☒	☐

If you are interested in sharing in the excitement and satisfaction of helping science improve the quality of life, write to Earthwatch for details.

American Youth Hostels Inc., National Campus, Delaplane, Virginia 22025, (703)592-3271. Are you interested in a way to build up your body, expand your horizons, and save money? There are over 4,500 youth hostels in sixty-one countries around the world, including more than 200 in the United States. Hostels are simple but comfortable overnight sleeping accommodations, often dormitory style; some offer accommodations for couples and families. Hostels are open to members only, and costs range from $1.50 to $3.50 per night. Most hostels provide cooking facilities; and European hostels offer meals at a nominal cost. The maximum stay is three nights. Members may be asked to help with the chores. AYH offers a comprehensive program of day, weekend, and extended holiday trips for both teen-agers and adults. Activities include bicycling, hiking, backpacking, Alpine and Nordic skiing, and canoeing. There are also bike repair courses, leadership training, ski instruction, films, and other social events. Memberships are $5.00 per year for those under eighteen, $11.00 for those eighteen and older, $12.00 for families, $25.00 for organization passes for nonprofit groups, and $110.00 for a lifetime membership pass.

A NEW BEGINNING

A Chinese philospher once said that even the longest journey begins with a single step. More than a thousand ways to improve yourself physically, intellectually, and emotionally are described in this book. You can embark on a new path to increase your enjoyment of life. Only the first step may be difficult.

Take that first step. Now is the time. You don't have to be strong, healthy, beautiful, rich, or young to start this journey. You may never reach your goal, but by accepting the challenge of self-improvement, you give yourself hope and a new interest in the world around you. You can change how the world looks at you and how you look to the world.

Begin! Then you'll be able to say, as the nineteenth-century poet Susan Chauncey Woolsey said:

Everyday is a fresh beginning.
Every morn is a world made new.